Journal of the American Revolution

JOURNAL
OF THE
AMERICAN REVOLUTION

ANNUAL VOLUME 2020

WESTHOLME
Yardley

Images are from the Library of Congress unless otherwise indicated.

Westholme Publishing, LLC
904 Edgewood Road
Yardley, Pennsylvania 19067
Visit our Web site at www.westholmepublishing.com

ISBN: 978–1–59416–340-1

Printed in the United States of America.

CONTENTS

EDITOR'S INTRODUCTION

The American Revolution and the Founding Era of the Unites States is remembered largely in terms of battlefields and assembly rooms, the places where soldiers fought and legislators sparred. Almost every aspect of these land-based activities, however, was connected in some way to the water—the rivers, lakes, seas, and oceans that afforded the best means of mass transportation.

During 2019, contributors to the *Journal of the American Revolution* remembered well the importance of the waterways, providing articles about ships, captains, sea battles, and waterborne trade. It is fitting that these articles feature heavily in this, our seventh annual compilation of selected articles: the revenue-raising Molasses Act directed at maritime trade of a critical commodity; a sea voyage by pamphleteer Thomas Paine before he gained fame; a businessman's exploits on the wartime Mississippi River; America's first warship, before a navy was even formed; the sufferings of American seamen held captive on a decommissioned hospital ship; the Revolutionary War service of the father of one of America's most famous admirals; gunboat diplomacy as practiced by an American naval captain; and some of the adventures of John Paul Jones. These and other topics are brought to life with the journal's emphasis on primary sources and personal accounts.

There's a lot about things on land too, from England's Magna Carta to Canada's *Habitants*, to the first Frenchman to serve in the war, to a slave-turned-bugler who earned a British pension. And of course John Hancock's signature—no book on the time period would be complete without a flourish.

And holding a book is a completely different experience from accessing an article on a computer or smart phone. While it is vitally important to provide well-researched history where it is convenient for today's readers (let alone the remarkable ability to add, correct, publish, and engage with research, writing, and a community of readers and writers in nearly real-time), having a selection of articles conveniently brought together in book form showcases the strength of a very old technology: here the articles are connected with a common thread, weaving a narrative that is impossible to duplicate online. We are pleased to be able to offer select articles from the *Journal of the American Revolution* in this fashion; while much on the internet can end up as ephemera, lost in electronic space, here some of the finest research and writing that first appeared on a screen is presented in a format as familar to an eighteenth-century reader as it is today.

The East India Company and Parliament's "Fateful Decision" of 1767

STEVEN NEILL

India, the fabled land of rubies, diamonds, gold, tigers, and mystery, captured the imagination of the British people in the mid 1700s. Robert Clive provided fodder for gossip when he returned to England in 1760 with a reported "£1,200,000 in cash, bills, and jewels. He is said to be the richest subject in the three realms"[1] Along with tales of unlimited wealth for those fortunate enough to go to India, were the stories of corruption, brutality, and profiteering by the employees of East India Company.

Founded in 1600 with a Royal Charter as a trade monopoly between Britain and the Mogul Empire of India, the East India Company would eventually make its directors more potent than most kings. The company's private army, built initially to guard their warehouses, conquered Bengal, the wealthiest state in India, during the battle of Plassey in 1757 under the leadership of Robert Clive. That victory made the company the controller and tax collector of over one hundred million people. Following the battle, Clive received "£2.5 million (over £250 million in today's currency) from the Bengal treasury for the Company and £160,000 for himself."[2] Following a victory at Buxar in 1766, the price of the company's stock increased 263 percent.[3]

Between the 1760s and the 1780s, two to three hundred English officials returned from India. Most enjoyed a very comfortable living,

1. Sir George Forrest, *The Life of Lord Clive* (London: Cassel and Company, LTD, 1918), 172.
2. William Dalrymple, "The East India Company: The original corporate raiders," www.theguardian.com/world/2015/mar/04/east-india-company-original-corporate-raiders, accessed July 14, 2019.
3. James Mill, *The History of British India*, 3rd edition (London: Baldwin, Cradock, and Joy, 1826), Vol. 3, oll.libertyfund.org/titles/842#MillJ_0381-03_485.

but several bought large estates and became members of Parliament.[4] Called Nabobs, they were despised by most Englishmen for their extravagant spending and excessive power. Prime Minister William Pitt said of the returning Nabobs in a January 22, 1770 speech:

> For some years past, there has been an influx of wealth into this country, which has been attended with many fatal consequences, because it has not been the regular, natural produce of labor and industry. The riches of Asia have been poured in upon us, and have brought with them not only Asiatic luxury but, I fear, Asiatic principles of government. Without connections, without any natural interest in the soil, the importers of foreign gold have forced their way into Parliament by such a torrent of private corruption, as no private hereditary fortune could resist. My Lords, not saying but what is within the knowledge of us all, the corruption of the people is the great original cause of the discontents of the people themselves, of the enterprise of the Crown, and the notorious decay of the internal vigor of the Constitution.[5]

WILLIAM PITT AND HIS TAX PLAN

While the lengthy and costly Seven Years War may have made England the mistress of the waves and holder of a worldwide empire, it left them with a national debt of £140,000,000, double what it was before the war. William Pitt became prime minister after George Granville's disastrous attempt to tax the American colonists through the Stamp Act. While he was secretary of state, Pitt had received a letter from Robert Clive stating that the East India Company could realize £2 million a year profit from its Indian conquests. Pitt saw India as the "greatest of all objects"[6] and believed taxing its profits was preferable to taxing the American colonies. Pitt, like the Americans, concluded that although Parliament could levy taxes on the colonies, it should not. Pitt was also not alone in regarding India as a way to balance the books. Privy Council President William Beckford wrote Pitt a letter that stated: "we must look to the East and not to the West," meaning looking at the East India Company as a means to fill British coffers.[7]

4. Philip Lawson and Jim Phillips, "'Our Execrable Banditti': Perceptions of Nabobs in Mid-Eighteenth Century Britain," *Albion: A Quarterly Journal Concerned with British Studies*, vol. 16 no. 3, (Autumn 1984): 225–241.

5. John Taylor, *The Identity of Junius with a Distinguished Living Character Established* (New York: Kirk & Mercein, 1818), 249-250.

6. Augustus Henry Fitzroy, *Autobiography and Political Correspondence of Augustus Henry, Third Duke of Grafton* (London: John Murray, 1898), 110-111.

7. William Hunt, *The Political History of England* (New York: Longman's, Green, and Co., 1905), 10: 80.

Pitt may have had other reasons for defending the colonists against taxes as well. During the Sugar Act of 1764 and the 1773 Tea Act, the colonists had used non-importation agreements to limit the number of products they imported from Britain. The effect of this cannot be understated; the colonists were buyers of more than forty percent of all British manufactured goods in 1774.[8] Also, American colonists owed British merchants almost £3 million, which the merchants were afraid of losing.[9] Additionally, Pitt was aware that numerous London merchants would be willing to pay a lot of money to the treasury if the government broke the East India Company's monopoly over trading in the East.

When Pitt proposed a Parliamentary inquiry into the affairs of the company, he believed that although it should retain its trading privileges while its charter was in force, it did not have the right to revenue generated in the territory nor should it have the responsibility to govern; both of which belonged to Britain. Pitt also stressed that the unrestrained corruption and subjugation prevailing in India called for parliamentary intervention. Pitt saw the revenue from the company as the "redemption of a nation, within reach of being saved at once by a kind of gift from heaven."[10] He proposed to look into taxing the vast wealth of the company to balance the national budget. He also intended the inquiry to examine the company's method for rewarding dividends and to look into the reports of corruption.

Pitt considered revoking the company's monopoly trade agreement in India, opening it to competition from other British merchants. The *London Political Journal* printed Pitt's impression of the company: "the lofty Asiatic plunderers of Leadenhall Street [location of the company headquarters] who were pouring the wealth of the east into the laps of Nabobs instead of the coffers of the British Exchequer."[11]

This inquiry divided the administration with Pitt and Lords Grafton, Shelburne, and Camden agreeing that sovereignty in India belonged to the Crown, and that open debate in Parliament was the best way to settle the issue. Pitt said of the matter:

8. "1754-1783: Business and the Economy: Overview," www.encyclopedia.com/history/news-wires-white-papers-and-books/1754-1783-business-and-economy-overview, accessed 07 15, 2019.

9. Richard B. Sheridan, "The British Credit Crisis of 1772 and The American Colonies," *The Journal of Economic History*, 1960: 161-186.

10. Fitzroy, *Autobiography and Political Correspondence*, 110-111.

11. John C. Miller, *Origins of the American Revolution* (Boston: Little, Brown, and Company, 1943), 244.

> On the whole, there is in substantial justice a mixed right to the territorial revenues between the State and the Company as joint captors; the State equitably entitled to the larger share as the largest contributor in the acquisition by fleets and men. Nor can the Company's share, when ascertained be considered as private property, but in trust for the public purposes of India and the extension of trade; never, in any case, to be portioned out in dividends to the extinction of the spirit of trade.[12]

Concern over the power of the Nabob's in Parliament was not limited to members of the cabinet; *Gentlemen's Quarterly Magazine* pondered in their April 1767 edition "whether the freedom or the slavery of this island shall result"[13] because of their [the East India Company] continued acquisition of power.

Lords Townshend, Grenville, and Conway however, believed the company's claim to sovereignty was stronger, and the issue was settled in private negotiations between representatives of Parliament and the company.

Sadly, at this time Pitt was bed-ridden with gout and barely able to receive visitors, let alone dictate policy. His inability or unwillingness to convey his intentions to Grafton, Shelburne, Camden, and others loyal to him left the door open for the demagogue Townshend (who was later a stockholder of the East India Company) to control the issue. Basil Williams would say of the Pitt and Townshend rivalry:

> Townshend had no high conceptions of State policy and was supremely indifferent to the question of right as between the Crown and the Company: but his responsiveness to popular feeling taught him that the public expected something out of the Bengal revenues, and he proceeded to obtain it in the manner least disagreeable to his friends in Leadenhall Street. He damped down Beckford's inquiry on the plea that he was making a private arrangement with the Company which was the method condemned beyond all others by Chatham: "the whole becomes a farce," he moaned, "and the Ministry a ridiculous phantom. not by the force of factions from without, but from a certain infelicity (I think incurable), which ferments and sours the councils of His Majesty's servants."

By Townshend's bargain with the directors, the Company retained all their old privileges and was left in undisturbed enjoyment of the new revenues, in consideration of a trifling payment to the public and

12. Basil Williams, *The Life of William Pitt, Earl of Chatham* (New York: Longmans, Green, and Company, 1914), 2: 233-236, 305.
13. Nick Robins, *The Corporation That Changed the World* (London: Pluto Press, 2012), 106.

restraint imposed on excessive dividends. The proposal, Chatham vainly told a friend, "deserves the highest disapprobation of Parliament. . . . It barters away in effect the great right and interest of the nation (which if duly and wisely asserted would have brought effectual relief) for the convenience of the present minute." But Townshend was now the master. No inquiry, such as Chatham had demanded, was held on the state of India, no abuses were redressed, and no conditions were attached to ensure the good government of the new provinces.[14]

Pitt's proposed Parliamentary inquiry faced several hurdles, not the least of which was that up to a third of the Members of Parliament had stock in the company.[15] The investigation also united several organizations created by royal charters, including the City of London, in opposition because they were unsure how a change in the charter of the East India Company might affect their own charters. Edmund Burke even resisted the inquiry because of how it might affect the people's rights to property: "To make a most important Revolution indeed in the whole Policy of this Country with regard to its Laws[,] its Commerce and its Credit" because it restricted "by a positive arbitrary Regulation the enjoyment of the profits which should be made in Commerce" and did so by taking profit from the East India Company, even though "it sinned against no rule prescribed by Law."[16]

At the same time, Charles Townshend offered his revenue acts as a way to quell the mutiny in the American colonies and force them to pay their way. Parliament lost interest altogether in Pitt's India concerns when the company agreed to pay £400,000 in duties and limit the amount of dividend they would pay their stockholders. Starting in June 1767, Parliament made what historian Oliver Morton Dickerson called its most "fateful decision" and they passed the Townshend Acts.[17]

Pitt said in his 1770 State of the Union address:

> The abolition of inland trade on private account is highly laudable, as far as that provision goes; but I would assuredly carry the prohibition further, and open again to the natives and other eastern merchants the inland trade of Bengal, and abolish all monopolies on the Company's account; which now operate to the unjust exclusion of an oppressed

14. Williams, *The Life of William Pitt*, 233-236, 305.
15. Lenny Flank, *The East India Company: A History*, www.dailykos.com/stories/2015/3/3/1365266/-The-East-India-Company-A-History, accessed July 15, 2019.
16. Paul Langford, *The Writings and Speeches of Edmund Burke* (Oxford: Clarendon Press, 1981), 2: 65-66.
17. Oliver Morton Dickerson, "England's Most Fateful Decision," *The New England Quarterly* Vol. 22 No 3 (1949), 388-394.

> people, and the impoverishing and alienating of those extensive and populous provinces. The hearts and good affections of Bengal are of more worth than all the profits of ruinous and odious monopolies.[18]

While Pitt fought for more Parliamentarian control over the East India Company, he also argued for moderation towards the American colonies, as he did in his last speech before Parliament in January 1775:

> An hour now lost may produce years of calamity—I contend not for indulgence but justice to America. Resistance to your acts was necessary as it was just. The Americans are a brave, generous, and united people, with arms in their hands and courage in their hearts: three millions of them, the genuine descendants of a valiant and pious ancestry, driven to those deserts by the narrow maxims of a superstitious tyranny. Of the spirit of independence animating the nation of America, I have the most authentic information. Destroy their towns and cut them off from the superfluities, perhaps the conveniences of life . . . And they would not lament their loss while they have—what, my Lords ?—their woods and their liberty. Such a united force, what force shall we muster to oppose it, a few regiments in America and 11,000 or 8,000 men at home? The idea is too ridiculous to take up a moment of your Lordships' time. Laying papers on your table or counting numbers on a division will not avert or postpone the hour of danger. It is not repealing this act Parliament; it is not repealing a piece of parchment, that can restore America to our bosom: you must repeal her fears and her resentments, and you may then hope for her love and gratitude.[19]

Several historians have cited Pitt's support towards the American colonies and his disdain for the East India Company as evidence that his 1767 plan intended to tax the revenues from the Company while leaving the colonies alone:

> The East India Company [whom] . . . British military forces had supported. . . . [William Pitt, the earl of] Chatham . . . it is proposed that the company should pay an annual rental to the government and that the dividend policy of the Company should be regulated by the government to prevent speculation in the company's stocks. [Furthermore], revenues from the Company could have made up the national deficit and averted the taxation issues with the American colonies.[20]

18. Kate Hotblack, *Chatham's Colonial Policy: A Study in the Fiscal and Economic Implications of the Colonial Policy of the Elder Pitt* (London: G. Routledge & Sons, Limited, 1917), 96.
19. Williams, *The Life of William Pitt*, 233-236, 305.
20. J. C. Long, *George III: The Story of a Complicated Man* (Boston: Little, Brown, and Co., 1960), 178.

Pitt sought to do justice to Ireland and Anglo-American colonies, to inaugurate Parliamentary reform in England and to secure the transfer of the government of British India from the East India Company to the British crown; but he was obliged to retire from public affairs because of ill-health.[21]

EAST INDIA COMPANY AND THE RETURN TO PLUNDER

As for the East India Company, employees continued to skim its profits, forcing the government to grant the company a £1.2 million loan, and to give support in selling its enormous stockpile of tea. "The Bailout in part demonstrated the extent to which Parliament itself had come under the sway of nabob money and influence because it had become clear from the previous decade how many were sitting members had significant shares, and often proprietary interests, in Company fortunes."[22] With the help of William Pitt, Parliament passed the Regulating Act of 1773, installing a series of economic and administrative reforms over the company.

WHAT IF?

The most crucial year between the French and Indian War and the Revolution was 1767. The colonies were content after the repeal of the Stamp Act and could have remained that way for the foreseeable future had Parliament followed Pitt's plan. So the questions remain: what if Parliament had taxed the East India Company and strengthened trade with the American colonies instead? How much did the company influence Parliament's decision to set aside Pitt's plans to instead demand a "rent" payment from the company? Could his plan have saved the Anglo-American Union?

21. John H. Clifford, *Library of World History: Containing a Record of the Human Race,* Vol. VII (Chicago: Western Press Association, 1914), 3192.

22. Dirks, Nicholas B. Dirks, *The Scandal of Empire* (Cambridge: Belknap Harvard, 2006), 15.

The Molasses Act: A Brief History

KEN SHUMATE

The Molasses Act of 1733 levied a duty of six pence per gallon on foreign molasses imported into British colonies in North America. The duty was not intended to raise revenue, but to be a prohibition against the importation of molasses from foreign sugar plantations. It was at first a nullity, a dead letter, but three decades later was enforced and amended into an act intended to produce revenue, thereby becoming part of the dispute over the authority of Parliament to tax the colonies.

Molasses was important; other duties were imposed by the Molasses Act, but the molasses prohibition was the motivation for its enactment. John Adams, in a reflective mood long after Britain and America went separate ways, wrote to a friend, "I know not why we should blush to confess that molasses was an essential ingredient in American independence."[1]

There is a backstory to the Molasses Act, beginning in the early eighteenth century.[2]

THE MOLASSES TRADE

British sugar colonies—islands in the West Indies—were in dire competition with foreign sugar islands (largely French). In addition to sugar, all these islands exported the by-product of sugar production: molasses. Over time, northern continental colonies had developed an economy dependent on plentiful and inexpensive molasses; it was there distilled into rum, an export necessary to obtain specie for further trade. These colonies imported molasses from all the sugar islands, most often in exchange for fish, lumber, horses, and other provisions necessary for the livelihood of the largely single-crop plantations. The British islands,

1. John Adams to William Tudor, Sr., August 11, 1818, Founders Online, founders.archives.gov/documents/Adams/99-02-02-6959.

2. For general background, see Frank Wesley Pitman, *The Development of the British West Indies, 1700–1763* (New Haven: Yale University Press, 1917). Pitman's work colors much of the following discussion of the economics of the molasses trade.

not faring well against the competition, resented that their sister colonies supplied the French with these indispensable provisions, and complained to British officials that the trade should be prohibited.

After decades of futile argument, the British sugar planters planned to bring the matter before Parliament. This was not good news for the Americans as the sugar interests held substantial influence in the House of Commons. A blizzard of pamphlets followed, leading up to the 1731 session of Parliament.

Here is the gist of the arguments. In late 1730 the Board of Trade read this essay supporting the sugar islands. The foreign sugar islands could not, "subsist without the horses from New England, nor ... without New England lumber, such as staves, hoops and beading especially, consequently [if they did not have such supplies] little sugar could be made among them."[3]

And British merchants submitted a petition on behalf of the American colonies.

> It would be very impolitic to obstruct the [northern colonies] from taking melasses, and even rum, from the French islands . . . as our own sugar colonies are unable to supply the immense quantities of melasses [necessary for American trade]. . . . The prohibiting the continental people from purchasing of the foreign colonies their sugar, rum, and melasses, or even laying high duties on them, would utterly destroy a commerce of ... great consequence to the northern colonies. . . . Neither could they dispose of the product of their lands and labour, a great part of the profits whereof centers in Great Britain, in payment of the manufactures they have from thence.[4]

THE MOLASSES BILL OF 1731

The sugar islands directly petitioned Parliament on February 23, 1731:

> That divers of his Majesty's subjects, residing within his dominions in America, and elsewhere, had of late years carried on a trade to the foreign Sugar-Colonies in America, from whence they were supplied with sugar, rum, molosses ... [the result being] injurious to the trade of this kingdom, and greatly impoverished the British Sugar-Colonies; and therefore the Petitioners prayed the consideration of the House, and such relief as the House should think fit.[5]

3. *Calendar of State Papers: Colonial Series, America and West Indies* (London, 1730), 300-301.
4. *Anderson's Historical And Chronological Deduction Of The Origin Of Commerce, From The Earliest Accounts: Containing An History Of The Great Commercial Interests Of The British Empire* (London, 1787), 180-82.
5. *Cobbett's Parliamentary History of England from the Earliest Period to the year 1803. Volume VIII. A. D. 1722-1733* (London, 1811), 856-57.

The result was a bill to prohibit American trade with foreign sugar colonies entitled, "An Act for the better Securing and Encouraging the Trade of his Majesty's Sugar Colonies in America." The preamble makes no bones about favoritism:

> Whereas the Welfare and Prosperity of his Majesty's Sugar Colonies in America, are of the greatest Consequence and Importance to the Navigation, Strength, and Wealth of this Kingdom: And whereas, of late Years a Trade has been carried on by divers of his Majesty's Subjects on the Continent of America to the Foreign Sugar Colonies there, to the great Prejudice and Discouragement of his Majesty's said Sugar Colonies. For remedy whereof . . . .
>
> Section 1. Enacted, that . . . no sugar, rum, or molasses, of [foreign sugar colonies] shall be imported into . . . his Majesty's colonies or plantations of America. . . .
>
> 7. And whereas great numbers of horses and great quantities of lumber have been exported [from North American colonies] to the foreign sugar colonies [such export is now prohibited][6]

This is an odd bill; although the right of Parliament to impose trade restrictions was well established, past restrictions had always been formulated in an evenhanded manner. This bill is different: it clearly favors one set of colonies over another. The bill passed the House of Commons on April 14, but was killed in the House of Lords as being detrimental to trade of the empire.

THE MOLASSES BILL OF 1732

Leading up to the 1732 session of Parliament (to again consider the bill of prohibition), there was another blizzard of argument regarding the trade involving molasses. The Board of Trade characterized the essays this way: "The papers . . . consist of many allegations, but of allegations only, and not of proofs, which has brought this matter hitherto no farther than to an issue upon the facts in dispute between the opposite parties."[7]

The debate on another bill to encourage "the Trade of his Majesty's Sugar Colonies in America" began on February 23, 1732 in the House of Commons. After a period of rancorous argument, James Oglethorpe made this point.

> There never was perhaps before this House an Affair of greater Moment, than the Affair which is now before us. The whole British Trade,

6. *The Political State of Great Britain*, Volume 42 (London, 1731), 639-43.
7. *Calendar of State Papers: Colonial Series, America and West Indies* (London, 1732), 45-46.

all our Colonies and Settlements in America, may be ruined and undone, or very much encouraged and strengthened by the Resolutions we come to upon the present Occasion.

He advocated balance, pointing out the advantages of both the sugar islands and New England. Then:

We ought not to encourage or raise one Colony upon the Destruction or Detriment of another; much less ought we to grant a Favour to any Subject, or to any particular Set of People, which may prove to be against the publick Good of the Nation in general.

Oglethorpe believed the bill was flawed; the Commons should not send, "up a Bill to the other House, so irregular or so improper, that they may find themselves under a Necessity of throwing it out."[8]

But on March 15, the bill passed and was sent up to the House of Lords. After careful deliberation, the Lords again killed the bill.

Richard Partridge (agent for Rhode Island and New York) wrote to Gov. Joseph Wanton of Rhode Island on April 3 to explain a change of direction in the strategy of the sugar planters—not a prohibition, but a duty intended to act as a prohibition" "But I am told that it is intended next Sessions of Parliam to lay a duty on Foreign Rum and Molasses imported into our North Colonies."[9] This was an ominous step. The duty would be a sham, embedded in what was claimed to be a revenue act, a money bill, thereby giving greater weight to desires of the House of Commons.

THE MOLASSES ACT OF 1733

Using the same title as the bill of 1731—"An Act for the better Securing and Encouraging the Trade of his Majesty's Sugar Colonies in America"[10]—the 1733 bill reaffirmed the essential nature of the act: prohibition, not revenue. The new preamble retained the flavor of favoritism.

Whereas, the welfare and prosperity of your Majesty's sugar colonies in America are of the greatest consequence and importance to the trade, navigation, and strength of this kingdom; and whereas, the planters of

8. *Cobbett's Parliamentary History Volume VIII*, 999-1002.

9. Gertrude S. Kimball, ed., *The Correspondence of the Colonial Governors of Rhode Island 1723-1775*, Volume I (Boston: Houghton Mifflin, 1902), 26.

10. 6 George II c. 13 (May 17, 1733), Danby Pickering, *Statutes at Large* (Cambridge, England: Joseph Bentham, 1762-1807), XVI: 374-379. Although the act imposed other duties, the molasses duty was the most important, and most resented. In contemporary writing, the act was known as the Sugar Act. In modern discourse, it is known as the Molasses Act.

> the said sugar colonies have of late years fallen under such great discouragements that they are unable to improve or carry on the sugar trade upon an equal footing with the foreign sugar colonies without some advantage and relief be given to them from Great Britain; for remedy whereof, and for the good and welfare of your Majesty's subjects, we, your Majesty's most dutiful and loyal subjects, the commons of Great Britain, assembled in Parliament, have given and granted unto your Majesty the several and respective rates and duties hereinafter mentioned.

Supporting the sham of a money bill, the preamble had words of donation usually associated with taxation: "have *given and granted* unto your Majesty."[11]

The molasses duty was:

> That from and after [December 25, 1733] there shall be raised, levied, collected and paid [duties on rum and other spirits, payable in money of Great Britain] and upon all molasses or syrups of such foreign produce or manufacture . . . the sum of sixpence of like money for every gallon thereof.

The prohibition against export of horses and lumber prominent in the 1731 bill was dropped since this prohibitive import duty was intended to effectively stop American trade with the foreign islands.

The bill included enforcement provisions:

> And be it further enacted, that in case any of the said commodities shall be landed . . . before the duties [are paid, all such goods] shall be forfeited; and all and every such goods as shall be so landed or put on shore, contrary to the true intent and meaning of this act, shall, and may be seized by the governor or [customs officials] and all and every such offence and forfeiture, shall, and may be prosecuted for and recovered in any court of admiralty in his majesty's colonies or plantations in America [or in a court of record] at the election of the informer or prosecutor. . . . Penalties and forfeitures so recovered there shall be divided as follows: one third part for the use of his majesty . . . to be ap-

11. Decades later, John Lind asserted that words of donation alone were sufficient to make this a revenue act, not a trade regulation. "The act uses the technical words of 'give, and grant.' Here then at least, one would think, was clearly a duty imposed for the purpose of raising a revenue." See *Remarks on the Principal Acts of the Thirteenth Parliament of Great Britain* (London, 1775): 219. Edmund Burke had a different view: "The title of this Act of George the 2nd, notwithstanding the words of donation, considers it merely as a regulation of trade." See *Speech on American Taxation*, April 19, 1774, in *The Parliamentary History of England, From the Earliest Period to the Year 1803. Vol. XVII A. D. 1771–1774* (London, 1813), 1235.

> plied for the support of the government of the colony or plantation where the same shall be recovered, one third part to the governor or commander in chief of the said colony or plantation, and the other third part to the informer or prosecutor, who shall sue for the same. [And on and on.]

In 1818, in private correspondence, John Adams quoted the enforcement provisions and called the act: "the most arbitrary among Statutes that were all arbitrary, the most unconstitutional among Laws which were all unconstitutional."[12]

DEBATE IN THE HOUSE OF COMMONS

Debate on the bill further muddied the water about whether it was intended to prohibit importation or to result in revenue. Our interest starts with this motion made by Colonel Bladen on February 21, 1733, "That a Duty of 6d. per Gallon, Sterling Money, be laid on all foreign Molasses and Syrups imported into any of his Majesty's Colonies or Plantations in America."

Sir John Barnard rose in opposition to ask if the duty was intended to be prohibitory, cutting off all trade with the foreign islands. Bladen replied:

> The duties proposed would not prove an absolute prohibition, but [they are intended] as something that should come very near it, for in the way the northern colonies are, they raise the French islands at the expense of ours, and raise themselves . . . to an independency.

After more resolutions and debate: "These Resolutions being all agreed to as above recited, a Bill was ordered to be brought in pursuant thereto."[13]

While the House of Commons was debating the bill, Partridge reported to Governor Wanton on February 28. Here he characterized the duty as a tax.

> This now comes to acquaint thee that thro the restlessness of the West India Gentlemen (who have the ministry on their side), the House of Commons have lately come into Resolutions to impose a duty upon Foreign Sugar, molasses and Rum that shall be imported into our Plantations . . . and it is generally thought the Bill will pass. . . . I am of the opinion if such a Law take place, (besides the present Injury it will do),

12. John Adams to William Tudor, Sr., August 16, 1818. Founders Online, founders.archives.gov/documents/Adams/99-02-02-6963

13. Leo Francis Stock, ed., *Proceedings and Debates of the British Parliaments Respecting North America: 1728–1739*, Volume 4 (Washington, DC: Carnegie Institution of Washington, 1937), 182.

> it will be rather worse in the consequence of it than the Bill of prohibition last year, because of the levying a Subsidy upon a free People without their knowledge against their consent, who have the libertys and immunities granted them [of] Natural born Subjects.

He explained why it was worse—and was prescient about the act being called a precedent for further taxation.

> . . . besides it may be drawn into a President for the future, for by the same Rule that a British Parliament imposes a duty on the Kings Subjects abroad, who have no Representatives in the State here, they may from 4/ advance to 20/— to £100, on different things, and so on ad infinitem which is an infringement on liberty and property and as I apprehend a violation of the right of the subject.[14]

This was a pivotal issue—the distinction between the right of Parliament to restrict trade (an accepted precedent), and the taxation of American imports for revenue (an innovation). In later years, this distinction became one of the central issues in the controversy over the authority of Parliament.

DEBATE ON A PETITION: MONEY BILL OR TRADE REGULATION?

On March 8, the House was asked to admit a petition from Rhode Island against the bill. The resulting debate primarily dealt not with the merits of the petition itself, but *whether the petition should be heard.*[15] Barnard argued that: "the Bill may absolutely ruin their trade, and since they were subjects of England, and were not represented, it was but just they should be heard."

Sir William Yonge was against hearing the petition.

> The petition [prays] for leave to be heard against a Bill now pending in this house, by which some certain duties are to be laid on several commodities mentioned in the Bill. I believe, Sir, it has been the constant usage of this house for many years, to receive no petitions against duties to be laid on.

He then objected to the nature of the petition.

> However, Sir, I must take notice of another thing, which I observe in the petition . . . They therein tell us, that as to the Bill now depending before us they apprehend it to be against their charter. This, I must say, is something very extraordinary, and, in my opinion, looks [as if] aiming at an independency, and disclaiming the authority and jurisdiction of

14. Kimball, *The Correspondence of the Colonial Governors of Rhode Island*, 34.
15. *Cobbett's Parliamentary History of England Volume VIII*, 1261-66.

> this House; as if this House had not a power to tax them, or to make any laws for the regulating of the affairs of their colony.

Thomas Winnington supported Yonge. "It has been a Custom always observed in this House, not to receive any Petitions against those Bills which were brought in for the laying on of any new Duties." He had more to say on charter.

> The honourable Gentleman near me took notice of the petitioners pretending, that the Bill now before us is against their charter; I hope, Sir, they have no charter which debars this House from taxing them as well as any other subject of this nation; I am sure they can have no such charter.

Back to Barnard.

> [Even if there] were a constant and perpetual rule not to receive petitions against such duties, yet certainly that rule could relate only to those duties which were to be laid on for raising money for the current service of the public; it could not be presumed to relate to those duties which were to be laid on for the regulation of trade only; and this last is the case now before us.

That was pretty blunt about the purpose of the duty. He next dealt further and even more explicitly with the hypocrisy of the bill.

> The duties to be laid on by this Bill are so far from being duties for the supply of the government, that I do not believe that even those gentlemen, who appear so fond of the duties to be laid on by it, so much as expect or wish that any money shall be thereby raised for the use of the public; the Bill is not intended for any such end; it is rather in the nature of a prohibition, and it was never pretended that no petitions were ever to be received against a Bill for prohibiting any sort of commerce.

He renewed his argument for hearing the petition.

> It may be the case that this House has sometimes refused to receive petitions from some parts of Britain against duties to be laid on; but this can be no reason why the petition I have now in my hand should be rejected . . . The people [of Rhode Island] have no particular representatives in this House; and therefore they have no other way of applying or of offering their reasons to this House, but in the way of being heard at the bar of the House by their agent here in England; therefore if that general rule of not receiving petitions against duties to be laid on, be ever to be receded from, the case now before us ought to be an exception to the general rule.

John Conduit returned to the argument against hearing the petition.

> I apprehend it has always been the custom of this House . . . to refuse receiving petitions against any duties to be laid on, and that without any distinction whether the duties to be laid on were for the raising of money, or for the regulation of trade. As our colonies are all a part of the people of Great Britain, they are generally represented in this House as well as the rest of the people are.

After more debate along these same lines, "The question being put for bringing up the petition, passed in the negative." This refusal to bring up the petition put the imprimatur of the House of Commons on the statute: a money bill. The bill passed in the Commons on March 21.

NOT A COMMON MONEY BILL

Agent Partridge, in an attempt to influence the House of Lords, wrote to the Duke of Newcastle on March 28. His plea went beyond condemning the proposed duty from an economic point of view, also alluding to "rights and privileges."

> Inasmuch as there is a bill lately passt ye House of Commons [for imposing] high duties on ye importation of sugar etc. into ye Northern Colonys from ye Foreign Sugar Plantations and [the bill] is likely to be brought up soon to ye House of Lords, the gentlemen of New York apprehend [i.e., in a petition] if it should pass into a law will be rather worse in the consequence of it than ye bill of prohibitions last year. Besides ye injury, it will be of in itself almost tantamount to a prohibition. It is divesting them of their rights and privileges as ye King's natural born subjects and Englishmen in levying subsidies against their consent when they . . . have no representatives in Parliament, nor any part of ye Legislature of this Kingdom, and that it will be drawn into a president hereafter whereby an incredible inconvenience may ensue . . . As it is not a common money bill for raising a duty out of ye Kingdom, we pray this petition may be presented to ye House of Lords in a proper time after the bill has been read a first time.
>
> I am, in behalf of the New York Gentlemen, Thy Friend, Richd. Partridge[16]

16. *Calendar of State Papers: Colonial Series, America and West Indies* (London, 1733): 66. On page xxxiii, the authors of the *Calendar* point out that the petition referred to by Partridge "raises in unmistakable words the constitutional plea of 'No taxation without representation,' which was to play such an outstanding part in the controversies preceding the American Revolution."

The letter highlighted the intrinsic ambiguity of the bill. The duty was an inappropriate invasion of American rights as a tax ("levying subsidies against their consent"), but yet the Lords could consider the petition since the duty was *not* a tax ("As it is not a common money bill").

CONSENT, ASSENT, EFFECT

The Lords did hear petitions, but consented to the bill on May 4; it received the royal assent on May 17, 1733.

The duty never did much to restrict American commerce (nor did it raise revenue); the Americans smuggled the molasses they needed. The strategy was successful, largely since the British, during the long period later called "wise and salutary neglect," made little effort (despite ongoing complaints from the sugar planters) to enforce the act. In addition, the act was difficult to enforce. A typical observation is this from the Massachusetts Governor to the Board of Trade, March 2, 1737: "The Sea Coast of the Province is so extensive & has so many Commodious harbours, that the small number of Customs House Officers are often complaining they are not able to do much for preventing illegal Trade."[17]

PARLIAMENT: RIGHT TO REGULATE? RIGHT TO TAX?

The Americans had contested furiously, but—with the exception of Partridge and his clients—on an economic basis only. The bogus duty created ambiguity—trade regulation vs. taxation—that cast a long shadow, contributing to the British-American controversy three decades later.

It was natural—since Parliament had been regulating the trade of the colonies almost from their first founding—that American protests against the bills of 1731 and 1732 were directed wholly against the economic burden that would result from the prohibition of trade. But there also was no constitution-based protest against the money bill of 1733.[18]

While the Lords were considering the bill, Pennsylvania submitted this protest:

17. *Calendar of State Papers: Colonial Series, America and West Indies* (London, 1737), 61.
18. Southwick, because of the unusually adverse effect of the prohibition, feels strongly about the lack of American protest. He points out that "The most striking thing about the whole affair, when we consider later colonial history, is the fact that the colonies made no claim whatsoever against the constitutionality of the proposed law." He concludes: they "did not question the authority of Parliament" to take such dramatic action. See Albert B. Southwick, "The Molasses Act—Source of Precedents," *The William and Mary Quarterly* 8, no. 3 (1951), 398-99. This paper also provides additional background on the genesis of the Molasses Act and the surrounding controversy.

> That a bill is brought up to [your lordships] named an act for the better securing and encourageing the trade of his Majestys sugar colonies in America, which bill, should be the same passed into a law, would have the same consequence as might have attended two former bills of the like title brought up to [your lordships] the two last sessions of Parliament but which [your lordships] did not think proper to pass.

This protest makes no distinction between the two earlier bills of prohibition and the new bill to levy a duty. The ambiguity of the bill, and the hidden nature of the taxation, resulted in there being no widespread American protest on a constitutional basis. Pennsylvania, for example, simply asserted that the bill "would fully and effectually prohibit the legal trade and commerce" of North America.[19]

ENDURING IMPORTANCE

From the British point of view, the Molasses Act was clearly a money bill, and hence a precedent for later taxation. From the American point of view, the act was trade regulation, and not a precedent for later taxation. Richard Price succinctly captured the nature of the Molasses Act and the American reaction.

> In this act, the duties imposed are said to be given and granted by the Parliament to the King; and this is the first American act in which these words have been used. But notwithstanding this, as the act had the appearance of being only a regulation of trade, the colonies submitted to it.[20]

In 1763, in order to derive a revenue from the American colonies, the British decided to enforce the Molasses Act. (George Grenville, the prime minister, also decided to reduce the molasses duty to three pence in order to encourage legal duty-paid importation of molasses in preference to continued smuggling. The amended Molasses Act is now known as the Sugar Act of 1764, and is a different story.[21])

The Board of Trade sent instructions to the governors on October 11. Because of "neglect, connivance and fraud, *not only the revenue is impaired*, but the commerce of the colonies is diverted from its natural course, and the salutary provisions of many wise laws are in great measure defeated." Therefore, "His Majesty has commanded us to require and enjoin you, in the strictest manner, to make the suppression of the

19. Stock, ed., *Proceedings and Debates*, 208-210.

20. Richard Price, *Observations on the Nature of Civil Liberty, the Principles of Government, and the Justice and Policy of the War with America* (London, 1776), 61.

21. Ken Shumate, "The Sugar Act: a Brief History," *Journal of the American Revolution*, September 17, 2018.

clandestine and prohibited trade with foreign nations, and the improvement of the revenue, the constant and immediate objects of your care."[22]

Gov. Francis Bernard of Massachusetts responded to the Board of Trade on December 26. He pointed out this problem: "[The Molasses Act] has been a perpetual stumbling-block to the Custom-house officers. . . . The question seems to be, whether it should be an Act of Prohibition, or an Act of Revenue."[23]

His next assertion, that it was "designed for the former," reflected the broad American understanding. In early 1764, the colonies remonstrated against enforcement. The action began with Boston merchants publishing a pamphlet of protest and writing to their counterparts in neighboring colonies.

> Boston, January 9, 1764
> [The Molasses Act] has long & justly been complain'd of by the Northern Colonies as a great Grievance; and should it be continued & put in Execution, with any Degree of Rigour (as is like to be the Case hereafter) it will give a Mortal Wound to the Peace of these Colonies.[24]

Three additional colonies—Connecticut, Rhode Island, and New York—published essays and petitions against the enforcement of the Molasses Act. All four protests objected only to the economic burden of the act, not its violation of the rights of Americans.

Charles McLean Andrews points out that "The vigorous protests of the New England merchants . . . do not contain a single word that can be construed as a denial of the legality of the act itself. . . . Not once did they say that parliament had no legal right to pass such a measure."[25]

Bernard Bailyn makes the same point: "The most striking fact about these addresses and petitions is their entire devotion to economic arguments: nowhere do they appeal to constitutional issues; nowhere was Parliament's right to pass such laws officially questioned."[26]

This lack of objection based on a constitutional argument was later brought forth to support the British rationale for taxation: a "Presi-

22. *Records of the Colony of Rhode Island and Providence Plantations, in New England: 1757-1769*, Volume VI: 375.

23. Francis Bernard, *Select Letters on the Trade and Government of America* (London, 1774), Letter II: 4.

24. *Publications of the Colonial Society of Massachusetts*, Volume 19, 380-81.

25. Charles M. Andrews, *The Colonial Background of the American Revolution* (New Haven and London: Yale University Press, 1931), 63.

26. Bernard Bailyn, ed., *Pamphlets of the American Revolution, 1750–1776; Volume I, 1750-1765* (Cambridge, MA: Harvard University Press, 1965), 358-59.

dent," just as Partridge had anticipated. Thomas Whately, trusted lieutenant and spokesman for Grenville, made the justification as explicit as could be.

> The Colonies have . . . acquiesced under several parliamentary Taxes. [The Molasses Act] lays heavy Duties on all foreign Rum, Sugar, and Melasses imported into the British Plantations. The Amount of the Impositions has been complained of; the Policy of the Laws has been objected to; but the Right of making such a Law has never been questioned.[27]

And therefore, the argument goes, Parliament has rightful authority to impose such duties for revenue.

The enforcement of the Molasses Act (and its amendment in 1764) was the first step in changing British colonial policy: from commercial regulation only, to the addition of parliamentary taxation.[28] Pitman states the consequence: "It was the serious attempt by the British government . . . to enforce this law [i.e., the Molasses Act], and again in 1764, by lower duties, to interfere with trade to the foreign West Indies, that ushered in the revolutionary movement."[29]

27. Thomas Whately, *The Regulations Lately Made Concerning the Colonies, and the Taxes Imposed Upon Them, Considered* (London, 1765), 104.
28. Burke (*Speech on American Taxation*: 1241) asserted that it, "opened a new principle: and here properly *began the second period of the policy of this country with regard to the Colonies;* by which the scheme of a regular Plantation Parliamentary revenue was adopted in theory, and settled in practice."
29. Pitman, *The Development of the British West Indies*, 272.

How the Magna Carta Influenced the American Revolution

JASON YONCE

In 1984, Ross Perot purchased a copy of the 1297 reissuance of the Magna Carta from the Brudenell family who had held the document for centuries. In 1988, it became a permanent fixture of the National Archives Museum where it stayed in the rotunda along with the American charters of freedom for several years. Nearly two decades later, in 2007, Perot sold the copy for twenty-one million dollars to David Rubenstein who also placed it again on long-term loan at the Archives as well as giving a generous donation for renovations to the rotunda.[1] The Archives re-encased the charter and placed in a new exhibit in 2010. The 2500-word Latin document is a remarkable sight. In many ways it is in better condition on vellum than the parchment copies of the Declaration of Independence and United States Constitution.[2]

The Magna Carta, and how the American founders viewed it, is fundamental to any Whig interpretation of the period. While economic interpretations are valid, it would be wrong to dismiss the founders' vision of the Magna Carta as a foundational text and patrimony, and its power in propaganda and legal argumentation. For patriot or loyalist, the Magna Carta took on a covenantal role to which all else was subordinate.

Nevertheless, the centuries-long history of the document before the Revolutionary War complicates the history for those in the present. It

1. A personal account of the auction can be found at David Rubenstein, "The Magna Carta Returns to the Archives," *Prologue Magazine* 42, no. 4 (Winter 2010).
2. "Perot Purchases a Copy of the Magna Carta," *New York Times*, September 27, 1984, www.nytimes.com/1984/09/27/us/perot-purchases-a-copy-of-magna-carta.html. Christopher Michaud, "Magna Carta fetches $21.3 million at Sotheby's auction," *Reuters*, December 18, 2007, www.reuters.com/article/us-magnacarta-auction/magna-carta-fetches-21-3-million-at-sothebys-auction-idUSN1854840520071219.

is difficult to draw a very straight of a line from 1215 to 1776 without losing focus and winding up in a thicket of legalese or mentioning every single colonial and founding figure who even once mentioned the charter in speech or letter. Yet despite unforgiving contemporary views of the charter's significance, and those in the Revolutionary period who saw it as a wellspring of everything it meant to be of English descent, we can see that the path may be quite tortuous but one can look backward from 1776 and see a clear beginning in the distant past.

ORIGINS

Histories of what occurred at Runnymede in 1215 can begin as early as the 900s with others starting after the Norman Conquest of 1066 under William I (the Conqueror). This was the ascent of the Norman and Angevin Kings in England. William the Conqueror's second son, Robert, was rightful heir to the throne because his older brother, William II, had died in 1100. Younger brother Henry, however, swiftly united the barons behind him and assumed the throne. This was accomplished with some conditions from the barons, which Henry outlined in a bilingual Charter of Liberties. Such promises were not unknown before this, but Henry's was the first of such great length. His charter was reaffirmed by his successors not only as originating with Henry but as a continuation of the rights and liberties of the English since before the Norman Conquest.

Henry made his promises to the Church first but then promised to ease the reliefs paid by the baronage that were required to "buy" back the lands they had inherited. He remitted debts owed to his predecessor and restored the "Law of King Edward."[3] Two generations later, in 1199, Henry II's youngest son—the infamous King John - rose to the throne. This was not an expected outcome throughout most of John's life. John spent much of his kingship at war with regions of France. War was costly and, as the story goes, John's barons had little patience with his fiscal policies to fund these massive campaigns. A new agreement was reached at Runnymede in 1215, called the Runnymede Charter for decades before the term *Magna Carta* became the standard.

Stephen Langton, then Archbishop of Canterbury, has long been considered the primary author of the charter, although it is unclear which provisions are his and which are not. Langton had the background to have crafted such a text. His education was primarily French and heavily influenced by his colleague Pierre Chanter or, Anglicized, Peter Cantor. Both held that monarchy was an element of Original Sin

3. Charter of Liberties of King Henry I, A.D. 1100.

and, while there were duties one owed to a monarch in the temporal realm, there were limits on what a monarch could exact from his subjects. Langton conditioned this obedience on a technicality: whether or not judges had ruled the king's actions to be just. Disobedience was not permitted if there was an affirming judgment. If, on the other hand, the king acted in his own will, that was another matter.

These types of debates, including the boundaries between ecclesial and political authorities, were commonplace in the academic world in medieval Paris. During the generation before Runnymede, English legal theory was dominated by the likes of John of Salisbury who was of Anglo-Saxon descent but educated, like Langton, in Paris under Abelard and who was a friend of the first and only English Pope, Adrian IV. In his *Policraticus*, Salisbury affirmed that kings were bound by the law and advanced his own somewhat unique solution of regicide in addition to mere disobedience.[4] Lawful kingship, however, was not a novel point of view during this period but a fairly commonplace one; the Magna Carta, far from being a watershed, reflected ideas that had already been long in place by 1215.[5] In 1291, Edward I declared the charter to have statutory force and it continued to do so for centuries.

1300-1600: AN INTERLUDE

The long-established narrative has been that the Magna Carta vanished from the English imagination from the fourteenth to the seventeenth centuries. Although many of the articles declined in relevance as laws changed during these three "dark" centuries, a seventeenth century writer asserted that the Magna Carta's mind was great even if the body was small.[6] Recent research on court documents of this era, long obscured by the archaic and inconsistent language they used, shows that many of these cases did cite the Magna Carta in some form or another. More formal treatises appear in the sixteenth century as well.

This dispels the notion that the charter grew irrelevant during the Late Middle Ages and disrupts another prevalent narrative, that Edward Coke democratized the meaning of the Magna Carta beyond what it could have possibly meant in its time. It is now evident that the

4. John of Salisbury, "The Statesman's Book" (*Policraticus* in the original Latin), in *Great Political Thinkers,* 3rd edition, ed. William Ebenstein (New York: Holt, Rinehart and Winston, 1964), 187-209.

5. John W. Baldwin, "Master Stephen Langton, Future Archbishop of Canterbury: The Paris Schools and Magna Carta," *The English Historical Review* 123, no. 503 (2008): 811-846. See also Lord Sumption, "The Magna Carta Then and Now," an address to the Friends of the British Library, March 9, 2015.

6. Richard H. Helmholz, "The Myth of Magna Carta Revisited," *North Carolina Law Review*, 94, (2015): 1475-92.

charter's *villiens tenementum*, those subject to a feudal lord, were partially included in the chapters concerning free men. To be fair, there was probably little recourse that a peasant would have against his lord.[7] However, it did not necessarily imply a lack of parity when acting *outside* the geographic bounds of his feudal domain. Rights were certainly limited weighed against one's lord but peasants nonetheless had rights under medieval readings of the Magna Carta particularly following the vast societal changes brought about by the Bubonic Plague of the fourteenth century. When writing about the Magna Carta's immemorial influence, recent discoveries have been a huge boon to those who look to the charter for its influence on American law and the founders' understandings of rights.

1600-1688

Stephen Langton, speaking for the barons, had attributed these rights to a very likely source: God. The barons, however, probably had a more terrestrial origin in mind: immemorial custom.[8]

Indeed, if there is a word which could contextualize the sentiments about English law during this period, particularly as it applied to the rights of individuals, the best choice would be *immemoriality*. While that may not actually be a word, it describes something that exists beyond memory. The Magna Carta had not been "forgotten" in the fifteenth and sixteenth centuries. However, a "revival" of its origin and meaning, especially of the twenty-ninth article, came during the seventeenth century. Its primary expositor, Edward Coke, is likely recognizable to most readers of American constitutional history. Its primary *exporter* was another name even more familiar to students of American history—William Penn. Penn, like Coke, would primarily concern himself with Article 29.[9]

In terms of immemoriality, Coke connected the Magna Carta to twelfth century origins, namely the coronation texts of Kings Henry I, II, and III. From there, Coke and his successors extended this law to Edward the Confessor, the last of the Anglo-Saxon Kings of the early eleventh century. An example of Coke's rendering of the Magna Carta, and one that would prove very important for his American acolytes in the next century, was the writ of Habeas Corpus. The notion itself pre-

7. Some peasants were willing to claim the rights of the charter against their lords. See John F. Nichols, "An Early Fourteenth Century Petition from the Tenants of Bocking to Their Manorial Lord," *Economic History Review* 2, no. 2 (January 1930), 300-7.
8. Sumption, "The Magna Carta Then and Now."
9. George Garnett, "Sir Edward Coke's Resurrection of the Magna Carta," in *Magna Carta: History, Context and Influence* (London: School of Advanced Study, University of London, Institute of Historical Research, 2018), 51-60.

dated the Magna Carta by nearly a half-century under Henry II.[10] The modern concept of Habeas Corpus is not clearly connected with the Magna Carta, rather, *Habeas corpus ad subjiciendum* had been a royal prerogative to have a prisoner called to the King's court. While Article 29 established that freemen cannot be imprisoned or dispossessed without some sort of due process, Article 28 of the Magna Carta established that no one (*aliquem*), not merely freemen (*liber homo*), could be charged without reliable witnesses presented in front of some sort of tribunal. From this, Coke extrapolated what many would consider a more contemporary notion of *habeas corpus*.[11]

Parliament passed the Habeas Corpus Act forty-five years after Coke's death in 1679 during Charles's reign. This was not understood as creating habeas corpus but, rather, strengthening it to prevent any arbitrary or capricious behavior from Charles's likely successor, his brother James. The act passed in a humorous back-and-forth between the Lords and Commons and Charles gave his assent.[12]

During the Stuart restoration in Britain, King Charles II and James were typically supportive of religious toleration. Unfortunately, the Parliament of the time did not share this sentiment and William Penn, as the story goes, found himself so at odds with supporters of the Church of England that he eventually fled to North America. With this background, Penn printed the Magna Carta in the North American colonies, expounding on the natural rights of Englishmen with particular reverence toward the ninth and twenty-ninth articles.[13]

10. A terrific account is available in J. Enoch Powell, *Great Parliamentary Occasions* (London: Queen Anne Press, 1966), 65.
11. From the text of the 1297 charter, Article 28: *Nullus ballivus ponat decetero aliquem ad legem manifestam vel ad juramentum simplici loquela sua, sine testibus fidelibus ad hoc inductis*, "No bailiff is henceforth to put any man on his open law or on oath simply by virtue of his spoken word without reliable witnesses produced for the same." Article 29: *Nullus liber homo decetero capiatur vel imprisonetur aut disseisiatur de aliquo libero tenemento suo vel libertatibus vel liberis consuetudinibus suis, aut utlagetur*, "No freeman is to be taken or imprisoned or disseised of his free tenement or of his liberties or free customs."
The two most commonly cited authors for those who oppose this reading are Edward Jenks who wrote his "Myth of the Magna Carta" in 1904 and William McKechnie whose own commentaries were published a decade later. Jenks declared false any claim that the document could apply to anyone outside of freemen who made up about one-sixth of the population. However, Richard Helmholz pointed out that much of the criticism of the Magna Carta rests on anachronistic assumptions about law and, although he doesn't use the word himself, a progressive view of English law's formation must be borne in mind to put it in its proper context. Helmholz, "The Myth of Magna Carta Revisited."
12. See the 1166 Assize of Clarendon, avalon.law.yale.edu/medieval/assizecl.asp.
13. The ninth article forbade land seizure for the payment of debt if there was sufficient money or property, or a willing surety, to cover the debt.

Most of Penn's commentary on the Magna Carta centered on the rights that it granted to *all* Englishmen. His introduction smacks of a warning and a call for all of the colonies, not just Pennsylvania, to pass resolutions affirming the rights of men, more akin to a call for a bill of rights than a constitution. With one exception in Maryland in the 1640s, key government documents like the *Fundamental Orders of Connecticut* (1639) were simply about governance and not about rights.

Marylanders had a stronger record of attempting to delineate their rights as Englishmen in addition to the marginally effective 1639 *Petition of Right*. The settlers asserted "the Inhabitants of this Province shall have all their rights and liberties according to the Great Charter of England." In a 1728 pamphlet, Daniel Dulany the elder re-asserted that these rights had their origin not only in the Magna Carta but also in other acts including the Bill of Rights of 1689 and the aforementioned Habeas Corpus Act of 1679. His son, Daniel Dulany the younger, though a loyalist, would nevertheless argue in a similar vein concerning taxation without representation decades later.[14]

In same decade as Penn's printing, comity between the colonial governments and the British Crown withered. Colonists had wearied not only of King James II's pro-Catholic power plays, but also of his royal governors in the colonies. Moreover, James used royal prerogative to dump the colonial charters that provided the later foundation for the patriot's argument that the North American colonists maintained the same rights of mainland Brits. The result, while not on the scale of war, did involve rebellion in a few of the colonies: Leisler's Rebellion (New York), Gove's Rebellion (New Hampshire), and the Boston Revolt of 1689.

Great Britain faced a two-front upheaval from the Dutch Low Countries against the Stuart Dynasty as well as discontent and revolt from its own North American colonies who were already rebelling to assert their rights nearly a century before the American Revolution. The Glorious Revolution of 1688 upended the Stuart Dynasty and began the rule of the House of Hanover under the William of Orange, a Dutch prince and stadtholder, and his first cousin Mary II.

14. Charles A. Rees, "Remarkable Evolution: The Early Constitutional History of Maryland," *Baltimore Law Review* 36, no. 2 (2007), 217-70. Dulany the Elder's Pamphlet *The Right of the Inhabitants of Maryland to the Benefit of English Laws* is difficult to locate but is reprinted in St. George Leaking Sioussat's "The English Statutes in Maryland," *Johns Hopkins University Studies in Historical & Political Science* (1903), 81-104. Dulany the Younger's pamphlet "Considerations on the Propriety of Imposing Taxes in the British Colonies, for the Purpose of rasing a Revenue, by Act of Parliament" was better known because of the revolutionary context in which it was written. An excerpt is available at www.let.rug.nl/usa/documents/1751-1775/daniel-dulany-considerations-october-1765.php.

AMERICANS AND THE RIGHTS OF ENGLISHMEN

The Founders' view of the Magna Carta was largely founded on such idealism of English law and identity. Far from its origins as a baronial document, the Magna Carta had its own mythos by the 1700s. In this high-minded idealism, the charter represented the rights of all Englishmen rather than just the peerage. As a legal matter the charter's relevance was far less clear.

Colonial grievances were against the policies of Parliament, not the monarchy, and rebelling against the British monarchy was not a focal point of protests before 1776. If anything, during the protests against Parliament, colonial political leaders remained deferent to the King. Historian Eric Nellis questioned the sincerity of the Olive Branch Petition in his book *The Long Road to Change* because it asserted allegiance to the King while rejecting Parliament's authority in the colonies.[15] However, its sincerity and logic is not as incoherent as it seems when taking into account the legal arguments of the 1760s and the appeals to the Magna Carta above any other major text of English history.[16] Having resorted to outright rebellion in 1776, the complaints of the Declaration of Independence could be addressed directly to the King. In fact, at that point, the Declaration seems to go out of its way to avoid acknowledging that Parliament owned any of the abuses cited therein.

In 1764 Parliament passed the Sugar Act to resolve the longstanding issue with American merchants evading import duties on molasses. While in the short run the act had some unpopularity with merchants, it failed to excite anti-parliamentary passions. The Stamp Act of 1765 was another matter: it was a new revenue tax that affected almost everyone. Here began the decade of discontent leading to secession.

The Glorious Revolution of 1688 had established greater parliamentary supremacy. This was a supremacy that would naturally have extended to the British colonies. While that revolution lessened the power of the British monarch to act in the absence of a convened parliament, and gave rise to the English Bill of Rights, it still occurred during a period of greater centralization of power throughout Europe. The absorption of Scotland into Great Britain under a single crown and parliament in the 1707 Act of Union was a natural consequence of this. Caution was taken in later colonial charters not to be as gener-

15. For an easy-to-read transcription of the Olive Branch Petition see Steven Thomas, "The Olive Branch Petition," *America's Homepage* (Georgia Tech), January 2009, ahp.gatech.edu/olive_branch_1775.html.

16. Eric Nellis, *The Long Road to Change: America's Revolution, 1750–1820* (Toronto: University of Toronto Press, 2007).

ous as in those granted in the earlier seventeenth century. Georgia, for example, entitled its colonists to the rights of Englishmen but no right of local governance.[17]

These matters came to a head during the Stamp Act Crisis in 1765. This was when the legal aspects of the charter came into question. Benjamin Franklin traveled to London to represent the colonies. Other recorded testimony came from Isaac Barre, an Irish soldier and member of Parliament supportive of the Americans, and Joseph Galloway, a lawyer and friend of Franklin's yet nevertheless an ardent loyalist pledged to defend the mother country.

Most of Franklin's associates agreed with Barre. Franklin combined his associates' *Declaration of Rights and Grievances*, undoubtedly written by John Dickinson, along with other municipal declarations to the House of Commons. In the course of questioning, the Magna Carta appears to have come up in a flurry of confusion between Franklin and the Prime Minister, Lord Grenville. The back-and-forth between Grenville and Franklin tested Franklin's patience and, as the ministers persisted in their interrogation, Franklin grew weary and testy.

> Q. Don't you know there is, in the Pennsylvania Charter, an express reservation of the right of Parliament to Lay Taxes there?
> A. I know there is a clause in the charter, by which the King grants that he will levy no taxes on the inhabitants, unless it be with the consent of the assembly, or by act of parliament.
> Q. How then could the assembly of Pennsylvania assert, that laying a tax on them by the Stamp Act was an infringement of their rights?
> A. They understand it thus; by the same charter, and otherwise, they are intitled to all the privileges and liberties of Englishmen; they find in the great charters, and the petition and declaration of rights that one of the privileges of English subjects is, that they are not to be taxed but by their common consent . . .
> Q. Are there any words in the charter that justify that construction?
> A. The common rights of Englishmen, as declared by the Magna Charta, and the petition of right, all justify it.

While it had been a pretty standard argument to invoke the older colonial charters, Grenville stood on firmer ground than Franklin here. The Pennsylvania Charter, ironically William Penn's own *Frame of Government*, stipulated exactly what Grenville had spoken. Franklin's rebuttal hyperextended a six hundred year old document that bore little relevance to the matter at hand.

17. "Charter of Georgia: 1732," *The Avalon Project* (Yale University Law School), avalon.law.yale.edu/18th_century/ga01.asp.

Notions of "inherited rights" get bandied about loosely in contemporary discourse but it is essential to understand how strong notions of "Englishness" existed for nearly a *millennium* before the American Revolution. Saint Bede the Venerable wrote a well-known history of England in the seventh century that formed the basis of an English identity apart from the fragmented continent in the post-Western Roman Empire realms. Englishness, and later Britishness, was extended generationally and, as far as the colonists were concerned, across all distances. In London, Edmund Burke made the same case for the colonists although he, like Joseph Galloway, would never claim colonial legislative supremacy over the Parliament.

Many British politicians, as well as many notable Americans, disagreed. Distance was a cause for differential treatment. Thomas Hutchinson was among the Americans who agreed that the colonies were not necessarily part of the British community insofar as rights were concerned. Here it is important to recall an important point in the chronology of the debates over "taxation without representation:" several colonies argued for their right for *their* representatives to tax themselves. That would put colonial legislative bodies on par with the British Parliament. If that seems like an unpalatable notion, also bear in mind that the Glorious Revolution was as close to their national memory as World War II is to ours. And from the ashes of the Glorious Revolution was the final subordination of the crown to the prerogatives of Parliament in most matters. One must keep this in mind when understanding the opprobrium of Parliament and American Tories. In sum: claiming rights of all post-1688 Britain while claiming further rights to autonomy from an inheritance from the 1215 charter frankly seemed absurd.

In 1776, in the spring preceding the Declaration of Independence, Chief Justice William Henry Drayton of South Carolina delivered a riveting address to a grand jury in Charleston. Drayton invoked the Magna Carta as a foundational document of justice in the English colonies and charged that George III's government had treated it with contempt. In this decade after the taxation crises, Parliament was no longer the main enemy and charges were increasingly made against the King signifying not only the offenses against the Americans—which Drayton and many others outlined—but the state of rebellion for which Englishness was no longer a sufficient bond to prevent. Drayton drew on numerous historical precedents including South Carolina's shedding of proprietary rule in a bloodless revolution in 1719.

While drawing parallels with King John would have been insult enough, Drayton took the approach of comparing George III to the final Stuart monarch, James II, who had been ousted during the 1688 Glorious Revolution. It was in these later years before 1776 that the colonial charters—which had been tampered with also under James II—were dissolved by George III. Other states, including New York, had their legislatures suspended. James II had broken the original contract between the Crown and Englishmen, and now George III had done so with the colonies; the response would be no different.[18]

While Drayton still paid some lip service to reconciliation, David Ramsay avoided any pretense in his July 4, 1778 address, also in Charleston. The language was extravagant and optimistic despite the state of war. In Ramsay's address one can see the beginnings of an "American Dream" in which even the lowest-born could succeed. "Whereas, in our present happy system, the poorest school-boy may prosecute his studies with increasing ardour, from the prospect, that in a few years he may, by his improved abilities, direct the determinations of public bodies, on subjects of the most stupendous consequence."[19] Ramsay's speech clearly wanted to boast of America's own glorious revolution. Naturally, it may be pointing out the obvious that the Siege of Charleston was still two years in the future from Ramsay's grandiloquent speech.

It is on this point we can return to 1776 when the Olive Branch Petition and other documents for reconciliation were addressed to George III. Thomas Jefferson and John Adams appealed to the rights that they believed extended from the pre-1688 Britain and tethered their loyalty to the King rather than to Parliament. However, taxation alone did not propel the colonists to outright rebellion. Rhode Island formally declared independence a month before the signing of the Declaration in 1776, citing the lack of trial by jury and habeas corpus. Harkening back to the Magna Carta: the fight was to remain free, not to become free.

But where the Declaration of Independence reflected ire over suspension of colonial charters and legislatures, and the Constitution's more immediate focuses were of habeas corpus and due process, the

18. "Judge Drayton's Address to the Grand Jury at Charlestown, South Carolina," April 23, 1776, digital.lib.niu.edu/islandora/object/niu-amarch%3A92538. Thomas Paine probably took the most radical approach of all: that the rights of all human beings derived not from statute but through their humanity. His notion of rights nearly had the same divine origination as Langton's. Paine went to great lengths in the early chapters of the first part of *Rights of Man* to dispose of any attempt to tie American rights to English rights via statute. Paine took Edmund Burke to task throughout the entire volume but never appeared to direct his ire toward Americans who espoused the statutory view.

19. David Ramsay, "An Oration on the Advantages of American Independence," July 4, 1776, name.umdl.umich.edu/N28767.0001.001.

Bill of Rights owed a massive debt not only to the English Bill of Rights but to the very wording of the Magna Carta:

> Fifth Amendment: "No person shall be held to answer for a capital or otherwise infamous crime . . . nor to be deprived of life, liberty, or property without due process of law . . ."
> Chapter Twenty-Nine: No freeman shall be taken, imprisoned, or disseized . . . or in any way destroyed, nor will we . . . prosecute him, except . . . by the law of the land."
> Fifth Amendment: "nor shall private property be taken for public use, without just compensation."
> Chapter Nineteen: "No constable or other bailiff of ours shall take anyone's grain or other chattels . . . without immediately paying for them in money"
> Sixth Amendment: "In all criminal prosecutions the accused shall enjoy the right to a speedy and public trial, by an impartial jury of the state and district wherein the crime shall have been committed"
> Chapter Fourteen: "A freeman shall not be [prosecuted] . . . except by the oaths of lawful men of the neighborhood"[20]

CONCLUSION

During the eight hundredth anniversary of the Magna Carta in 2015, British jurist and medieval historian Jonathan Sumption—Lord Sumption—took on legal and historical interpretations of the charters. "Its practitioners have a natural tendency to legitimise their ideals by asserting their antiquity. But they have, on the whole, been bad historians."[21] Sumption assailed Coke and the exceptionalist mythos that persisted until the early twentieth century. "But I do have a problem with the distortion of history to serve an essentially modern political agenda. Claims like those which I have just cited are high-minded tosh." There is little to nothing wrong to be found in Lord Sumption's analysis. However, even if much of the tradition that the Founders saw was a cooked-up historical fiction it would be foolish to deny the power of the idea and how it came to shape the political thinking of the period. In that sense, the Magna Carta's placement with the charters of freedom is reasonable even if the ultimate, parallel truth is much more complicated. However, there is some reason to believe that it is *un*complicated. The recently-translated court documents from the fourteenth and fifteenth centuries cast doubt on the idea that Coke's—and the

20. William Swindler, *Magna Carta* (New York: Grosset & Dunlap, 1968), 101-17.
21. Lord Sumption, "The Magna Carta Then and Now."

American Founders'—views of the Magna Carta and the rights of Englishmen were mythical. Exaggerated, perhaps, but far from baseless. As Justice Felix Frankfurter put it in 1953, the Magna Carta "was the beginning, not the end, of the struggle for the principles it enunciated."

Thomas Paine Goes to Sea: A Pre-Revolutionary Tale

JETT B. CONNER

Coming up rapidly from behind the British privateer, the frigate suddenly lowered one national flag and raised another, the customary ruse of switching colors, swung about and unleashed a fury of cannon fire directly at the stern of the enemy ship. Although it had done its best to prepare for just such an attack, the privateer suffered damage and heavy losses. Above deck, limbs of masts and men went flying. But what must have been happening below was even a greater nightmare for Thomas Paine—the fear of being struck down "not by cannon balls, but by splinters from inside the ship that fly in all directions."[1] The privateer managed to come about and return fire, taking many lives on the French ship. Soon, though, the British ship, overwhelmed, out gunned and out manned, struck its colors. For real.

Fortunately, young Paine missed all the action this time. On the crisp November morning in 1756 that the British privateer *Terrible* put out to sea, he was not aboard. He certainly had meant to be, but just in the nick of time his father tracked down his runaway son in London and talked him out of sailing off with the rest of the crew. Good thing he listened. As he recalled later: "From this adventure I was happily prevented by the affectionate and moral remonstrance of a good father, who, from his own habits of life, being of the Quaker profession, must begin to look upon me as lost."[2]

Growing up in Thetford, England, a market town northeast of London of about 2000 inhabitants at the time, Thomas Pain (he would add the "e" later in life) was provided a grammar school education by his working-class family. His father was a staymaker, a maker of whalebone

1. Thomas Paine, *The Complete Writings of Thomas Paine*, 2 vols. ed. Philip S. Foner (New York: The Citadel Press, 1969), 2: 1068.
2. Ibid., 1: 405.

components for women's corsets. His mother was the daughter of a civil servant. Around age thirteen, his formal education having come to an end, Paine began an apprenticeship with father to become a staymaker. He worked in the trade for six years until suddenly running away from home to seek his adventure at sea.

It must have been a dull existence, making whalebone stays. Descriptions of Thetford at the time do not paint a bleak picture of the town or surrounding countryside, although like many English towns of the period stark inequality was everywhere and little opportunity existed for those not well connected to the town's ruling family, named Grafton. Paine attended the Anglican church of his mother, but nonetheless was exposed through his father to the bland uniformity of the Quaker religion which he mildly poked fun of years later: "Though I reverence their philanthropy, I cannot help smiling at the conceit, that if the taste of a Quaker had been consulted at the creation, what a silent and drab-coloured creation it would have been. Not a flower would have blossomed its gaieties, nor a bird been permitted to sing."[3]

So, the young bird flew the coop: "At an early period, little more than sixteen years of age, raw and adventurous, and heated with the false heroism of a [school] master who had served in a man-of-war, I began the carver of my own fortune."[4] (Paine's recollection of his age was off. He was nineteen in 1756, the year he left home to seek adventure—the same year the Seven Years War between England and France began in Europe.)

After running away, Paine quickly found work as a staymaker in London. But he soon answered an advertisement that appeared in London's *Daily Advertiser* in the fall of 1756: "To cruise against the French, the *Terrible* Privateer, Capt. William Death . . . All Gentlemen Sailors, and able-bodied Landmen, who are inclinable to try their Fortune, as well as serve their King and Country, are desired to repair on board the said Ship."[5] Paine's dream of going to sea was finally coming true, or so he thought.

Privateers were "ships with a license to rob."[6] Outfitted as a privateer in October and granted its license soon after, a letter of marque, the *Terrible* carried twenty-four guns, a combination of six and nine pounders and smaller carriage-guns. After posting its advertisement

3. Moncure D. Conway, *The Life of Thomas Paine* (New York: G.P. Putman's Sons, 1893), 498.
4. Ibid., 405.
5. Alyce Barry, "Thomas Paine, Privateersman," *The Pennsylvania Magazine of History and Biography*, Vol. 101. No. 4 (October, 1977), 454.
6. Barbara W. Tuchman, *The First Salute* (New York: Alfred A. Knopf, 1988), 47.

for a crew, the one that Paine saw and responded to, the privateer ship sailed from London in November. It quickly spotted and boarded a vessel which likely held contraband goods and, after dropping it off and hoping it would be declared a prize, continued making its way to Plymouth to lay over for additional supplies. What might have happened to Paine had he sailed off on that fateful cruise soon unfolded.

The names of the captain and the ship were certainly ominous enough. Aboard the *Terrible* in addition to its captain, William Death, was a second officer, a cousin to the captain also named Death and several other officers with names such as Ghost and Devil. The privateer ship, which sailed from Execution Dock, was about to live up to those names. As it happened, there was also aboard a lieutenant of Marines named Samuel Stokes, who survived the ship's fateful battles and capture, and later published an account of the events.[7] It is by his account that much of what happened to the *Terrible* is known. Also, aboard as the ship departed Plymouth in early December to begin its cruise was a very dangerous passenger—a deadly fever with a presence much more menacing than the frightful names of the ship and its crew.

Even before its first battle the *Terrible* already had become a ship of death. Only 116 of the crew of 200 were able to "stand the guns" of the ship, "the rest being either dead or sick below with a distemper called spotted fever [likely typhus] that raged among the ship's company."[8] About two weeks after departing Plymouth, the privateer ship spied a sail and gave chase. It belonged to a French cargo ship named *Alexander le Grand* (which the English translated The Great Alexander). Finally catching up to the French ship, the *Terrible* subdued it after a two-hour battle. Then the *Terrible* with its prize in tow started making its way toward Plymouth to drop it off. Unfortunately, William Death's cousin—the second officer named Death—and several other crew members on the *Terrible* were killed during this first battle, further weakening the ship's already spare crew.

After a few days, the *Terrible* spotted two distant sails at dusk. The next morning, one of those ships bore down on the *Terrible* at a high rate of speed. Alarmed but forced to slow down while awaiting her prize to catch up, the *Terrible* prepared for battle. Soon the approaching

7. Samuel Stokes, "An Narrative of the Many Unparalle'd Hardships and Cruel Sufferings, While in France, of the Crew of the TERRIBLE Privateer, Commanded by Captain WILLIAM DEATH (London: J. Towers). Printed in Sarah and John Exshaw, The Gentleman's and London Magazine," vol. 26 (Dublin: John Exshaw, 1757), 490-492, books.google.com/books?id=SmFFAAAAYAAJ.

8. E.P. Statham, *Privateers and Privateering* (New York: James Pott & Co., 1910), 106-107.

ship, which turned out to be the *Vengeance*, a French privateer of thirty-six guns, switched its colors from British to French and attacked.

The *Terrible* fought fiercely against its attackers, killing the captain and many crew on the *Vengeance*, but in the end the French were the victors. And in spite of striking his ship's colors signaling surrender, Capitan Death, who was wounded several times early on but continued to fight, was shot in the back and killed as soon as the French boarded the defeated ship. Stripped of his watch and other personal belongings, he was tossed overboard. New horrors now faced the few remaining survivors of the *Terrible*. Because Lieutenant Stokes was among those who managed to survive dreadful imprisonment conditions later, he was able eventually to return to England and publish his account of the battle and the survivors' treatment. Among his descriptions:

> I come now to relate the most melancholly Scene of all . . . the Deck was cover'd with our Men, some dead, and many with their Arms and Legs off, and otherwise wounded . . . these barbarous Villains, having no more Regard to the Living than the Dead, tumbled all overboard, in Spite of their Dismal Cries for Mercy . . . After they had beat us unmercifully with their Cutlasses, they put some of us in double Irons on board the Terrible, and the rest on board the Vengeance . . . The next Morning, being the 28th of December [1756] . . . they hawl'd Twenty-seven of the poor Wretches out of the Hole, who were smothered to Death . . . and threw them overboard, like so many Dogs, taking no more Notice of it, than if nothing had happen'd.[9]

Years later, Paine wrote that the *Terrible* had "stood the hottest engagement of any ship" during the Seven Years War.[10] But soon after that ship had sailed, young Paine—not knowing of the *Terrible*'s fate at the time—brushed off his father's warnings which "began to wear away," and sought out another adventure at sea. This time he boarded the *King of Prussia*, a 340 ton multi-decked privateer with a crew of 250 and over fifty guns, and "went in her to sea."[11] The ship left London, sailed down the Thames in early January 1757 and, after picking up additional crew in Dover, put out to sea in February to cruise the English Channel and nearby waters.[12]

Interestingly, there were two privateers named *King of Prussia*, the one that Paine joined and another that sailed out of Liverpool. The ship Paine boarded had a six month's cruise; the ship sailing out of Liv-

9. Stokes, *An Narrative of the Many Unparalle'd Hardships*.
10. Paine, *The Complete Writings of Thomas Paine*, 1: 33.
11. Ibid., 1: 405.
12. John Keane, *Thomas Paine: A Political Life* (New York: Little, Brown, 1995), 38.

erpool returned to port after two years at sea. This has caused confusion in retelling Paine's adventure as a privateer sailor, some authors believing that Paine spent two years at sea.[13]

Next to nothing is known about Paine's experiences on this voyage. Even though it lasted six months, he barely mentioned the event later in life. The ship captured prizes and brought back plenty of booty. There is no record of Paine's responsibilities, so whether he took up arms against enemy ships, which was typical of hired crews' responsibilities, or performed other duties, no one really knows. Perhaps he put his staymaking skills to good use keeping lines and sails repaired.

But danger lurked aboard all privateer ships and he certainly saw death and destruction. Whatever his role on the *King of Prussia*, he experienced violent battles, felt fear and found plenty to fulfill his ambition for adventure. He particularly feared splinters flying around underneath the decks like little unguided missiles during cannon bombardments, because that's what he mentioned later. At the very least, he learned some survival skills that helped him achieve the independence he was seeking from home and family. And he took part in the Seven Years War, the same war that across the Atlantic was called the French and Indian War, a conflict that a young George Washington helped start in 1754.

For a time after disembarking from the cruise and with the help of his portion of the ship's bounty, Paine was able to live in London, attend scientific lectures and hobnob with some of London's elite and literati in the various social clubs of the city. It was a brief respite from the world of tradesman work, and it proved to be a period of education and enlightenment. But before long, his seafaring earnings depleted, he was forced to face the world of regular work again and consider his options, which weren't many. Going back to sea, however, was not among them. He didn't sign up for another privateer's cruise.

While living in Lewes where he served as a tax collector Paine penned his first pamphlet, *The Case of the Officers of Excise*. It was a forcefully written petition urging Parliament to improve wages and working conditions for England's excisemen. Many of them collected the funds necessary to get the pamphlet printed. Distributing it himself, Paine lobbied members of both houses of Parliament personally, but in the end his efforts failed and cost him his job, most likely for his political agitating though officially for neglecting his duties in Lewes as a tax collector while leaving his job to lobby the government in London.

13. For further details about the *King of Prussia,* see threedecks.org/index.php?display_type=show_ship&id=27009.

But Paine's pamphlet revealed his skills for persuasion and a way with words, and it caught the attention of some of London's movers and shakers, including such people as playwright and novelist Oliver Goldsmith.

At some point around this time Paine was introduced to Benjamin Franklin who was in London serving as an American agent for several colonies. The two got on well enough, because toward the end of 1774, at age thirty-seven and with numerous career failures and two failed marriages behind him, but carrying a letter of introduction from Franklin to his son-in-law Richard Bache in Philadelphia recommending the "ingenious, worthy young man," Paine went to sea once again for a second adventure. This time it was to start life anew in America and perhaps to fulfill a dream. He had always wanted to see America since grammar school: "I happened, when a school boy, to pick up a pleasing natural history of Virginia, and my inclination from that day of seeing the western side of the Atlantic never left me."[14]

Unfortunately, that old seafaring passenger and foe which had appeared on the *Terrible*, the dreaded Deadly Fever, was also aboard for this voyage. By the time the ship docked in Philadelphia in December, Paine was deliriously sick, unconscious, and unable to get out of his berth to set foot on the land of his new country. Still, in spite of acquiring the illness, he survived the crossing. Luckily, Franklin's letter worked its magic as a friend of his, a doctor, came aboard to help Paine get off the boat, carry him ashore and restore his health. Within a month, having recovered enough to get out and about, Paine began to explore his new opportunities. Virginia would have to wait.

He struck up a friendship with Robert Aitken, a Philadelphia printer, bookseller, and recent Scottish immigrant, and was hired in January 1775 to help edit Aitken's brand new publication, the *Pennsylvania Magazine: or, American Monthly Museum*. Paine's career as a revolutionary writer was about to take off. One year later, he published *Common Sense*, a pamphlet that created a sensation and would soon make its anonymous author famous for spurring the movement for independence.

Paine crossed the Atlantic several more times during the rest of his life. But it's likely he was able to do so only by the good fortune of being talked out of that first attempt to go to sea on the *Terrible* by his father, and later surviving his first ocean crossing. His lucky breaks were certainly critical for his own future and, as it turns out, for America's too.

14. Paine, *The Complete Writings of Thomas Paine*, 1: 88n.

"Monsr Dubuq," the First French Officer to Serve the American Cause?

FREDERICK C. DETWILLER

To historians of the American Revolution, the date of 1775 for French participation in the Patriot cause may seem incredible. The enigmatic "Monsr Dubuq," "Dubuc," or "Dubuque" was nonetheless, one of the first French officers to assist in the American Revolution, before envoy M. Julien Bonvouloir,[1] and two years prior to the arrival of Baron de Kalb and Marquis de Lafayette in July 1777. As early as July 6, 1775, Maj. Stephen Kemble reports "A Frenchman came this day from the Rebels says a French Man, one Dubuc, is their Chief Engineer, as Gridley cannot act from his Wound. Sent the French Man to the Provosts."[2] A July 8 report states, "I am told ye French rebel that came ye other ev'g speaks English though he pretends otherwise . . . which he [General Howe] takes to be string proof he came over with some design."[3] On August 17 Kemble reports, "The Capt. of the Man of War that Conveyed the inhabitants to Salem returned, and brought with him Monsieur Dubuque, a French Man, who had been employed by the rebels as an Engineer."[4]

So just who was this mysterious French engineer Dubuq? The engineer who served the rebels at Boston in June, July and August 1775 was probably Jean-Baptiste du Buq (1752-1787), son of Louis XVI's

1. Bonvouloir was the secret envoy of Vergennes, the French minister of state, through whom negotiations were opened in1775 that resulted in French intervention for American independence.
2. "Journal of Stephen Kemble," *Collections of the New York Historical Society* (New York: New York Historical Society, 1883), 47; MA Archives 137-8. Col. Richard Gridley, Chief U.S. Engineer, was wounded at Bunker Hill on June 17, 1775.
3. Dubuq to Thomas Gage, August 21, 1775, Thomas Gage Manuscripts, William L. Clements Library, University of Michigan.
4. "Journal of Stephen Kemble," 55.

Intendant des Colonies J-B "le Grand" Dubuc and a member of the Noailles Regiment (which, coincidentally, was led by Lafayette's brother-in-law).[5] Dubuq sailed for Beverly, Massachusetts, from La Trinité, Martinique in late April 1775. His contact was Josiah Batchelder, a merchant member of the Committee of Correspondence at Beverly, who had traded pine lumber and building materials, along with salt cod, from Massachusetts for sugar cane products (molasses and rum, etc.) with the Dubuq family at Galion, La Trinité, Martinique, as early as 1769.[6] Dubuq's schooner, captained by Nathaniel Leach, a Batchelder associate, was intercepted by the British sloop of war *Nautilus* off Cape Cod before he was allowed to make his way to Beverly and Salem. Dubuq wrote that Gen. Israel Putnam brought him to the American Camp at Cambridge in a chaise on June 4, 1775.[7]

At General Putnam's request, Dubuq went to New London, Connecticut, in early June 1775 on a mission seeking gunpowder suppliers and returned to the "Rebel" camp just after the Battle of Bunker Hill. He then served as "chief engineer" in the place of Richard Gridley who had been wounded in the thigh during the June 17 battle. Dubuq wrote about his construction of earthworks at Winter Hill and Prospect Hill under Putnam in June. In early July, Gen. Charles Lee ordered him to view the New Hampshire lines under the command of Gen. John Sullivan and Col. John Stark, with headquarters at the Royall Mansion in Medford.[8]

Dubuq then visited Danvers, Marblehead, and Newburyport, and heard Pres. Samuel Langdon's speech at Harvard revealing the colonists' ambitions for "Free Trade." Dubuq wrote to the French

5. Arbres Généalogiques sur Toujoursla, GeneaNet.org. Dubucs who served during this era include Abraham du Buc de Marcussy (de Marentille, 1761-1825), a sous-lieutenant in the Agenois Regiment which sailed with de Grasse from Martinique to Yorktown, and his brother Jean-Baptiste de Buc de Marcussy (1752-1787). Gilbert Bodinier, *Dictionnaire des officiers de l'armée royale qui ont combattu aux États-Unis pendant la guerre d'Indépendance* 3d ed. (Château de Vincennes, 2001), 172-73.

6. Dubuq apparently went to Beverly with an introduction by Dubuq de Bellefond, commandant of the battalion of the Trinity of Martinique, a correspondent and trading partner of Josiah Batchelder. Batchelder was on the Committee of Correspondence and Safety in Beverly, Massachusetts from 1773 until the end of the Revolution. Josiah Batchelder Papers, Series 3, B and C, 36 and 37 Correspondence and Bills in French: 1769-1776, and 1777-1792, Beverly Historical Society, Cabot House.

7. Dubuq to Gage, August 21, 1775.

8. Charles Lee quartered early in July with his famous dog Spado at the Royall Mansion, that he christened 'Hobgoblin Hall' in Medford. John Sullivan and John Stark were also quartered there. Washington later moved Lee and his dogs headquarters to the Oliver Tufts House, still standing nearby. Somerville Historical Society.

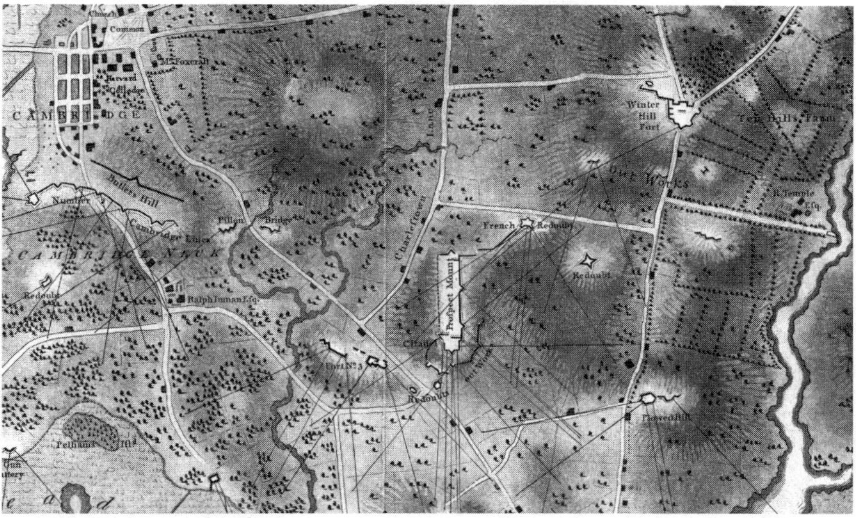

Detail from Henry Pelham's 1777 map of Boston, showing Dubuq's "French Redoubt" (center right) built from June to August 1775 on Central Hill between the works on Winter Hill and Prospect Hill. Note Cambridge and Harvard University at the upper far left. (*Library of Congress*)

colonies in the Caribbean for powder, some of which arrived from St. Domingue (Haiti) for the Provincial Massachusetts Committee on Supplies soon after August 8.[9]

A "French Redoubt" is clearly shown between Prospect and Winter hills in Medford on the 1775 Map of Boston and Environs by Henry Pelham, showing that the work bore that name in August.[10] The redoubt is shown in other detailed drawings of the "Rebel Works" on Prospect and Winter hills.[11] Washington had visited the new entrenchments soon after his arrival in the area, and wrote from Cambridge to John Hancock, President of Congress on July 10: "I arrived safe at this

9. James Swan recorded on August 8, 1775 that the first foreign military supplies (probably those ordered by Dubuq), in which the Committee of Safety had an interest, were soon to arrive from Cap François, St. Domingue. The Committee Appointed to State the Disbursements of this Colony in the Defense of American Liberty for the consideration of the Continental Congress: Col. James Swan account, 1775 Provincial Committee Accounts, Massachusetts Archives.

10. "A Plan of Boston in New England with its Environs . . .With the MILITARY WORKS constructed in those places in the Years 1775-1776," Henry Pelham. The pass that he was granted to do the survey for this map was dated August 21, 1775.

11. These were likely re-drawn by British Engineer Col. John Montresor based upon Dubuq's plans. See John Montresor, "Draught of the Towns of Boston and Charlestown and the Circumjacent Country shewing Works thrown up by his Majesty's Troops,"Map Division, Library of Congress.

place on the 3rd instant . . . Upon my arrival I immediately visited the several posts occupied by our troops . . . on our side we have thrown up intrenchments on Winter and Prospect Hills . . .the enemy's camp in full view, at a distance of a little more than a mile."[12]

After leaving the rebels and coming in to Boston, on August 20 "Monsr Dubuq" wrote two letters to British Gen. Thomas Gage, with several pages of detailed observations identifying his family connections and describing his visit to New England from April to August in service of his King (Louis XVI) and the American rebels including the construction of the "French Redoubt." In an apparent ruse to gain passage back to Europe he even offered his service to Gage himself.[13] The first letter, from "Monsr. DuBuq, A Frenchman who left the rebels among whom he served in quality of an Engineer," written in French and translated by this author, began as follows:

> To His Excellency General Gage, Commandant of His Majesty's Troops . . . My journey in this country was to have been for only two or three months after which time I planned to return to my country. I had the misfortune to let myself be deluded into the cause of the Americans and my services were received. I was employed by them in the quality of an engineer. The works I made were situated on Winter's Hill adjacent to Prospect Hill on the Medford side.14 The slopes of Prospect dominate the Cambridge river [and] are very well fortified by the works and the situation. The rear would be little accessible . . . As to whom the entrenchments are for in particular I could not tell in all exactitude as to proportions and their situation, but the plans which I could make in giving perhaps an idea. . . . Dubuq.[15]

Included was a four-page report, along with his offer to serve in British forces.

A second letter written by Dubuq to Gage in English the same day, August 20, gave details of his visit in a letter of introduction (in French) with his family connections:

12. *Final Report of the Boston National Historic Sites Commission* (Washington, DC: Government Printing Office, 1961), 232-236. Also "Forts built prior to Washington's Arrival" in Somerville Historical Monographs "George Washington in Somerville" by George Hill Evans, Librarian, Somerville Public Library, 1933, sub-committee on Study and Research of the George Washington Bi-Centennial Commission, appointed by Mayor John J. Murphy in 1932. Somerville Public Library.
13. Dubuq to Gage, August 21, 1775.
14. The "French Redoubt" is shown on Henry Pelham's map.
15. Dubuq to Gage, August 20, 1775, Thomas Gage Manuscripts, William L. Clements Library, University of Michigan.

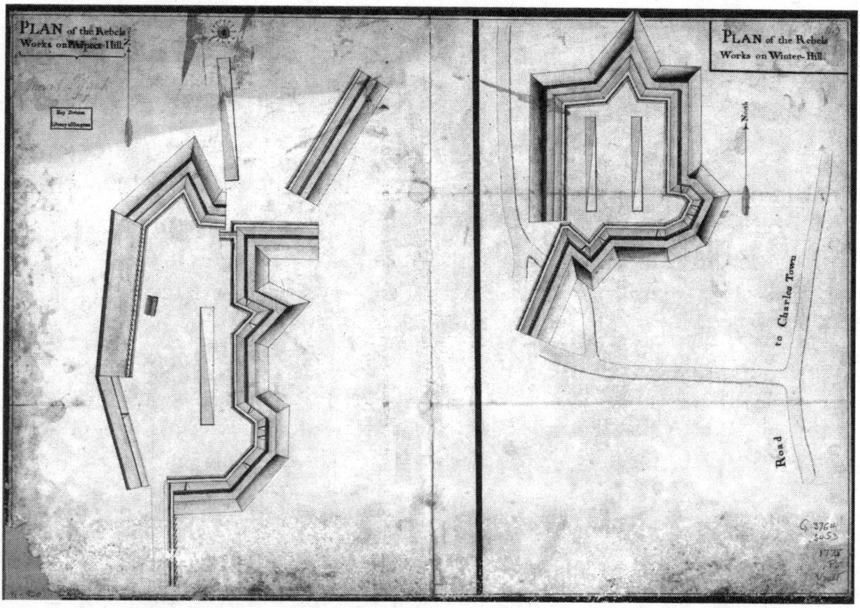

Plans of the "Rebel" Works on Prospect Hill and Winter [Central] Hill, 1775. Dubuq to Gen. Gage August 20, 1775: "As to whom the entrenchments are for in particular I could not tell in all exactitude as to proportions and their situation, but the plans which I could make in giving perhaps an idea." (*Library of Congress*)

> Dear Sir,
> As for further information in my regard you will please be able to take in receipt of Mr. Dubuq de Bellefond Commandant of the battalion of la Trinité of Martinique, Mr. the Count of Choiseul-Meuse, Brigadier of the armies of the King and governor of Martinique, Mr. Dubuq Superintendent of Commerce of the Colonies to enable to assure you, I flatter myself, Sir, That by saying to you that I belong to them, they will add advantageous accounts on my behalf. I have the honor to be with profound respect, Dear Sir, of your excellency, The very humble and very obedient servant,
> Dubuq[16]

16. "Monsieur, Quant à de plus amples informations à mon égard s'il vous plait En prendrez vous pourrez en reçevois de Mr Dubuq de Bellefond Commandant du battaillon de la Trinité de la Martinique, Mr le Comte de Choiseul-Meuse brigadier des armies du Roi et gouverneur de la Martinique, Mr Dubuq surintendant du commerce des colonies pourer encore vous en donner, je me flatte, Monsieur Qu'en vous disant que je leur appartiens, ils ajouteront des comptes avantageux sur ma conduite. J'ai l'honneur d'etre avec un trés profound respect, Monsieur, De vôtre excellence, Le trés humble et trés obéisant serviteur, Dubuq."

Dubuq continues with his lengthy account in English documenting his role as engineer and his sourcing of powder supplies for the rebels.[17]

Dubuq—Boston August 20th 1775

To His Excellency General Gage commanding his majesty's forces in America

I have already the honour to write you some reflections about the rebels and their measures, but I shall believe to have quite satisfied but when I shall have given you a more particular account on the same subject and my behaviour since I left my country. I shall begin if you will give me leave.

Departed from Martinico the twenty third of April with a mere desire of traveling and being back in three months. Captain Leach was the master of the vessel, and was bound for Beverly. Off Cape Cod, we were brought to the sloop of war the Nautilus, Captain John Collins. The Lieutenant, Mr. Will Brown, took charge of the schooner which he carried into Boston. We cruised three days more, and came to anchor in the harbour. The schooner was cleared and brought by the Nautilus under the protection of another sloop of war at Marblehead. The day after we had leave to go to Beverly; the kindness I received from Captain Collins and all the officers on his board afforded me sufficient reasons to engage my coming and offer you my services; but deprived of any acquaintance who could protect that resolution, I durst not get into Boston and I followed my former idea. The day after my arrival in Beverly, I went in Salem where I settled to spend the time I purposed. Many persons suspecting that I had served in France engaged me to offer my services; young and inexperienced, their impressions prov'd it and I wrote to Mr. Putnam. He answered and fournished me a chaise to go in the camps. His letter is dated June the fourth and is now in the hands of Mr. Lee.[18]

I rode to Cambridge the same day. He [Putnam] enquired a great deal from me about the quantity of powder which could be in our French Islands, and engaged me to write for getting some from thence. About eight days after, I departed for New London. I wrote in Martinico to Mr. Olivier St. Pierre, Guadeloupe to Mr. Caramajor Basseterre and Hispaniola to Mr. Brocas, Port au Prince. A merchant in New London was to dispatch a vessel in the fortnight.[19] I heard in that

17. *Final Report of the Boston National Historic Sites Commission,* 232-236. Also "Forts built prior to Washington's Arrival" in Somerville Historical Monographs.

18. Gen. Charles Lee.

19. "By a vessel which arrived here on the 30th ult. from Cape François [St. Domingue, now Haiti], we are informed that the Captain of the vessel sent from this port to the Cape

town the new[s] of the Battle at Charleston [Bunker Hill] and soon departed for Cambridge where I found faces quite disturbed; they were then entrenching on Prospect Hill; Mr. Putnam ordered me to fortify with some intrenchments [on] Winter's Hill. When I did I was encamped with two other Frenchmen, one Mr. de Longchamp. Then arrived in Cambridge Mr. Washington and Mr. Lee.[20] Mr. Lee sent me the day after his arrival to survey the lines of New Hampshire which I have already had the honour of speaking to you of. As I was going I met with Mr. de Longchamp who was a-coming from Medford and made his escape in your camps on Bunker's Hill. Since that day, I conceived the resolution to fetch for an occasion of coming and offer you my services in the Kin[g]'s army. I reflected on the inconsequent proceeding which has brought me amongst the rebels but I could not effect my design by the same way as Mr. de Longchamp, I mean thro' their guards. Besides not willing to go off as a coward deserter. I wrote a letter to Mr. Lee whereby I presented him of my retreat and asked him for a pass to go to Canada, hoping that it could serve me to go to Portsmouth where I intended to get aboard the Scarborough, Captain Barclay. Mr. Lee and Mr. Putnam assured me they suspected no connection betwixt Mr. de Longchamp and me and promised me a commission if I agreed to stay. I resoluted to take it to support me in the meantime I would find an occasion to come to you. Then I left the camp and lived in Medfort [Medford]. I have always been there since and walked sometimes in Cambridge and the camps. The last time I have been is Monday last week. I departed the Wednesday to go and get a passage in Newburyport for Martinico. I found it by a vessel which was to sail in but three weeks. Hearing that a sloop of war was come to Salem to escort the transport which brought the poor of Boston I resoluted to try every mean[s] to go aboard, and the vessel for Martinico was but my camp-de-reserve. I returned to Medfort on Saturday morning. The foggy weather made me hope that the man of war could not sail; but at my

for a quantity of warlike stores, in which the Committee of Safety for the Colony of Massachusetts had interested themselves, had executed his commission and was to sail with a large quantity in a day or two so that she may be hourly expected." Nicholas Cook to George Washington, Providence, August 8, 1775, Revolution Miscellaneous 1774-83 Vol. 138 p. 262-9; Reports 1774-83, Vol.137 p. 19, Massachusetts Archives. Correspondence between John Adams and Massachusetts Provincial Council president James Warren confirmed a shipment of 7,000 pounds of powder was en route to Boston between July 24 and August 9, 1775. John Adams to James Warren, July 24, 1775, in "Journal of Stephen Kemble," 52-54; Warren to Adams, August 9, 1775, Adams Papers, Massachusetts Historical Society.

20. "Forts built prior to Washington's Arrival" in *Final Report of the Boston National Historic Sites Commission*, 3, 232-236.

return in the afternoon I found I was quite deceived. I went to Danvers to wait for an occasion of going by sloop to Marblehead where I heard the man of war had sailed. The sailors of that little town were too much kept by their arming a dozen of privateers. They employed to that work all last Sunday. I have yet heard a noise that they would have the same week six hundred men to mount them. I embarked then at Marblehead Tuesday in the afternoon. I went thro' the ferry in a little boat to get where that of the Merlin was taking water. I went on the frigate and left in the town of Marblehead a bundle of some of my cloathes. I was very much flattered with all the politeness I proved from Captain Barnaby and all his officers. I felt them a very great difference between the gentlemen amongst whom I was and the coarse rebels I had lived among before at the dock. The Captain made me the kindness to lend me his man to go ashore and try could I get the things I had left in the inn. What gave me that confidence is that I had been thought in the morning by all the peasants to belong to the man of war. We were stopped three times by their guard and seeing how much I was in danger to be catched I gave up my design and went aboard the frigate.

As to the epoch of the going off of Mr. Longchamp, the day after the rebels seeing the floating batteries mounting the river drummed an alarm. 'Twas over all on Prospect Hill which Mr. Putnam commanded when they perceived that the King's Troops were not going to form the attack, every soldier went in his tent. I think if they had not so soon come from that alarm they would have been in the plain to face the regular troops at their landing. As for their gathering together they do it very quick—as soon as the drums beat they are under arms. They use to fear an attack when they see floating batteries mounting the river.

For the number of their guards at night reinforcements, I can give you but conjectures as it was a service very different from that wherein I was employed. They relieve it in the morning and I doubt very much it be reinforced in the night. It is pretty numerous, but I think they inspect not very exactly when going upon that duty. The soldier arms are in general in a pitiful state. I have seen some which were not of caliber and others garnished with unfiring flints. The little discipline which does not subject the soldier to clean his arms shall support more and more that abuse; 'tis yet thought very common among them that the suns reflection on the bright arms of the King's Troops disturb them from taking a just sight.

They have on Winter's Hill two brass field pieces taken at Quebec. They have four pounders in the main road from Cambridge to Watertown. They have eight pieces of cannon, some field pieces and all the different pounders. They have lately received from the north two very large guns of four and twenty to six and thirty pounds. They minded to place them on Prospect Hill in the Bastion which commands the river. As for chevaux de frise they have but five or six in all the intrenchments in Cambridge. Tis not, as far as I could discover, a means of defense they are very fond of using of. Since the light horses are arrived they order'd for fifteen hundred halberds eight feet long. They placed them all by the entrenchments for the case they should be attacked by that corps.

Tis any ground to believe they shall feel misery very soon. The most part of the soldiers are very unclean, often without stockings, and lying in straw what gets them very lousy. Great many amongst them who are sick, over all of the troops of Mr. Putnam, if I recollect well, but this fortnight one of his rebel officers is dead with the small pox.

Powder is pretty scarce. I doubt of the new I have heard the last days, they had received such and many other falsehoods the less poor wits amongst them find to support the spirit of the crowd. They fancy they will make a free trade with all the nations of the world, and the strangers will fight to enter into their ports. Such was the respectable talk of the president of the college in his free enthusiasm.[21]

As for the generals, there is but General Lee who has any experience; he is a very alert man, always surveying the lines and posts. He walked about all the night of the attack by the riflemen. General Putnam is a very good soldier, and General Washington a very rich man.

In all the time I have spent amongst those rebels I have been but once to Roxbury in the intrenchments which command the river of Cambridge [Charles River]. Then they had no gun there and I have perceived it was protected westwards but by the situation.

They generally reckon a greater number of troops in Roxbury than in Cambridge, but I don't believe in all, the army of the rebels over goes twelve thousand men amongst which a great many of a mean age.

For conclusion, Sir, they are but a parcel of rebels governed by a tyranny of which they can't fail to know soon the difference from the happy constitution under which reason ought to maintain them. I know the inconsiderate proceeding which engaged me amongst them. I am more to complain than to be condemned on it. My account is but the

21. Samuel Langdon acted as chaplain to several American regiments on August 15, 1775 including that of Col. John Glover. (Langdon Papers, Harvard University Archives.) Dubuq may also have seen a sermon by Langdon published as *Government corrupted by vice, and recovered by righteousness: A Sermon preached before the honorable Congress of the colony of the Massachusetts-Bay in New England, assembled at Watertown, on Wednesday the 31st day of May, 1775. Being the anniversary fixed by charter for the election of counsellors*, Samuel Langdon, D.D. president of Harvard College in Cambridge (Watertown, MA: Benjamin Edes, 1775).

interpretation of my changement of my sentiments, I pray you to be persuaded of it and to believe that I am yours to command, to expose my life for the defence of this cause I esteem the best.

I am with a very great respect, Sir, Your Excellency's The most Humble and most obedient Servant,

Dubuq

The appearance of M. Dubuq and his "French Redoubt" built at Boston during the siege in June 1775, predates by two years the landing of Lafayette on June 13, 1777 at Charleston, South Carolina. In 1885, the City of Somerville built a memorial at the site in a park on Central Hill, that was subsequently destroyed. The site is now occupied by Somerville High School and Library. The Dubuq family "operations" open new insight into the causes and foreign resources of the American Revolution.

Les Habitants: Collaboration and Pro-American Violence in Canada, 1774–1775

SEBASTIAN VAN BASTELAER

The fleeting invasion of Canada in 1775, though often consigned to a bit part in the American Revolutionary drama, proved vital to the emergence of American nationhood. An abortive attack at the walls of Quebec City on New Year's Eve was one of the first of many major setbacks for the Continental Army and ensured there would be no further incursions into the would-be "fourteenth colony." Yet the misbegotten campaign, which began with a two-pronged assault the preceding summer, provided a vital learning experience for a fledgling force that had to overcome numerous obstacles. Soldiers earned experience and learned difficult lessons, while the military careers of some of the leaders who oversaw the operation were forever altered.[1]

These military outcomes were not the only useful lessons to the Americans, however. The plains of Quebec were also the scene for a political and ideological struggle for the loyalties of the people in the province. The class of peasants known as the *habitants*, a largely illiterate group that worked the land they occupied and rarely left their parishes, weighed heavily on the minds of both rebel and Loyalist leaders. Soldiers and their officers relied on these people's support in order to secure shelter, rations and logistical aid. As a result, both sides sought to cultivate and retain the favor of the *habitants*. Their help could sustain an army indefinitely; failing to secure this endorsement could, conversely, lead to ruin.

1. Benedict Arnold and Aaron Burr both saw their earliest action in the war in this campaign. Their valor won them praise and eventual promotion.

Scholars have long sought to determine the political sentiments of the populace in Canada. Most groups of citizens can easily be sorted into respective camps without much difficulty. The clergy were pleased with the passage by the British government of the Quebec Act (or "An Act for making more effectual Provision for the Government of the Province of Quebec in North America") in 1774, which established support for Catholicism in Canada and reinstituted French legal practices. These religious leaders pledged their allegiance to the British and nearly unanimously remained loyal. The nobility of the province also backed the British and feared the potential social consequences of an American victory; they thus opted to maintain the status quo. British and Anglo-American merchants, many of whom were disappointed to not receive exclusive commercial privileges, were more generally sympathetic to the revolutionaries (though the extent to which they would help the American Patriots eventually became a divisive issue).[2]

The peasants (or *habitants*), however, are much more difficult to classify. This stems in part from a lack of sources. Low literacy rates ensured that few records exist of these people's inner thoughts. Some historians, then, have to rely on other sources, often written by authors with clear biases toward the American cause on the one hand or the British on the other. Undeterred by these obstacles, scholars have attempted to make assumptions about the peasants' loyalties, often concluding this class of people, weary of warfare after the Seven Years' War and generally pleased with British rule, chose to remain neutral.[3] Canadian historian George F.G. Stanley concurred, saying, "French Canadian support for the invasion was more apparent than real and more imaginary than apparent. Most of the French Canadians remained neutral and non-committal."[4] Concurring, Sir John George Bourinot wrote in his *A Manual of the Constitutional History of Canada*, "while the American War of Independence was in progress the French Canadian people remained faithful to their allegiance and resisted all the efforts of the Americans to induce them to revolt against the English."[5]

2. According to Clark, the merchants "were not more than a few hundred in number," and were almost exclusively concentrated in the towns of Montreal and Quebec. S.D. Clark, *Movements of Political Protest in Canada, 1640-1840* (Toronto: University of Toronto Press, 1959), 75.

3. This group includes Sir John George Bourinot, Martin I.J. Griffin, John C Miller, George F.G Stanley and others; their views and works are outlined below.

4. George F.G Stanley, *Canada Invaded, 1775-1776.* (Toronto: A.M. Hakkert Ltd., 1973), 109-110.

5. Sir John George Bourinot, *A Manual of the Constitutional History of Canada.* (Montreal: Dawson Brothers, 1888), 17.

This scholarly conclusion would have come as a surprise to those who experienced the Canadian campaign firsthand. Their letters, diaries and reminiscences are punctuated by references to varied *habitant* collaboration efforts. The most common form of assistance was of a logistical nature. This included providing directions, food, shelter and supplies; performing *corvée* (unpaid manual labor usually organized by militia leaders); executing acts of espionage and recruiting American sympathizers; and occasionally physically accompanying soldiers through the wilderness.[6] Gustav Lanctot cited a British administrator who claimed that much of "the countryside south of the river was at the service of the *Bostonnais* who got [the militiamen] to mount guard for them . . . and who were supplied with fresh food and carts by the farmers."[7]

Soldiers' journals and diaries, in addition to letters from officers to their colleagues in the Thirteen Colonies, furnish countless examples of this help. For instance, Caleb Haskell, a "plain man" in Benedict Arnold's expeditionary force (one of the two main invasion groups), received aid from numerous Canadians on his journey. He constantly noted the magnanimity of his hosts: on November 3 he remarked, "The people are all French and Indians, but they are exceedingly kind to us. Here we have provisions provided for us."[8] The next day, he and his men "got liberty of one of the inhabitants to sleep in his house. The people are kind to us."[9] Four days thereafter, he again highlighted the welcoming disposition of the *habitants*: "The inhabitants have been very kind to us since we have been among them."[10]

Haskell was not the only foot soldier to come across kind Quebecois denizens; others recounted more specific acts of succor in their own journals. Matthias Ogden, a stepbrother of Aaron Burr and a volunteer in the 1st New Jersey Regiment under Arnold's command, recalled a time of hunger and suffering in early November. When all appeared lost, the men were

> blessed with the finest sight my eyes ever beheld; no sensation could be equal to it. Scarce one of us but with tears of joys expressed the grat-

6. Richard Ouellet and Jean-Pierre Therrien, eds. *L'Invasion du Canada par les Bastonnois: Journal de M. Sanguinet (suivi du Siège de Québec)* (Quebec: Ministère des Affaires culturelles, 1975), 137.
7. Quoted in Gustave Lanctot, *Canada and the American Revolution 1774-1783*, translated by Margaret M. Cameron (Toronto: Clarke, Irwin & Co., 1967), , 67.
8. Caleb Haskell, *Caleb Haskell's Diary: Revolutionary Soldier's Record Before Boston and with Colonel Arnold's Exhibition* (Newburyport, MA: William H. Huse and Co., 1881), 12-13.
9. Ibid., 13.
10. Ibid.

> itude of his heart at seeing five horned cattle and two birch canoes loaded with mutton and flour brought forward by French men. They appeared glad to see us and welcomed us to Canada. After taking off the meat and flour enough to satisfy our hunger, we hastened them on to the main body of the detachment.[11]

Other soldiers, such as Capt. Henry Dearborn of New Hampshire, also made note of this specific act of kindness. Much like Haskell, Dearborn also noted how "kind" the inhabitants were on several occasions, adding that "The Canadians are Constantly Coming to us, and are expressing the Greatest satisfaction at our coming into the Country."[12] Return J. Meigs of the 2nd Connecticut Regiment wrote, "the Canadians very hospitable."[13] George Morison, a volunteer rifleman, wrote:

> The Canadians were highly rejoiced at our arrival among them; they were constantly in our camp, and never failed to bring us a present of some eatables, such as potatoes, turnips, and such things as we stood in need of. Our camp furnished a pretty good market. We enjoyed ourselves well.[14]

Examples of this form of aid abound in the reports of everyday soldiers who witnessed firsthand the willingness of Canadians to support the passel of greenhorns entering their province.

Leaders of the American expeditions also gave reports of unstinting Quebecois kindness in the early weeks of the invasion. Reminiscing in April 1776, officer Moses Hazen recalled "the friendly disposition of the *Canadians* when General *Montgomery* first penetrated into the country. The ready assistance which they gave on all occasions, by men, carriages, or provisions, was most remarkable."[15] Benedict Arnold also

11. Matthias Ogden, *Journal of Mathias Ogden on the March to Quebec with Benedict Arnold, 1775* (Morristown, NJ: Washington Association of New Jersey, 1928), 3.
12. Henry Dearborn. *Journal of Captain Henry Dearborn in the Quebec Expedition, 1775* (Cambridge: J. Wilson, 1886), 11-14.
13. Return J. Meigs, *Journal of the Expedition Against Quebec: Under Command of Col. Benedict Arnold, in the Year 1775.* (New York, privately printed, 1864), 21.
14. George Morison.,*An Interesting Journal of Occurrences During the Expedition to Quebec Conducted by the Celebrated Arnold at the Commencement of the American Revolution*, (Hagerstown, MD: James Magee, 1803), 21.
15. "Colonel Hazen to General Schuyler," Peter Force, ed. *American Archives: Consisting of a collection of authentick records, state papers, debates, and letters and other notice of publick affairs, the whole forming a documentary history of the origin and progress of the North American colonies; of the causes and accomplishment of the American revolution; and of the Constitution of government for the United States, to the final ratification thereof,* Vol. 5 (Washington: M. St. Clair Clarke and Peter Force, 1853), 869; General Montgomery led the second of the two prongs in the assault. After capturing Montreal, he perished in the attack on Quebec City.

wrote several letters with a similar message. On November 7, 1775, he recorded, "We have been very kindly received by the inhabitants who appear very friendly, and willing to supply us with provisions." The following day, he said, "the Canadians, by whom we have been very friendly received . . . will be able to furnish us with a number of canoes."[16] Other distinguished persons noted the alacrity with which the *habitants* helped the Continentals. Col. Ethan Allen "found the Canadians . . . friendly; they guarded me under arms night and day, escorted me through the woods as I desired, and showed me every courtesy I could wish for."[17]

Evidence of the *habitants'* aid to rebel forces is not confined to American sources; the British, too, noted the loyalties of the French peasants. The account of François Baby, Gabriel Taschereau and Jenkin Williams provides perhaps the best glimpse at the ubiquitous aid to the rebels. A postmortem analysis conducted by the British administration, it was presented after the three men completed an exhaustive trans-province journey documenting each parish's actions. It found parties guilty in practically every parish, leaving detailed reports of collaboration. In Beauport, for example, "most of the *habitants* . . . stood guard and assisted the rebels in various ways."[18] In St. Henry, "Almost everyone from this parish seems to have aided and assisted the rebels with much zeal."[19]

A few leaders and scholars have attempted to quantify the extent of the assistance. One analysis of the Baby journal found that out of 4492 people investigated, 757 had collaborated, and in some areas over one-quarter of residents were guilty of subversive behaviors.[20] In a similar vein, John E. Hare of the University of Ottawa examined data from the Baby journal, concluding that nearly one in five habitants were considered "bad subjects.'"[21] He showed that "more than one-third of Carleton's 1775 militia officers and sergeants were accused of supporting the Continentals to some degree." He also highlighted "seven 'bad

16. Benedict Arnold, "Arnold's Letters," *Collections of the Maine Historical Society*, Vol. 1 (Portland, ME: Maine Historical Society, 1831), 371.

17. "Report by Colonel Ethan Allen, to General Schuyler," *American Archives,* 3: 742.

18. François Baby, Gabriel-Elzéar Taschereau, and Jenkin Williams. *Québec During the American Invasion, 1775-1776: The Journal of François Baby, Gabriel Taschereau, and Jenkin Williams,* edited by Michael P. Gabriel, translated by S. Pascale Vergereau-Dewey (East Lansing, MI: Michigan State University Press, 2005), 8.

19. Ibid., 58-59.

20. Jacques Lacoursière,, *Histoire Populaire du Quebec: Des origins à 1791*, Vol. 1 (Sillery, QC: Septenentrion, 1995), 433.

21. John Hare, "Le comportement de la paysannerie rurale et urbaine dans la region de Québec, pendant l'occupation américaine, 1775-1776," *Revue de l'Université d'Ottawa* 47, nos. 1-2 (janvier et avril 1977): 146.

parishes' . . . where more than 30 percent of militia-age men were 'bad subjects.'"[22] These numbers demonstrate the pervasive pro-American sentiment in Quebec and, as we shall see later, they also mirror in some ways the extent of pro-revolutionary sentiment in the thirteen colonies at the same time.

Most historians are willing to concede that the peasants provided various forms of logistical aid, while insisting that very few went beyond such transactional deeds. Again, the evidence paints a different picture: in many cases the *habitants* did more than offer provisions and logistical aid; many chose brazenly to take up arms in support of the American cause. The British, hoping to avoid a widespread insurrection, urged the people to join militias to fight the invaders, or to at least adopt a "neutralité bienveillante [benevolent neutrality]," but many Canadians risked their lives and livelihoods to resist British colonial rule.[23] They marched with the American forces, provided them with arms, intimidated Loyalists and authority figures, and even fought against other Canadians. Dispensing with any semblance of neutrality, these rebels expressed their affinity for their southern brethren in defiance of their clergy and government officials.

Colonial administrators in Canada endeavored in various ways to compel the *habitants* to reject the Americans. Benedict Arnold reported to the Continental Congress, "every artifice is used by Governour *Carleton* to procure provisions, and induce the *Canadians* to take arms against us . . . seconded by the clergy, our bitter enemies."[24] The British themselves acknowledged their desperation in their dealings with the *habitants.* In late September 1775, Governor Carleton wrote, "no means have been left untried to bring the Canadian peasantry to a sense of their duty and engage them to take up arms in defense of the Province."[25] Some of these means included offering land in the Thirteen Colonies to all who would participate in Quebec's defense. James Livingston, an American-born merchant in Quebec at the start of the campaign, wrote to Gen. Philip Schuyler announcing that Carleton "has made a proposition to the *Canadians*, in case they would enlist under the Crown of *Great Britain*, to gratify every man that will turn out upon this occasion with one hundred acres of land, at *Boston, New-*

22. Ibid., 264.
23. Ouellet and Therrien, eds., *L'Invasion du Canada par les Bastonnois,* 137.
24. "Letter from Colonel Arnold to the Continental Congress," *American Archives,* 4: 838.
25. Victor Coffin, "The Province of Quebec and the Early American Revolution: A Study in English-American Colonial History," *Bulletin of the University of Wisconsin, Economics, Political Science and History Series,* Vol. 1, no. 3 (1896), 275-562.498.

York, &c."[26] While the practicability of such a grant is unclear, it is patently clear that few *habitants* accepted Carleton's initial offer.

In fact, few French Canadians accepted the commissions of any sort given to them by the government. A man described only as "A Virginian" wrote an epistle published in the *Middlesex Journal* in the Thirteen Colonies. He repeated the widespread notion that "The Canadians have used General Carleton extremely ill" in refusing to join and provision the local militias.[27] In his letter to Schuyler, James Livingston recounted that a British officer, "Colonel *McLean*, who arrived here with Colonel *Johnson*, has orders from the King to raise a Regiment of *Canadians* . . . I can assure you, from *Three Rivers* to *Chambly*, he got not a single man."[28] Not only pro-American agents reported this intransigence. J.B. Badeaux, a Loyalist notary in the area between Montreal and Quebec City, reported in his journal: "almost the entirety of Trois-Rivières refused to march, with the exception of a few volunteers."[29] Clearly proponents of the both Loyalist and revolutionary causes could see the colonial administrators' shortcomings when it came to winning over the public.

Men were not the only agents of resistance. Some women of *habitant* society stood up to the British, sometimes surpassing their male counterparts in fervency. The Baby report noted that several women held meetings and urged neighbors not to support the British, while in the St. Vallier district, a widow "caused more trouble . . . than anyone" in fomenting insurrection.[30]

Many *habitants* went beyond merely abstaining from serving the British and maintaining a "prudent neutrality;" they sowed chaos throughout the countryside, terrorizing opponents and threatening people of all ranks.[31] The Baby report is punctuated with charges of overt acts of violence. One such incident in St. Féréol included three brothers who "stood guard and . . . reported the names of those who refused to do so to the rebels. Almost all the *habitants* of this parish stood guard at the Sault armed with rifles. Several young men loaded

26. "James Livingston to General Schuyler," *American Archives,* 3: 469.

27. Frank Moore, ed., *The Diary of the Revolution: A Centennial Volume Embracing the Current Events in Our Country's History from 1775 to 1781 as Described by American, British, and Tory Contemporaries* Vol. 1 (Hartford: The J.B. Burr Publishing Company, 1875), 209.

28. "James Livingston to General Schuyler," *American Archives,* 3: 469.

29. J.B. Badeaux, *Journal des Operations de l'Armée Américaine lors de L'Invasion du Canada en 1775-1776* (Montreal: Eusebe Senécal, 1871), 3.

30. Baby et al., *Quebec During the American Revolution,* xxxvii.

31.Michel Brunet, *French Canada and the Early Decades of British Rule, 1760-1791* (Ottawa: The Canadian Historical Association, 1981), 10.

their rifles before leaving the village, swearing that they would fire on anyone who tried to pursue them."[32] In another instance, the insubordination was even more direct:

> When the Governor's delegates on the Ile d'Orléans [right outside Quebec City] tried to raise fifteen men in the parish of Saint-Famille, and threatened to set fire to the village if they were opposed, a young man called Drouin, who had refused to accept a commission immediately retorted: 'We are ready for you.' Then, setting out with the rebels from Saint-Famille, he gathered recruits from Saint-Pierre and Saint-François and set up a camp at the end of the island where about twenty men from Saint-Jean joined the group.[33]

Non-military authority figures were not exempt from intimidation. Local priests, who purportedly exerted great influence on their parishioners, were determinedly pro-British as a result of the Quebec Act's reestablishment of the Catholic Church. In 1774, following the legislation's passage, a group of clergymen assured Carleton, "you will always find the Clergy to be good and faithful subjects."[34] From the outset, they upheld their vow. While it certainly cemented their good relations with the administration—Bishop Briand, the bishop of the Diocese of Quebec was close with Carleton—this loyalty made them easy targets for unruly *habitants*.[35] Mark Anderson explains,

> habitants . . . would not form as a militia. Priests took a prominent role in addressing this issue, yet incorrigible parishioners defied both the governor and the Church, arguing that they would not fight colonial brethren and that they considered themselves permanently relieved from armed duty once the militia was disbanded in the 1760s.[36]

The fractious Canadians refused to budge, flouting the wishes (and in some cases direct orders) of the two groups that traditionally provided order and authority in colonial Quebec. Baby and his colleagues committed numerous pages to this disobedience towards the clergy. Some reports were rather unexceptional: several peasants were charged with rebelling "despite the good counsel of their priest."[37] Other re-

32. Baby et al., *Quebec During the American Revolution,* 11.
33. Lanctot, *Canada and the American Revolution,* 70.
34. "Address of the Clergy to Guy Carleton, Governour of Quebeck," *American Archives,* 1: 792.
35. Brunet, *French Canada and the Early Decades of British Rule,* 9.
36. Mark R. Anderson, *The Battle for the Fourteenth Colony: America's War of Liberation in Canada,* 1774-1776 (Lebanon, NH: University Press of New England, 2013), 115.
37. Baby et al., *Quebec During the American Revolution,* 63.

ports, however, involved explicit actions against the clergy. The commission chided one district's parishioners for making "a reprimand and threats to Father Louis, their parish priest."[38] Other *habitants* resented their priests' involvement in secular affairs. In one parish, Sainte Croix, a man, "upon leaving church last summer after having heard a sermon by the parish priest extolling obedience to the King, shouted in front of everyone 'What is our priest talking about now? What business is he meddling in, talking like an Englishman?'"[39]

Going beyond verbal harassment, rebels did not forbear using force against the clergy. A partisan in St. Thomas encouraged the ransacking of a priest's house, from which Continental soldiers pilfered three barrels of Bordeaux wine.[40] In St. Thomas, government messengers carrying a proclamation of amnesty for rebel sympathizers spent the night at a priest's house. A group of approximately two dozen partisans surrounded the house to harass the agents. They threatened to set the house ablaze if the priest did not hand over the operatives. When a servant peeked out a window, a rebel shot and killed her.[41] These incidents show the manifestly violent and passionate support for the Americans in parishes throughout Quebec.

Military activity was not limited to sowing chaos and intimidating innocent priests. Many partisans attempted to join the Americans or formed fighting forces of their own. Various contemporary reports recounted a migration to the American camp. Ethan Allen and his famous Green Mountain Boys succeeded in recruiting a sizable number of peasants to join their ranks. He wrote to General Montgomery in September, "I have two hundred and fifty *Canadians* under arms; as I march, they gather fast."[42] A sympathizing merchant named Baker, who lived in Montreal, reported to a captain of the Green Mountain Boys that he had "1,500 Canadians ready to fight for the Americans."[43] General Montgomery, in announcing the surrender of the town of Chambly in October, described how 300 Canadians, aiding a force of only 50 Americans, helped to take the town through their bravery and knowledge.[44] Benedict Arnold, ascribing a strong ideological fervor to the

38. Ibid., 49.
39. Ibid., 57.
40. Ibid., 92.
41. Lanctot, *Canada and the American Revolution,* 66-67.
42. Quoted in Brunet, *French Canada and the Early Decades of British Rule,* 96.
43. Claude-Nicolas-Guillaume de Lorimier, *At War with the Americans: The Journal of Claude-Nicolas-Guillaume de Lorimier*, translated and edited by Peter Aichinger (Victoria, B.C.: Press Porcepic, 1981), 28.
44. "Letter from General Montgomery to General Schuyler," *American Archives,* 3: 1132.

habitants, summarized: "The inhabitants are generally in our favor, and many of them have taken up arms for us, or rather, for themselves."[45]

J.B. Badeaux's journal recounts a particularly humorous episode of military sabotage. In this incident, *habitants* from the Chambly region reported to the British camp under the pretense of joining the militia defending the province. Having been provided with arms, however, the group promptly deserted, marched to the "Bastonnais" camp, and used these weapons on behalf of the rebels. The pro-British author, petrified by this brazen treason, concluded: "we have every reason to fear for our poor province."[46]

In some cases, this support was enduring. Some militants even stayed with the American force as it retreated south across the border in 1776, demonstrating their commitment to the revolutionary cause long after it was no longer convenient. The 1st and 2nd Canadian Regiments, under the command of James Livingston and Moses Hazen, respectively, were known for their fighting quality discipline, earning affectionate nicknames such as "Congress's Own."[47] They took part in some of the decisive battles of the war, including the Battles of Long Island, Saratoga, Brandywine, Germantown and the final *coup de grâce* at Yorktown.[48]

When they would not or could not join the Americans, some *habitants* simply created their own fighting forces. In one instance, a baker from Charlesbourg "attempted to form a company" to support the Americans.[49] As previously detailed, groups of men roamed the countryside, intimidating others and advocating for the Americans. Canadians also physically fought one another. One such example is the Battle of Longue-Plante, in the Montreal area, in September of 1775. In early 1776, a small clash occurred in St. Pierre-du-Sud at the house of a Loyalist named Michael Blay (also spelled Michel Blais). This pitted against one another two small detachments of largely Canadian militia members, some Loyalist and some pro-American. The skirmish ended with a victory for the rebels.[50]

As a wealth of evidence illustrates, and in spite of some historians' claims to the contrary, a sizable bloc of the French-Canadians in Quebec in 1775-1776 were open to and even supportive of the American

45. Quoted in Baby et al., *Quebec During the American Revolution*, xxxvi.
46. Badeaux, *Journal des Operations*, 8
47. Allen S. Everest, *Moses Hazen and the Canadian Refugees in the American Revolution* (Syracuse, NY: Syracuse University Press, 1976), 47.
48. Baby et al., *Quebec During the American Invasion*, xxxvi.
49. Baby, *Quebec During the American Revolution*, 6.
50. Anderson, *The Battle for the Fourteenth Colony*, 118.

invaders. Their assistance took many different forms: while many provided logistical aid and performed *corvée* for the revolutionaries, an oft-overlooked group actively took up arms, jeopardizing their own livelihoods and security. These deeds reflected conscious decisions to reject the appeals of the British leaders and, perhaps more importantly, the clergy whose counsel they were supposed to heed. Armed with the knowledge of these brave acts, one can better understand the fluid nature of revolutions and, more specifically, the tenuous bands that tied the French-Canadians to their British rulers. For a brief but momentous period for people on both sides of the border, the addition of the Fourteenth Colony seemed no pipe dream at all.[51]

51. Continental Congress, *Letter to the Inhabitants of the Province of Quebec* (1774).

“That Damned Absurd Word Liberty”: Les Habitants, the Quebec Act, and American Revolutionary Ideology, 1774–1776

SEBASTIAN VAN BASTELAER

The American invasion of Quebec of 1775-1776 failed to achieve its primary objective: to bring into the fold what the Continental Congress referred to as “the only link wanting, to compleat the bright and strong chains of union.”[1] While Canada would not join its southern brethren in outright rebellion, the Americans’ campaign furnishes important insight into the early stages of the Revolution and the appeal it held both in the thirteen colonies and abroad.

Pro-American sentiment was widespread and polymorphous. In the early stages of the invasion, French-Canadian *habitants* (peasants) provided assistance in various ways to the Continental troops, even if it meant turning on neighbors and flouting traditional societal hierarchies. But why? Were the *habitants*, as some claim, merely opportunistic? Did they simply choose whichever side appeared to be winning in order to personally prosper and avoid punishment from the victorious army? Did the transatlantic political debates that provided the impetus for the Revolution have any bearing on the *habitants*’ decisions? And if so, were they merely fooled by the war of words between the two sides? One study claims that the peasants’ acted as they did because they were “frightened, misled and completely demoralized by American propaganda.”[2] This view, however, reduces the large group of peasants to one ignorant bloc. It also echoes some of the elitist rhetoric of the

1. Continental Congress, *Letter to the Inhabitants of the Province of Quebec* (1774).
2. Gustave Lanctot, *Canada and the American Revolution 1774-1783*, translated by Margaret M. Cameron (Toronto: Clarke, Irwin & Co., 1967), 74.

time period: one letter written by an administrator in June 1775 read, "one need not be a great orator to persuade these poor fellows."[3] It also runs counter to historical evidence, which shows that a thoughtful rejection of the 1774 Quebec Act and a partial embrace of the revolutionary ideology of liberty did in fact take place in the province in response to American appeals. The *habitants,* it appears, were not blindly committing acts of wanton violence or simply transacting out of economic and military expediency. Instead, they were often making considered choices about the belligerents' ideologies and taking risks to fight for the American cause.

The Quebec Act, which reestablished various French civil and governmental norms in addition to reinstituting Catholicism, is a vital factor in understanding the *habitants'* loyalties. It created a Governor's Council to help administer the province; extended the boundaries of Quebec south into the Ohio Valley—a region for which Anglo-Americans had fought and died less than two decades prior; reestablished the Catholic Church; and granted French law to the populace. Though one can easily see why Protestant, land-hungry Americans to the south were leery of the act,[4] what did the *habitants* make of it? Scholars often credit the Act for preventing a full-scale provincial uprising, often portraying the peasants as rigidly religious. Griffin Martin argued that "the main cause, the great reason why Canada did not join in the Revolution was … [that] Bishop Briand [the head of the Roman Catholic Diocese of Quebec] was loyal to England."[5] Historian Victor Coffin called the view that the Quebec Act secured the *habitants'* loyalty to Britain "generally accepted," and other studies bear this claim out.[6] In the introduction to a report from British administrators on *habitant* collaboration, Louis Balthazar opined that the Quebec Act "had much to please Canadians who had become attached to their old laws, to their seigniorial regime, and, above all, to their Catholic religion."[7] Finally,

3. *Lettres Ecrites pendant L'Invasion Americaine en 1775 et 1776* (Montreal: Eusebe Senécal, 1872).

4. Protest against the Quebec Act in the Thirteen Colonies was strident; even the Declaration of Independence decried it as a concession aimed at making the Canadians "fit instruments" to subjugate the Americans.

5. Martin I.J. Griffin, *Catholics and the American Revolution*, Vols. 1-3 (Ridley Park, PA: self-published, 1907), 219.

6. Victor Coffin, "The Province of Quebec and the Early American Revolution: A Study in English-American Colonial History," *Bulletin of the University of Wisconsin, Economics, Political Science and History Series,* Vol. 1, no. 3 (1896), 275-562.

7. François Baby, Gabriel-Elzéar Taschereau, and Jenkin Williams, *Québec During the American Invasion, 1775-1776: The Journal of François Baby, Gabriel Taschereau, and Jenkin Williams,* edited by Michael P. Gabriel, translated by S. Pascale Vergereau-Dewey (East Lansing, MI: Michigan State University Press, 2005), xiv-xv.

in his *Thrust for Canada,* Robert McConnell Hatch asserted that the Act "enabled non-English people to become part of the empire without losing their identity, their religion, or their voice in government—a historic achievement, greatly to [Governor General of Canada Guy] Carleton's credit."[8]

Yet the eighteenth-century evidence fails to support this established narrative. Historian Mark Anderson has written "that the habitants' first practical experience with the Quebec Act was the distinctly distasteful imposition of martial law."[9] Moreover, the religious reforms were not what they seemed. Though the Canadians remained uniformly Catholic, the church leadership had lost some of its grip on the peasants, many of whom began to reject the supreme authority of the clergymen. The disdain for ecclesiastical authority, however, predated the Revolution. There were signs prior to the American invasion that Catholicism held only a diminished sway over parishioners. Many residents hated the compulsory taxes (called tithes) paid to the church. A practice that had declined since the end of the Seven Years' War, the tithes were unpopular. Many peasants wanted to see them abolished forever. In the 1760s, Gov. Gen. James Murray (Carleton's predecessor) lamented, "they [the *habitants*] do not submit as tamely to the yoke, and under sanction of the capitulation they every day take an opportunity to dispute the tithes."[10] Michel Brunet summarized, "Living for more than a century on American soil, the Canadian had imbibed much of the spirit of freedom of his frontier environment. He had come to resent the oppressive controls of an absolutist state and a puritanical church."[11]

The problem, therefore, was that the Quebec Act did not materially improve the lives of the *habitants* in any way. As Lanctot showed, the Quebec Act in effect "did not change the lives of the country people, who had never ceased to practice their religion nor to follow" French legal customs.[12] The one principal change was the reinstitution of the tithe system. This tax was the most tangible impact of the Quebec Act's passage. It reinforced old customs and forced the peasants to subordinate themselves to the clergy once again. The Act's other changes were essentially nominal to the everyday French-Canadian, who did not par-

8. Robert McConnell Hatch, *Thrust for Canada: The American Attempt on Quebec in 1775-1776* (Boston: Houghton Mifflin, 1979,) 13.
9. Mark R. Anderson, *The Battle for the Fourteenth Colony: America's War of Liberation in Canada*, 1774-1776 (Lebanon, NH: University Press of New England, 2013), 81.
10. Quoted in Coffin, "The Province of Quebec and the Early American Revolution," 284.
11. Clark, *Movements of Political Protest in Canada,* 89.
12. Lanctot, *Canada and the American Revolution,* 74.

ticipate in the government and cared little about the boundaries of the province. In the eyes of many, then, the Quebec Act was simply an arbitrary tax—the sort of imposition that had rankled the "Bostonians" for over a decade.

The passage of the Quebec Act, therefore, did not elicit a jubilant response from the *habitants*. William Hey, the Chief Justice of Quebec, expressed with some surprise, "it may be truly said that Gen. Carleton had taken an ill measure of the influence of the seigneurs & Clergy over the lower order of people." He continued, explaining that the Act had been "passed for the express purpose of gratifying the Canadians," and yet instead had "become the first object of their discontent & dislike."[13] A rare epistle from a Canadian village added that the reaction to the Quebec Act was "so great a consternation, that the most violent storm of thunder and lightning could not have produced a greater effect upon a people."[14] Another letter, written in Quebec City, noted, "The new arrangement of government under the Quebeck-bill, met with a general disapprobation ... the Canadians in general were displeased with it, and declared that it was not at their desire or sollicitation that it was passed."[15]

This resistance sometimes took concrete forms. In spring 1775, a Loyalist in Montreal wrote to a contemporary about vandalism directly linked to the Quebec Act. The legislation was due to go into effect on May 1, and on the night of April 30, "some malicious and mischievous person or persons disfigured the King's bust on the parade, by blacking its face, hanging a chaplet of potatoes about its neck, with a wooden cross and a label, on which was wrote, '*Le Pape de Canada ou le sot Anglois*' [the Pope of Canada or the English fool]."[16] This caused a fight to break out, during which enemies exchanged physical blows. Evidently, the inhabitants of Quebec were not as pleased by the new law as the administration had hoped—or as scholars tend to suggest.

While the Quebec Act made many *habitants* frustrated with the British, it may not have been enough on its own to convince such a large segment to aid actively the invading, anti-Catholic army. To better

13. Quoted in Anderson, *The Battle for the Fourteenth Colony*, 86.
14. Quoted in Coffin, "The Province of Quebec and the Early American Revolution," 91.
15. Ibid., 91-92.
16. "Copy of an Intercepted Letter, Dated Montreal, May 6, 1775," Peter Force, ed. *American Archives: Consisting of a collection of authentick records, state papers, debates, and letters and other notice of publick affairs, the whole forming a documentary history of the origin and progress of the North American colonies; of the causes and accomplishment of the American revolution; and of the Constitution of government for the United States, to the final ratification thereof* (Washington: M. St. Clair Clarke and Peter Force, 1853), 2: 518.

comprehend the motives that actuated this conduct, we have to look at the efforts of American leaders to appease and convince the peasants of the revolutionary cause's benevolence and righteousness. It would not be easy; many scholars have pointed out the bald hypocrisy in attempting to propitiate a group of people against whom Anglo-Americans had long fought. John C. Miller declared the efforts moot: "[The Americans' appeals] fell upon barren soil. The Canadians were reluctant to fling themselves into the arms of the Pope haters to the south … even the most expert phrase turners might well have found themselves at a loss in addressing the Canadians."[17] Yet once again, archival evidence undermines the assertion that the conservative *habitants* rejected wholesale the Americans' appeals.

American political and military leaders quickly grasped the importance of appeasing the peasantry, who constituted a sizable portion of the population. The most well known (and widely distributed) set of appeals to the Canadians came from the Continental Congress. It published three public declarations to the populace over the course of the Revolution. The first and most important came in October of 1774. Titled *Letter to the Inhabitants of the Province of Quebec,* it tactfully yet convincingly made several arguments against the Quebec Act while threatening the use of force. Further, it deftly skirted underlying religious issues by making anodyne statements about the importance of religious liberty. The document, drafted by John Dickinson, Thomas Cushing and Richard Henry Lee, praised French thinkers and ideas before delving into a summary of British rights, particularly those that the Canadians could stand to lose under the Quebec Act. It warned that the decision-makers in London had eliminated rights of habeas corpus and trial by jury; moreover, they pointed out, the British could easily raise taxes, pointing out the Quebec Act had essentially denied the Canadian people the right to set their own taxes.

The drafters then questioned the benefits of the Act. Addressing the establishment of Catholicism, they asked, "what is offered to you by the late Act of Parliament in their place? Liberty of conscience in your religion? No. God gave it to you."[18] It also warned the inhabitants that the granted rights were only temporary, pointing out a line in the Act itself that read, "those 'laws shall be the rule, until they shall be *varied* or *altered* by any ordinances of the Governor and Council.'"[19]

17. John C. Miller, *Origins of the American Revolution,* 4 (Palo Alto: Stanford University Press, 1959), 456-457.
18. Continental Congress, *Letter to the Inhabitants of the Province of Quebec,* (1774).
19. Ibid.

Artfully glossing over centuries of anti-Catholic animus in the thirteen colonies, the writers of the appeal reminded their readers of the "Swiss Cantons," whose "union is composed of Roman Catholic and Protestant States, living in the utmost concord and peace with one another, and thereby enabled . . . to defy and defeat every tyrant that has invaded them."[20] They finished by inviting the Canadians to send delegates to the Second Continental Congress, set to convene the following May.

Two more entreaties followed from the Congress, and several others came from different American leaders. These all carried similar messages. The second letter from Philadelphia, sent in May 1775, again pointed out the impermanence of the Quebec Act's benefits. Highlighting the lack of self-representation as well as the flimsy freedom of religion granted by Parliament, the authors noted, "the enjoyment of your very religion, in the present system, depends on a legislature in which you have no share, and over which you have no control."[21] It also asserted, "we perceived the fate of the protestant and catholic colonies to be strongly linked together."[22] The final letter, written in January 1776, thanked the *habitants* specifically for their zeal in assisting the American effort, and urged them to organize politically and send delegates to the Congress. It concluded, "We flatter ourselves with the prospect of the happy moment when the standard of tyranny shall no longer appear in this land; and we live in full hopes that it will never hereafter find shelter in North America."[23] Congress were not the only ones to send letters to convince the Canadians. Generals Schuyler and Washington both sent proclamations as well; these, too, were intended to flatter the Canadians and impel them to aid the American cause.

So, did these appeals fail in the inhospitable and "barren" Canadian political landscape, as scholars have suggested? On the contrary, accounts show that many copies of the addresses were distributed throughout Quebec, and that they did not fall on deaf ears. Over 2,000 copies were made of the first address from the Congress.[24] Since many *habitants* could not read, word-of-mouth was a vital means whereby the message could spread. The account written by colonial administrators François Baby, Gabriel Taschereau and Jenkin Williams reported numerous incidents of peasants reading American addresses aloud in

20. Ibid.
21. Continental Congress, *Letter to the Inhabitants of Canada* (1775).
22. Ibid.
23. Continental Congress, *Letter to the Inhabitants of the Province of Canada* (1776).
24. Coffin, "The Province of Quebec and the Early American Revolution," 496.

public and attempting to communicate with the Americans.[25] An unsigned letter written in Montreal reported,

> The Address from the Continental Congress attracted the notice, of some of the principal Canadians; it was soon translated into very tolerable French. The decent manner in which the religious matters were touched; the encomiums on the French Nation, flattered a people fond of compliments.[26]

Some *habitants* themselves were able to report their satisfaction. In November 1775, a group of *habitants* peasants near Montreal wrote a letter to Gen. Richard Montgomery, who was on the verge of taking the city. Providing perhaps the best glimpse at how some inhabitants responded to American appeals, it exulted:

> Sir, The darkness in which we were buried is finally dissipated - the day shines, our chains are broken, a happy freedom has been returned to us...we accepted union in our hearts from the moment that the address of the 26th October 1774 reached us, to which we could have replied if we had dared.[27]

The appreciation for liberty and freedom among the *habitants* evident in this letter appears in numerous pieces of evidence from the time—what's more, it is clear that the American entreaties did not spawn sentiments where none had existed prior. S.D. Clark argues, "this spirit of independence grew from within and was fostered from without. American propaganda, disseminated by local British residents, at least strengthened ideas of freedom which had long been growing up among the Canadians."[28] The Badeaux journal reports a similar desire for freedom among some *habitants*: some people in "the parishes of Chambly who were on the side of the *Bastonnais* [Bostonians] announced to all the other parishes to not take arms against the *Bastonnais*, for these men had come to save us from oppression."[29]

Further illustrating the ubiquity of these beliefs is a series of letters written by British administrators and religious officials. Though they could understandably have downplayed the chaos and pro-American agitation, several of these leaders were frank. Assessing the effectiveness

25. Baby et al., *Quebec During the American Invasion,* 11-12.
26. "Extract of a Letter from Canada, Dated Montreal, March 24, 1775," *American Archives,* 2: 281.
27. Quoted in Marcel Trudel, *La Tentation Américaine 1774-1783* (Québec City, QC: Presses de L'Université Laval, 1968), 102.
28. S.D. Clark, *Movements of Political Protest in Canada, 1640-1840* (Toronto: University of Toronto Press, 1959), 89.
29. J.B. Badeaux, *Journal des Operations de l'Armée Américaine lors de L'Invasion du Canada en 1775-1776* (Montreal: Eusebe Senécal, 1871), 3.

of Congress's appeals, William Hey reported, the Canadians' minds had been "all poisoned by emissaries from New England . . . [and] corrupted and persuaded by the circular letters" from Congress.[30] Fifteen years after the invasion, Bishop Jean-François Hubert of the Archdiocese of Quebec, concurred in a letter to Carleton. He recalled "the progress among the Canadians of the spirit of liberty and independence, brought about by the circulation of manifestoes by the Anglo-Americans at the beginning of the last war."[31]

It was Carleton himself, the man in charge of defending Quebec, who most emphatically sounded the alarm over *habitant* disloyalty to the Crown. In 1777, he reminisced, "these people were too penetrated by the American ideas of emancipation and independence."[32] At another moment, he discussed "that spirit of licentiousness and independence that has pervaded all the British Colonies upon this continent, and was making, through the endeavors of a turbulent faction here, a most amazing progress in this country."[33]

There are also examples of collective political action in favor of the Americans. The most famous of these is the formation of the so-called "Seditious Assembly" in Pointe-Levy on the south shore of the Saint Lawrence River. This was a rare early case of popular organization in Canada, in which "perhaps a hundred men," all peasants it seems, gathered to resist collectively the British forces. As Anderson has recounted, after they heard of this assembly, "four hundred habitants from nine different parishes gathered from as far as thirty miles away" within twenty-four hours. Furthermore, "Many were unarmed; the 'assembly' was as much a political demonstration as it was a show of force."[34] Though a sparsely populated, geographically spread out and largely illiterate population was unlikely to form a lasting political infrastructure for themselves, they were still able to muster a large gathering of like-minded partisans to advocate opposition to British conscription and coercion. Importantly, the "Seditious Assembly" belies the assertion that the French-Canadians had no desire for self-determination, an imputation occasionally made by historians.[35]

30. Quoted in Anderson, *The Battle for the Fourteenth Colony,* 86.

31. *Mandements, Lettres Pastorales et Circulaires des Évêques de Québec* (Quebec: Imprimerie Générale, 1888), 430.

32. Quoted in Lionel Groulx, *Histoire du Canada Français Depuis le Découverte.* Vol. 3 (Quebec City, QC: Ligue d'Action Nationale, 1952), 85.

33. Quoted in Coffin, "The Province of Quebec and the Early American Revolution," 509.

34. Ibid., 139-140.

35. Louis Balthazar, in his introduction to the Baby report, relayed the notion that the *habitants* "much preferred the certainty of recognition by the crown to the uncertain future of an American republic" (xv).

Clearly, the Quebec Act was far less effective initially in propitiating the Canadian people. Furthermore, the American appeals were not rejected out of hand; rather, they encouraged and strengthened an existing eleutheromania within the province. One therefore can conclude that much of the collaboration that occurred in Quebec was not merely borne of economic concerns or congenital violent tendencies. For many *habitants,* it was a thoughtful, peaceful and ideologically-driven decision made in spite of the risks it engendered. As Thomas Gamble, a deputy quartermaster, concluded: "In short, the Quebec Bill is of no use; on the contrary the Canadians talk of that damned absurd word liberty."[36]

36. Quoted in ibid., 495.

Massachusetts Privateers During the Siege of Boston

ALEXANDER R. CAIN

Following the Battles of Lexington and Concord, the Massachusetts Grand Army surrounded Boston and began to lay siege to it. The Massachusetts Committee of Safety quickly recognized that in order to drive the British army from the town, it had to starve them out.[1]

The British military had a longstanding practice of acquiring fresh provisions from local farmers. At first, Gen. Thomas Gage contemplated purchasing supplies from American farmers who lived on the islands in Boston Harbor. Unfortunately, many yeomen were reluctant to cooperate.[2] As a result, the general decided he would initiate military operations to forcefully seize necessary resources. Of course, the harbor islands only provided a limited amount of supplies. As a result, Gage was forced to rely heavily upon the long and tenuous communication lines to British possessions in Nova Scotia and the West Indies, and ultimately, back to England.

The Massachusetts Committee of Safety saw this logistical nightmare as an opportunity to loosen Gage's hold on Boston. Massachusetts had a long history of privateering during the previous French wars and almost immediately turned to the practice as a method to drive His

1. On May 7, 1775, the Massachusetts Committee of Safety passed a resolution ordering selectmen from the towns located near Boston "to take effectual methods for the prevention of any Provisions being carried into the Town of Boston." Minutes of the Massachusetts Committee of Safety 1775, in *American Archives*, Fourth Series, 6 vols., comp. Clarke M. St. Clair and Peter Force (Washington: U.S. Congress, 1837–46), 2: 753.

2. Farm manager William Harris noted he was "very uneasy, the people from the Men of War frequently go to the Island to Buy fresh Provision, his own safety obliges him to sell to them, on the other Hand the Committee of Safety have threatened if he sells anything to the Army or Navy, that they will take all the Cattle from the Island, & our folks tell him they shall handle him rufly." William Harris quoted in H. Prentiss to Oliver Wendell, May 12, 1775, *Essex Institute Historical Collections* (Salem: Essex Institute, 1877), 13: 181.

Majesty's troops out of the town. Privateering, or "lawful piracy," was the act of seizing enemy supply or military vessels by civilian-owned warships. Privateers operated under the authority of "Letters of Marque" issued from governmental authorities and were often, if not solely, motivated by the opportunity for profit.[3] Massachusetts authorities actively encouraged just about any person with a seaworthy vessel to partake in privateer operations and placed no limits on the number of ships receiving Letters of Marque.[4]

Within a very short time, Gage's Atlantic supply lines fell prey to the privateer fleets of Newburyport, Salem, Beverly and Plymouth. According to reports from the *Essex Gazette*, Massachusetts privateers were far more successful in cutting off British supplies than their land-based counterparts. As early as September 9, 1775, the newspaper reported that "Last Saturday a privateer belonging to Newburyport carried into Portsmouth a schooner of forty-five tons, loaded with potatoes and turnips intended for the enemy in Boston."[5]

Many of these privateers traveled in groups that varied in size from a few ships to over twenty. One such squadron from Newburyport consisted of twenty-five vessels and over 2,800 men. A second from the same town boasted thirty vessels.

Perhaps one of the most successful American supply interdictions during the Siege of Boston occurred on November 25, 1775 when the *Lee*, a privateer under the command of Capt. John Manly of Marblehead, captured the British vessel *Nancy*. According to a December 7, 1775 description, "Captain Manly, in the *Lee*, a vessel of war, in the service of the United Colonies, carried into Cape Ann a large brig called the *Nancy* which he took off that place, bound from London to Boston, laden with about three hundred and fifty caldrons of coal; and a quantity of bale goods, taken by Captain Manly, was carried into Salem. She is about two hundred tons burthen, and is almost a new ship." Of course, the *Nancy* was a military ordnance vessel from Woolwich, England that carried no less than 2,000 muskets, 31 tons of mus-

3. The objective was to capture prizes and sell the vessels and cargo for profit to the ship's owner, her officers and crew.

4. According to a November 1775 resolution, Massachusetts privateers were authorized to "equip any vessel to sail on the seas, attack, take and bring into any port in this colony all vessels offending or employed by the enemy." *An Act For Encouraging The Fixing Out Of Armed Vessels To Defend The Sea-Coast Of America, And For Erecting A Court To Try And Condemn All Vessels That Shall Be Found Infesting The Same*, Massachusetts General Court, November, 1775, State Library of Massachusetts, Acts and Resolves of the Massachusetts General Court (1692-1780), archives.lib.state.ma.us/handle/2452/117010.

5. *Salem Gazette*, September 9, 1775, in *Proceedings of the Massachusetts Historical Society* (Boston, Massachusetts: Massachusetts Historical Society, 1885), 1: 21.

ket shot, 30,000 round shot of "various sizes," 100,000 musket flints, 11 mortar beds, and a 2,700-pound 13-inch mortar.[6]

A few weeks after the capture of the *Nancy*, the *Essex Gazette* announced Captain Manly had struck again. "Captain Manly has, within a few days past, taken another valuable prize, a sloop from Virginia bound for Boston, loaded with corn and oats; fitted out and sent by Lord Dunmore."[7]

Towards the close of 1775, Massachusetts privateers were not only preventing much-needed supplies from reaching Boston but were also seizing enemy vessels in rapid succession. According to one newspaper report, "several vessels loaded with fuel, provisions of various kinds, &c, bound to Boston, have been carried into Salem and Beverly within a few days past."[8] By mid-December, reports of successful captures by Massachusetts privateers were pouring into the colonies.[9] As Benjamin Hichborn noted to John Adams, "Our privateers have made so many Captures that, it is impossible for me to be particular, most of those from Europe I am informed have considerable quantities of Coal in them."[10] Likewise, James Warren, president of the Massachusetts Provincial Congress, wrote about the success of privateers against British supply lines. "Several Prizes have been taken in the week past, & among the rest a fine Ship from London, with coal, Porter Cheese Live Hoggs &c &c and a large Brigt [brigantine] from Antigua with Rum Sugar &c all the Country are now Engaged in prepareing to make salt Petre fixing Privateers, or Reinforceing the army."[11]

The activities of the Massachusetts privateers did not go unnoticed by British military officials. The spy Benjamin Church warned General Gage that "unless some plan of Accommodation takes Place immediately their [harbors] will swarm with Privateers."[12] Maj. Gen. William

6. *Salem Gazette*, December 7, 1775, ibid.

7. *Salem Gazette*, December 21, 1775, ibid.

8. Ibid.

9. For example on Christmas Day, a Plymouth-based privateer successfully intercepted a supply sloop from New York. "On the 25th of December last [1775] was taken by a Plymouth privateer and carried in there a small sloop from New York, Moses Wyman, Master, laden with provisions fur the ministerial army in Boston, consisting of thirty-five fresh hogs, one hundred barrels of pork, fifty barrels fine New York pippins, twenty firkins hog's feet, some quarters of beef, turkeys, &c., &c." *Proceedings of the Massachusetts Historical Society*, 21.

10. Benjamin Hichborn to John Adams, December 10, 1775, in James Richard Wils, *In Behalf of the Continent: Privateering and Irregular Naval Warfare in Early Revolutionary America* (Greenville, NC: East Carolina University, 2012), 65-66.

11. James Warren to John Adams, December 11, 1775, ibid., 66.

12. Benjamin Cowell, *Spirit of '76 in Rhode Island, or Sketches of the Efforts of the Government and People in the War of the Revolution* (Boston: A. J. Wright, 1850), 29.

Howe openly complained about the interdiction efforts when he stated, "I am also concerned to observe the Uncertainty of defenceless Vessels getting into this Harbour is rendered more precarious by the Rebel Privateers infesting the bay, who can take advantage of many Inlets on the Coast, where His Majesty's Ships cannot pursue them, and from whence they can safely avail themselves of any Opportunities that offer."[13] Similarly, Admiral Graves wrote about the difficulty of protecting vital supply lines, "Notwithstanding the utmost Endeavors of the Cruizers to protect Vessels arriving with Supplies, the Rebels watch the opportunity of the Kings Ships and Vessels being off the Coast, slip out in light good going Vessels full of Men, seize a defenceless Merchant Ship and push immediately for the nearest Port the Wind will carry them to."[14] Eventually, Commodore Marriot Arbuthnot, who oversaw the Royal Navy's North American station at the outset of the war, was forced to concede the early success of the Massachusetts privateers. "I am sorry to inform their Lordships, that I have it from pretty good Authority that the Rebels have many Armed Vessels . . . I have great reason to believe their Orders are to interrupt the trade of this Country, by preventing them from sending lumber & other Necessary's to the West Indies, or Great Britain, & particularly to stop all supplies for Boston."[15]

Even as the British army was preparing to evacuate Boston, Massachusetts privateers were still harassing Crown shipping lanes. On March 6, 1776. "the *Yankee Hero* sent into Newburyport another prize, a fine brig of about two hundred tons burthen, laden with coal, cheese, &c, bound for White Haven, for the use of the ministerial butchers, under the command of General Howe, Governor of Boston. This is the fifth prize out of eight which sailed from the above port."[16] A little over a week later, Massachusetts sailors successfully intercepted a pair of vessels that carried artillery, ammunition, food and necessary medical supplies.[17]

13. William Howe to Lord Dartmouth, December 13, 1775, in Wils, *In Behalf of the Continent*, 67.
14. Samuel Graves to Philip Stephens, December 8, 1775, ibid.
15. Commodore Marriot Arbuthnot to Philip Stephens, December 26, 1775, ibid., 68.
16. *Salem Gazette*, March 6, 1776, in *Proceedings of the Massachusetts Historical Society*, 21.
17. On March 14, 1776, "a transport brig of sixteen guns, laden with naval stores and provisions bound from Boston for the ministerial fleet at the southward was taken. A ship of two hundred and forty tons also captured by Captain Manly about this time was shipped with six double fortified four-pounders, two swivels, and three barrels of powder, while the cargo consisted of one hundred and seventy-five butts of porter, twelve packages of medicine with large quantities of coal, sourkrout, &c, besides a great number of packages for the officers in Boston. She also brought out sixty live hogs, but only one of them was alive

According to historian George Clark, over a period of five months between November 1775 and March 1776, the number of British vessels captured en route to Boston "amounted to thirty-one, their tonnage to 3,045 tons."[18] A similar study conducted by James Richard Wils revealed that New England privateers seized £1,575,500 worth of ships and supplies during the first two years of the war.[19]

The introduction of privateering had the desired result. The British encountered increasing difficulty in provisioning its army in Boston. Moreover, with the capture of supply vessels destined for the British garrison, the Americans gained muskets, ammunition, and provisions for themselves, affording them the potential ability to launch a land assault on the city. Worse still for the British, the soldiers and people in Boston began to starve.

Both General Washington and rebel authorities recognized the important contributions of privateers towards the war effort. As a result, less than one week after the evacuation of Boston, the Continental Congress passed the *Privateer Act of 1776.* The act expanded privateer operations and authorized the vessels to "attack, subdue, and take all Ships and other Vessels belonging to the Inhabitants of Great-Britain, on the High Seas … You may, by Force of Arms, attack, subdue, and take all Ships and other Vessels whatsoever carrying Soldiers, Arms, Gun-powder, Ammunition, Provisions, or any other contraband Goods, to any of the British Armies or Ships of War employed against these Colonies."[20] In response, Massachusetts privateers, as well as those from other colonies, expanded their war efforts. According to the National Park Service, approximately 800 vessels were commissioned as privateers throughout the American colonies during the American Revolution. These ships were responsible for capturing or destroying over 600 British ships and inflicting approximately $18 million in damage, which translates to approximately $300 million today.[21]

when she was carried in." *Salem Gazette*, March 14, 1776, in *Proceedings of the Massachusetts Historical Society*, 22.

18. *Proceedings of the Massachusetts Historical Society*, 22.

19. Wils, *In Behalf of the Continent*, 128.

20. *Instructions to the Commanders of Private Ships of Vessels of War, Which Shall Have Commissions or Letters of Marque and Reprisals, Authorizing Them to Make Captures of British Vessels and Cargoes* (Philadelphia, 1776), www.sethkaller.com/item/1337-23701.99-John-Hancock-Signed-1776-Privateering-Act&from=5.

21. John Frayler, "The American Revolution," *National Parks Service*, U.S. Department of the Interior, www.nps.gov/revwar/about_the_revolution/privateers.html.

"Under God": Understanding its Revolutionary Usage

BRIAN PATRICK O'MALLEY

The words "under God" have been part of America's fabric since its inception; any school child will recognize the words in the Pledge of Allegiance. But did the Founding Generation use this phrase the same way we do today?

In 1775, Col. Benedict Arnold led a detachment of Continental forces into Canada. George Washington admonished Arnold to respect all the people of Canada, as "the Success of this Enterprize (under God) depends wholly upon . . . the favourable Disposition of the Canadians & Indians."[1] George Washington often used the phrase "under God." In his General Orders for July 2, 1776, Washington reminded his troops, "The fate of unborn Millions will now depend, under God, on the Courage and Conduct of this army." Washington counseled Col. Fisher Gay: "Your own Reputation—the safety of the Army, & the good of the Cause depends, under God, upon our vigilance & Readiness." In July 1776, Washington observed that the safety of the United States "depends (under God) solely on the success of our arms."[2]

Americans also used "under God" in their messages to George Washington. Edward Rutledge, one of the South Carolina delegates to the Continental Congress, wrote to Washington, "Our Reliance continues. . . to be (under God) on your Wisdom & Fortitude & that of your Forces." Asa Douglas compared Washington to Parliamentarian

1. George Washington to Benedict Arnold, September 14, 1775, *Founders Online*, National Archives, founders.archives.gov/documents/Washington/03-01-02-0356.
2. George Washington, General Orders, July 2, 1776, *Founders Online*, National Archives, founders.archives.gov/documents/Washington/03-05-02-0117; George Washington to Colonel Fisher Gay, September 4, 1776, *Founders Online*, National Archives, founders.archives.gov/documents/Washington/03-06-02-0174.; George Washington, General Orders, July 9, 1776, *Founders Online*, National Archives, founders.archives.gov/documents/Washington/03-05-02-017.

Oliver Cromwell, whose takeover of England led to the 1649 execution of King Charles I. Douglas exclaimed, "Great *Cromwell*, under *God*, I rest upon you to save this country from ruin!"[3]

In practice, "under God," literally, meant "after God" or "other than God." Depending on the moment, the Revolution's only hope, *other than God*, was the strength of the currency, the conduct of the army, or the wisdom of George Washington. In 1777, for instance, John Adams wrote, "The success of our Cause appears to me to depend intirely, under God, on our Supporting the Credit of our Currency."[4]

The *Oxford English Dictionary* (*OED*) offers two definitions for "under God." The first is "under God" denoting rank. On a ship, as any sailor knows, there was God and then, immediately under God, the captain.[5] Second, "under God" indicates a person or thing that is a secondary cause, or a secondary recipient of thanks. This second meaning of "under God" can also signify "with God's permission." In this respect, "under God" was an apotropaic measure (having the power to avoid evil or bad luck) analogous to "God willing" (*Deo volente* in Latin, *inshallah* in Arabic). Such precautionary sayings avert misfortune by blunting excessive praise or tempering high expectations.[6]

On October 18, 1774, the Continental Congress approved a plan for a Continental Association to enforce a boycott of British goods. The measure called for local committees on the town or county level. Each committee was to monitor residents, publish the names of resi-

3. Edward Rutledge to George Washington, September 11, 1776, *Founders Online*, National Archives, founders.archives.gov/documents/Washington/03-06-02-0228; Asa Douglas to George Washington, June 7, 1776 (?), in Peter Force, *American Archives*, 3rd Series, 6:746, Northern Illinois University Digital Library, digital.lib.niu.edu/islandora/object/niu-amarch%3A80847.

4. John Adams to Joseph Palmer, February 20, 1777, in *Letters of Delegates to Congress, 1774-1789*, ed. Paul H. Smith, Gerard W. Gawalt, Rosemary Fry Plakas, and Eugene R. Sheridan, vol. 6 (Washington, D.C.: Library of Congress, 1980), 327, Library of Congress, American Memory, memory.loc.gov/ammem/amlaw/lwdg.html; Scott Bomboy, "Thomas McKean: A Founding Father with a Double Life," March 19, 2019, Constitution Daily, National Constitution Center, constitutioncenter.org/blog/thomas-mckean-looking-at-a-most-interesting-founding-father; Thomas McKean to John Dickinson, December 25, 1780, in Smith, et al. *Letters*, 16:481; Hugh Williams and William Blount to the Chevalier de La Luzerne, August 14, 1782, in Smith, et al., *Letters*, 19: 65.

5. *Oxford English Dictionary*, www.oed.com/ (*OED*).

6. *OED*; Weight of Gunpowder shipped at St. Eustatius, June 29, 1776, enclosed in James Smith to the Committee of Safety of Any Port or Place, except Philadelphia, June 28, 1776, Peter Force, *American Archives*, 6:1114 digital.lib.niu.edu/islandora/object/niu-amarch%3A105140. Joseph T. Shipley, *The Origins of English Words: A Discursive Dictionary of Indo-European Roots* (Baltimore: The Johns Hopkins University Press, 1984), 418; Margo DeMello, *Faces Around the World: A Cultural Encyclopedia of the Human Face* (Denver: ABC-CLIO, 2012), 89.

dents buying British goods, and announce a boycott of offenders.[7] Over the course of 1775, Americans pledged their support for the congressional boycott of British imports, producing a number of documents that often featured the phrase "under God."

In the founding charters of local and provincial associations, Americans often invoked the phrase "under God." On January 12, 1775, for instance, the Committee of Darien, Georgia, established a committee of the Continental Association, "Being persuaded that the salvation of the Rights and Liberties of *America* depend, under *God*, on the firm union of its inhabitants." Likewise, the May 4, 1775, town meeting of Newark, New Jersey, also established a committee of the Continental Association, "firmly convinced that the very existence of the rights and liberties of *America* can, under *God*, subsist on no other basis than the most animated and perfect union of its inhabitants."[8]

A search of two databases for "under God" in documents from 1776 confirmed a marked preference in the Founding Generation. Of forty-four usages of "under God," a total of thirty-two (seventy-three percent) signify a secondary recipient of thanks, "after God" or "other than God."[9] Preaching before the General Assembly of Connecticut, Rev. Judah Champion assured officers of the militia, "Your country reposes the highest confidence (under GOD) in your wisdom, prudence . . . and heroic valour." In other words, the country put its greatest faith, *after God*, in the officer corps. Likewise, Rev. Eleazar Wheelock said of American unity, "the continuance of it will, under GOD, be our best defence and security." In other words, the best protection, *other than God*, is unity.[10]

7. Ford, *Journals of the Continental Congress*, 1: 75, 79; T. H. Breen, *American Insurgents, American Patriots: The Revolution of the People* (New York: Hill and Wang, 2010), 18, 160-183.

8. "Darien, Ga., January 12, 1775" in Gehrke and Buchmuller, "Texts of Associations," in Maria Gehrke and Caren Buchmuller, "Texts of Associations, 1774-1776," in *The Revolution of the People: Thoughts and Documents on the Revolutionary Process in North America, 1774-1776*, ed. Hermann Wellenreuther (Gottingen, Germany: Gottingen University, 2006), 154; New York Association, April 29, 1775, in Gehrke and Buchmuller, "Texts of Associations," 170; "Town-Meeting, Newark, New-Jersey, May 4, 1775," in Gehrke and Buchmuller, "Texts of Associations," 174.

9. The documents derive from two digitalized collections, *American Archives*, Librarian of Congress Peter Force's collection of documents from the Revolutionary War; and Early American Imprints, Series I, Charles Evans's collection of historic books published in America. *American Archives* provided thirty usages of the phrase, Early American Imprints the remaining fourteen. Several authors contributed more than one document.

10. Judah Champion, *Christian and Civil Liberty and Freedom Considered and Recommended: A Sermon* . . . (Hartford: E. Watson, 1776), Early American Imprints, Series 1, no. 14675, 28.

Seven (almost sixteen percent) of the references suggested *God willing* or *with God's permission*. Gen. Griffith Rutherford, for example, pleaded with the North Carolina Council of Safety, "Pray, gentlemen . . . send us plenty of powder, and I hope, under *God*, we of *Salisbury* district are able to stand them."[11]

Three references proved too ambiguous to assign only one connotation exclusively. One reference signified an oath or exclamation comparable to "by God!" Samuel West exclaimed, "UNDER GOD, every person in the community ought to contribute his assistance" to the resistance movement.[12] Another single usage was an identification of rank. This was a customary bill of lading (i.e., a list of items in a shipment). In the standard phrasing of a bill a lading, the document identified the captain as "master, under *God*" of a ship.[13] A few documents used "under God" more than once. Rev. Samuel West, for instance, used "under God" three times in one sermon, and he used the phrase a different way each time.[14]

With the Treaty of Paris (1783), Britain recognized the independence of the United States. Americans acknowledged any human contribution to the Revolution as secondary to God. Delivering a sermon in Lexington, Massachusetts, in 1783, Rev. Zabiel Adams told members of the local militia, "To your conduct, under GOD, we are much indebted for the present independent station we hold among the nations of the earth."[15]

Americans gave much credit to Washington, while still recognizing his secondary role. In August 1783, for instance, a town meeting of Killingworth, Connecticut, declared that Washington "may justly be reputed under God, the *saviour* and *deliverer* of his country." In a 1783 address to Washington, the trustees and faculty of the University of

11. General Griffith Rutherford to the Council of Safety of North-Carolina, July 14, 1776, *American Archives*, 1: 613 digital.lib.niu.edu/islandora/object/niu-amarch%3A83853.
12. William Foster, *True Fortitude Delineated: A Sermon* . . . (Philadelphia: John Dunlap, 1776), Early American Imprints, Series 1, no. 14758, page 8; West, *A Sermon Preached*, 41, 67; George Washington, General Orders, June 30, 1776, *American Archives* 6: 1150 digital.lib.niu.edu/islandora/object/niu-amarch%3A102705.
13. John Taylor, Bill of Lading for Five Hundred Weight of Gunpowder shipped at St. Eustatius, June 29, 1776, enclosed in James Smith to the Committee of Safety of Any Port or Place, except Philadelphia, June 28, 1776, *American Archives*, 6: 1114, digital.lib.niu.edu/islandora/object/niu-amarch%3A105140; "Shippers by Sea Godfearing Men in Old Colonial Days," *Chicago Tribune*, January 2, 1927.
14. West, *A Sermon Preached*, 41, 61, 67.
15. Zabiel Adams, *The Evil Designs of Men Made Subservient by God to the Public Good*. . . (Boston: Benjamin Edes & Sons, 1783), Early American Imprints, Series 1, Number 17807, 9.

Pennsylvania wrote, "Long may you live, to enjoy the . . . prosperity and peace, which your arms have, under God, given to America."[16]

During the American Civil War (1861–1865), Unionists and secessionists agreed on the meaning of "under God." In an 1861 letter to a Raleigh, North Carolina, newspaper, "J.B." declared himself "devotedly attached to the Union, which under God, has been instrumental in giving us civil and religious liberty." In an 1862 tract, Rev. James Henley Thornwell called on men to enlist in Confederate ranks. Since the Confederacy could not depend on foreign assistance, Thornwell asked his readers "to see that all under God, depends on ourselves." Abraham Lincoln reportedly used "under God" in the Gettysburg Address (November 19, 1863), but whether or not he did, its distinction by commas in his handwritten recreation of the speech concurs with contemporary usage, when he hoped, "that this nation, under God, shall have a new birth of freedom. . . ."[17]

Only in the twentieth century did "under God" lose its earlier meaning when the words became a component of longer slogans rather than a parenthetical expression. In 1934, the National Conference of Christians and Jews (NCCJ) launched an annual observance of "Brotherhood Day" to combat religious bigotry. In 1936, Brotherhood Day became "Brotherhood Week." In the 1940s, the NCCJ repeatedly made "brotherhood under God" the theme of Brotherhood Week. Sermons, speeches, and newspaper columns promoted "brotherhood under God." In 1945, influential syndicated journalist Jay Franklin supported the effort by promoting "brotherhood under God" over the "racial supremacy embraced by Germany and Japan."[18]

16. "At a Town-Meeting, Held in Killingworth," *The Connecticut Courant and Weekly Intelligencer*, September 2, 1783; "The Address of the Trustees and Faculty of the University of Pennsylvania," *The Independent Gazette* (Philadelphia), December 20, 1783.
17. Abraham Lincoln, Address Delivered at the Dedication of the Cemetery at Gettysburg, First Draft, in Abraham Lincoln, *The Collected Works of Abraham Lincoln*, ed. Roy P. Basler, vol. 7 (New Brunswick, NJ: Rutgers University Press, 1953), 18 (*Collected Works*); Abraham Lincoln, Address Delivered at the Dedication of the Cemetery at Gettysburg, Second Draft, in Lincoln, *Collected Works*, 19; *The Weekly Raleigh Register*, February 13, 1861; "Thinks Lincoln Revised Speech at Gettysburg: Man Who Heard Talk Doesn't Recall Words 'Under God' as Part," *The Brooklyn Daily Eagle*, February 12, 1930; *The Weekly Raleigh Register*, February 13, 1861, J. H. Thornwell, "Our Danger and Our Duty," *North Carolina Argus* (Wadesboro, NC), April 22, 1862; Benjamin Morgan Palmer, *The Life and Letters of James Henley Thornwell: Ex-President of the South Carolina College* (Bedford, Mass.: Applewood Books, 2008 [1875]), 513.
18. Abraham H. Feinberg, "Hitler and the German Situation," April 8, 1934, in Marc Saperstein, ed., *Agony in the Pulpit: Jewish Preaching in Response to Nazi Persecution & Mass Murder 1933-1945* (New York: Hebrew Union College Press, 2018), 183; Brotherhood Week Throughout U.S. Has Been Decreed, *Rushville* (Ind.) *Republican*, January 26, 1940; Jay Franklin, "Race Supremacy Is Basic Issue," *The Decatur Herald*, January 26, 1945.

In 1951, pastoral organization Spiritual Mobilization used its magazine and its national radio show to promote the week of July 4th as "Freedom Under God Week." Over the next several years, Spiritual Mobilization continued Freedom Under God Week as an annual event. Throughout the early 1950s, several governors and hundreds of mayors issued proclamations honoring "Freedom Under God Week."[19]

In February 1953, Washington, DC, powerbroker fellowship organization The Family held the first National Prayer Breakfast. The theme of the event was "Government Under God." The Committee on the Uniform Series, a source of pastoral Bible study plans since 1872, established the sermon subject for Sunday, December 6, 1953, as "Government Under God." Across the United States, Protestant clergy of various denominations delivered sermons on the theme.[20] As a rebuttal to "godless" communism during the Cold War, Americans welcomed nonsectarian acknowledgements of God.

In 1954, the Senate and the House of Representatives passed a joint resolution adding "under God" to the Pledge of Allegiance. President Dwight D. Eisenhower signed the change into law on Flag Day, June 14, 1954. Almost immediately, "one nation under God" became a popular compound phrase that did not reflect the Founding Generation's usage of "under God." Newspapers branded the change with the headline, "One Nation Under God." On Sunday, July 4, 1954, preachers delivered sermons on "one nation under God."[21]

19. "Nation's Leaders Urge Freedom Under God," *Monroe Morning World* (Monroe, LA), July 3, 1955; "Churches Plan Observance; 'Freedom Under God' Topic," *The Cincinnati Enquirer*, July 3, 1955Eckard V. Toy, "*Faith and Freedom*, 1949-1960," in *The Conservative Press in Twentieth-Century America*, ed. Ronald Lora and William Henry Longton (Westport, CT: Greenwood Press, 1999), 153; Kevin M. Kruse, *One Nation Under God: How Corporate America Invented Christian America* (New York: Basic Books, 2015), 27-31, 92.
20. "Fellowship of Prayer," *The Orlando Sentinel*, February 15, 1953; Julien C. Hyer, "Government Under God," *Dayton Daily News*, December 5, 1953; "Trinity Lutheran," "St. John's Lutheran," "First Baptist, Pennsville," and "Church of God, Indian Head," *The Daily Courier* (Connellsville, PA), December 5, 1953; History: Committee on the Uniform Series: A Brief History, National Council of Churches, nationalcouncilofchurches.us/cus/?page_id=9.
21. Kruse, *One Nation Under God*, 102-104, 110; Richard J. Ellis, *To The Flag: The Unlikely History of the Pledge of Allegiance* (Lawrence: University of Kansas Press, 2005), 130, 255-256n26; *Daily Independent Journal* (San Rafael, CA), July 3, 1954; "One Nation, Under God," *Elmira Advertiser*, June 22, 1954 "'One Nation Under God' Inserted in Pledge to Flag," *The News* (Paterson, NJ), June 9, 1954; "One Nation Under God," *Daily Mountain Eagle* (Jasper, Alabama), June 24, 1954; "Diamond Methodist" and "Emmanuel's Ev. [Evangelical] & Reformed," *The Plain Speaker* (Hazelton, PA), July 3, 1954; "Fourth Street Methodist Church" and "Newfield Methodist Church," *The Daily Journal* (Vineland, NJ), July 3, 1954; "The Central Union Church," *The Honolulu Advertiser*, July 3, 1954.

Harry S. Truman was the last president who consistently used "under God" as the Founders used it. By the time Truman left office in 1953, the older usage of "under God" retired with him. Through radio, print, and sermons, recurring public awareness campaigns conditioned Americans to think of "under God" as merely a component of slogans like "brotherhood under God," or "freedom under God," or "one nation under God." In 1776, however, "under God" was the Founding Generation's equivalent of "God willing" or "after God."[22] How different is the meaning of "one nation, God willing, indivisible, with liberty and justice for all"? Is there a simple piousness reflected in Revolutionary-era usage that has been lost to the certitude of our own?

22. Harry S. Truman: "Message to the Congress on the State of the Union and on the Budget for 1947," January 21, 1946. Online by Gerhard Peters and John T. Woolley, *The American Presidency Project*. www.presidency.ucsb.edu/ws/?pid=12467; "Vote Your Convictions: President," *The Oneonta Star* (Oneonta, NY), November 2, 1948.

The Declaration of Independence: Did John Hancock Really Say That about His Signature?—and Other Signing Stories

J. L. BELL

When we picture the Declaration of Independence, most of us immediately think of the document handwritten on parchment and signed at the bottom by fifty-six members of the Second Continental Congress. Few individuals from the first two generations of Americans shared that view, however. The vast majority of those citizens never saw the Congress's document, which was kept safe in the nascent national government's archive. For them the Declaration existed as a printed text or as words read aloud. It was a piece of writing, not a piece of parchment.

The first engraved copies of the handwritten Declaration were published in 1818 and 1819, followed by a government-endorsed facsimile in 1823.[1] Many more reproductions followed. (In fact, the process of making copies caused the original to become so faded that modern images and souvenirs are based on the 1823 reproduction rather than the original.) Eventually the elegantly signed handwritten document became Americans' shared conception of the Declaration.[2]

That made the signatures on the Declaration, especially John Hancock's, icons of patriotism. The signing of the document became more important than the Congress's actual votes to approve independence and the Declaration's text, though a lot of authors forgot that the signing did not begin until August 2 and assigned that action

1. Pauline Maier, *American Scripture: Making the Declaration of Independence* (New York: Alfred A. Knopf, 1997), 175-6.
2. Catherine Nicholson, "The Stone Engraving: Icon of the Declaration," *Prologue*, 35 (2003), 3: 24-5.

to July 4.[3] Those fifty-six members of the Congress were labeled the Signers, elevated in public memory above other delegates. Dramatic stories of just how they put their names on the parchment became significant to the nation.

After the Colonial Revival of the late 1800s, however, historians became more skeptical about those stories. Often authors would retell one of those anecdotes—they really are good stories—but add a note that the tale was probably just a legend. In this article I reexamine four of those stories, trying to identify how early they appeared in print and how reliable they really are. The results vary.

"I SHALL HAVE A GREAT ADVANTAGE OVER YOU"

The first anecdote is about is Benjamin Harrison, one of several oversized Virginians at the Congress, joking with slender Elbridge Gerry about long it would take each of them to hang. The Course of Human Events blog listed this among "a number of quotations from the signing for which we have no evidence."[4] A recent Weekly Standard essay called the story "probably apocryphal."[5]

In fact, we can trace that story back to one of the men in the room where it happened. Dr. Benjamin Rush recounted that anecdote in a July 20, 1811, letter to John Adams, a fellow Signer:

> Do you recollect the pensive and awful silence which pervaded the house when we were called up, one after another, to the table of the President of Congress, to subscribe what was believed by many at that time to be our own death warrants? The Silence & the gloom of the morning were interrupted I well recollect only for a moment by Col: Harrison of Virginia who said to Mr Gerry at the table, "I shall have a great advantage over you Mr: Gerry when we are all hung for what we are now doing. From the size and weight of my body I shall die in a few minutes, but from the lightness of your body you will dance in the air an hour or two before you are dead." This Speech procured a transient smile, but it was soon succeeded by the Solemnity with which the whole business was conducted.[6]

3. Some Signers added their names after August 2, 1776, the last being Thomas McKean of Delaware sometime between 1777 and 1782. See Emily Sneff, "Unsullied by Falsehood: The Signing," Course of Human Events: Declaration Resources Project Blog, July 27, 2016, declaration.fas.harvard.edu/blog/signing, accessed June 19, 2019.
4. Ibid.
5. Richard Samuelson, "The Fighting Spirit of the Declaration," *Weekly Standard*, July 2, 2016, www.weeklystandard.com/richard-samuelson/the-fighting-spirit-of-the-declaration, accessed June 19, 2019.
6. Benjamin Rush to John Adams, July 20, 1811, in *Letters of Benjamin Rush*, Eric Crahan, ed. (Philadelphia: American Philosophical Society, 1951), 2:1090. See also Rush to Adams,

This was a private letter between friends, written before the handwritten Declaration became an icon and thus not concocted to please the public.

Dr. James Thacher published a version of the same story in 1823 in his Military Journal, a book that combined his actual notes from the war years with later recollections and material from other sources. In an entry pegged to 1776, Thacher wrote:

> I am credibly informed that the following anecdote occurred on the day of signing the declaration. Mr. Harrison, a delegate from Virginia, is a large portly man—Mr. Gerry of Massachusetts is slender and spare. A little time after the solemn transaction of signing the instrument, Mr. Harrison said smilingly to Mr. Gerry, "When the hanging scene comes to be exhibited I shall have the advantage over you on account of my size. All will be over with me in a moment, but you will be kicking in the air half an hour after I am gone."[7]

Thacher might well have heard the story from Rush, with whom he corresponded. Yet his wording of Harrison's remark is obviously different from what Rush wrote down for Adams. Rush also said Harrison spoke "at the table" while Thacher said he did so "A little time after the solemn transaction of signing the instrument." Nonetheless, this is obviously the same story being passed along.

It is notable that John Adams, who could be quite cranky about Revolutionary myth-making when he wasn't indulging in it himself, did not object to the story from either Rush or Thacher. His reply letter to Rush took no issue with the tale even though he disliked Harrison and came to see Gerry as a political foe.[8] In 1824 Adams told Thacher: "I have had read to me, your valuable Journal of your Campaigns in the American revolutionary war, and I have no hesitation in saying, that it is the most natural, simple, and faithful narration of facts, that I have seen in any history of that period."[9]

July 20, 1811, Founders Online, National Archives, founders.archives.gov/ documents/ Adams/99-02-02-5659, accessed June 19, 2019.

7. James Thacher, *A Military Journal during the American Revolutionary War, from 1775 to 1783* (Boston: Richardson & Lord, 1823), 57-8.

8. Adams to Rush, July 31, 1811, in *Old Family Letters*, Series A, Alexander Biddle, ed. (Philadelphia: J. P. Lippincott, 1892), 342-4. See Adams to Rush, July 31, 1811, Founders Online, National Archives, founders.archives.gov/documents/Adams/99-02-02-5666, accessed June 19, 2019.

9. Adams to Thacher, September 11, 1824, in Thacher, *Military Journal*, 2nd edition (Boston: Cottons & Barnard), iv. See also Adams to Thacher, September 11, 1824, Founders Online, National Archives, founders.archives.gov/documents/Adams/99-02-02-7915, accessed June 19, 2019.

Of course it is possible that Rush's recollection was not accurate. For example, Harrison could have come up with the witticism days later instead of at the dramatic moment of signing. The story had obvious appeal for Adams and Rush in burnishing their egos, emphasizing how the Congress delegates signed despite fear that they might be executed for doing so. Nevertheless, for a story from the Revolution not written down at the time, the agreement of two documented witnesses is about as strong as our evidence can get.

"YOU WILL BE VERY APT TO HANG SEPARATELY"

Another oft-told story first appeared in the biographical sketch of Benjamin Franklin that historian Jared Sparks published in 1840:

> There is also another anecdote related of Franklin, respecting an incident which took place when the members were about to sign the Declaration. "We must be unanimous," said Hancock; "there must be no pulling different ways; we must all hang together." "Yes," replied Franklin, "we must, indeed, all hang together, or most assuredly we shall all hang separately."[10]

Sparks did not cite any source for this anecdote. However, we can trace the witty line back to a book first published in 1811. Unfortunately for our picture of the signing, that book attributed the witticism to a different man who had left the country by 1776.

In his memoirs, Alexander Graydon wrote:

> Both the brothers, John and Richard Penn, had been governors of Pennsylvania; the former being in office at the beginning of hostilities. By yielding to the torrent, which it would have been impossible to withstand, he gave no offence, and avoided reproach; though it was deemed expedient to have him secured and removed from Philadelphia, on the approach of the royal army in the year 1777. Mr. Richard Penn, having no official motives for reserve, was even upon terms of familiarity with some of the most thorough-going whigs, such as general [Charles] Lee and others: An evidence of this was the pleasantry ascribed to him, on occasion of a member of Congress, one day observing to his compatriots, that at all events "they must hang together:" "If you do not, gentlemen," said Mr. Penn, "I can tell you that you will be very apt to hang separately."[11]

10. Jared Sparks, ed., *The Works of Benjamin Franklin* (Boston: Tappan & Whittemore, 1840), 1: 408.

11. Alexander Graydon, *Memoirs of a Life, Chiefly Passed in Pennsylvania, within the Last Sixty Years* (Harrisburg: John Wyeth, 1811), 115-6. Graydon's name did not appear in this first edition, but it did in the 1846 edition, retitled *Memoirs of His Own Time*. Richard Penn

The way Graydon presented the witticism as "ascribed to" former governor Richard Penn indicates that he had no direct knowledge of the conversation. Many people were probably passing around the story. It is also notable that Graydon mentioned Franklin several times in his book but did not credit him with this line.

In American culture Franklin became a magnet for witty remarks and clever ideas. Of course, he did come up with many such remarks and ideas, but he also gets credit for all the sayings in Poor Richard's Almanac, most quoted from earlier publications; for suggestions he clearly made in jest, such as daylight saving time; and for schemes that probably duped him as much as everyone else, such as Baron de Steuben's claims of a marvelous career in the Prussian army.

The "hang separately" line is good dark humor; American authors like Sparks wanted it to come from Franklin, and at a significant moment. In the mid-1800s the signing of the Declaration became the most important act of the Continental Congress. Furthermore, the anecdote about Harrison and Gerry suggested that the Signers did speak about hanging on August 2. Unfortunately, the evidence that Franklin responded with a witticism of his own is weak, and if he did he was most likely quoting lukewarm Loyalist Richard Penn.

"IF MY HAND TREMBLES, JOHN BULL WIL FIND MY HEART WON'T!

Two more stories about the signing surfaced in an 1840s article headed "Revolutionary Anecdotes," printed in many American newspapers. At the time it was common for editors to run this type of historical material, which was of public interest but did not become dated. Editors copied texts from other papers whenever they needed to fill space, occasionally with credit but usually without. Such items circulated so thoroughly that a newspaper could run the same tidbit a year or two later with no suggestion that readers might have seen it before.

The earliest newspaper I have seen offering these "Revolutionary Anecdotes" was the July 10, 1841, *Public Ledger* of Philadelphia. One states:

> When I visited Mr. [John] Adams in November, 1818, his hand trembled similar to that of Stephen Hopkins, the Quaker patriot from Rhode Island, who had been afflicted with a paralytic stroke. Mr. Adams acted as his amanuensis, and asked him if he should sign his

(1735-1811) left Philadelphia in the summer of 1775, carrying the Continental Congress's Olive Branch Petition to London. He settled in Britain, returning to Philadelphia only for a visit in 1808.

> name to the Declaration of Independence for him. "No! I will sign it myself—if we are hung for signing it, you shall not be hung for it for me." Mr. Adams, then, in imitation of Hopkins, took his pen, clasped his wrist with his left hand, went through the tremulous motion of signing his name, and in the language of Hopkins, emphatically said, "If my hand trembles, John Bull will find my heart won't!" which Mr. Adams said electrified all Congress, and made the most timid firm in their purpose.

There is no author name attached to this story as published in the *Public Ledger*.[12] But within the telling itself are signs of a provenance: from John Adams, present at the signing, to a writer who visited him in late 1818. We know that Adams remembered Hopkins with respect and fondness, which offers support for this story. At the same time, Adams's anecdotes are not always reliable.

An earlier publication of the story might offer more hints about the writer, which in turn would make it easier to assess the tale. Even as it is, however, this story comes to us with a provenance leading back to a Signer. That may not be enough to make everyone certain that it happened, but it is evidence to be reckoned with.

"JOHN BULL CAN READ MY NAME WITHOUT SPECTACLES"

The other of the two "Revolutionary Anecdotes" is much less solid on its face. Although published in Philadelphia alongside the story about

12. The editor of Philadelphia's *Public Ledger* at this time was Russell Jarvis (1790-1853), who had New England roots and a background in the law. He went into journalism as editor of the *Boston Patriot*, a newspaper that John Adams favored with many long reminiscences in 1809-12. On October 20, 1818, the *Boston Patriot* published remarks from "a correspondent" about the virtues of Stephen Hopkins. Five years later, Jarvis was a strong proponent of John Quincy Adams for the presidency. It is plausible, therefore, that Jarvis paid a friendly visit to former President Adams in 1818, heard the anecdote about Hopkins, and recalled it for publication in 1841.

However, Jarvis's most famous interaction with the Adams family was not so pleasant. Frustrated at not receiving a government appointment from President J. Q. Adams, he became an opposition journalist in Washington. In April 1828 the president's son and secretary made a critical remark about Jarvis in front of his wife and in-laws. The journalist demanded satisfaction and then tried to provoke the younger man into a duel by pulling his nose. (See Samuel Flagg Bemis, "The Scuffle in the Rotunda: A Footnote to the Presidency of John Quincy Adams and to the History of Dueling," *Massachusetts Historical Society Proceedings*, 71 [1957], 156-66.) Even a decade later, Jarvis's memories of the Adams family were undoubtedly mixed.

Nonetheless, the "Revolutionary Anecdotes" did appear in the *Public Ledger*. If further research uncovers an earlier publication of that article or the Hopkins story alone, the context could provide further clues about provenance. Both tales concern New England politicians, so they may have originated in that region. If no earlier version can be identified, then Russell Jarvis appears to be the most likely author.

Hopkins and Adams, it did not come with the same sort of internal sourcing. Most likely, an early newspaper editor put the tales together because they were both about the signing.

That anecdote is:

> It will be remembered that a reward of £500 was offered for the head of John Hancock. When he signed the Declaration of Independence, he did it with a bold hand, in a conspicuous manner, and rose from his seat, pointing to it, and exclaimed, "there, John Bull can read my name without spectacles, he may double his reward, and I put him at defiance."

In fact, there is no evidence that the British government offered a £500 reward to capture Hancock by the summer of 1776, though this article implies that most readers would already believe that. For such a reward to be effective, it would have had to be widely publicized, and no example of such an offer appears in newspapers or letters of the time.

This tale is so far the earliest version of the story of Hancock signing his name on the Declaration so large that someone "can read my name without spectacles." In this version that figure is John Bull, the personification of England also reportedly mentioned by Hopkins. Later authors changed that imagined reader to King George III or his ministers. Likewise, the wording of Hancock's exclamation changes slightly from one recounting to another.

All versions of this story about Hancock's signature collapse under one crucial fact: the Continental Congress never planned to send the signed parchment to Britain. As noted above, that document remained carefully guarded in the American government's archive. The Congress had already published its Declaration with Hancock's name printed at the bottom and sent copies of that printed version to Britain and elsewhere. Hancock's ornate signature was for his fellow delegates, or for history.

The anecdote about John Hancock's signature and King George's spectacles is therefore not reliable in the least. But, like the three other stories of the signing, two of which rest on more solid foundations, that patriotic tall tale has lasted—some authors are still repeating it today.

1776—The Horror Show

BRIAN PATRICK O'MALLEY

The British Army held New York City from 1776 to November 25, 1783. In prisoner exchanges, royal forces in New York periodically released prisoners of war who were "sickly and emaciated." Sometimes the prisoners numbered a few dozen, sometimes a few hundred. In 1776, however, British military commander Lt. Gen. Sir William Howe released more than 2,000 prisoners. The sudden appearance of 2,000 dying men was a national trauma for the United States.[1]

In a series of clashes, from the Battle of Long Island (August 27, 1776) to the capture of Fort Lee (November 20, 1776), Howe secured New York City. Joshua Loring, a Massachusetts Loyalist, served Howe as commissary general of prisoners. According to Loring, Howe captured 4,101 privates, 304 officers and 25 staff of the Continental Army. Historian Edwin G. Burrows noted Loring's list overlooked an unsuccessful Patriot raid on Montresor's Island, now Randall's Island (September 23, 1776), that brought the number of captive soldiers to 4,114 and captive officers to 305.[2]

On October 7, Howe extended to Continental officers the customary right of parole. On their pledge as officer-gentlemen to not escape British lines, the American officers found lodging on British-held sec-

1. *The Continental Journal, and Weekly Advertiser* (Boston), February 4, 1779; *The Connecticut Gazette; and The Universal Intelligencer* (New London), August 24, 1781; Paper From Lieutenant Colonel William Walcott, April 2, 1777, *Founders Online*, National Archives, founders.archives.gov/documents/Washington/03-09-02-0049 (Walcott Paper); Edwin G. Burrows, *Forgotten Patriots: The Untold Story of American Prisoners of War During the Revolutionary War* (New York: Basic Books, 2008), 64-65; Jabez Fitch, *The New-York Diary of Lieutenant Jabez Fitch*, ed. William H. Waldon Sabine (New York: Colburn & Tegg, 1954), 93n1; David Hackett Fischer, *Washington's Crossing* (New York: Oxford University Press, 2004), 378.

2. Joshua Loring, "Return of Prisoners taken during the Campaign, 1776," enclosed in Sir William Howe to Lord George Germaine, December 3, 1776, *The New-York Gazette; and the Weekly Mercury*, March 17, 1777; Burrows, *Forgotten Patriots*, 296n1.

tions of Long Island. Continental soldiers, however, remained warehoused in prison ships, and in sugar refineries, non-Anglican churches, and other large buildings appropriated by Howe. Many paroled Continental officers visited the captive soldiers. As the health of the soldiers deteriorated, however, some officers found it unbearable to witness suffering they could not alleviate.[3]

From late December 1776 through January 1777, Howe released just under 2,300 Continental soldiers on parole, an arrangement usually reserved for officers. On January 29, Howe informed Gen. George Washington that only an "inconsiderable Number" of prisoners remained in New York. There was a discrepancy between the 4,114 soldiers Howe captured and the remnant he released. Several hundred had joined Loyalist regiments like the Royal Highland Emigrants, but one sarcastic Patriot nonetheless remarked that Howe sent out all the soldiers, but "one half he sent to the world of spirits for want of food."[4]

Former-prisoners recalled the spike in prisoner deaths that prompted Howe's frantic mass-release. Pvt. John Adlum wrote, "In the churches and sugarhouse the mortality was dreadful in the latter part of the month of December and January." Pvt. William Darlington recalled the moment prisoners "began to die like rotten sheep" from "cold, hunger, and dirt." Likewise, Pvt. Thomas Boyd's fellow-prisoners "began to die in heaps."[5]

To preserve a claim on British soldiers held by Patriot forces, Howe loaded prisoners by the hundreds onto transport ships. The *Glasgow*, for instance, dropped about 200 soldiers near Milford, Connecticut. Two ships carried about 300 prisoners to South Amboy, New Jersey. Col. Ethan Allen, an officer on parole in New York, recalled several

3. John Nice, "Extracts from the Diary of Captain John Nice, of the Pennsylvania Line," ed. Edward Burd, *The Pennsylvania Magazine of History and Biography* 16 (1893): 404; Burrows, *Forgotten Patriots*, 21-26, 50-53; *Fitch Diary*, 54, 148; Alexander Graydon, *Memoirs of a Life. . .* (Harrisburg, PA: John Wyeth, 1811), 211-212; Ethan Allen, "Narrative of Colonel Ethan Allen's Treatment during His Captivity," *The Pennsylvania Packet or the General Advertiser*, November 16, 1779.

4. Walcott Paper; William Howe to George Washington, January 29, 1777, *Founders Online*, founders.archives.gov/documents/Washington/03-08-02-0189; Extract of a Letter from Peeks kill (Peekskill, New York), January 19, 1777, *The Continental Journal, and Weekly Advertiser* (Boston), February 13, 1777.

5. John Adlum, *Memoirs of the Life of John Adlum in the Revolutionary War*, ed. Howard H. Peckham (Chicago: The Coxton Club, 1968), 125 (*Adlum Memoirs*); affidavit of William Darlington, February 27, 1777, *Pennsylvania Evening Post*, May 3, 1777; affidavit of Thomas Boyd, February 27, 1777, *Pennsylvania Evening Post*, May 3, 1777 (Boyd Affidavit).

prisoners "fell dead in the streets of New York, as they attempted to walk to the vessels in the harbor, for their intended embarkation."[6]

Several prisoners died on their voyage. Pvt. Oliver Woodruff recalled twenty-eight prisoners passed away on the *Glasgow* in the several days it took to reach Milford; the *Connecticut Journal* put the number at twenty. The two ships bringing prisoners to South Amboy anchored only one night off Staten Island. In that night, six prisoners died, three on each vessel, recalled John Adlum, one of the prisoners dumped at South Amboy.[7]

Once ashore, the prisoners kept dying. Woodruff recalled nineteen prisoners died the first night after landing at Milford. Adlum helped a tottering prisoner off a boat, only to find him dead moments later.[8]

Many prisoners languished for weeks where they landed. Based on information from Col. William Humpton, the Continental Congress Executive Committee reported to John Hancock, president of Congress, that most prisoners in South Amboy were too "weak & sickly" to travel any further. The *Connecticut Journal* published the names and hometowns of thirty-two returned Connecticut residents who "lie sick at Milford."[9]

The unexpected arrivals tested a town's resources. South Amboy residents were "carting" the prisoners from house to house, "to get the burthen of them from one to another." The Executive Committee asked William Shippen Jr., director of hospitals for the Flying Camp in New Jersey, to secure medicine and provisions for the "poor Creatures," who "perish for want of Physick & food."[10]

Sadly, John Adlum wrote, "Numbers of those who were prisoners died on the road in going home." Writing from Wethersfield, Connecticut, Col. John Chester described returning prisoners "dying along the road." In their joint deposition, privates William Houston and Samuel Young of Pennsylvania claimed that "many of those who were released died upon the road before they reached home."[11]

6. Burrows, *Forgotten Patriots*, 63; Allen, "Narrative," *Pennsylvania Packet*, November 20, 1779; *The Connecticut Journal* (New Haven), January 8, 1777; *Adlum Memoirs*, 135-137.
7. Oliver Woodruff, Revolutionary War Pension Application, September 27, 1832, Pension Number s14885, National Archives, at Fold3 by Ancestry.com, www.fold3.com/image/28402390 (Woodruff Application); *Connecticut Journal*, January 8, 1777; *Adlum Memoirs*, 137.
8. Woodruff Application; *Adlum Memoirs*, 137.
9. Executive Committee to John Hancock, January 30, 1777, *Letters of Delegates to Congress, 1774-1789*, vol. 6, *January 1, 1777-April 30, 1777*, ed. Paul H. Smith (Washington, DC: Library of Congress, 1980), 163; *Connecticut Journal*, January 8, 1777.
10. Executive Committee to Hancock, January 30, 1777.
11. *Adlum Memoirs*, 143; *Webb Correspondence*, 184; Affidavit of Samuel Young and William Houston, December 15, 1776, in *Pennsylvania Evening Post*, May 3, 1777.

As prisoners struggled to return home, shock rippled through the country. According to John Chester, returnees were "mere skeletons." Chester wrote, "Humanity cannot but drop a tear at sight of the poor, miserable, starved objects." In a 1777 sermon in Lancaster, Pennsylvania, Continental Army chaplain Hugh Henry Brackenridge cried, "We saw them—oh spectacle of horror and commiseration!" Brackenridge described the typical figure with "belly contracted to the ribs," "the eye sunk and hid within the head" and "the voice shrill, feeble and not to be distinctly heard." Brackenridge even mentioned swollen lower extremities of famine edema, "legs swollen, and from the ankle to the knee of an equal shape."[12]

Quaker diarist Christopher Marshall documented the gradual arrival of returnees in Philadelphia. Marshall's moral indignation steadily sharpened. On December 30, 1776, "many" former prisoners "returned to this City very poorly and weak." The next day, Marshall recorded, "More of our poor prisoners coming into town." On January 2, 1777, "A number of sick soldiers arrived from New York, being discharged by Gen. Howe, after a tedious imprisonment, being starved by the enemy."[13]

Brackenridge described what might have been a typical experience for survivors who reached home. The chaplain described townspeople crowding around a returnee, begging to know about missing loved ones. "Ask one of these what became of his companion whom we see not? He died the first week partly with hunger and partly with cold. He recommended his wife and infant children to God . . . What became of another whom we see not? He died the second week on board the ships by the badness . . . of the food which was served to us."[14]

The mass prisoner release ended January 27, 1777. James McHenry, a surgeon with the Continental army captured at the Battle of Fort Washington (November 16, 1776), left New York on parole with eighty-one Continental soldiers. These, McHenry wrote, were "the sick

12. John Chester to Samuel Blachley Webb, January 17, 1777, in *Correspondence and Journals of Samuel Blachley Webb*, vol. 1, ed. Worthington Chauncey Ford (Lancaster, PA: Wickersham Press, 1893), 184 (hereafter *Webb Correspondence*); Hugh Henry Brackenridge, "The Bloody Vestiges of Tyranny," in Hugh Henry Brackenridge, *A Hugh Henry Brackenridge Reader, 1770-1815*, ed. Daniel Marder (Pittsburgh: University of Pittsburgh Press, 1970), 66 (*Brackenridge Reader*); Joseph Stein and Henryk Fenigstein, "Pathological Anatomy of Hunger Disease," Myron Winick, ed., *Hunger Disease: Studies by the Jewish Physicians in the Warsaw Ghetto*, trans. Martha Osnos (New York: John Wiley & Sons, 1979), 227; Todd Tucker, *The Great Starvation Experiment: Ancel Keys and the Men Who Starved for Science* (Minneapolis: University of Minnesota Press, 2007 [2006]), 140.

13. Christopher Marshall, *The Diary of Christopher Marshall*, ed. William Duane (Albany, NY: Joel Munsell, 1877 [1839]), 110.

14. *Brackenridge Reader*, 66-67.

privates and those that remained of the well." From Hightstown, New Jersey on January 31, McHenry reported, "Six have died since our leaving New-York."[15]

A month after the mass release ended, most of the returnees were probably dead. Two Continental officers, recruiting in different regions of the United States, offered George Washington two similar assessments in February 1777. From York, Pennsylvania, on February 12, Col. Thomas Hartley reported that most returning prisoners lived just long enough to see their families again. The prisoners "return Home to tell the doleful Story of their Captivity and Distress" and "almost all these Die in a few Days after they have joined their Families." Reporting from Lyme, Connecticut, on February 19, Brig. Gen. Samuel Holden Parsons estimated "about Three Quarter parts" of returnees in that area were already dead.[16]

On January 23, before sending out the last returnees, Howe appointed a British officer, Lt. Col. William Walcott, to negotiate for Washington's release of an equal number of Redcoat prisoners. Washington authorized Continental Lt. Col. Robert Hanson Harrison to negotiate what proportion of the returnees were fit to consider for exchange. Meeting Walcott on February 17 and March 10, 1777, Harrison explained that Continental forces would not release a number of British soldiers equal to the number of prisoners Howe released, because so many of the returnees died on their way home, or shortly after arriving, "owing to their close & rigorous confinement."[17]

Walcott observed the returnees were "delivered over alive." For Walcott, it hardly mattered that prisoners died a month or a minute after

15. James McHenry to Washington, January 31, 1777, *Founders Online*, National Archives, founders.archives.gov/documents/Washington/03-08-02-0214.

16. Thomas Hartley to Washington, February 12, 1777, in George Washington, *The Papers of George Washington*, Revolutionary War Series, vol. 8, *January-March 1777*, ed. Dorothy Twohig (Charlottesville: University Press of Virginia, 1998), 317-318, also in *Founders Online*, founders.archives.gov/documents/Washington/03-08-02-0341; Samuel Holden Parsons to Washington, February 19, 1777, in *Founders Online*, founders.archives.gov/documents/Washington/03-08-02-0406.

17. [Alexander Hamilton], List of Questions Regarding a Prisoners Exchange, undated, enclosed in Washington to the Continental Congress, March 18, 1777, The Papers of the Continental Congress, 1774-1789, National Archives Microfilm Publication M247, roll 167, item 152, Record Group 360, at Fold3 by Ancestry.com, www.fold3.com/image/395942 (Washington to Congress, March 18, 1777), William Walcott and Robert H. Harrison, Objections, etc., undated, enclosed in Washington to Congress, March 18, 1777, www.fold3.com/image/395973. Harold C. Syrett, editor of the Papers of Alexander Hamilton, supposed Hamilton's list dated from 1778; Questions Concerning A Proposed Cartel for the Exchange of Prisoners of War, [April 10-11, 1778], *Founders Online*, founders.archives.gov/documents/Hamilton/01-01-02-0426.

their return. The prisoners were alive the instant Howe released them. Besides, Walcott added, Howe could not prevent high mortality among the returning prisoners, if prolonging their lives was "contrary to the will of the Supreme Being in whose Hands only are life and death."[18]

The mass release preempted an official exchange, but Howe and Walcott implied the returnees were virtually exchanged. Walcott, however, sabotaged this pretense. When talks with Harrison stalled, Walcott relayed a note to Washington through British officer Lt. Gen. Charles, Earl Cornwallis. The officers and privates released on parole were subject to recall to New York at Howe's discretion, until they were formally exchanged. Walcott no doubt meant to threaten the officers with recall to New York when he reminded Washington that the officers, as well as the privates, were still considered Howe's prisoners "untill They shall be regularly exchanged."[19]

Washington capitalized on Walcott's slip. Washington informed Howe, "It is confessed . . . on all sides, that after their delivery they still continued your prisoners & would be so, till regularly exchanged." Even if paroled Continental soldiers died at their homes, they were still Howe's prisoners when they died. Hastily dumping prisoners just before they expired hardly exonerated Howe in the "speedy death of a large part of them."[20]

Washington wished Howe released the prisoners on humanitarian grounds much sooner, "before these ill fated men were reduced to such extremity." Washington's expectation was not outlandish by the standards of the age. In his 1758 work *The Law of Nations*, first published in English in 1760, Swiss jurist Emmerich de Vattel wrote that if prisoners of war are too numerous "to be kept or fed with safety," even if it strengthens the enemy, "These prisoners are sent back on their parole, not to carry arms for a certain time, or to the end of the war."[21]

The dispute over the returnees lasted for the remainder of Howe's command. The protracted dispute provided several estimates of returnee numbers. In January 1778, Henry Hugh Ferguson, the Scottish-born Loyalist who served as commissary of prisoners in Philadelphia, listed 1,701 privates as "Returned by Sir William Howe

18. Walcott and Harrison, Objections.

19. Walcott Paper.

20. Washington to Howe, April 9, 1777, *Founders Online*, founders.archives.gov/documents/Washington/03-09-02-0103.

21. Washington to Howe, April 9, 1777; M. [Emmerich] de Vattel, *The Law of Nations; or Principles of the Law of Nature: Applied to the Conduct and Affairs of Nations and Sovereigns* (Dublin: Luke White, 1787), 528.

and for whom none are sent back in exchange."[22] Howe and Walcott offered an estimate higher than Ferguson offered. Walcott insisted Howe released "upwards" of 2,200 Continental privates. Writing to British Gen. John Burgoyne on November 16, 1777, Howe mentioned the 2,200 Continental soldiers "that I sent in last Winter, in full Confidence of receiving an equal Number in Return, which . . . has been pointedly refused under the most frivolous Pretences."[23]

In March 1778, American commissary of prisoners Elias Boudinot mentioned "1821 Privates in dispute." This figure was a subset of the returnees. Joshua Loring showed his ledger of prisoners to Ambrose Serle, the civilian secretary of Royal Navy Adm. Richard, Viscount Howe, a brother of General Howe. In his diary, Serle raged that "above 2000 of them have been released (1800 & upwards of those taken at Fort Washington) upon their Parole, and the Rebels refuse to return us a man in their Room—such is their insult towards us!" By March 1778, Howe apparently only demanded a full return for the Fort Washington soldiers.[24]

With the surrender of Fort Washington, 2,607 Continental privates became prisoners. About two months later, Howe released only 1,821 of those soldiers. From death and recruitment, soldiers from Fort Washington lost thirty percent of their number.[25]

Walcott indicated the returnees totaled over 2,200, implying the number did not reach 2,300. Allowing for 2,299 returnees leaves 1,815 (about forty-four percent) who disappeared from Howe's custody. Some prisoners escaped. Historian Francis D. Cogliano estimated about eight percent of the Patriots held at Mill Prison, in Plymouth, England, escaped during the war. The British military prisons of New York left no comparable records, but Edwin G. Burrows documented several escapees who met little resistance. Patriots detained in Britain, however, had the sympathy of nearby civilians. The care of the civilian populace

22. Henry Hugh Ferguson, "A General Return of Prisoners," January 10, 1778, Peter Force Collections, Series 7E, item 12: Elias Boudinot Papers, Library of Congress (hereafter Boudinot Papers); Elias Boudinot to Washington, June 28, 1778, Boudinot Papers.

23. Walcott Paper; Howe to John Burgoyne, November 16, 1777, in Jane Clark, "The Convention Troops and the Perfidy of Sir William Howe," *The American Historical Review* 37 (July 1932): 722.

24. Boudinot to Washington, March 2, 1778, *Founders Online*, founders.archives.gov/documents/Washington/03-14-02-0015; Ambrose Serle, *The American Journal of Ambrose Serle*, ed. Edward H. Tatum, Jr. (New York: New York Times, 1969 [1940]), 305.

25. Loring, "Return of Prisoners."

also meant captive Patriots in Britain were in better condition than prisoners in British-occupied New York.[26]

Royal recruiting officers siphoned off some prisoners. In his memoirs, Continental Ens. Isaac Van Horne recalled "a great number" of soldiers "enlisted with the enemy" to escape starvation. Lt. William Sterett, however, indicated Royal recruiters had little success with prisoners. Thomas Boyd even "thanked heaven" that most prisoners preferred to die rather than serve "the emissaries of the *Prince of Darkness*."[27]

Loring claimed "upwards" of 700 Continental soldiers in 1776-77 offered to enlist, but Howe refused the offer. Loring was probably incorrect about Howe refusing prisoner-enlistees, but probably right about the numbers. If 799 prisoners enlisted with Howe, then perhaps 1,016 (24.7 percent) of captive Patriot soldiers died in 1776. The figure drops below seventeen percent if, as in Mill Prison, eight percent of prisoners escaped from New York facilities.[28]

By the customs of European warfare, Patriot authorities owed Continental soldiers pay and clothes during their custody. On December 5, 1776, Howe warned Washington that prisoners, namely the sick and wounded, needed "Accomodation, Refreshments, & Attendance" that Howe could not provide. After releasing the prisoners, though, Howe claimed he provided them "proper Habitations, sufficient and wholesome Food, and Medicines." In 1777, Howe claimed Patriot prisoners lacked only money and clothes, items Patriots owed the prisoners.[29]

Washington noted that returnee testimony was unanimous. Prisoners alleged they received insufficient food, and what they did get was

26. Burrows, *Forgotten Patriots*, 107-109; Francis D. Cogliano, *American Maritime Prisoners in the Revolutionary War: The Captivity of William Russell* (Annapolis: Naval Institute Press, 2001), 94-112; 147; Ferguson, "General Return;" Boudinot to Gouverneur Morris and Henry Knox , March 14, 1782, *Letters of Delegates*, 17: 397.

27. Isaac Van Horne, "Isaac Van Horne Memoirs," August 1776-May 1778, in Dennis P. Ryan, ed, *A Salute to Courage: The American Revolution as Seen through the Wartime Writings of Officers of the Continental Army and Navy* (New York: Columbia University Press, 1979), 52; Affidavit of Lt. William Sterett, January 19, 1777, in *The Pennsylvania Evening Post*, April 29, 1777; Boyd Affidavit (emphasis in original).

28. Joshua Loring, "State of the Prisoners," undated, Boudinot Papers.

29. Howe to Washington, December 5, 1776, *Founders Online*, founders.archives.gov/documents/Washington/03-07-02-0199; Howe to Washington, April 21, 1777, *Founders Online*, founders.archives.gov/documents/Washington/03-09-02-0211; Erica Charters, *Disease, War, and the Imperial State: The Welfare of the British Armed Forces during the Seven Years' War* (Chicago: University of Chicago Press, 2014), 177; Erica Charters, "The Administration of War and French Prisoners of War in Britain, 1756-1763," in Erica Charters, Eve Rosenhaft and Hannah Smith, ed., *Civilians and War in Europe, 1618-18152* (Liverpool: Liverpool University Press, 2014), 93.

often "bad in quality." Washington believed returnee testimony was "confirmed by their appearance." Washington repeatedly claimed proof of neglect was in the "emaciated bodies" or "miserable emaciated" faces of returnees.[30]

A third party, however, neglected its duty in 1776. Historians found the British public sustaining French prisoners in Britain during the Seven Years' War (1756-1763). A 1777-78 fundraiser for Patriot prisoners in Britain had the support of students from a Quaker boarding school and patrons of a London tavern. During the American Revolution (1775-1783), the death rate for Patriots in two English prisons was below five percent.[31]

Patriots knew Britain's reputation for compassion toward enemy prisoners. Consequently, Patriots were slow to respond to reports of prisoner suffering. In 1777, the Board of War of the Continental Congress claimed that "a Remembrance of what Britons once were lull'd us into an Inattention to what they now are."[32]

The prisoners themselves were shocked. Thomas Boyd claimed death "stared each [prisoner] in the face, in a city possessed by pretended Christians." Pvt. James Stuart found "the inhabitants of the city were implacably cruel and hard hearted to the prisoners." A committee of the Continental Congress, appointed to investigate war crimes by royal forces, asserted the lack of charity from "inhabitants who remained in or resorted to the city of New-York" was "never known to happen in any similar case in a Christian country."[33]

30. Washington to Howe, June 10, 1777, *Founders Online*, founders.archives.gov/documents/Washington/03-09-02-0657; George Washington to William Livingston, February 14, 1777, *Founders Online*, founders.archives.gov/documents/Washington/03-08-02-0359; Washington to Howe, January 13, 1777, *Founders Online*, founders.archives.gov/documents/Washington/03-08-02-0063; Washington to the Continental Congress Executive Committee, January 12, 1777, *Founders Online*, founders.archives.gov/documents/Washington/03-08-02-0047.

31. "American Prisoners: King's Arms Tavern, Cornhill, Jan. 26," *The Public Advertiser*, January 26, 1778; Charters, *Disease, War, and the Imperial State*, 182-184, 186; Cogliano, *American Maritime Prisoners*, 61-63; 149, 156-158; Jesse Lemisch, "Listening to the 'Inarticulate:' William Widger's Dream and the Loyalties of American Revolutionary Seamen in British Prisons," *Journal of Social History* 3 (1969): 10.

32. Board of War to Boudinot, June 24, 1777, in Paul Hubert Smith, ed., *Letters of Delegates to Congress, 1774-1789:* Vol. 7: *May 1, 1777-September 18, 1777* (Washington, D.C.: Library of Congress, 1986), 242-243, American Memory, Library of Congress, memory.loc.gov/ammem/amlaw/lwdg.html.

33. Boyd Affidavit; Affidavit of James Stuart, February 27, 1777, in *Pennsylvania Evening Post*, May 3, 1777; Worthington Chauncey Ford, ed., *Journals of the Continental Congress, 1774-1789*, Vol. 7, *January 1-May 21, 1777* (Washington, D.C.: Government Printing Office, 1907), 278, American Memory, Library of Congress, memory.loc.gov/ammem/amlaw/lwjclink.html.

The Loyalists who "resorted to" New York City were hostile toward Patriot prisoners. Most New Yorkers fled the city before the British occupation. Based on information from British Maj. Gen. James Robertson, the British press reported that Howe's forces found New York City "almost without Inhabitants." Thanks to an influx of Loyalists from the rest of the United States, by February 17, 1777, the city had "upwards of 11,000" inhabitants.[34]

John Witherspoon was a Presbyterian minister, a New Jersey delegate to Congress, and the sixth president of the College of New Jersey (now Princeton University). Witherspoon believed Loyalists were "insensibly biassed" from overusing the word "rebel." Signifying an illegal combatant, "rebel" was a powerful slur in the eighteenth century. In his 1582 work, *De Jure Officiis Bellicis et Disciplina Militari Libri Tres* (Three Books on the Law of War and on the Duties Connected with War and on Military Disciple), Spanish jurist Balthazar Ayala claimed the customary rules governing prisoners of war did not extend to rebels, "any more than they apply to pirates and robbers." Writing in the eighteenth century, Vattel advocated clemency toward rebels. Despite Vattel's argument for leniency, the traditional doctrine on rebels seemed to prevail among Loyalists crowding into New York.[35] Witherspoon also knew many Loyalist were "roughly handled by the multitude" early in the conflict. The combination of indoctrination and resentment radicalized many Loyalists to militance.[36]

People least able to help were the most likely to try. Ethan Allen wrote, "Some poor women contributed to their necessity, till their children were almost starved." Continental Lt. Robert Troup recalled that prisoners had the assistance of "some poor persons and common prostitutes."[37]

Historian John Fabian Witt suggested most prisoners in 1776-77 died from smallpox, not starvation. Privation, however, facilitates ill-

34. *Public Advertiser* (London), March 24, 1777.

35. Balthazar Ayala, *De Jure et Officiis Bellicis et Disciplina Militari Libri III* ed., James Brown Scott and John Westlake, trans. John Pawley Bate (Baltimore: The Lord Baltimore Press, 1912), 11-12; Vattel, *Law of Nations*, 623-624.

36. Jeffrey H. Morrison, *John Witherspoon and the Founding of the American Republic* (Notre Dame, Indiana: University of Notre Dame, 2005), 2-4; John Witherspoon, *The Works of the Rev. John Witherspoon*, ed. John Rodgers, vol. 3, (2nd ed., Philadelphia: William W. Woodward, 1802 [1800]), 75 (*Witherspoon Works*); *Witherspoon Works*, 4: 445; Burrows, *Forgotten Patriots*, 34-36, 141-142.

37. Allen, "Narrative," *Pennsylvania Packet*, November 20, 1779; Affidavit of Robert Troup, January 17, 1777, in *Journals of the Provincial Congress, Provincial Convention, Committee of Safety and Council of Safety of the State of New-York, 1775-1776-1777* (Albany: Thurlow Weed, 1842), 2: 411, Hathi Trust Digital Library, babel.hathitrust.org/cgi/pt?id=nnc2.ark:/13960/t0ks9fh9v;view=1up;seq=421.

ness. Smallpox is more damaging to the undernourished than to the sated. Starvation benefits lice-borne diseases like typhus, by causing lethargy and heightening sensitivity to cold. Washing clothes at least once per week breaks the life cycle of lice. Even if prisoners had water and soap for washing clothes, starving people might neglect the chore, especially in winter. Alas, an unsympathetic observer blamed sickness among prisoners on "their own Laziness and Filth."[38]

Patriots recognized the interaction of hunger and disease. Oliver Woodruff spoke of "disease occasioned by hard treatment and hunger." A Patriot editorial from 1779 claimed it "requires no great sagacity" to predict "crowding people together" and "starving them" would "unavoidably produce a contagion."[39]

The trauma of 1776 lingered with many Patriots. John Adams was rattled in 1777, as Congress investigated prisoner abuse. Adams lamented, "I who would not hurt the Hair of the Head of any Animal . . . am obliged to hear continual Accounts of . . . the most tormenting Ways of starving and freezing, committed by our Enemies." As late as November 1782, Adams mentioned "the Prison Ships, and the Churches at New York, where the Garrisons of Fort Washington were starved in order to make them inlist."[40]

In November 1782, John Witherspoon also remembered the gaunt figures of 1776. Delivering a sermon in New Jersey, Witherspoon said every part of the United States knew prisoners suffered, "But we in this state, through which they passed to their homes, can never forget the appearance of the emaciated spectres."[41]

38. Elizabeth A. Fenn, *Pox Americana: The Great Smallpox Epidemic of 1775-82* (New York: Hill and Wang, 2002 [2001]), 22; Violetta Hionidou, "Why Do People Die in Famines? Evidence from Three Island Populations," *Population Studies* 56 (2002): 65-80, www.jstor.org/stable/3092942; Arthur Allen, *The Fantastic Laboratory of Dr. Weigl: How Two Brave Scientists Battled Typhus and Sabotaged the Nazis* (New York: W. W. Norton & Company, Inc., 2014), 13-14; Julian Fliederbaum, Ari Heller, Kazimierz Zweibaum, Jeanne Zarchi, "Clinical Aspects of Hunger Disease in Adults," in Winick, *Hunger Disease*, 14, 27, 36; *Politicus*, "Case of the Rebel Prisoners Truly Stated," *Public Advertiser* (London), August 13, 1777; Victoria A. Harden, "Typhus, Epidemic," Kenneth F. Kiple, *The Cambridge World History of Human Disease* (Cambridge: Cambridge University Press, 1993), 981-982.

39. John Fabian Witt, "Ye Olde Gitmo: When Americans were Unlawful Combatants," *Slate*, December 9, 2008, slate.com/news-and-politics/2008/12/when-new-york-harbor-was-guantanamo-bay.html; Woodruff Application; *Continental Journal*, February 4, 1779.

40. John Adams to Abigail Adams, February 17, 1777, *Founders Online*, founders.archives.gov/documents/Adams/04-02-02-0118; November 17, Sunday [1782; from the Diary of John Adams], *Founders Online*, founders.archives.gov/documents/Adams/01-03-02-0001-0004-0012.

41. *Witherspoon Works*, 3: 77.

Christmas Night, 1776: How Did They Cross?

WILLIAM M. WELSCH

When the two columns of the Continental Army slammed into Trenton at 8 a.m. on Thursday, December 26, surrounding and capturing most of the Hessian garrison, new life was breathed into a faltering revolution. But how did they get there?

In late 1776, Washington's greatest fear was that a hard freeze of the Delaware River would enable the British to march across and capture the colonial capital at Philadelphia. The river had frozen over lightly on December 23, but had broken up 48 hours later.[1] He also realized that enlistments for many of his troops expired at the end of the year. He and his advisors were cognizant of the need for a bold stroke to revive the war effort. In mid December, the commander-in-chief began to formulate that bold strike—an attack against the 1500 Hessians garrisoned at Trenton. He wrote, "Christmas-day at night, one hour before day is the time fixed upon for our attempt on Trenton."[2] Washington's plan called for three coordinated, simultaneous river crossings, with two columns attacking Trenton, while the third provided security against an enemy counter-thrust from the south. Those efforts led by Col. John Cadwalader and Gen. James Ewing below Trenton were mostly unsuccessful.[3]

1. David Hackett Fischer, *Washington's Crossing* (New York: Oxford University Press, 2004), 398.
2. Dorothy Twohig, editor, *The Papers of George Washington*, Revolutionary War Series, Vol. 7 (Charlottesville: University Press of Virginia, 1997), 423.
3. There are many comprehensive studies of the Trenton campaign that detail Washington's plans. The best are Fischer (see above); William S. Stryker, *The Battles of Trenton and Princeton* (New York: Houghton, Mifflin, and Company, 1898) and subsequent editions; Samuel Stelle Smith, *The Battle of Trenton* (Monmouth Beach, NJ: Philip Freneau Press, 1965); William M. Dwyer, *The Day Is Ours!* (New York: The Viking Press, 1983); and William L Kidder's *Ten Crucial Days* (Lawrenceville, NJ: Knox Press, 2018).

While many participants wrote of the crossing in letters and memoirs, most soldiers mentioned only the weather or the icy river. Almost nothing seems to have survived about the actual mechanics of the event. I've arrived at many of the conclusions in this article after years of studying the literature of the crossing, many visits to the site, and conversations and correspondence with professional and avocational historians. Unfortunately, many of the details of this historic night will never be known.

The main element of the Continental Army under Washington was to cross the Delaware above Trenton and then march the approximately ten miles to their objective.[4] This would be a river crossing, not a contested amphibious assault such as the Normandy landing. Given the obstacles encountered, it's amazing that this part of the plan worked as well as it did.

The Delaware River at the point of crossing is estimated to have been between 850 and 1,000 feet wide and between 5 1/2 and 7 1/2 feet deep, with a current of 11 to 12 miles per hour. Richard Paterson, director of the Old Barracks Museum, posits that the river was in flood, rising to the current visitor's center on the Pennsylvania side and over the current lower parking lot on the New Jersey side.[5] As water was not then removed from the river for other purposes as is now the case, the width and depth were likely greater than today.[6]

Two ferries and their adjacent houses or taverns served the traveling population at this site—McKonkey's[7] (the lower ferry) on the Pennsylvania side and Johnson's (the upper ferry, sometimes referred to as John's, but operated by James Slack) on the Jersey side. As ferries were licensed by the individual states, it was not unusual to have two such ferries in such close proximity with different names. But essentially, this was one ferry crossing, just north of the current bridge. The current stone walls along the bank are later additions, and there were no docks, but rather roads that sloped down to the landing to accommodate teams and wagons as they rolled on or off the ferry boats.

4. See Fischer, 403, for the best description of distances and routes.

5. George Athan Billias in *General John Glover and his Marblehead Mariners* (New York: Henry Holt and Company, 1960), 8, says 1,000 feet. The late Harry Kels Swan of New Jersey's Washington's Crossing State Park, a long time scholar of the campaign, estimates the river was 850 feet. Conversations with Swan and Richard Paterson.

6. Paul Taylor, New Jersey Department of Environmental Protection, email, November 15, 2000

7. McKonkey's Ferry is referred to in the historical records as both McKonkey and McConkey, although McKonkey's appears to be the more used designation during the revolution.

The ferry or flat boats themselves, which were to play a crucial role in the crossing, were usually between 40 and 50 feet long and up to 12 feet wide—large enough to accommodate the freight wagons and teams as well as the smaller farm vehicles that would constitute their regular customers. The boats were flat-bottomed scows with low sides and hinged front and rear ramps. Ferrymen propelled them across the river using cables fixed to the shore and a system of pulleys, ropes, and setting poles.[8]

Mort Kunstler's recent painting of the crossing clearly shows a cable connected to the ferry, as would have been the case under normal circumstances. However, as part of securing the river crossings, such cables would probably have been earlier cut or simply removed to deny access to the British. Whether they were restrung for Christmas night will likely never be known.

The boats most associated with the crossing are Mr. Durham's Boats, the work horses of the Delaware. Tradition says that Robert Durham built the first such craft in 1757, to serve the Durham Iron Works in Riegelsville, Pennsylvania. There is, however, no hard evidence to support this, and historian Richard Hulan suggests that the sleek craft were initially developed by Swedish and Finnish river men, not Durham. Either way, by the time of the revolution, perhaps as many as 100 such vessels served as the chief cargo boat on the Delaware, hauling iron, grain, whiskey, and produce.[9] William Stryker estimates the number much lower at forty.[10]

With both a sharp bow and stern, the boats varied in length from 40 to 66 feet, with the average probably about 60 feet, drawing between 20 and 30 inches of water when loaded. The beam was about 8 feet, the hold 3 to 3 1/2 feet deep, and the bottom flat. Eighteen foot oars, iron tipped setting poles, and sails propelled the craft, although there is no record of the latter having been used during the crossing. A 30-foot-plus stern sweep controlled the direction. The captain's name was usually painted on the hull.[11] The current reproduction boats at Washington's Crossing State Park in Pennsylvania are approximately 40 feet in length.

8. Jack Davis, "Crossing the Delaware—Before Washington," *Hopewell Valley Historical Society Newsletter*, Vol. XXV, No. 3, Winter 2007, 484-485.

9. The best description of the Durham boats is Marion V. Brewington's "Washington's Boats at the Delaware Crossing," *American Neptune*, Vol. 2, 1942, 167-70. Also very useful are "History of the Durham Boat," Durham Township Historical Society web site DurhamHistoricalSociety.org/history2.html; and Frank Dale, *Delaware Diary, Episodes in the Life of a River* (New Brunswick: Rutgers University Press, 1996), 32-40.

10. Stryker, 129, note 2.

11. Dale, 33.

The Durham was typically manned by a crew of five to seven. With the captain at the stern sweep, the rest would work the oars or walk the 12-inch wide boards along the gunwales, using the setting poles—much like a keelboat. If weather and current cooperated, a sail could be used.

One observer offered that, "She left the water almost as calm as she found it."[12] Washington wrote of the boats breaking a passage through the ice.[13] He had first seen these vessels in Philadelphia in 1775. Despite the depiction in the movie *The Crossing*, Washington did not wait until his retreating army reached the banks of the Delaware to begin collecting the Durhams. As early as December 1, from Brunswick, New Jersey, he wrote to Col. Richard Humpton of Pennsylvania, ordering: "You are to proceed to the two ferries near Trenton and to see all the boats put in the best order, with a sufficiency of oars and poles and at the same time to collect all the additional boats that you can from above and below and have them brought to these Ferries and secured for the purpose of carrying over the Troops and Baggage. . . . You will particularly attend to the Durham Boats which are very proper for this purpose."[14]

Through purchase, hiring, and confiscation, Humpton, with the assistance of Hunterdon County, New Jersey, militia and New Jersey and Pennsylvania river men, did just that. Shortly after, similar orders were also dispatched to Brig. Gen. William Maxwell above Trenton.[15] These craft would first deliver the Continental Army out of harm's way into Pennsylvania on December 7-8, would then bring that same army back across the Delaware on Christmas night, and finally return soldiers and prisoners back to safety after the victory. They would also be used to return to New Jersey for the second phase of the winter campaign.

The boats were collected not only to transport the army across the river, but also to keep them out of British hands. Most were berthed in Knowles Creek (now Jerico Creek) and behind Malta Island (now connected to the mainland) below Coryell's Ferry (today's New Hope, Pennsylvania). Many histories speak of the boats as being "hidden" in these areas. As the British knew that the Americans had cleared the river of all serviceable craft and since there were spies up and down the banks, it seems less likely that they were hidden as much as simply collected in these locations. Plus, trees in December would be bare, offering little foliage for concealment.

12. John A. Anderson, "Navigation of the Upper Delaware, A Paper Read before the Bucks County Historical Society," Doylestown, PA, 1912, 18.
13. *Papers of George Washington*, Vol. 7, 450.
14. Ibid, 248.
15. Ibid, 278.

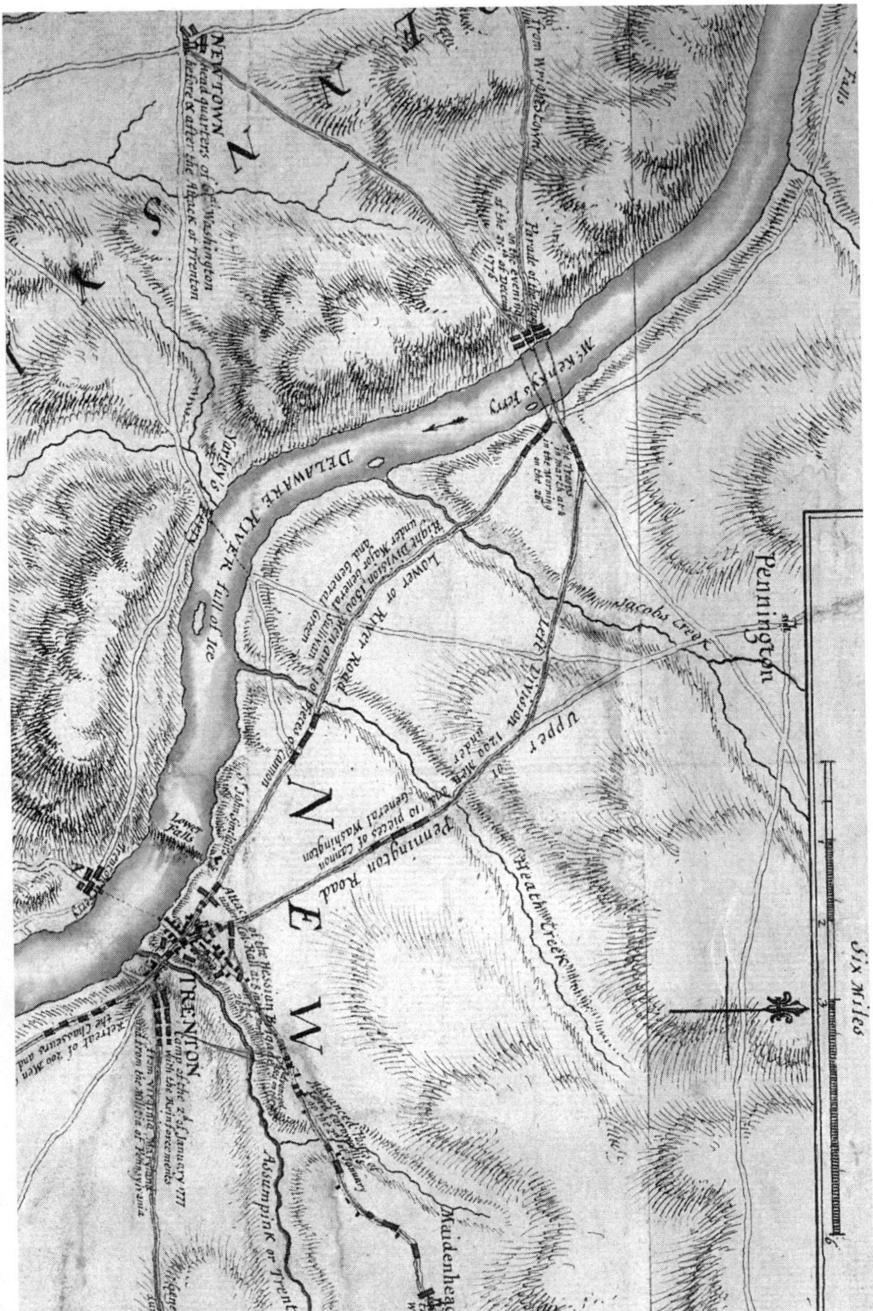

Detail from "Plan of the operations of General Washington against the King's troops in New Jersey, from the 26th of December 1776 to the 3d of January 1777," c. 1777, showing the three river crossings north of Trenton and the two columns making the attack. (*Library of Congress*)

On December 19, at Washington's direction, Maj. Gen. Nathanael Greene wrote to Brig. Gen. Ewing from Bougart's Tavern in Buckingham, Pennsylvania: "Sir I am directed by his Excellency General Washington to desire you to send down to Meconkea ferry, sixteen Durham Boats & four flats. Youl send them down as soon as possible. Send them under the care and direction of some good faithful Officer. I am Sir your most obedient & very humble servant."[16]

While this document gives us the number of boats planned for the crossing, we are still uncertain about the exact number, as we cannot determine if the sixteen were actually sent and if McKonkey's and Johnson's flats were already on the scene or part of the four mentioned. A safe estimate is sixteen Durhams and four or five flats.

Some writers claim that any available small boat was used in the crossing. This makes little sense, as the artillery and horses would be too big for such vessels and the Durham boats were quite sufficient for the infantry. Plus, manning small craft would be an inefficient use of the experienced mariners, who would be better employed on the larger craft. But there is no way to know for certain. Maybe some small boats were used.

The Durhams and ferry boats would be crewed by the 177 officers and enlisted men of the 14th Continental Infantry, experienced mariners, supplemented by river men from New Jersey and Pennsylvania, who assisted in both the crossing and the landing on the Jersey side.[17] The 14th—Glover's Marblehead Regiment—were the Grand Banks fishermen who in late August had evacuated the Continental Army across the mile wide East River from Brooklyn to New York. Capt. Alexander Graydon praised them, "There was an appearance of discipline in this corps. . . . Though deficient, perhaps, in polish, it possessed an apparent attitude for the purpose of its institution and gave a confidence that myriads of its meek and lowly brethren were incompetent to inspire."[18]

16. *Papers of General Nathanael Greene*, Vol. 13 (Chapel Hill: University of North Carolina Press, 2005), 712. Greene's order concerning the boats was initially reported by W.W.H. Davis in an 1880 article in the *Pennsylvania Magazine of History and Biography*. It then apparently disappeared from historical view for 100 years, resurfacing in 1984, when it was rediscovered purely by accident. While Davis dated the document Dec. 10 (the writing on the document is blurry), the editors of the *Papers of Nathanael Greene* verified the authenticity of the letter and confirmed the date as Dec 19, which makes more sequential sense.
17. Stryker, 355.
18. Alexander Graydon, *Memories of His Own Time, with Reminiscences of the Men and Events of the Revolution* (Philadelphia, 1846), 149.

Although never mentioned as such, the 27th Continental Infantry, under Maj. Ezra Putnam, was another unit of experienced seafarers who could have also contributed seasoned mariners, as did Capt. Joseph Moulder's Philadelphia artillery company.

According to Henry Knox, eighteen guns were moved across the Delaware on that historic night. These cannon would be the deciding factor in the battle of Trenton, but would present the biggest difficulty at the crossing. The ferry boats would be critical in moving the guns and their accompanying ammunition wagons safely over the river, with each gun taking as much as an hour to load, secure, transport, and unload. Authors who write of the cannon being moved in the Durham boats are incorrect. They were hauled to the ferry landing and rolled or driven, not lowered, into the flats.

In addition to the men and guns, the critical horses had to be transported. Estimates vary as to just how many animals crossed. Historian Kemble Widmer suggests between 64 and 90.[19] Most other writers make no mention of the topic. My own estimate is a bit higher, broken down as follows: the artillery, 29 to 32; senior officers and aides, 35; Philadelphia Light Horse troop, 24; ammunition carts, 7 to 14. That totals 95 to 105, an estimate at best and perhaps a bit low. Given horses' difficulty with open running water,[20] moving this many animals over the river would have been one of the major challenges and delays of the night, with estimates that three men were needed to control each horse. The flats would have been used for this purpose, not the Durhams as suggested by some chroniclers.

The weather initially cooperated with the American movement, but eventually turned nasty. The recorded temperature at 3 p.m. was 29 degrees. According to US Naval Observatory calculations, the sun set at 4:40 p.m. on December 25, with the moon rising at 5:31 p.m.[21] The moon had been full the previous day, so there was initially sufficient light to assist the troop movements, with a waning gibbous with 99 percent illumination.[22] Some snow from previous storms lay on the ground.

19. Kemble Widmer, "A Severe Ordeal," unpublished paper, the Swan Historical Foundation, 1995, 11. I wish to thank my friend Clay Craighead of New Jersey's Washington's Crossing State Park for years of good conversations, outstanding assistance, and great observations about the crossing and for providing a copy of Kemble Widmer's paper. Although I do not agree with all of that author's conclusions, this is one of the finest examinations of the topic available.

20. Widmer, 8-11.

21. US Naval Observatory Astronomical Applications Department, http://mach.usno.mil/cgi-bin/aa_pap.pl.

22. Donald Olson, astrophysicist, Texas State University, email correspondence, Dec. 2000.

According to Henry Knox, "Floating ice in the river made the labor almost incredible."[23] Ice moving from upriver presented a challenge, especially along the shores where passages for the boats had to be broken. The boat crews would battle the floes all night—but successfully.

Weather quotes abound. Sergeant Thomas McCarty said that the 26th was "the worst day of sleet rain that could be."[24] Knox wrote of a cold and stormy night "that hailed with great violence."[25] Another writer stated that, "About eleven o'clock at night it began snowing, and continued so until daybreak when a most violent northeast storm came on, of snow, rain, and hail together."[26] "The storm is changing to sleet and cuts like a knife."[27] Fifer John Greenwood wrote, "After a while it rained, hailed, snowed, and froze, and at the same time blew a perfect hurricane."[28] At about 11 p.m., a nor'easter had struck, hiding the moon and considerably hampering visibility. Weather historian David Ludlum describes the events as a cyclonic disturbance that created a storm beginning as snow, but soon changing to a mixture of snow and sleet.[29]

By 2 p.m. on Christmas day, the first troops were in motion toward the river, with all moving by 3 p.m. The brigades of Brigadier Generals Lord Stirling and Roche deFermoy moved down from the north, while Brig. Gen. Hugh Mercer's came from the south. Maj. Gen. John Sullivan's division of three brigades moved in from the west. Brig. Gen. Adam Stephen's brigade was already in the area of McKonkey's. The troops assembled about a mile back from the ferry in the area of the Wright's Town Road to await darkness. Maj. James Wilkinson said that the, "route was easily traced, as there was a little snow on the ground, which was tinged here and there with blood from the feet of the men who wore broken shoes."[30]

23. Francis S. Drake, *Life and Correspondence of Henry Knox: Major General in The American Revolutionary Army* (Boston, 1873), 36. This and what follows are from a Dec. 28, 1776, letter from Knox to his wife describing the crossing and subsequent action at Trenton.
24. Jared C. Lobdell, editor, "The Revolutionary War Journal of Sergeant Thomas McCarty," *New Jersey Historical Society Proceedings*, January 1964, 41.
25. Drake, 36.
26. Frank Moore, compiler, *Diary of the American Revolution*, Vol. 1 (New York: Charles Scribner, 1859), 365.
27. Stryker, 362. This is "From Diary of an American Officer on Washington's Staff." Dated Dec. 26, 3 a.m, it is somewhat suspect. The description is still accurate.
28. John Greenwood, *A Young Patriot in the American Revolution: The Wartime Service of John Greenwood 1775-1783* (Westvaco Corporation, 1981), 80. Written by Greenwood in 1809, first published in 1922.
29. David M. Ludlum, *The New Jersey Weather Book* (New Brunswick: Rutgers University Press, 1983), 206.
30. James Wilkinson, *Memoirs of My Own Times*, Vol. 1 (Philadelphia, 1816 and reprint 1973), quoted in Dwyer, 231.

In total, 28 infantry regiments in seven brigades, seven companies of artillery, and a troop of light horse needed to be moved over the icy waterway. While 2,400 is the usually quoted number of men who marched on Trenton, the actual number is harder to determine. Force's Archives, William S. Stryker, and *Sinews of Independence* all present detailed breakdowns of the troop numbers, and none of them agree![31] One count is as high as 4,500. On December 28, Henry Knox wrote to his wife that "about 2500 or three thousand pass'd the River."[32] If Knox, who supervised the crossing, was uncertain, it's unlikely that an exact count will ever be known. Not all men on a regiment's muster role participated, but only those who were physically able and minimally equipped.

Gen. Greene's second division crossed first, in the following brigade order: Stephen, Mercer, and Stirling. DeFermoy, who would initially operate independently, crossed next. The three brigades of Gen. Sullivan's first division followed, Gen. Arthur St. Clair's first, followed by Col. John Glover's, and finally Col. Paul Dudley Sargent's.[33] As soon as darkness partially covered their movements, probably around 5 p.m., the troops marched to the ferry landing, eight men abreast. Each man carried sixty rounds of ammunition and three days rations. Officers affixed a piece of white paper in their hats to mark their rank; and according to John Greenwood, everyone, including officers, carried a gun.[34]

Gen. Stephen's initial assignment was to secure the landing area on the Jersey side, detaining anyone attempting to either enter or exit the perimeter. This security net would expand as more of his troops landed, eventually reaching a mile beyond Johnson's Ferry, forming "a chain of sentries round the landing place at a sufficient distance from the river to permit troops to form."[35] They would also protect the in-progress crossing. Torches and lanterns likely lit the scene once Stephen was across, as maintaining any degree of secrecy would be impossible with 2,400 men and 100 horses involved. There was now no real need or means to maintain silence, although it was mandated. The old military axiom of "hurry up and wait" would have certainly applied.

31. *Force's American Archives*, series 5, vol. 3, 1401-02; Stryker, 351-58; Charles H. Lesser, editor, *The Sinews of Independence: Monthly Strength Reports of the Continental Army* (Chicago: University of Chicago Press, 1976), 43.
32. Drake, 36.
33. *Papers of George Washington*, Vol. 7, 436.
34. Greenwood, 80.
35. *Papers of George Washington*, Vol. 7, 436.

The larger-than-life figure charged with overall supervision of the crossing and the main architect of its success was Col. Henry Knox, commander of the artillery regiment. Wilkinson wrote of Knox's stentorian lungs and deep voice that could be heard above the storm's roar.[36] Col. John Glover was the other prime mover, with responsibility for the boats, and he usually receives due credit along with Knox. Glover was also a brigade commander, responsible for five regiments, so it is impossible to know just where his main efforts lay. Tradition offers that Knox and Ferryman Samuel McKonkey "tested" the water at the start. It's unclear what that entailed.

Again, tradition suggests that Washington crossed early in the evening on a boat commanded by Capt. William Blackler of the 14th with Private John Russell as an oarsman. There is no evidence as to whether this was a Durham or a flat. There is also an anecdotal story that suggests Knox crossed with Washington.[37]

This raises the vital question of when Knox, with overall responsibility, actually crossed. Again while no documentary evidence exists, Clay Craighead, Senior Curator at Washington's Crossing State Park in New Jersey, has posited that Knox made a number of trips back and forth across the river to monitor the critical action on both banks. This is a logically reasoned possibility.[38]

So did the troops stand or sit? As with many other aspects of the night, we just do not know. David H. Fischer says that they would not sit due to the slush and icy water in the boat bottoms.[39] But given the Durham's stability, standing troops could be a problem. Perhaps they stood, squatted, and sat. The ferry boats would also offer all these options.

Washington had hoped for the operation to be complete by midnight, but it quickly fell behind schedule. It was likely the artillery and its wagons and the horses that caused the greatest delay. Subtracting approximately 300 to 400 artillerymen in the seven companies and the light horsemen leaves about 2,100 infantry to move. Using Greene's number of sixteen boats, each Durham needed to ferry about 130 to 135 men. Taking a low average capacity of 30 to 35 troops, each boat would need to make four or five round trips to move all the infantry. The average crossing time is hard to determine, with estimates ranging from ten to fifteen minutes, although the rough river conditions could

36. Wilkinson, 232.
37. Howard Fast, *The Crossing* (New York: Pocket Books, 1971), 135-6.
38. Conversations with Clay Craighead, Washington's Crossing State Park.
39. Fischer, 216-7.

certainly have extended the trip. We can, I believe, safely speculate that loading, crossing, unloading, and returning could take an hour for each trip. It's unknown how wide a front the crossing encompassed—how many boats were crossing at one time and how quickly the next wave pushed off.

Knox later wrote that all the troops were in New Jersey by 2 a.m., without the loss of a man.[40] But a few did take an unwanted swim. Washington stated that the artillery was over by 3 a.m. That means the entire crossing lasted between nine and ten hours, or three hours longer than planned.

An intriguing question is just how difficult was the crossing. With no intention of disparaging the heroic efforts of the boat crews and realizing the icy conditions they faced, this might not have been a particularly arduous task for these experienced mariners and fishermen who regularly plied the stormy Atlantic. This crossing was about one-fifth the length of the earlier East River crossing, also made under difficult weather conditions.

What of the commander-in-chief, after landing in Jersey? According to a suspect "Diary of an Officer on Washington's Staff," he stood on the bank wrapped in his cloak supervising the landings. Another account says that he sat on an old beehive, but staff on the New Jersey side can find no such documentation.[41] As the hours passed and the crossing fell behind schedule, he contemplated cancelling the entire operation, but decided, "As I was certain there was no making a Retreat without being discovered, and harassed on repassing the River, I determined to push on at all Events."[42] He need not have worried. Again Greenwood, "The noise of the soldiers coming over and clearing away the ice, the rattle of the cannon wheels on the frozen ground, and the cheerfulness of my fellow-comrades encouraged me beyond expression, and, big coward as I acknowledge myself to be, I felt great pleasure."[43]

By 4 a.m., with a small rear guard likely remaining at the river to protect the boats, the troops were on the march to Trenton. It is possible that the 260 men of the 6th Battalion of Connecticut State troops under Col. John Chester of Sargent's Brigade filled this role. They did not march to Trenton. Washington would certainly never leave the critical boats and landing site without protection, for even a small enemy raiding party could have easily torched any unguarded boats.

40. Drake, 36.

41. Stryker, 362. Nancy Ceperley is the historian at the Johnson Ferry House.

42. *Papers of George Washington*, Vol. 7, 454, in a Dec. 27, 1776 letter to John Hancock.

43. Greenwood, 80-1.

"Victory or Death!" Dr. Benjamin Rush observed Washington writing this on a scrap of paper before the crossing.[44] With that as the watchword for the night, and after marching the ten miles to Trenton, the army would ultimately capture over 900 Hessians and then re-cross the Delaware using those same boats. The return trip was supposedly more difficult.

At a dinner after Yorktown, Lord Cornwallis toasted Washington with, "When the illustrious part that your Excellency has borne in this long and arduous contest becomes a matter of history, fame will gather your brightest laurels rather from the banks of the Delaware than from those of the Chesapeake."[45] Certainly well spoken.

44. Benjamin Rush, *Autobiography*, George W. Corner, editor, Princeton, 1948, 124.
45. George Washington Parke Custis, *Recollections and Private Memoirs of George Washington*, 1859, 250-51. These writings by Washington's step-grandson and adopted son should be viewed with caution. In a recent email, Ian Saberton, the editor of the *Cornwallis Papers* was unable to verify this quote from Cornwallis. But he did offer that it was in the style of Cornwallis and sounded right.

Captain Lambert Wickes and "Gunboat Diplomacy, American Revolution-Style"

RICHARD J. WERTHER

The Continental Navy. Words that didn't exactly strike fear into the heart of the mighty British Royal Navy. For most Americans, knowledge of the early American Navy likely begins and ends with the daring exploits of John Paul Jones, starting in 1778. Indeed, it was not the Continental Navy, but the French Navy, that was decisive in defeating the British at Yorktown. But why were the French there? Conventional wisdom identifies the American victory at Saratoga in 1777 as a major reason. While it may have been the triggering event, sealing French aid for the American rebels was not a one-event story; it was a process involving diplomatic as well as military maneuvers.

Historians debate the contribution of the Continental Navy to the success of the Revolution and France's entrance into the conflict. Some, acknowledging that naval actions were instrumental to the outcome, dismiss the notion that the Continental Navy had much impact at all, contending it was the Royal Navy and the French Navy that determined outcomes. In terms of size, the Continental Navy acquired nearly sixty ships over the course of the war, but there were fewer than forty owned in any one year and many fewer in service.[1] The Continental Navy, even before Jones had yet begun to fight there, played a pivotal role in this process through their activities in the European theater in 1776 and 1777. And while many people were involved in this effort, this story is focused on one. His name was Captain Lambert Wickes.

1. Overview of the Continental Navy, Oxford Reference, www.oxfordreference.com/view/10.1093/oi/authority.20110803095634985?rskey=G3kiyt&result=3, accessed October 16, 2018.

The Continental Navy had no pretensions about confronting the British Navy head on. This would have been suicide. It did play two overlapping roles. First, to keep the Continental Army supplied, covering for shortfalls in American manufacturing capacity. Much of this work was with the illicit cooperation of the French. Second, to stoke further conflict between the British and French by preying on British shipping from the shelter of French ports. What ensued was a kind of brinksmanship, as the Americans continually pushed the two countries close to war and then backed off. American success in the effort is an interesting study which could be called "Gunboat Diplomacy, Revolution Style." The activities of Wickes and his naval brethren were critical in positioning the French to eventually ally with America in the Revolution.

Unfortunately, Wickes would not be around to see the fruits of his labors. His ship, the *Reprisal,* on its return trip to America, was wrecked in early October 1777, swamped by a Nor'easter off Newfoundland which killed all aboard except the cook. Jonathan Williams, Ben Franklin's grandnephew, writing to the American Commissioners in France late in 1777, reported, "I have just heard a melancholy Accot of Capt Wickes having foundered on the Banks of Newfdland. This I am much disposed to disbelieve, and the more so as I think the accot does not carry with it an air of certainty . . . a man arrived in a french Vessell from the Banks who called himself the Steward of the *Reprisal*, and said that when the Ship foundered he saved himself by the gang Ladder which supported him, 'till french Vessell took him."[2] Alas, Williams' report was true, and the life of one of the most successful and notorious of the Continental Navy's captains came to a premature end that early October day. But Wickes left a remarkable list of accomplishments that have been overshadowed by the later adventures of Jones.

Born in 1735, Maryland native Wickes took a visible role early in the rebellion. He first caught the attention of Rebel leaders when, despite British pressure, he refused to carry British tea into Baltimore on his merchant ship the *Neptune*. Two weeks earlier, one ship that did carry British Tea to Annapolis, the *Peggy Stewart*, was burned by Rebels in the less-celebrated "Annapolis Tea Party."

This notoriety secured Wickes an appointment to the new Continental Navy, where he was listed eleventh in seniority among the original twenty-four ranked commanders and captains (Jones was

2. Jonathan Williams, Jr. to the American Commissioners in France, November 29, 1777, in *Naval Documents of the American Revolution*, Michael J. Crawford, et al. ed. (Washington, DC: Government Printing Office, 1962–), 10: 1050-1051 (NDAR).

eighteenth). He was assigned to the *Reprisal*, a vessel purchased for the Navy by the Continental Congress. The schooner was about 200 tons, one hundred feet long and thirty feet wide. It carried eighteen 6-pounder carriage guns and was served by a crew of 130 seamen.[3] Wickes' first engagement became known as the Battle of Turtle Gut Outlet. An American ship, the *Nancy*, returning from the Caribbean with a much-needed supply of nearly 400 barrels of gunpowder, as well as other military materials, ran aground in the Capes of Delaware. In this vulnerable position, it came under attack by HMS *Kingfisher*. Wickes and the *Reprisal*, along with John Barry and the *Lexington*, held off the British ship long enough for the crew to off-load about half the gunpowder and other items. As the British closed, a trail of gunpowder was set as a fuse, which detonated the remaining gunpowder as the British boarded the *Nancy*, destroying both ships and killing several British sailors.[4] Unfortunately, Richard Wickes, Lambert's brother and 3rd lieutenant, was also killed by a cannonball near the end of the fight. "We have this Consolation," Lambert Wickes wrote his elder brother Samuel, "that he fought like a brave Man & was fore most in every Transaction of that Day."[5]

Next, Wickes was assigned the important mission to transport Continental Congress envoy William Bingham, who working with the French would help obtain supplies for the American war effort from his post in Martinique.[6] They set out on July 3, 1776, and upon arrival encountered HMS *Shark* in the harbor. After shuttling Bingham safely to shore, Wickes engaged the *Shark*, a conflict that was eventually broken up by the firing of French shore batteries, causing the *Shark* to withdraw. This was the first of many instances where Wickes would provoke conflict between the two superpowers, causing British protests and sometimes testing French tolerance, anxious though they were to avenge losses from the Seven Years' War, but nominally neutral in the American rebellion.

En route to Martinique, armed with privateering commissions backed by the firepower of the *Reprisal*, Wickes had started privateering by nabbing three British merchant ships, carrying mostly commercial goods (rum, cocoa, etc.). The ships and goods were returned to the United States for sale, escorted by a large portion of his crew. He also

3. Gordon Bowen-Hassel and Dennis Michael Conrad, *Sea Raiders of the American Revolution: The Continental Navy in European Waters* (University Press of the Pacific, 2004), 1.
4. Pennsylvania Ledger, Saturday, July 6, 1776, NDAR, 5: 952.
5. Lambert Wickes to Samuel Wickes, July 2, 1776, NDAR, 5: 883.
6. Richard J. Werther, "William Bingham, Forgotten Supplier of the American Revolution," *Journal of the American Revolution*, June 7, 2017.

captured a fourth ship, this one the *Duchess of Leinster*, headed for Ireland. Reluctant to retain this prize, due to his shortage of (trusted) crew, Wickes sent the ship its way. But instead of divulging the true reason for their release, he told their captain he was letting them go because they were Irish property and the United States was not at war with Ireland. His hope was that this information would get back to Ireland, which it appears to have done. A bit of positive public relations never hurts, even for a privateer!

Wickes received a hero's welcome upon his return to Philadelphia, as well as kudos from the Secret Committee of Correspondence of the Continental Congress on September 21, 1776, which wrote that "Capt Wickes's behaviour meets the approbation of his Country & Fortune seems to have had an Eye to his Merit when She Conducted his three prizes safely in."[7]

Wickes' next human cargo would be even more valuable. His heroism earned him the assignment of carrying the venerable Dr. Benjamin Franklin (along with two of his grandsons) to France to be the American Commissioner. An October 24, 1776 letter from the Committee of Secret Correspondence to the current commissioners in France states,

> The Congress having Committed to our charge and Management their Ship-of-War Called the Reprisal commanded by Lambert Wickes Esq. . . . we have allotted her to carry Doctor Franklin to France and directed Captain Wickes to proceed to the Port of Nantes where the Doctor will land and from thence proceed to Paris, and he will either Carry with him or Send forward this letter by express as to him may then appear best. The Reprisal is a fast Sailing Ship and Capt Wickes has already done honor in Action to the American Flagg.[8]

On the same day, the Continental Marine Committee of Congress informed Wickes of his heretofore secret cargo:

> The Honourable Congress having thought proper to Submit the Ship Reprisal under your command to our direction for the present voyage or Cruize. You are to be governed by the following orders. The Honble Docter Franklin being appointed by Congress one of their Commissioners for negotiating some publick business at the court of France. You are to receive him and his Suite on board the Reprisal as passengers

7. Committee of Secret Correspondence of the Continental Congress to William Bingham, September 21, 1776, NDAR 6: 937.

8. Committee of Secret Correspondence to the American Commissioners in France, October 24, 1776, NDAR, 6: 1,405.

> whom it is your duty and we dare Say it will be your inclination to treat with the greatest respect and Attention and your best endeavours will not be wanting to make their time onboard the Ship perfectly agreeable.[9]

While the instructions were straightforward about the need to deliver Franklin with all due haste, they provided Wickes leeway to take some prizes, if Franklin approved. The opportunity arose near the end of the voyage, and on November 27, 1776, the *Reprisal* captured two British merchant ships, the *Vine* and the *George*, both of which would later be sold upon arrival in Nantes, France. With this, Wickes became the first Continental Navy captain to capture prizes in European waters. The *Reprisal* approached the coast of France in November, but contrary winds prevented it from reaching Nantes. An impatient Franklin disembarked December 3 to complete the rest of the trip by land.

Thus began the delicate dance of selling American-captured British prizes, operating out of French harbors, as France strived to maintain its neutrality. In his writings, Wickes was quite clear that his orders were to continue patrolling and capturing British prizes. Wrote Wickes: "those orders [to depart] from the French Ministry I look on as Fenness [finesse] and only given to Save appearances and gain time, as they are not yet quite ready for a Warr."[10] He was correct, the French weren't ready; as well as needing some evidence that the American cause was winnable, they also were stalling for time to get their navy built up to a level where it could at least be competitive with the British. In the meantime, they would alternately ignore, disclaim knowledge of, explain away, or indignantly condemn (but without much action to back it up) American privateering activities out of their ports.

Wickes for his part was all in, and over the first half of 1777 conducted two voyages circumnavigating Ireland, the first with the *Reprisal* alone, the second a three-boat squadron of Continental Navy vessels. Collectively, these two voyages seized twenty-three ships, pursued many more, slowed or halted much commercial shipping in the region, and generally terrorized coastal areas. Reported Williams:

> The little american Squadron under Commodore Wickes have made very considerable havoc on the Enemys Vessells in the Irish Channel, this has created universal Terror in all the Seaports throughout Ireland and on that side of England and Scotland. In some places they muster'd

9. Continental Marine Committee to Captain Lambert Wickes, October 24, 1776, NDAR, 6: 1,400-01.

10. Lambert Wickes to the Committee of Secret Correspondence, February 28, 1777, NDAR, 8: 624.

> their militia in apprehension of a Descent, and their fears have taught them to respect our naval Force.[11]

However, not all ships seized were to be sold. Of the twenty-three captured, seven were sunk and two belonging to smugglers were released.[12] When seized ships were taken to France, they had to be sold, but the problem arose of what to do with the British prisoners. Having gathered about seventy-seven prisoners during the first cruise, Wickes made port at Port Louis, near L'Orient, France, arriving February 13, 1776. Once ashore, he paroled five British captains with the understanding they would not leave Port Louis or contact England. The latter promise was broken by Captain Charles Newman, who sent a letter to Britain's Lord Stormont "to inform you of the taking the *Swallow* Packet, (lately under my Command) by the *Reprisal* an Arm'd Ship belonging to the American Congress."[13]

Wickes' first inclination was to trade the prisoners for American captives held in England. To that end he had Franklin write to Stormont inquiring

> whether an Exchange may be made with him for an equal' Number of American Seamen now Prisoners in England? We take the Liberty of proposing this Matter to your Lordship & of requesting your opinion . . . whether such an exchange will probably be agreed to by your Court. If your People cannot be soon exchanged here, they will be sent to America.[14]

To complicate this negotiation, and reacting to British outrage, the French gave Wickes twenty-four hours to depart L'Orient, rendering an exchange impracticable time-wise. Another of the paroled prisoners, John Hunter, wrote Stormont that

> The reason that induced Capt Newman to be so precipitate in demanding The prisoners without waiting for Your Excellencys instructions, was a Report that was circulated in L'Orient, & supposed to be pretty well founded that Wickes had received orders to quit the Port in 24 hours—Had this been the case, there was no other expedient left to save 77 British subjects from being carried to America, & possibly prevailed on to serve against their Country.[15]

11. Jonathan Williams to Committee of Foreign Affairs, Nantes, Aug 10, 1977, NDAR, 9: 561.
12. News from Whitehaven, June 26, 1777, NDAR, 9: 429.
13. Charles Newman to Lord Stormont, February 21, 1777, NDAR, 8: 602.
14. American Commissioners in France to Lord Stormont, Feb 23, 1777, NDAR, 8: 605.
15. John Hunter to Lord Stormont, Feb 23, 1777, NDAR, 8: 606-7.

Wickes cannily evaded the twenty-four hour deadline by claiming that the *Reprisal* had leaks, was not seaworthy, and needed to remain in port for repair. To make sure the case was convincing, he had carpenters sign a second opinion certificate that "they thought The Ship Would be in Emminent Danger If Sent to See Without Carreanig and Repairing." Wickes, to support these opinions, allegedly had "pumped water into the hold to simulate a leak."[16] I will spare the reader the twists and turns of the ensuing diplomacy, where the passive-aggressive French Foreign Minister Vergennes vacillated between denying that any prize sales took place or that Wickes was even still in France, to decrying the situation and promising to take immediate action. The result was that the prizes were sold (for 90,000 livres)[17] and the prisoners released (seventy-two of whom returned to Britain while five elected to join Wickes' crew).[18]

The second cruise around Ireland accounted for eighteen of the twenty-three ships captured, a high number facilitated by the fact the Wickes was commanding a three-ship convoy. He was joined by the sixteen-gun, 110-man *Lexington*, commanded by Henry Johnson, and the *Dolphin*, under Samuel Nicholson, with ten guns and 64 men. This cruise was also mired in controversy, which began even before its May 28, 1777 departure. Initially, Wickes' crew refused to go, not having been paid prize money since the start of the voyage. Wickes made promises to mollify them for the time being "with much threats and a promise that the prize Money should be paid before they left Nantz, have prevailed on them to go to Nantz, but do not expect to get them from there till they are paid."[19]

Once underway, success came fast. Nicholson wrote to the American Commissioners, "Just before taken A Snow Under the Lizard, bound for Falmouth, from Giberalter, loaded with Cork, we sent 8 prizes forward for the first Port they cou'd make in France or Spain, 7 we Sunk 1 we gave the Prisoners & 2 Smuggelers we gave their Vessells again, 3 Briggs loaded with Coals we Sunk in Sight of Dublin harbor."[20]

16. Lambert Wickes to Benjamin Franklin, February 28, 1777, Founders Online, founders.archives.gov/documents/Franklin/01-23-02-0257.

17. August Caron de Beaumarchais to Comte de Vergennes, March 7, 1777, NDAR, 8: 650. Beaumarchais, who played a prominent role in the French arms trade with the Americans, bemoaned having arrived in L'Orient after the sale took place, claiming he could have gotten 600,000 livres. This was the sacrifice made to expedite the sale.

18. Extract of a Letter from France, March 10, 1777, NDAR, 8: 660.

19. Lambert Wickes to the American Commissioners, L'Orient April 27th. 1777, Founders Online, founders.archives.gov/documents/Franklin/01-23-02-0424.

20. Samuel Nicholson to American Commissioners in France, St. Malo, June 28, 1777, NDAR, 9: 442.

Heading back to L'Orient with their haul, they spotted one more ship to go after, but this intended prize was discovered to be British warship HMS *Burford*, a ship of the line and well above the weight class of any of the American vessels. Time for a full retreat. As Wickes described it,

> Saw a large Ship of War off Ushant, Stood for her at 10 A M discovered her to be a large Ship of War standing for us,3 Bore away and made Sail from her, She Chased us till 9 P M, and Continued fireing at us from 4 till 8 at Night, she was Almost within Musquet Shott.[21]

To escape, Wickes got creative. To lighten the *Reprisal*, he "ordered her Guns to be Thrown over Board and four Beams sawed out which orders were executed accordingly and the said Privateer was carried into the Port of Saint Maloes [St. Malo] in the said Kingdom of France under the directions of a French Pilot."[22] Wickes was ecstatic, stating to Johnson that "our late Cruize has made a great deal of Noise & will Probably Soon bring on a Warr between France and England which is my Sincere Wish."[23]

The American convoy was safely back in port, but this being a French port, the diplomatic sparks again flew, reducing the furor following their last foray to a minor spat in comparison. What angered the British even more was an additional set of prizes taken by another American privateer, Gustavus Conyngham, operating his ship, the *Revenge,* out of Dunkirk, on questionable authority (the orders of American Commissioner Silas Deane had been verbally countermanded).[24] Operations out of Dunkirk were prohibited by treaty, and were a bridge too far even under the shaky British-French neutrality. The fact that Conyngham operated with a predominately native French crew drove the final nail for the British. Vergennes, perhaps with a wink, excoriated the American actions in a letter to Franklin and Deane:

> After such repeated warnings, the motives of which have been explained to you, we had no reason to expect, Gentlemen, that the said Wickes would continue Cruising in European Waters, and we could only be greatly Surprised that, having joined the privateers the Lexington and the Dolphin in order to harass the English coast, they should, all three, then come in to take refuge in our Ports.[25]

21. Lambert Wickes to the American Commissioners in France, June 28, 1777, NDAR, 9: 440.
22. Deposition of William Newell, James Newell, and John Harrison, July 25, 1771, NDAR, 9: 528.
23. Lambert Wickes to Captain Henry Johnson, July 20, 1777, NDAR, 9: 515.
24. Jonathan Dull, *A Diplomatic History of the American Revolution* (New Haven, Yale University Press, 1985), 83.
25. Vergennes to Franklin and Deane, July 16, 1777, NDAR, 9: 501-502.

In response to British protests, King Louis XVI ordered the American warships detained in port, and all captains to sign paroles agreeing not to leave France without permission. This was inadequate to satisfy the British, and the crisis came to a head when Lord North sent a special envoy to France to threaten war if the situation were not rectified to Britain's satisfaction. Vergennes and the American Commissioners were shocked when, after the French had thrown the American purchaser of the *Revenge* in the Bastille for the Dunkirk escapade, the only additional action needed to defuse the situation was for France to dismiss the two American ships, the *Reprisal* and the *Lexington*, from all French ports.[26]

The immediate threat of war between Britain and France blew over for now. The American ships were sent off to meet their fates, with the *Lexington* captured by the British cutter HMS *Alert* just two days out of port, and the *Reprisal,* as noted previously, meeting its demise off the coast of Newfoundland. Conyngham, for his part, was eventually arrested by the French in Dunkirk and due to be extradited to Britain before Franklin negotiated his release.[27]

Was Lambert Wickes a diplomat, Naval Officer, privateer, or pirate? Along this continuum of roles, some distinctions are clear, others are a bit blurry. Clearly because of the battle action he saw, Wickes was not merely a diplomat. Said one naval historian, "to call him a diplomat is a little too high praise, except in the sense that every naval officer who conducts himself with credit in ticklish diplomatic situations is a diplomat"[28] Yet, his actions drove, and were specifically intended to drive, diplomatic outcomes. Hence one biography is titled *Lambert Wickes, Sea Raider and Diplomat.*[29]

On the other end of the scale, it would be difficult to classify him as a pirate, though it's not much of a stretch to think that the terrorized people living along the British and Irish coasts regarded him as such. His operations appear to have been largely self-funding, and he likely did not make the personal profits that might be associated with a pirate.

26. Dull, *A Diplomatic History*, 85. The third ship, the *Dolphin*, was re-fitted and retained for use by the American Commissioners.

27. Louis Arthur Norton, "Captain Gustavus Conynham: America's Successful Naval Captain or Accidental Pirate?," *Journal of the American Revolution*, April 15, 2015.

28. Louis H. Bolander, "Review of Lambert Wickes, Sea Raider and Diplomat: The Story of a Naval Captain of the Revolution," *The American Historical Review*, Vol 38, No. 1 (October 1932), 129.

29. William Bell Clark, *Lambert Wickes, Sea Raider and Diplomat: The Story of a Naval Captain of the Revolution* (New Haven: Yale University Press, 1932).

Beyond this, distinctions are less clear. Some have called privateering nothing but legalized piracy, but many scholars have disputed the conflation of the two terms; privateers engage in warfare which nations authorize and consider legitimate, while pirates are international outlaws.[30] As an officer of the Continental Navy, Wickes initiated attacks that were military in nature, and performed them using a ship owned by the U.S. government. This would place them in the category of naval warfare with a declared enemy. His targets, however, were commercial rather than naval vessels, and were sold as privateering prizes. That the British government did not consider the Continental Congress as legitimate further complicates the question of what to call Wickes's activities. Let's just say he acted in expediency, shielded by the fog of war.

Most of the material I have read regard Wickes as a privateer, and I think that title fits, though later officers in this theater (e.g. John Paul Jones) would chafe at this label. Jones denounced privateers, stating, "Publick Virtue is not the Characteristick of the concerned in privateers," calling them "licensed robbers."[31] Critics of privateers question the morality of their behavior, their sapping of human resources available to the Continental Navy, private profitability versus patriotic motives, and one of Jones's major peeves, their failure to use their prisoners to trade for American captives. On the other hand, supporters regard privateers as brave and patriotic, their warfare legitimate based on prevailing international norms, and were practical in that they represented a major tactic for an outmanned America against the Royal Navy.

Regardless of how you classify him, Wickes had an almost unrivalled record of success in serving the American cause. Historian Steven Howarth, in his book *To Shining Sea: A History of The United States Navy*, states,

> Had [Wickes] lived, he might well have outshone his more celebrated colleague John Paul Jones; and of the two, it could be argued that Wickes was the more courageous, for when he conducted his pioneering raids, he (unlike Jones), had no guaranteed safe port in France. Wickes paved the way for Jones. Today Jones is far more widely remembered, and in the context of the U.S. Navy's whole history, that is right . . . But at the time, Wickes's contribution to the immediate cause of American independence was far greater.[32]

30. Michael Crawford, "The Privateering Debate in Revolutionary America," *The Northern Mariner*, XXI No.3 (July 2011), 222.

31. John Paul Jones to Robert Morris, December 11, 1777. NDAR, 10: 1091-93. This letter, a rant on several issues, trails off at the end, unsigned.

32. Steven Howarth, *To Shining Sea, a History of the United States Navy:1775-1998* (Norman, OK: University of Oklahoma Press, 1999), 31.

One can only speculate what Wickes and Jones might have done together, but that was not to be, and Jones's stature is altogether appropriate. Wickes' impact and that of the Continental Navy during his time are certainly underappreciated. He was instrumental in nudging (and sometimes shoving) France closer to its eventual alliance with America.

The Wickes name has lived on in the Navy's memory. Two destroyers named for Wickes were commissioned, one each in World War I and World War II. Each was christened by a Wickes descendent.[33]

33. Naval History and Heritage Command, www.history.navy.mil/content/history/nhhc/research/histories/ship-histories/danfs/w/wickes-ii.html, accessed October 16, 2018. Lambert Wickes never married nor had children, thus the descendants were those of one of his six Wickes siblings.

The *Liberty*: First American Warship Among Many Firsts

MICHAEL R. GADUE

One might think that the first American warship, named the *Liberty*, would be showered with accolades and articles touting its significant place in American history. It isn't. Whether this deficit is because she was first owned by Loyalist Philip Skene under another name, captained by later traitor Benedict Arnold, or recaptured by the British in 1777, she seems to fall from the pages of history, likely prejudiced and dismissed by the U.S. Navy as an inland, shallow-water craft before there was a deep, blue-water, Continental Navy. But minimizing her exploits is wrong—the *Liberty* was and is a unique part of American naval history.

LITTLE RED TRADING-SLOOP, 1771–1775

Philip Wharton Skene (1725–1810) was one of the more interesting immigrants that had come to northern New York in 1756. English born, Scotsman-soldier, and entrepreneur, he was a veteran military officer. He married in Ireland, came to America to take part in Gen. James Abercromby's unsuccessful attack against Fort Ticonderoga in 1758 where he was wounded. The following year he was appointed Major of Brigade in the campaign that took Crown Point.

After all this war, Skene was captivated by the possibility of becoming a major land-baron. He acquired land patents from many British soldiers settling in the area around his plantation at Skenesborough, New York, now known as Whitehall, which even today is touted as the "Birthplace of the United States Navy."[1] In 1761, Skene was recalled to British active duty and served in the Caribbean, after

1. Doris Begor Morton, *Birth of the United States Navy* (Whitehall, NY: The Whitehall Independent, 1986). Morton, the Whitehall Town and Village Historian, begins with the capture of the *Katherine* and follows the history of Whitehall (former Skenesborough) through the construction there of the American lake navy by Benedict Arnold.

which he returned to his plantation and entrepreneurial interests near Lake Champlain.

The idea for a north-woods settlement or plantation may have been suggested to Skene by Sir Jeffrey Amherst, not only because of commercial and profit motivation, but also because it might establish a kind of buffer-state or stronghold of former British soldiers near the border of French Canada[2] before the end of the French and Indian War. Skene's military campaigns had made him well travelled in the Fort Anne, Fort Edward, South Bay, Wood Creek, and Crown Point areas of northern New York and the Hampshire Grants of Vermont. Skene's various successful land amalgamations totaled in excess of 56,000 acres.[3]

In order to populate his plantation, Skene recruited settler-tenants from England, Scotland, and America that eventually totaled some two-hundred.[4] His labor force constructed a blockhouse and barracks, houses, saw-mill, grist-mill, iron forge, barns and stables for commercial sale of horses and cattle, and slave housing. By 1771, Skene had been appointed Post Master by Benjamin Franklin, entitled to collect twenty percent of proceeds of the post office.[5]

Situated next to Lake Champlain, Skene was engaged in transport and sale to Montreal of potash, lumber and iron goods. Additionally, he was selling horses and cattle internationally. By April of 1771, Skene wrote his New York City Agent that he would have ready a sloop by August of that year, "to convey horses to the West Indies, as well as to carry the produce of staves and lumber to Montreal." Further, Skene postulated that he might offer the schooner, to be made of locally available red-cedar (*Junipperus virginiana*) to the Crown for "passenger-service," even though the King had already decided to build his own vessel.[6]

Oscar Bredenberg has written that the red-cedar sloop *Katherine* underwent some construction delays but was apparently fully operational by early 1774.[7] It was a square topsail schooner, likely of

2. Doris Begor Morton, *Philip Skene of Skenesborough,* (Granville, NY: Ms.Cellaneous Enterprises, 1995), 22.

3. Morton, *Skene of Skenesborough*, 26.

4. Ibid., 24.

5. Ibid., 34.

6. The *Betsey,* referred to in original contemporaneous documents as the "Kings' sloop" and the "armed sloop of George the Third." Russell P. Bellico, *Sails and Steam in the Mountains: A Maritime and Military History of Lake George and Lake Champlain* (Fleischmanns, NY: Purple Mountain Press, Revised edition, 2001), 116.

7. Philip Skene referred to his civilian mercantile ship as a sloop, but once captured by the Americans and re-named *Liberty,* and employed in a military capacity, reference was appropriate as a schooner.

Marblehead design and influence, "forty tons burden, length of deck forty-one feet, length of keel for tonnage thirty-one feet; extreme breadth fourteen feet nine inches; depth of hold three feet one inch."[8] Though small, her construction using red cedar made her extremely buoyant due to resinous oils, and the wood was almost impervious to rot. It is thought that the sloop *Katherine* was named after Skene's sickly wife, Katherine Hayden of Ireland, appropriately a "red-haired colleen."[9]

In 1774, Philip Skene returned to England hoping to straighten out a number of vexing issues with his businesses and land holdings, and to establish his proposed new County of Charlotte separate from Albany County. He left his estate in the capable hands of his son, Capt. Andrew Skene, as a going concern.[10]

ENTER ETHAN ALLEN AND BENEDICT ARNOLD

Capitalizing on the morale effect of the Battles of Lexington and Concord to cement colonial fervor for separation and revolution, the next offensive effort by the colonies was to strike a strategic, offensive-blow by capturing Fort Ticonderoga. Benedict Arnold of Connecticut and Ethan Allen of the Hampshire Grants worked together, albeit reluctantly, to effect a passage across Lake Champlain that would put them near the gates of the fort. Key to the plan was obtaining water transport to conduct the men assembled at Hand's Cove near Shoreham on the lake's eastern shore across about a mile of open water, the first offensive amphibious operation of the Revolution, allowing them to attack the unsuspecting and unprepared British garrison, thought to comprise fifty old and worn-out British Regulars.

"WHERE'S THE *Katherine*?"

To obtain water transport, a "Skenesborough Raid" was authorized on May 9 against Skenesborough to seize the *Katherine*, sail her back to Hand's Cove some nine miles distant, and then load up the Allen-Arnold force to deliver them for an early morning assault. This raid by

8. Oscar Bredenberg, "The Champlain Fleet, 1775-1777," *Bulletin of the Fort Ticonderoga Museum* 12 No. 4 (September 1968), 249.
9. Sources that name the Skene schooner as *Katherine* before American capture on May 9, 1775 include: Brendan Morrissey, *Quebec 1775* (Osprey Publishing, 2001), 10; *Lake Champlain, An Illustrated History* (Adirondack Life, Lake Champlain Quadri-centennial Celebration, 2009); Bellico, *Sails and Steam in the Mountains*, 115. Interestingly, the fictional '*Kathi' of Skenesborough*, written by May Bell Curtis in 1914 (re-published, Peru, NY: Bloated Toe Publishing, 2013) indicates that the schooner was referred to by Skene's Black slaves in 1774 as *Liberty,* which seems highly unlikely.
10. Morton, *Skene of Skenesborough*, 34-35.

"The *Liberty* off the Palisades," showing the schooner heading north, across from Basin Harbor, with the Palisade rocks in the background, taking stores to Benedict Arnold's fleet in October 1776. (*Original painting by maritime artist Ernest Haas*)

some thirty men, under the command of Capt. Samuel Herrick, was perfectly executed, but the *Katherine* was out on Lake Champlain when troops arrived and could not be delivered to transport the American troops assembled at Hand's Cove.

Ethan Allen and Benedict Arnold used other commandeered watercraft and seized Fort Ticonderoga in the early hours of May 10, 1775. Only eighty-three men were put ashore before a heavy squall put an end to further ferrying operations. But it was enough, and the fort and garrison surrendered.

Eleazer Oswald, one of Captain Herrick's men attacking Skenesborough, made an entry in his journal on May 11, 1775: "We set sail from Skenesborough in a schooner belonging to Skene, which we christened *Liberty*."[11] It appears that Oswald and Marine Capt. Johnathan Brown were responsible for the re-naming of the *Katherine* to *Liberty*.

Between Allen and Arnold, whatever cooperation there may have once been was soon replaced by unbridled attempts to best the other

11. *Naval Documents of the American Revolution* (Washington, DC: 1964-2019), 1: 312, (*NDAR*).

in correspondence and deed. On May 12, Ethan Allen advised Jonathan Trumbull, governor of Connecticut:

> Herrick has seized a Schooner of Skene's, I expect in ten days-time to have it rigged, manned and armed with 6 or 8 pieces of cannon which with the Boats in our Possession I Purpose to make an Attack on the armed Sloop of George the Third [the *Betsey*] which is now cruising Lake Champlain and is about twice as bigg as the Schooner. I hope in a Short Time to be authorized to acquaint Your Honor that Lake Champlain & the fortifications thereon are subjected to the Colonies.[12]

On May 14, Arnold wrote to the Massachusetts Committee of safety from Ticonderoga, taking credit for the capture of the now renamed *Liberty.* Arnold advised them, "I intend setting out directly in the small sloop seized from Skene, which has just arrived here, together with a Batteau and 50 men to take possession of the British sloop, *Betsey,* which we are advised this morning by the post, is at St. Johns, Quebec, loaded with Provisions and waiting for this Place."[13]

Obviously men both could not be commanders of the same vessel. There was an almost comical aspect of one-upmanship practiced by Allen and Arnold in their race to gain bragging rights in the next iteration of offensive combat against the Crown. Although it can be argued that the *Liberty* was not really a ship of the Continental Navy because that navy did not yet formally exist, the attack on St. Johns was in fact conducted under auspices and for the benefit of the thirteen colonies that were soon to become the United States.

THE ATTACK OF THE *Liberty* AGAINST SAINT JOHNS, QUEBEC

The *Liberty* sailed back to Fort Ticonderoga carrying the captured Capt. Andrew Skene and his daughters. They were disembarked and sent with the captured garrison of Fort Ticonderoga to Hartford, Connecticut, as prisoners of war. On May 12 Seth Warner, third in command of the Fort Ticonderoga assault force, took the *Liberty* to capture Fort Crown Point, which had only a weak garrison. The *Liberty* reached Crown Point on May 14, and it was there that the brass cannon captured at Skenesborough were mounted and the ship slightly reconfigured to make it into a fighting vessel.[14] The armament consisted of four carriage guns and six swivel guns.[15]

12. *NDAR*, I: 319; also appearing in Bredenberg, "The Champlain Fleet," 3, 65.
13. *NDAR* 1: 330; *Massachusetts Archives* 193: 186; Bredenberg, "The Champlain Fleet, 1775-1777," 249. Oscar Bredenburg touts that Arnold feared if word of Ticonderoga's capture reached St. Johns, Quebec, the post would be reinforced. Bredenberg, "The Champlain Fleet, 1775-1777," 250.
14. Morton, *Birth of the United States Navy*, 4-5.
15. Bellico, *Sails and Steam in the Mountains*, 116.

There is room for some disagreement about the following events, but Benedict Arnold was so anxious to spearhead the attack against St. Johns (present-day St. Jean sur Richelieu) that he pushed north on Lake Champlain in a small boat with thirty men, leaving Oswald and Capt. John Sloan to follow with fifty armed troops aboard the *Liberty*, both leaving Crown Point on May 16.[16] At some point the *Liberty* overtook Arnold, and they proceeded north until in the vicinity of Isle La Motte where the attacking force disembarked onto smaller craft, less obvious, and proceeded up the Richelieu River.

Arnold and the troops paddled to Saint Johns and caught the small garrison by surprise at 6 o'clock in the morning on May 18. They captured a sergeant and twelve soldiers, the village of St. Johns, the King's seventy-ton sloop *Betsey* with two brass 6-pounders and crew of seven, five large bateaux, and substantial naval stores. They destroyed five bateaux and took the timbers of a cutter that were subsequently used in building the American ship *Lee.*[17] Arnold had achieved the strategic objective of neutralizing British naval forces at St. Johns, thereby gaining control of Lake Champlain, which could not be challenged until the British re-built their lake navy during the winter and spring of 1775–1776.[18]

Ethan Allen, after discovering that Arnold had taken off from Crown Point to attack St. Johns, put together his own force of some ninety men in four rowed bateaux, chasing Arnold. Humorously, Arnold met Allen's small flotilla about six miles south of St. Johns as Arnold returned with the prizes from the successful St. John's Raid.

Allen was bedraggled, as his force had set out with little provisions and he and his men were starving.[19] Allen may have even been a little seasick as he certainly was no mariner like Arnold. Arnold made available what rations he had, but Allen was still adamant that he too would push on to St. Johns to occupy the town. Arnold correctly advised that it was a fool's errand, and that the strong garrisons at Montreal and Fort Chambly were sure to be dispatched after news of his attack. Allen could not be dissuaded.

Of course, Allen accomplished little but went on to take the lion's share credit for the capture of Fort Ticonderoga, and his impetuosity later caught up with him when he captained a weak force to attempt an assault against Montreal. He recruited some fifty French Canadians who paddled over to Lachine, Quebec, where they promptly abandoned

16. Morton, *Birth of the United States Navy*, 5.

17. Bellico, *Sails and Steam in the Mountains*, 116; Morton, *Birth of the United States Navy*, 5.

18. Bredenberg, "The Champlain Fleet, 1775-1777," 250.

19. Bellico, *Sails and Steam in the Mountains*, 116, citing *NDAR* 1: 539, 366, 358.

him, and he was captured by the British. He was sent in irons to London, with serious discussion whether he should be executed as traitor, but he was released in an exchange in 1778.

THE REST OF THE *Liberty*'s STORY

By mid-August 1775, the American lake navy on Lake Champlain was comprised of the schooner *Liberty*, sloop *Enterprise*, gondolas *Hancock* and *Schuyler*, and two large bateaux armed with swivel cannon. These vessels patrolled the lake as well as collected intelligence and reports of activity in British dockyards. The vessels also supported transportation of the American army in an invasion attempt made against Canada. Brig. Gen. Richard Montgomery commanded, and embarked from Ticonderoga with some 1,200 troops on August 12, several hundred of which had become ill by the time the Army landed at Isle La Motte on September 2. The American Lake Champlain fleet including the *Liberty* operated in the vicinity of Isle aux Noix in September and October, supporting the capture of Fort Chambly and Fort St. Johns. These victories resulted in the capture of the schooner *Royal Savage*, raised after the British had scuttled her, and the schooner *Revenge*. Both vessels joined the American lake navy returning to Ticonderoga.

Both the British and Americans spent the early part of 1776 building up their respective navies with which to engage in a decisive battle. The British concentrated their construction at Chambly and St. Johns. The Americans built at Skenesborough, for which reason it is called "Birthplace of the American Navy." Capt. Jacobus Wynkoop, formerly of the 4th New York Regiment, was assigned in early summer of 1776 as commander of the Lake Champlain fleet. He had charge of the construction and upgrade of the fleet, but his inspiration and commitment were found lacking in comparison to the effort of Benedict Arnold. Arnold was effective in finding supplies, crews, and materials based on his general knowledge of ship construction and seamanship. When Arnold was made the new commander of the fleet, Wynkoop refused to accept Arnold as his replacement. On August 17, 1776, Arnold ordered the *Revenge* and *Liberty* to proceed north to scout and provide support to the Americans at Crown Point. Wynkoop, operating from the *Royal Savage*, fired a swivel gun at *Revenge* and *Liberty* in an unsuccessful attempt to prevent them from raising sail to perform their assigned mission, giving *Liberty* the unusual distinction of having been fired on by a friendly ship.[20]

20. Bellico, *Sails and Steam in the Mountains*, 139-141. Wynkoop was allowed to withdraw from the forces, but was not cashiered, even though General Gates ordered his arrest.

On August 24, "the American fleet commanded by Benedict Arnold departed Crown Point, comprised of *Royal Savage* and *Enterprise*, followed by the gondolas *New Haven*, *Boston*, *Providence*, *Spitfire*, *Philadelphia*, and *Connecticut*, with schooners *Revenge* and *Liberty* in the rear, as well as a large number of bateaux."[21] After being joined by the cutter *Lee* and gondola *New Jersey*, and finally by the galleys *Congress* and *Trumbull*, the American fleet was ready for battle.

At Valcour Bay, adjacent to present-day Plattsburg, New York, Arnold prepared for a defensive action to delay the British fleet's move toward Forts Crown Point and Ticonderoga. The schooner *Liberty* was employed to make repeated runs back to Ticonderoga for supplies and last-minute components of hardware and rigging for several of the hurriedly-completed American craft.[22]

The British fleet consisted of ship *Inflexible*, schooners *Maria* and *Carleton*, radeau *Thunderer*, gondola *Loyal Convert*, and twenty or more gunboats, longboats, bateaux, and canoes. The British had difficulty locating Arnold's fleet but when they finally made contact on October 11, 1776, the battle generally went badly for the Americans, prompting Arnold to make a secretive, night-time escape south toward Crown Point.

The British pursued the remnants of the American fleet across and up Lake Champlain. The *Liberty*, sailing northward down the lake from Ticonderoga, met up with the retreating American ships on October 13, the sloop *Enterprise*, schooner *Revenge*, row galley *Trumbull*, gondola *New York*, and joined them in sailing to Ticonderoga. The British, however, because of the lateness of the season with snow in the air, determined to go into winter quarters and headed back down the lake towards Quebec.

During the fall and winter the Americans constructed a floating bridge that connected Fort Ticonderoga with Fort Independence directly across the lake. All of the surviving American vessels, including *Liberty*, were placed behind the floating bridge and did not venture further north.[23]

Forts Ticonderoga and Independence were abandoned on the night of July 5-6, 1777, in the face of an advancing British army. Six hundred American troops in 200 batteaux accompanied the five armed galleys (including *Liberty*), heavily laden with supplies and artillery, invalids and women, as they made their way to Skenesborough[24] while the main

21. Bellico, *Sails and Steam in the Mountains*, 143.

22. Ibid., 147.

23. Bredenberg, "The Champlain Fleet, 1775-1777," 262.

24. Bellico, *Sails and Steam in the Mountains*, 172.

American army sought retreat to Hubbardton and Manchester in Vermont.

Within an hour of the arrival of the Americans at Skenesborough, British gunboats closed on the Skenesborough channel and brought about the sad end of the American lake fleet: "*Trumbull* Galley—Taken; *Revenge*—loaden with powder—Blown up; *Gates* Galley—Blown Up; *Enterprize* Cutter—laden with provisions—Burnt; *Liberty*—schooner—loaden with Powder -Taken."[25]

The *Liberty* became part of the British fleet, and supposedly transported British troops who escaped capture at Saratoga back down the lake later in 1777. For the remainder of the war she patrolled the lake with British Marines on board.[26] A March 1784 list based on a "Return of Vessels at St. Johns, Quebec, 3rd Sept 1783", recorded the *Liberty* as "Ha[u]led up on the stocks not worth the trouble." It appears that most of those vessels left at St. Johns "settled to the bottom of the Richelieu River, or were broken up in the vicinity of St Johns." "Remnants of the British fleet were found at St. Johns when the Chambly Canal was constructed during the nineteenth century,"[27] but no artifacts specifically attributable to the *Liberty* are known. On May 31, 1790, Capt. John Schank, commanding at Quebec, reported that the *Liberty* was "old but still repairable."[28]

WHAT FIRSTS FOR THE *Liberty*?

Although not officially recognized as the first Unites States naval vessel, the *Liberty* can claim a number of firsts during the Revolutionary War:
First private ship captured by American forces.
First re-named and or christened American warship.
First American warship transporting prisoners of war, the Skene family.
First ship to land attacking American troops on foreign soil.
First American warship to capture a British fort, Crown Point, New York.
First American warship involved in the capture of a foreign town (St. Johns), a Royal Naval vessel (the *Betsey*), and British Naval installation (Fort St. Johns's Dockyard).

25. Bellico, *Sails and Steam in the Mountains*, 172, citing "A Journal of Carleton's and Burgoyne's Campaigns," *Bulletin of the Fort Ticonderoga Museum* 11 (September 1965) Part 2: 231. This list is identical to one published in the *Connecticut Gazette*, December 5, 1777, in *NDAR* 9: 225.
26. Bellico, *Sails and Steam in the Mountains*, 183; Bredenberg, "The Champlain Fleet, 1775-1777," 262-3.
27. Bellico, *Sails and Steam in the Mountains*, 199-200.
28. Bradenberg notes that Ethan Allen's brother, Levi Allen, a Tory, considered purchasing the *Liberty* but declined as her bottom was then rotten. Bredenberg, "The Champlain Fleet, 1775-1777," 263.

First American warship to patrol and control an inland waterway (Lake Champlain).
First American Sailors' and Marines payroll ratified by Congress, August 23, 1775.[29]

The history of the *Liberty* is more intriguing and varied than almost any other of Arnold's Lake Champlain ships. Her service evolved from commercial sloop, to American warship involved in some of the nation's first offensive operations, to British schooner patrolling the Lake Champlain corridor. But through it all there is another first that should not be minimized. Throughout the whole of her service from capture by the Americans on or about May 9, 1775, until her demise, she was always referred to as *LIBERTY*, even when in British service.

29. The British sloop *Betsey*, seized in the St. Johns Raid, was re-named as the American ship *Enterprise* while being sailed back to Fort Ticonderoga by Capt. John Sloan. En route, Sloan drew up a ship's company payroll for the "Sloop Interprise" which covered the period from May 3 to July 12, 1775. The sixteen men on the roll were referred to as "Marines," and these men must have served initially on the *Liberty*. Ratification by the Congress shows that their service was approved, formally "adopting all men under arms, placing them under public service on 14 June 1775." Morton, *Birth of the United States Navy*, 5-7.

James Willing and the Mississippi Expedition

JEFF DACUS

The story of the Revolutionary War tends to focus on operations and events east of the Appalachian Mountains, with good reason as most of the war took place in at area. West of the mountains, the story of George Rogers Clark in the Ohio Valley is famous and found in many history books. The expedition of James Willing on the Mississippi River is not as well known but is full of adventure, intrigue, and piracy.

Born to a well-to-do family in Philadelphia, James Willing opened a store in 1770 in Natchez, then part of British West Florida. A poor businessman and reckless with his money, he soon was on the verge of poverty. The Mississippi was bordered by Spanish Territory to the west and the British to the east. When the Revolutionary War began, Willing tried to rouse the local population, a mix of Spanish, French, and other backgrounds, against the British but failed.

Returning to Philadelphia in 1777, Willing lobbied Congress for command of an expedition to eliminate the threat of the British closing the Mississippi to trade. Congress agreed. He later described his instructions to the American agent in New Orleans: "the following Extracts will serve to specify their Tenour—After being ordered to make prize of all British property on the Mississippi River I was instructed to apply to the Governor of this Province [Spanish Louisiana] for Liberty to make sale of them, that obtained I am again instructed to pay one moiety [share] of the Net proceeds into Your Hands as agent for the Congress."[1] It is not clear what property was included in these instructions.

1. James Willing to Oliver Pollock, May 30, 1778, in Charles R. Smith, *Marines in the Revolution, A History of the Continental Marines in the American Revolution, 1775-1783* (Washington, DC: Government Printing Office, 1975), 182.

Willing arrived at Fort Pitt on December 12, 1777, with instructions for Gen. Edward Hand, the local commander: "You will receive this from the hands of Mr. James Willing who is charged with some P[rivate?] dispatches for New Orleans and . . . require from you one of the Continental Boats properly manned, armed and provisioned to carry him from Fort Pitt to New Orleans and hereby request that you immediately comply with this order . . . it is of great Importance that Mr. Willing get speedily down."[2]

Given a captain's commission in the Continental Navy, Willing purchased a small craft from a local merchant. The boat, named the *Rattletrap*, was a galley of some sort with long oars, a small sail, and a sweep in the stern. Its armament consisted of two small swivel guns. When considering that the expedition was to clear the Mississippi of British control, the cost of outfitting of the craft was a bargain: "payment of a Bill drawn by Capt James Willing . . . for Three hundred pounds, as also for payment of an account for sundry Articles he furnished Capt James Willing for the use of the armed Boat Rattle Trap's Crew, amounting to Two hundred and fifteen pounds."[3] Hand helped Willing enlist Marines for his boat. First to enlist was a group of twenty men from the 13th Virginia Regiment, another fourteen came from a variety of other regiments. Willing appointed Robert George and Robert Elliott as lieutenants.

The little vessel set out down the Ohio River on January 10, 1777. Along the way to the Mississippi the Americans seized cargoes of pelts and brandy from French traders. Approaching the Mississippi, Willing recruited ten more men and two canoes. With the reinforcements, Willing proceeded to take property that appeared to be owned by British Loyalists along the banks of the Mississippi.

By February 19, the expedition had reached Natchez. The population, with no means of defense and far from any support by Spanish or British officials, was cowed by the presence of so many armed men. The local citizens agreed to remain neutral, proposing to Willing: "That we will not in any fashion take arms against the United States of America, nor help to supply, nor give any assistance to the enemies of said States. That our persons, slaves and other property of whatever

2. Commercial Committee to Edward Hand, November 21, 1777, in Edmund C. Burnett, ed., *Letters of Members of the Continental Congress, Volume II, July 1, 1776 to December 31, 1777* (Washington, DC: Carnegie Institute, 1923), 565.
3. Committee of Commerce to Hand, February 28, 1778, in Worthington Chauncey Ford, ed., *Journals of the Continental Congress, 1774–1789, Volume X, 1778, January 1–May 1* (Washington, DC: Government Printing Office, 1908), 183.

description shall be left secure, and the least molestation during our neutrality."[4] In return, the residents would provide supplies for Willing's men.

Many men unofficially joined his force, swelling the ranks to at least one hundred adventurers. Moving into the countryside, his followers took livestock and slaves, and destroyed property of British citizens or those perceived to be British sympathizers. One British planter, who had known Willing when the young swashbuckler had been a merchant in Natchez, wrote a description of Willing's raids: "a young man . . . perfectly & intimately acquainted with the Gentlemen upon the river at whose houses he had often been entertained in the most hospitable manner . . . they have taken from the Natchez Col. Hutch[ins] with his Negroes; they plundered Harry Stuart's House and have seized the negroes & other property at Cumming's Plantation; they divide the property at Castles' . . .wantonly killing the Hogs & other stock upon the plantation . . . The Houses were immediately rummaged & every thing of any value secured . . . the Heroick Captain ordered his people to set fire to all the houses & indigo works." The planter did not think that Willing's motives were purely patriotic: "Cap. Willing conceived the design of making his fortune at one Coup upon the ruin and destruction of his Old Friends & Intimates."[5] For the most part, those who declared themselves neutral or American sympathizers were untouched by the destruction.

A British sloop of war, the *Rebecca*, was sent upriver from the Gulf of Mexico to stop the American advance. The vessel mounted fourteen small cannon and six swivels. The advanced guard of Willing's expedition surprised the British short of Natchez and captured the ship. Renamed the *Morris*, in honor of Robert Morris who was a friend of the Willing family, the small craft was used to raid British possessions in the lower Mississippi. With each success, more locals joined his force. Only a few of them were actually enlisted as Marines, the rest hung on to the edges of the expedition looking for plunder.

A few weeks later Willing's forces, now over 200 strong, reached Spanish New Orleans. Pushing on toward the gulf, they captured British vessels and goods. In the forays into British plantations in West Florida, there were excesses. This led Willing into clashes with Louisiana's Spanish governor, Bernardo Galvez, who was a covert supporter of the overall American revolutionary effort but also trying to maintain neutrality with his powerful British neighbors.

4. Smith, *Marines*, 184.
5. Diary of William Dunbar, in Smith, *Marines*, 185.

Using the *Rattletrap* and the *Morris*, Willing's men continued to raid the countryside up and down the Mississippi. Unfortunately, many of the men associated with his force were nothing more than bandits, using the raids to plunder for their own benefit. Spanish citizens as well as other neutrals were pillaged and Galvez asked Oliver Pollock, the Continental agent in New Orleans, to end Willing's services. Frustrated, Pollock wrote Congress: "The Small Party you sent hereunder the Commander of Captn. James Willing without any Order or subordination, has only thrown the whol river into confusion and created a Number of Enemies and a heavy Expence which would not have happened had they been otherwise Governed and a Proper number sent, however the only Remedy for what has past is a speedy dispatch."[6]

The British were not idle, sending troops to take Natchez and blockading New Orleans. Representatives of the British government pressured Galvez to cease his support of the raiders. Willing interfered with the treatment of paroled British prisoners in New Orleans, usurping Galvez's authority. Pollock fell out of favor when he was unable to financially support Willing's efforts. Pollock wrote to Congress again: "What his next Pretence for tarrying here will be God knowns, but there is a clear Passage for him and his Party to go up, part by Land and Part by Water through the Spanish territories by way of the Appelousa & Nachetosh and join Colo Clark, I am determined to stop all Supplies in order to get him away."[7]

Pollock managed to get most of Willing's men, about sixty, to leave in August 1778. They would join George Rogers Clark at Kaskaskia. Eventually the *Morris* set sail into the Gulf as a privateer but sank in poor weather along with eleven of her crew. When Pollock ended his support of Willing, the pillagers and thieves who had lurked alongside the American expedition skulked away.

Finally, in October 1778, Willing set sail for Philadelphia but his ship was captured and he was taken prisoner. He remained in British custody in New York for several years. He tried to escape; thrown into solitary confinement he was apparently abused by his captors. George Washington implored Congress in the spring of 1781 to facilitate a deal for Willing's freedom: "Should there be no Naval Officer of Captain Willins Rank who has prior right of exchange, I shall be very glad to see his effected, as he has been peculiarly severely treated by the enemy."[8] He was finally exchanged in September 1781.

6. Pollock to Commerce Committee, July 6, 1778, in ibid., 190.

7. Pollock to Commerce Committee, August 11, 1778, in ibid., 191.

8. George Washington to the Board of War, May 1, 1781, in John C. Fitzpatrick, ed., *The Writings of George Washington, 1745-1799, Volume 22, April 27, 1781-August 15, 1781* (Washington, DC: Government Printing Office, 1937), 22.

Meanwhile, Spain declared war on Great Britain on June 21, 1779, and Galvez launched an invasion of British West Florida. Capturing the major towns and forts in the British province, Galvez ended the threat of Britain's control over the Mississippi River. Some of the men Willing had enlisted as Marines remained in West Florida, assisting the Spanish against the British. Willing returned to Pennsylvania and resumed his business activities. He died in Havorford in 1801.

The "Hynson Business"—The Story of a Double Agent

RICHARD J. WERTHER

Wars have a way of creating strange alliances, and the American Revolution was no exception. I encountered one such unusual relationship while researching my earlier article in this volume on American naval officer Lambert Wickes, who completed many daring privateering captures in European waters in 1776-77 before relinquishing the stage to John Paul Jones. By all accounts, Wickes was an upright and trustworthy man, with a mission to foment conflict between the British and the French, to drive the French to support the American cause.

Wickes' brother in law, Joseph Hynson, was another story entirely: an American sea captain, like Wickes, but one who turned double-agent. He accomplished one of the more notorious and least known sleights of hand in early American diplomatic history.

Joseph Hynson, born in 1750, was one of eighteen children in the extended Wickes-Hynson family. It is difficult to ascertain how close he was to his half-brother Lambert, as the written record reveals little formal correspondence between the two. The only such correspondence I found provides no hint of familiarity or informality you would expect when dealing with a family member. Both were sea captains, though only Wickes received a commission in the Continental Navy.

If France provided the decisive edge to America in the Revolution, that edge was won through the diplomatic and intelligence work that swirled around and through the American commissioners to France. That group consisted of Silas Deane, the first on the scene to start supply chain activities, Benjamin Franklin (delivered to France by Wickes), and Arthur Lee, as well as a staff of secretaries and assistants.

One of the biggest obstacles the commissioners faced was communication with the American Congress, which ostensibly directed their activities. In addition to extended communication lags in both directions, information didn't always get through, as we shall see. Conversely, the geographical proximity of France and England allowed for relatively quick communications, as well as easy movement of intelligence operatives, from one country to another. In other words, it facilitated espionage between the belligerents, England and America (as represented by the Commission).

The Commission's operations out of the Paris suburb of Passy were heavily compromised. Though he hardly ran a tight ship, Franklin was without question the man to lead the American Commission. His international experience and stature were un-paralleled among Americans, and his abilities as a diplomat and a relationship builder were second to none. Nevertheless, so porous was security at the Passy office of the commissioners that, "From 1776 to 1781, it is not too much to say that the British Foreign Office was for better informed of American activities than was Congress itself Franklin's embassy at Passy, it now appears, was almost a branch office of the British Secret Service."[1]

Franklin either didn't care about, or had no time for, the administrative structures needed to successfully operate a secure diplomatic enterprise. He was a little too trusting of some of the people he engaged to support the operation and did little to intervene in the rifts that ultimately developed between members of his team. Some of this may have been Franklin being smart like a fox, given there is a certain strategic value to diplomatic leaks, both of misinformation (to confuse the enemy) and even correct information. If one goal of Franklin's presence in France was to further enflame British and French relations, driving the French to the American side, the British had to know what the French were doing. Granted, such leaks would not please the French, but they were necessary to the American cause.

Edward Bancroft (aka Edward Edwards), Franklin's American secretary, was in the pay of the British, a fact not discovered until he had been dead nearly seventy years. Handsomely compensated by the British, Bancroft received a salary of £500 a year, a recruitment bonus of £400, and, later, a pension of £200 per year.[2] By 1780, his annual salary had increased to £I,000. He was also promised a future baronetcy and seat in Commons after the war, neither of which ever materialized. Bancroft made a weekly drop of documents placed in a sealed bottle

1. P. K. Rose, "A Counterintelligence Debacle: British Penetration of America's First Diplomatic Mission," *Studies in Intelligence*, 41, 4 (1997), 60. This publication is an in-house CIA journal. The quote is footnoted as originating from Burton J. Hendrick, *The Lee's of Virginia* (Boston: Little, Brown & Co., 1935), 279.
2. Rose, "A Counterintelligence Debacle," 59.

and left in a hole at the foot of a tree on the south terrace of the Tuileries every Tuesday.[3]

Bancroft, though prolific, was hardly the only leaker. Arthur Lee was highly critical of the security practices of the Commission, to the extent that the other members considered him a paranoid crank. To his credit, he was the only one who identified Bancroft as a security problem, though it is unclear whether this was his insight or simply his suspicion of everyone. But even Lee was not immune to slipshod security. On a trip to Berlin seeking financial aid, he made the mistake of leaving his journal in his hotel room when he went to dinner. British operatives broke into his room, stole the journal, and proceeded to frantically transcribe the contents. When Lee returned early, they unsuccessfully attempted to stall him until the journal could be put back. They later returned it to the hotel staff, who in turn handed it back to Lee with some vague explanation about a theft.[4] The journal information, not in code, significantly increased difficulties in shipping military supplies to America and resulted in the abandonment of a shipbuilding project.[5] Lee would also later hire a secretary of his own who, like Bancroft, was a British agent.

Several other Americans, including Reverend John Vardill, Paul Wentworth, and a cast of other smaller players (including, according to some rumors, John Williams, a distant relative of Franklin), were also utilized by British intelligence. It was Vardill who recruited Hynson and another American, Jacobus Van Zandt into the service of the British. Both were living a generally profligate life in England at the time and shared the same boarding house there.

Nevertheless, Hynson gained the trust of the Americans, working mainly with Deane. In the course of that relationship, he was recruited by Deane to shuttle six months of diplomatic correspondence from the American commissioners to the United States Congress on the *Duc De Chartres*, under a French flag and nominally commanded by a French captain.

Hynson and his handlers set up a plan by which the ship would be navigated into a choreographed British ambush. The British would seize the documents from (passenger) Hynson. In a letter, a British intelligence agent advised Sir John Hamilton, captain of HMS *Hector*, of what to do once Hynson's ship was captured:

3. Julian P. Boyd, "Silas Deane, Death by a Kindly Teacher of Treason?," *William and Mary Quarterly*, Vol. 16, No. 3 (July 1959), 324.
4. Rose, "A Counterintelligence Debacle," 63.
5. Helen Auger, "Benjamin Franklin and the French Alliance," *American Heritage*, Vol. 7, No. 3 (April 1956).

> her real Master or Owner, whose name is Hynson, who is a lusty black looking man, and will, as it is expected, endeavour to pass for a Passenger . . . And, upon your discovering the said Hynson, or any other Englishman, to search very closely & narrowly their Persons, Cabbins, Chests &c (but more particularly Hynson's) for dispatches and Papers, and to secure all such as you shall find in their custody or any where else on board the sd vessel[6]

Was it overkill, then, to acquire the actual documents, since the British were receiving regular summaries of all diplomatic activity between France and the American Commission from Bancroft? Maybe, but the King and Lord North did not fully trust that they were getting the right story, or the whole story from the American, Bancroft. The adage of "trust but verify" comes to mind and Hynson's hijacked documents were the King's verification of authenticity. King George called the operation "the Hynson business," yet even bringing Hynson into the game and getting the original documents didn't erase his distrust of intelligence. In one communication, he wrote "I have ever doubted whether any trust could be reposed in Hynson; I am now quite settld in my opinion that he as well as every other spy from N. America is encouraged by Deane and Franklin and only gives intelligence to deceive me".[7]

The American commissioners appeared to unintentionally thwart the British plan when they sent the dispatches earlier than expected, with Capt. John Folger on his ship *Benjamin*. Just to add another familial connection to the mix, Folger was a distant relative of Franklin (Franklin's mother was Abiah Folger). The earlier send date resulted in a British workaround that was much riskier and would cost Hynson his cover as a double agent. Providentially, Hynson had been assigned by Deane to deliver the dispatches to Folger. Before he gave the packet to Folger, Hynson removed the dispatches, substituted an equal amount of blank paper, and resealed the pouch as best he could. The tampered pouch of dispatches was then taken by an unsuspecting Folger, who had no reason to look at the content and likely was instructed not to do so. For this deed and other smaller ones, Hynson received a one-time payment of £200 and was promised an annual pension of the same amount.[8]

6. Philip Stephens to John Hamilton, March 8, 1777, *Naval Documents of the American Revolution*, William Bell Clark, et, al, ed. (Washington, DC: U.S. Government Printing Office, 1964-), 8: 650-651.
7. Wrapper with Eden's Endorsement on which is added a Note by the King, in Benjamin Franklin Stevens, *Facsimiles of Manuscripts in European Archives relating to America, 1773-1783*, Volume 3 (January 1890), Item No. 249.
8. Rose, "A Counterintelligence Debacle," 61.

The commissioners usually didn't depend on a single source, making multiple copies of communications and sending them on separate ships. This tactic was a two-edged sword—it increased the probability of a communication getting to its target, but it also increased the probability of a copy being intercepted. Some copies didn't make it at all. An example occurred in 1777 when two American privateering vessels, Wickes' *Reprisal* and Capt. Henry Johnson's *Lexington*, were ejected from French ports and set out for America carrying copies of some of the dispatches included in the Hynson batch.[9] *Lexington* was captured by a British cutter two days into its voyage. Johnson tossed all the correspondence overboard. *Reprisal* sunk in a storm off Newfoundland, taking the documents down with it. As such, it is hard to know which of the documents Hynson intercepted got through to Congress anyway (five different copies of the document mentioned above were sent).

We do know that all passed into British hands, which was really the point. Keeping them away from Congress was a secondary benefit. Communications from Congress were subject to similar risks, so the commissioners were often lacking in direction from Congress, at one point writing,

> It is now more than 4 Months since Mr. Franklin's Departure from Philadelphia, and not a Line from thence written since that time has hitherto reached either of your Commissioners in Europe . . . Our total Ignorance of the truth or Falsehood of Facts, when Questions are asked of us concerning them, makes us appear small in the Eyes of the People here, and is prejudicial to our Negotiations.[10]

Folger, as ordered, made haste to the American continent, making a less-than-precise landfall at Wilmington, North Carolina, still a fair distance from Congress. With little in the way of money and credentials, he drew the attention of authorities in North Carolina. His story about transporting documents for the Continental Congress quickly fizzled when the document pouch was opened by North Carolina governor Richard Caswell, and only blank paper was discovered. Folger was, nonetheless, allowed to make his way to Congress, then convening in York, Pennsylvania. He knew he was innocent as far as the missing documents, but he also knew the finger of blame would immediately point at him. Congress was not amused by the blank paper gambit:

9. Richard J. Werther, "Captain Lambert Wickes and 'Gunboat Diplomacy, American Revolution Style'," *Journal of the American Revolution*, January 3, 2019, allthingsliberty.com/2019/01/captain-lambert-wickes-and-gunboat-diplomacy-american-revolution-style/.
10. The American Commissioners to the Committee of Secret Correspondence, March 12 [–April 9, 1777], Founders Online, founders.archives.gov/documents/Franklin/ 01-23-02-0305, accessed December 19, 2018.

> Not having received any letters from you since the 26 of May we were severely chagrined yesterday upon the arrival of Capt. John Folgier, who, under the name of dispatches from the Commissioners at Paris, delivered only an enclosure of clean white paper with some familiar letters, none of which contained any political intelligence.[11]

Congress's response, written by John Witherspoon and James Lovell, went on to question the commissioners' choice of courier, as well as casting the initial light of suspicion on Folger:

> You will see by the within examination of Folgier that he was by no means a discreet person fit to have the charge of what you trusted to him; but, we cannot yet prove that he was wilfully connected with the robbers of the Packet . . . We shall endeavour to find whether the roguery was committed after Folgier left France; but, we must depend upon you to trace the circumstances from the time of your sealing till that of his embarking.[12]

Congress immediately set up an investigatory committee:

> The committee appointed to examine J. Folger, respecting the despatches with which he was charged by the commissioners at Paris, laid before Congress his examination, reduced to writing, which was read; Whereupon, Ordered, That the president inform governor Caswell, of North-Carolina, of the purport of the said examination, and request him to examine the persons who came over in the vessel with J. Folger, and inform Congress of every circumstance that may come to his knowledge respecting the said despatches. That the board of war be directed to confine the said John Folger in close prison, till advice can be received from gov. Caswell, or till further orders from Congress.[13]

I was unable to find the committee report, the conclusion of which was that "on the whole, have no proof of any guilt in Mr. Folger: Whereupon, Resolved, That Mr. Folger be permitted to go home, and that his expenses be paid him, as well such as have been already incurred as such as may necessarily accrue on his journey home."[14] Folger was

11. The Committee for Foreign Affairs to the American Commissioners, January 12, 1778, Founders Online, founders.archives.gov/documents/Franklin/01-23-02-0305, accessed December 19, 2018.
12. Ibid.
13. Minutes of January 12, 1778, *Journals of the American Congress From 1774 to 1788, Volume II: From January 1, 1777, to July 31, 1778, inclusive* (Washington: Way and Gideon, 1823), 402.
14. Minutes of May 8, 1778, ibid., 546.

released May 8, 1778, though the commissioners did not know it yet. The ever-suspicious Lee had already raised doubts about Hynson's fidelity to the American cause. Hynson pretty much gave up the game when he fled to England, though at this time the commissioners were still not aware he had the dispatches or that he had sent a batch of blank paper received by Congress. Said Deane, who had assigned Hyson in the first place "The wrong-headed, conceited Fool [Hynson] has at last turned out one of the most ungrateful of Traitors . . . has fled into England, there to help himself by telling all & much more than he had knowledge of."[15]

It is unclear when the commissioners received the letter from Congress concerning the missing dispatches, but because of Hynson's flight to England and whatever they were hearing through their own intelligence channels, they probably had already suspected, if not knew, that Hynson had stolen the documents. This explains the cool reception he received upon his return to Paris in late October. Incredibly, he continued to hound Deane for assignments. He was shunned by Deane and the other commissioners, the former of whom tartly informed him by letter, "I do not write you to reproach you for the ungrateful and treacherous past you have acted;—I leave this to your own Reflections . . . to propose the betraying your new Patrons, in the manner you have wickedly but in vain attempted to betray our form, & with them your Country, I must tell you that no Letters from you will hereafter be received by [signed] Deane."[16] When Deane was subsequently recalled by Congress for suspected financial malfeasance, they (specifically Committee on Foreign Affairs secretary Thomas Paine) would use the stolen dispatch incident as another factor with which to attack Deane's reputation.

This brings us to the question of which and how many communications Hynson may have successfully pilfered. We don't know for sure, as no complete list exists; we do have lists of the major items, courtesy of the correspondence of British Intelligence Director William Eden.[17] It was a valuable haul that included letters from the Commission to Congress as well as an exchange with French Foreign Minister Comte de Vergennes over the near state of war between France and Britain

15. Silas Deane to Jonathan Williams, October 24, 1777, *The Deane Papers*, Charles Isham, ed. (New York Historical Society, 1887), 200.
16. Silas Deane to Captain Joseph Hynson, October 26, 1777, Stevens, *Facsimiles*, Volume 2 (January 1890), Item No. 208.
17. Eight Wrappers with Eden's Endorsements covering Papers relative to Hynson's Business, Stevens, *Facsimiles*, Volume 2 (January 1890), Item No. 223.

precipitated by Wickes's privateering activities. I reviewed these letters, and found among other things, the following information:

•Details of weapon and military supply purchases, purchases about which Vergennes had claimed ignorance when pressed by the British causing a huge embarrassment for the French. In one letter, the commissioners wrote "For tho' the fitting out may be cover'd and conceal'd by various Pretences, so as at least to be wink'd at by Government here, because those pretences afford a good Excuse for not preventing it."[18]

•Evidence of the growing fissures between members of the American Commission, and some indications of a willingness by Franklin and Deane to accept a compromise agreement with Britain (before the British surrender at Saratoga).[19]

•Lists of French military officers volunteering to aid the American cause. One letter notes that "The Desire military Officers here of all Ranks have of going into the Service of the United States, is so general and so strong as to be quite amazing. We are hourly fatigu'd with their Applications."20 Although these lists yielded stalwarts like Lafayette and De Kalb, the flow of officer candidates from France became an irritation stateside for George Washington. The deluge of volunteers sent by the Commission, many of whom sought high rank, caused understandable discontent among American officers and a glut of officer contenders (some deserving, most not).

•Updates of activities to finance the war, including funding promises from the French as well as diplomatic activities to enlist the help of other countries (Spain, Prussia, Portugal among others).

•Information on naval and privateering activities (of which the British, having been the victims, were likely already keenly aware). This included, eventually, a discussion of French plans to expel American cruisers from its ports (though only when it was safe to do so). There was also discussion, probably unrealistic, of getting even more aggressive: "Burning or Plundering Liverpool or Glascow would do us more essential Service than a Million of Treasure and much Blood spent on the Continent."[21]

18. The American Commissioners to the Committee for Foreign Affairs, May 25, 1777, Founders Online, founders.archives.gov/documents/Franklin/01-24-02-0052, accessed December 19, 2018.

19. Samuel F. Bemis, "British Secret Service and the French-American Alliance," *The American Historical Review*, Vol. 29, No. 3 (April 1924), 483.

20. The American Commissioners to the Committee of Secret Correspondence, 12 March [–9 April 1777], Founders Online, founders.archives.gov/documents/Franklin/01-23-02-0305, accessed December 19, 2018.

21. The American Commissioners to the Committee for Foreign Affairs, May 26, 1777, Founders Online, founders.archives.gov/documents/Franklin/01-24-02-0055, accessed December 19, 2018.

•Details of French preparations, particularly ship-building, for a possible war with Great Britain.

•A long, rambling rumination by Franklin comparing American and British credit-worthiness across seven criteria and (amazingly) rating the United States as superior in all. This was possibly to use as selling points when trying to pry credit out of other European countries.

Continuing to be shut out by the commissioners in Paris and fearing for his life, Hynson eventually returned to England. Those fears were justified: One French supporter of the American Revolution, for example, stated that he "intend[ed] to get Hynson command of a frigate . . . if I catch him by this bait, he certainly will not take it to England."[22] He completed a few more espionage assignments on behalf of the British, took a position in the British Navy and settled in England after the war. After courting Isabella Cleghorn, he ended up marrying her sister Elizabeth in 1783 (perhaps proving that once a traitor always a traitor!). They went on to have five children. Hynson died in England on January 19, 1817.

Constant leaks from people like Bancroft, as well as one-time events like "the Hynson business" and others, often allowed the British to know what was happening in as close to "real time" as possible in the eighteenth century. There was at least one reported instance where the British reacted to things Vergennes was planning to say before he said them.[23] They also had summaries of the key points of the treaties before they were announced. With their ability to track the illicit French-American trade in military supplies so closely, it is somewhat of a mystery why, with the most powerful navy in the world at their disposal, the British did not, or could not, do more to stop the privateering and military supplying activities, the latter of which made a big difference at Saratoga. This may indicate that British naval readiness was not what it was reputed to be, at least not in certain theatres of action. Nevertheless, as one historian put it, "the greatest irony . . . is that while British intelligence activities were highly successful, British policy was a total failure."[24] Resulting partly from this failure, the Commission succeeded in striking the alliance helped win the war for America.

22. Donatien Le Ray de Chaumont to Vergennes, April 18, 1778, Stevens, *Facsimiles*, Item No. 308. De Chaumont was a French aristocrat and major supporter of the Revolution.
23. Boyd, *Silas Deane, Death by a Kindly Teacher of Treason?*, 324
24. Rose, *A Counterintelligence Debacle*, 57.

Death Had Almost Lost Its Sting: Disease on the Prison Ship *Jersey*

KATIE TURNER GETTY

"There, rebels, there is a cage for you."[1]

Forced to row under guard of British marines, a boatload of captured American sailors approached the forbidding black hulk of the old British warship, HMS *Jersey*. Nicknamed "The Hell Afloat,"[2] the *Jersey* and other decommissioned British warships were moored in Wallabout Bay, just off Brooklyn, New York, where they served as floating prisons for captives taken at sea by the Royal Navy.

In one of the small rowboats sat "universally detested" David Sproat, a Loyalist who had been named Commissary of Prisoners and whose responsibility it was to oversee the captives.[3] As they approached the prison ships, Sproat gloated about the imminent confinement of his rowing prisoners.[4]

One of the men rowing Sproat's boat was Capt. Thomas Dring, a twenty-three-year-old American sailor captured off the privateer *Chance* from Rhode Island. As Sproat exulted at the sight of the filthy, black hulk looming before them, Dring quickly averted his eyes—but not before catching sight of the shuffling masses of imprisoned men moving about the upper deck in the twilight.[5]

1. Thomas Dring, *Recollections of Life on the Prison Ship Jersey*, ed. David Swain (Yardley: Westholme Publishing, 2010), 21. Captain Dring's manuscript was published by Albert G. Greene in 1829 and is available on Google Books. However, in this writer's opinion, the Greene version of Captain Dring's story should not be relied upon as Greene substantially re-wrote the work so that it no longer reflects the voice or word choice of Captain Dring. For this article, the manuscript as edited by David Swain has been relied upon.
2. Ebenezer Fox, *The Adventures of Ebenezer Fox, in the Revolutionary War* (Boston: Charles Fox, 1847), 96, archive.org/details/adventuresebene00foxgoog/page/n10.
3. Dring, *Recollections*, 20.
4. Ibid.
5. Ibid., 21.

Decades after surviving their imprisonment aboard the prison ships, many men in writing their memoirs recalled their immediate impressions upon seeing the *Jersey* for the first time.

The *Jersey* was a gigantic sixty gun warship built in 1736 that had been converted into a hospital ship in 1771. In 1779, being repurposed from a warship to a prison, the *Jersey* had been stripped of almost all sails, spars and rigging. "Nothing remained but an old, unsightly, rotten hulk. Her dark and filthy external appearance perfectly corresponded with the death and despair that reigned within."[6]

The derrick and bowsprit, however, remained intact, their skeletal outlines extending from the decaying carcass of the *Jersey* like bones picked clean by carrion birds. Typically used for hoisting supplies on deck, the derrick stood out from the blighted hulk, putting prisoners in mind of a gallows.[7] Captain Dring saw men clambering out upon the bowsprit, in a desperate bid to temporarily escape the close confines of the decks and perhaps savor a momentary breeze.[8]

The *Jersey*'s portholes had all been sealed shut. Iron-barred breathing holes were drilled the length of the ship about ten feet apart.[9]

Ebenezer Fox, imprisoned on the *Jersey* as a seventeen-year-old in the late spring of 1781, recalled that, "The idea of being a prisoner in such a place was sufficient to fill the mind with grief and distress. The heart sickened, the cheek grew pale with the thought."[10]

It was now sunset and Captain Dring and the other prisoners had reached the *Jersey*. A sickening miasma emanated from the ship. The men whom Captain Dring had glimpsed shuffling on the deck had tasted their last breath of fresh air for the evening and were now locked down below, in the fetid, suffocating hold of the ship. Captain Dring happened to be facing one of the airholes which dotted the side of the ship and out of which "came a current of foul air . . . with accumulated nauseousness which it's impossible for me to describe."[11]

Prisoners locked within the hold called out to Dring and the others through these airholes. One prisoner, whose face Dring couldn't see in

6. Thomas Andros, *The Old Jersey Captive: Or a Narrative of the Captivity of Thomas Andros On Board The Old Jersey Prison Ship At New York, 1781* (Boston: William Peirce, 1833), 8, books.google.com/books?id=sTZPAAAAYAAJ&dq=Narrative%20of%20Thomas%20Andros%20on%20board%20the%20Jersey%20Prison%20Ship&pg=PA1#v=onepage&q&f=false.

7. Fox, *Adventures*, 96.

8. Dring, *Recollections*, 21.

9. Ibid., 8.

10. Fox, *Adventures*, 97.

11. Dring, *Recollections*, 22.

the gloaming, expressed regret that such young, healthy men were about to join the ranks of sick and starving sufferers aboard the *Jersey*. Captain Dring recalled that the man told him that, "Death had no relish for their skeleton carcasses and that he would now have a feast upon fresh comers."[12]

To be imprisoned on the *Jersey* was to inhabit a hell on earth of sickness, contagion, and misery. Once on board, the health of a prisoner was doomed to deteriorate due to a myriad of factors—rampant disease, rotten food, contaminated water, infestations of lice, and suffocating heat or frigid cold. According to prisoner Thomas Andros, who had been captured on the brig the *Fair American* in 1781, the *Jersey* "contained pestilence sufficient to desolate a world; disease and death were wrought into her very timbers."[13]

Every evening at dusk, the prisoners were herded below deck. The clang of the grate as it closed over the hatchway behind them signaled the start of yet another hellish, interminable night. Allowed no fire or light, the prisoners languished in darkness. Though unable to see each other, the moans and lamentations of suffering men comprised a perpetual and maddening cacophony, haunting what few precious moments of rest a prisoner could steal. "But silence was a stranger to us. There was a continual noise during the night . . . some the effects of pain and some from delirium but mostly the effects of heat or suffocation."[14]

Any attempt at finding comfort below deck proved futile. Desperate for fresh air, Captain Dring often competed with other prisoners to find a place to sleep near the barred breathing holes. Lying down along the sides of the ship "not only secured us from being trod upon by night but also afforded a breathing place, which was very desirable, particularly by night when the nauseous smell was scarcely to be endured."[15]

Locked in the netherworld of the hold, the men who were still somehow clinging to health were intermingled with gravely ill and dying men. Contagion and illness were simply inescapable. "All the most deadly diseases were pressed into the service of the king of terrors, but his prime ministers were dysentery, small-pox, and yellow fever."[16]

DYSENTERY

Of the hundreds of men confined in the hold overnight, only one or two men at a time were ever permitted to climb up on deck during the

12. Ibid.
13. Andros, *The Old Jersey Captive*, 16.
14. Dring, *Recollections*, 42.
15. Ibid.
16. Andros, *The Old Jersey Captive*, 12.

night. The most pressing reason to ascend would be to relieve oneself—which, owing to the rampant disease on the *Jersey*, often took on an unprecedented urgency.

Prisoner Christopher Hawkins, who was about seventeen years old during his imprisonment, recalled that "We had a great deal of sickness on board the *Jersey*, and many died on board her. The sickness seemed to be epidemic and which we called the bloody flux or dyssenterry."[17]

Dysentery, a highly contagious disease often spread by contaminated food or water, resulted in severe stomach cramps and uncontrollable, bloody diarrhea. According to Christopher Vail, who was confined on the *Jersey* in 1781 at age twenty-three, "many of the prisoners was troubled with the disentary and would come to the steps and could not be permitted to go on deck, and was obliged to ease themselves on the spot, and the next morning for twelve feet round the hatches was nothing but excrement."[18]

Hawkins echoed Vail's complaint. "Only two prisoners were allowed to visit the upper deck at the same time in the night let the calls of nature be never so violent, and there was no place between decks provided us to satisfy those calls. This induced an almost constant running over me by the sick, who would besmear myself and others with their bloody and loathesome filth."[19]

Captain Dring, during his time on the *Jersey*, could at least avail himself of the "necessary tubs" that had been placed below deck—but the tubs proved noisome "and it was with difficulty they could be reached . . . in utter darkness, particularly as we had to tread over many who were strewn along the deck to sleep, though all had avoided, as far as in their power, a place of repose near those tubs."[20]

YELLOW FEVER

In addition to dysentery, prisoners were also susceptible to the mosquito-borne illness yellow fever. Thomas Andros recalled the horror of trying to sleep below deck amidst men in the throes of fever and accompanying delirium. At any given moment, according to Andros, the man sleeping next to him "would become deranged and attempt in darkness to rise and stumble over the bodies that every where covered the deck."[21] In an effort to prevent the man from roaming deliriously

17. Christopher Hawkins, *The Adventures of Christopher Hawkins* (New York: Privately Printed, 1864), 66, archive.org/details/adventureschris00bushgoog/page/n6

18. John O. Sands, "Christopher Vail, Soldier and Seaman in the American Revolution," *Winterthur Portfolio, The University of Chicago Press on behalf of the Henry Francis du Pont Winterthur Museum, Inc.* vol. 11 (1976): 53-73, www.jstor.org/stable/1180590.

19. Hawkins, *Adventures*, 67.

20. Dring, *Recollections*, 41.

21. Andros, *The Old Jersey Captive*, 13.

through the hold, stepping on others and adding to the chaos, Andros said he would "hold him in place by main strength."[22] If his exertions failed and the man was able to rise, Andros would be forced to "trip up his heels and lay him again upon the deck."[23]

Sometimes, a man in the grip of delirium might manage to break free from the grasp of his well-intentioned bedfellows and restlessly wander, disoriented and hallucinating, through the hold. Or even worse, slashing and swiping with a weapon. "To increase the horror of the darkness that shrouded us, (for we were allowed no light betwixt decks,) the voice of warning would be heard, "Take heed to yourselves. There is a mad man stalking through the ship with a knife in his hand."[24]

Other times, the man sleeping next to Andros would prove to be preternaturally still and silent during the night. Only in the morning would Andros find that the man beside him was not sleeping, but dead.

SMALLPOX

Captain Dring passed his first night on the *Jersey* in misery. Finally, the desolation of night gave way to the slow creep of dawn and sunlight filtered into the hold. The hatches sprang open, and Captain Dring and the other prisoners, in anticipation of moving about the deck for the day, climbed out of the darkness.

As the sun rose higher in the morning sky, it flooded the *Jersey*'s deck with light and illuminated the faces of his fellow prisoners. Captain Dring suddenly noticed a nearby man whose flesh bore the unmistakable signs of smallpox. He quickly scanned faces of the other men around him and realized, with dawning horror, that he was "surrounded by many with the same disorder."[25]

Ichabod Perry, though confined on a different prison ship in Wallabout Bay, also endured an outbreak of smallpox. "To add to our misery, we soon got the smallpox among us, which was some alarming, as but few of the prisoners had ever had it . . . All that was taken with it soon died . . . I put the vituals into a fellow's mouth (which was the last he ever ate) who was blind with the smallpox but I did not take it then; our situation had got so hopeless that Death had almost lost its sting."[26]

22. Andros, *The Old Jersey Captive*, 13.
23. Ibid.
24. Ibid.
25. Dring, *Recollections*, 25.
26. Ichabod Perry, *Reminiscences of the Revolution* (Lima, New York: Ska-Hage-Ga-O Chapter Daughters of the American Revolution, 1915), 16, archive.org/details/reminiscencesofr00perr/page/n5.

Placing food, morsel by morsel, into the mouth of a person infected with smallpox was altruistic indeed, especially considering that part of the progression of the disease is the breaking open of sores in the mouth, spreading large amounts of virus into the mouth and throat.[27]

Rather than risking catching smallpox naturally from one of the other men, Captain Dring decided to inoculate himself against the disease. Inoculation usually, though not always, increased one's chances of surviving the illness and obtaining the one benefit that smallpox bestowed—the welcome after-effect of lifelong immunity.

To inoculate himself, Captain Dring obtained some "matter" from the oozing pustules of a fellow prisoner he deemed sufficiently "full" with pox.[28] "Having no one to do it for me, it was my task to stand my own doctor."[29] Using a pin, he scratched the flesh of his hand between the thumb and forefinger. He then loaded the smallpox material into the scratch, and bound it up. The next day, the wound began to fester—a sure sign that the virus had been effectively transferred.

One of Captain Dring's messmates, a twelve-year-old boy whom he had known on the *Chance*, was suffering from severe case of smallpox. The boy had been inoculated but the disease took a fierce turn and the prognosis was dire. One night, in the final throes of the illness, the boy suffered extreme agony—writhing and screaming. Captain Dring sat up with the boy in the blackness of the hold and cradled him in his arms until dawn.

Decades later, Captain Dring recalled "This night was truly a painful one to me, most of which was spent in holding him in his convulsed state, and that in utter darkness."[30] His attempts to soothe the boy were in vain. "It was truly heart-piercing to me to hear the screeches of this amiable boy calling in his delirium for the assistance of his mother and others."[31]

The boy passed away in Captain Dring's arms. In the morning, the bodies of the prisoners who died overnight would be ferried to the sandy shore of Wallabout Bay, where they would be hastily interred under a few shovelfuls of sand.[32] Captain Dring wanted to help bury the boy, but could not—by then, he had broken out with smallpox due to his inoculation.[33]

27. Centers for Disease Control and Prevention, "Smallpox Signs and Symptoms," Cdc.gov, www.cdc.gov/smallpox/symptoms/index.html.

28. Dring, *Recollections*, 25.

29. Ibid.

30. Ibid, 56.

31. Ibid.

32. Ibid., 51-52.

33. Ibid., 57. Dring also indicates that in addition to his poor health precluding him from attending the boy's burial, he was unsure if he would have been granted to permission to attend.

Luckily for Captain Dring, his case of smallpox proved to be fairly light and he recovered fully. At least, his body recovered. His mind, however, still rankled four decades later with memories of the *Jersey*, the scar on his hand serving as an immutable memento of his imprisonment. Writing his memoir as a sixty-five-year-old man, he mused, "I often since (after a lapse of more than forty years) look at the scar it has left upon my hand. It brings fresh to my recollection the dread upon my mind upon that occasion."[34]

Two months after his capture, Capt. Thomas Dring was released from the *Jersey* in a prisoner exchange. On the day of the exchange—hardly daring to hope—Captain Dring and the surviving crew of the *Chance* waited anxiously to hear their names called. He remembered, "Our hearts beat hard with joy, fear, and apprehensions at the same time . . . My name was soon called, and I cheerily answered "here." The commissary pointed to the boat. I believe I never stepped quicker. It certainly was to me the most happy moment I had ever experienced in all my life."[35]

Captain Dring stepped aboard the cartel which would take him home to Rhode Island. But he and the other crew members silently worried that their freedom might be snatched back at the last second and that they would be forced back on board the *Jersey*. "The very thought of again being put on board the hulk was terrifying to us, and I believe that an event of this kind would have been immediate death to most of us."[36]

At long last, the prisoner exchange was officially completed. Aboard the cartel, finally free from the horror of the *Jersey*, Captain Dring looked back at the old hulk. It was sunset, just as it was when he first caught sight of the *Jersey* two months before.[37] Yet again, he saw the shuffling masses of imprisoned men moving about the upper deck in the twilight, preparing to descend into the hold for the night. But this night, Capt. Thomas Dring would not be among them.

34. Ibid., 26.
35. Ibid., 104.
36. Ibid., 105.
37. In his manuscript, Captain Dring states that he spent almost five months on board the Jersey. But, the extensive research of editor David Swain has revealed that Dring's imprisonment was actually about two months. According to Swain, "Clearly Dring's memory, filled with the horrors of the Jersey, stretched out the duration of his imprisonment to fit his concept of the magnitude of those horrors (Dring, xxxiii—xxxiv).

Continental Congress vs. Continental Army: Paying for It All

STUART HATFIELD

When the Second Continental Congress met in June 1775, they were not prepared for what they found. Several months earlier on April 19 the war of words with Great Britain had become a shooting war. The individual colonies found themselves at war with one of the greatest military powers of the age. It would fall on the delegates of the Continental Congress to lead them the best they could with a strong united voice that would see them through the crisis, or maybe not. Congress was not really prepared to become a governmental body. These men who were sent to discuss issues and send petitions suddenly found themselves placed in the position of having to create a united front from thirteen separate entities. They would be tasked with coming up with a military response, building an army, and finding some way to pay for all of it. They were, to say the least, not always up to that task. While many of the men that served in congress had experience running business or even colonial government, the task set ahead of them was more than they had ever done before. In many of the tasks set before it, Congress either failed or nearly failed, nearly causing the still birth of the great republic.

Nowhere did Congress fail as abysmally as it did in trying to create some way to generate money that would support the war. There were several sources they would look to in an effort to pay the bills. Getting support from the states and foreign powers was one path they took. Steps were even taken to try and build a real economy that would see them through the war and perhaps thereafter. Each came with its own set of difficulties.

FROM THE STATES

Not even a week after starting his term in Congress, James Madison wrote a letter to his friend, mentor and governor of Virginia, Thomas Jefferson, where he summed up what he found.

> From a lack of adequate Statesmen, [Congress is] more likely to fall into wrong measures and of less weight to enforce right ones, recommending plans to several states for execution and the states separately rejudging the expediency of such plans, whereby the same distrust of concurrent exertions that has dampened the ardor of patriotic individuals must produce the same effect among the States themselves.[1]

Congress was in a very unique position when it came to the states. While they were acting on behalf of the thirteen former colonies, they had no power to compel them into action. As such, no matter how much Congress needed money or supplies, they could not simply take them from the states and they had no power to create any sort of national tax to raise revenue. It was this lack of being able to raise revenue that caused Congress to decide on a paper-based currency for their use.

While the states themselves did have the power to impose taxes, many chose not to. It was difficult to fight a war that started because of taxes and then turn around and impose new ones on the people. Congress would have to rely on most of the support for the army being provided by the states themselves.[2]

What had started as a Congress that spoke with one voice for all the colonies had been defeated by its thirteen partners, each of whom now stood as if on their own.[3] In effect, after a brief period of actually having power, Congress was rendered subservient to thirteen masters. This lack of authority placed the nation and the war on seriously shaky ground.

Part of the problem came from the fact that as the war went on, the reputation of Congress was so threadbare that many of the states preferred to put their resources into maintaining their militias rather than supporting the "national" army. This desire to ensure their own safety over that of the United States was very hard to overcome.[4] Militias had the pick of the food and supplies from each state and often the Continental Army would find itself competing with the militias for recruits because the states could pay more. More importantly they could actually pay. Congress had a very difficult time actually paying their soldiers, something that would have horrible consequences as the war progressed. To add insult to injury, when the Continental Army did find

1. Jack Rakove, *Revolutionaries* (Boston: Mariner Books, 2010), 349.
2. Benson Bobrick, *Angel in the Whirlwind* (New York: Penguin Books, 1997), 395.
3. Joseph Ellis, *American Creation* (New York: Alfred A. Knopf, 2007), 71.
4. Christopher Hibbert, *Redcoats and Rebels* (New York: Norton Books, 1990), 257.

itself in a position where militia units could be useful, they were forced to provide for their supplies out of their dwindling stocks. Many, many times General Washington was forced to send sorely needed men in militia units home because they could not be fed from Congress's meager supplies.

As stated, state militias often could and would pay recruits more than Congress was able to. This not only had the effect of the Continental Army constantly searching for men, unable to fill the ranks, but it also led to another sort of drain. As men and officers fulfilled their enlistments in the Continental Army, they would go home, rest and recuperate and instead of re-enlisting would join their state militias because the pay was better and actually existed. This sort of dichotomy had a very strange effect, an almost good and bad. The bad was that not only could the Continental Army not fulfill its quota for new troops, it could not keep the ones it had. The good was that as the war progressed, the militias were able to take advantage of this influx of talent and become a much more effective fighting force. The victories and pseudo victories in the south later in the war, such as Cowpens and Guilford Courthouse saw the benefits of this talent drain into the militia.

If anything could be said to have come from this conflict with the states it is that the idea of a confederation was shown to be a shallow husk. Washington himself, in the years after the war, would be one to take up the cause of a strong central government.[5] Without the experience that he had in the war, dealing with what amounted to fourteen separate governing bodies, he may have been one of the many that saw a strong central government as anathema to what the revolution had been fought for. After all, the colonists had rebelled from just such a structure and if left to their own devices would not have willingly moved back towards it.

Numerous times, Congress attempted to raise money from the states by issuing resolutions for the raising of men, money and supplies. As late as 1781, Congress was still passing these resolutions:

> Resolved, That it be recommended to the several states to lay taxes for raising their quotas of money for the United States, separate from those laid for their own particular use, and to pass acts directing the collectors to pay the same to the commissioner of the loan office, or such other person as shall be appointed by the superintendent of finance, to receive the same Within the State, and to authorize such receiver to recover the moneys of the collectors, for the use of the United States, in the

5. Ellis, *American Creation*, 92.

> same manner, and under the same penalties, as state taxes are recovered by the treasurers of the respective states, to be subject only to the orders of Congress, or the superintendent of finance.[6]

Notice the wording of the resolution. Congress could only *recommend* that the states carry out the actions in the resolution. They could choose not to and most did. At the time of that resolution being passed, the southern states were occupied, the middle states (New York specifically) played host to a large British army embedded into New York City and even though the French were becoming more involved, the states were more concerned with providing for themselves.

As Congress struggled in getting cooperation from the states, the value of continental currency collapsed. The only way out would have been for the states to cooperate. In a debate on the floor of Congress, this was discussed and laid out by one delegate.

> To raise the value of our paper money and to redeem it, will not, we are persuaded, be difficult, nor to check and defeat the pernicious currency of counterfeits impracticable; both require a far less share of public virtue and public vigilance than have distinguished this arduous conflict. . . . Without public inconvenience or private distress, the whole of the debt incurred in paper emissions to this day may be cancelled by taxes; it may be cancelled in a period so limited as must leave the possessor of the bills satisfied with his security.[7]

For want of cooperation from the States, the national economy very nearly became still born.

FOREIGN SUPPORT

It did not take Congress very long to realize that they would need the help of foreign allies if they were going to defeat the British. The colonies themselves did not have the resources to create the war machine necessary. Immediately, Congress dispatched agents to Europe to start rounding up as much support as possible. The early search for support was difficult as most European powers were not prepared to go to war with the English over what seemed like an internal struggle. This was one of the reasons that the push for independence was so important. Once Congress passed the independence resolution and declared themselves free of Britain, the task became much easier. In October 1776, Congress sent the following instructions to the agents in France.

6. *Journals of the Continental Congress, 1774-1789. Edited from the original records in the Library of Congress* (U.S. Government Printing Office, 1904-37), 21: 1091.
7. Ibid, 13: 60.

> You shall endeavor, when you find occasion fit and convenient, to obtain from them a recognition of our independency and sovereignty, and to conclude treaties of peace, amity and Commerce between their princes or states and us, provided, that the same be not inconsistent with the treaty you shall make with his most Christian majesty, that they do not oblige us to become a party in any war which may happen in consequence thereof, and that the immune ties, exemptions, privileges, protection, defense and advantages, or the contrary, thereby stipulated, be equal and reciprocal. If that cannot be effected, you shall, to the utmost of your power, prevent their taking part with Great Britain in the war which his Britannic majesty prosecutes against us, or entering into offensive alliances with that king, and protest and present remonstrance's against the same, desiring the interposition, mediation and good offices on our behalf of his most Christian majesty, the king of France, and of any other princes or states whose dispositions are not hostile towards us. In case overtures be made to you by the ministers or agents of any European princes or states for commercial treaties between them and us, you may conclude such treaties accordingly.[8]

From the early days of the conflict, Congress put itself into the position of dealing with potential foreign allies in order to gain the supplies and funds that it needed to carry out the war.

In 1777, John Adams took the time to lay out for his wife the possibilities of getting more loans from Europe to help fund the war:

> As to America, in the present state of affairs, it is not probable that a loan is practicable, but should it appear evident that we are likely to support our in dependency, or should either France or Spain acknowledge it, in either of these cases, we might have money, and when it shall be seen that we are punctual in our first payments of the interest, we shall have as much as we please.[9]

In the same letter he broke down all the possible sources of potential revenue that the Congressional agents in Europe were hoping for. While the issuance of loans was a trickle into the treasury, many foreign powers projected interest in potential commercial treaties. None, however, would move before a major power officially recognized the United States.

While the idea of asking for help from France, the natural enemy of all Englishmen, stuck in the throats of many of the delegates, it was necessary. Congress appointed Silas Deane of Connecticut to that task

8. Ibid, 6: 1404.
9. Charles Francis Adams, *Letters of John Adams, Addressed to His Wife. Edited by His Grandson, Charles Francis Adams* (New York: Hurd and Houghton, 1876),1: 205.

and he was very successful in that endeavor. At first his mission was a secret one, as the goal of the revolution was still up in the air. He could not be seen requesting aid from the French and for their part the French government could not be seen supplying the rebels for fear of ending up in a war with England.

A system of covert aid was set up with the help of the French playwright Beaumarchais, who was acting with the wink and nod support from the French court. Beaumarchais used much of his own money to set up a fake merchant company that would provide arms, powder and other military supplies to the Americans. This material would be "purchased" from the armories of the French Army under the table. For his part Beaumarchais and Deane arranged a fair trade, military stores for tobacco and other goods.[10]

Such an agreement was an incredible boon to the Congress and it was always struggling to come up with hard currency that deals like this would normally require. Beaumarchais used his profits to purchase more stores in return for more crops and this cycle helped supply the Americans and ostensibly keep the French king's hands clean. Unfortunately Congress had a knack for making such easy things incredibly difficult.

The difficulty came based on false information provided by Arthur Lee, Congress's appointed representative to Prussia. Lee spent time in London and Paris feuding with not only Silas Deane but Benjamin Franklin. In a series of reports to Congress Lee was able to convince them that the military stores Beaumarchais was providing were a gift to the new country and urged them to not pay for the "gifts."[11] Lee was lying and did much to undermine his "rivals" and to make himself look good to the Congress. Being more of a political animal than a diplomat, Lee had many supporters in Congress who fell for what he said. Eventually his duplicity was uncovered, but the damage was done.

Over the course of the agreement and prior to the official alliance, Beaumarchais had arranged for almost $46 million in goods, partially financed from his own pocket and partially from the French court, to be sent to the United States to support the war. After many years of fretting and delay and promise of some sort of payment, Congress never sent one shipment of tobacco or anything else to Beaumarchais as payment. Eventually the entire scheme came crumbling down. For his pains, Beaumarchais gained nothing and lost everything.[12]

10. Joel Richard Paul, *Unlikely Allies* (New York: Riverhead, 2009), 193.
11. Ibid, 193.
12. Ibid, 335.

As for the French, the amount of support they provided to the Americans was one of the worst kept secrets on the continent. When word got around of the American victory at Saratoga, which led to the surrender of an entire British army, France was ready to come out of the darkness and support the Americans with men, troops, ships, supplies and, most importantly, money. Millions and millions in hard currency were loaned to the United States during the war. Spain and the Netherlands would also provide loans to the new nation in an effort, more than anything, to cause injury to Great Britain. How did Congress repay these loans? They did not. France spent so much money on the Continental Army that it caused economic problems that only a few years after the war, led them into a revolution of their own.

A question that was hotly debated in Congress was the amount of trade that should be conducted with other countries during the war. The more ships they sent out for trade, the more revenue they could generate to pay for the war, but there was a catch: fighting against one of the largest navies in the world meant losing many ships, many goods and much revenue. As Roger Sherman of Connecticut said in the course of a debate on the subject on February 16, 1776, "I fear we shall maintain the armies of our enemies at our own expense with provisions. We can't carry on a beneficial trade, as our enemies will take our ships. A treaty with a foreign power is necessary, before we open our trade, to protect it."[13]

The support that was gained from the foreign powers, especially France, was indispensable. It allowed the army to fight and survive and kept the nation going. While Congress and its committees did much to secure what support they could, it was eventually the spirit and victories of the army that created an atmosphere that allowed other nations to want to invest in the cause. Washington's victories at Trenton and Princeton, along with those of Gates and Arnold at Saratoga, did more to help the cause with foreign powers that Congress ever did. As far as diplomacy goes, because of the distance involved the agents in Paris often were left to their own designs and as such were able to arrange for an incredible amount of support, much of which was done without any input from Congress. In fact it could be said that thanks to men like Lee, Congress really had very little control over the support that was gained from across the sea.

13. *Journals of the Continental Congress,* 6: 1071.

BUILD AN ECONOMY

One of the best things that Congress could have done to provide the men and material necessary to carry on the war effort would have been to create and maintain an economic system that instilled confidence in the people of the country. This confidence was lacking and only became worse as the war raged on. In December 1778 General Washington observed to a member of Congress that action had to be taken to strengthen the economy:

> That party disputes & personal quarrels are the great business of the day whilst the momentous concerns of an empire—a great & accumulated debt—ruined finances—depreciated money—& want of credit (which in their consequence is the want of everything) are but secondary considerations & postponed from day to day—from week to week as if our affairs wore the most promising aspect[14]

Congress was not doing its job and confidence in them suffered.[15] This lack of confidence found several outlets. The decision was made early on in the conflict that Congress would carry out all of its financial business using paper scrip that Congress itself produced. Paper currency is only as valuable as what stands behind it. In the best case scenario, the paper is backed by hard specie, such as gold. As long as there is gold available to back up the currency, the currency has value. The worst case scenario is when there is nothing backing up the value of the currency, except for the confidence of the people that it can be exchanged. Congress based its currency on the promise that once the war was over, it would be able to generate enough revenue to pay off the scrip. In effect, they attempted to fund the war with promissory notes, the value of which was almost totally dependent on how the fortunes of war were going for the American side. As the Continental Army faced defeat after defeat and the war dragged on, the value of congressional scrip dropped and dropped. This created a vicious circle where the army could not be supplied or presented in numbers to win battles, but by not winning battles, there was not enough confidence to support the currency and as such, the currency would lose value making it more difficult to field and fund the army.

In December 1776, George Washington began planning his foray against the Hessians stationed in Trenton. He knew that to do it he

14. Edward G. Lengel, *This Glorious Struggle George Washington's Revolutionary War Letters* (New York: Harper Collins, 2007), 171.

15. Frank Moore, *Diary of the American Revolution. From Newspapers and Original Documents* (New York: Scribner & Son's, 1859), 2: 343.

would need men. The problem was that at the end of the month the majority of his army had expiring enlistments. Washington asked for volunteers to extend their enlistments for several weeks until replacements could be found. None came forward. Finally he offered ten dollars each if they would stay on six more weeks. This was enough for many, but they would not accept the Continental currency for their bounty; instead Washington promised to pay them out of his own fortune.[16] Such was the confidence in congressional scrip even that early in the war.

As the value dropped, Congress had no choice but to print more, driving the value down even further. By 1781 the exchange rate was $225 to $1 ($225 in paper money for $1 of hard specie). This was at a time when the average Continental Army private made $5 a month in Continental scrip, when they were paid at all.

Joseph Plumb Martin, a soldier from Connecticut, relayed in his memoirs a story where to earn a little extra (having not been paid in many months) he assisted in a roundup of runaway slaves that had fled to British service after the siege at Yorktown in 1781:

> the fortune I acquired was small, only one dollar; I received what was then called its equivalent, in paper money, if money it might be called, it amounted to twelve hundred (nominal) dollars, all of which I afterwards paid for one single quart of rum; to such a miserable state had all paper stuff, called-money—depreciated.[17]

This devaluation meant that many people who had goods that Congress and the army needed would not take the paper money. Instead they were more than happy to sell their goods to the British army who paid in specie. While it would be easy to hold these people in contempt for not supporting the Congress or at least the Continental Army, it should be remembered that these people had families to support regardless of who won the conflict. Faced with the choice of taking scrip or selling to the enemy they really had no choice. As the war progressed the Continental Army had to adapt to these issues. At first it was the desire of Washington that any supplies taken from the people be paid for with specie. As the supply of specie dried up the Continental scrip became the preferred method of payment. As the value of the scrip bottomed out the army was forced to simply take what was needed, often

16. Bobrick, *Angel in the Whirlwind*, 231.

17. Joseph Plumb Martin, *A Narrative of a Revolutionary War Soldier* (New York: Signet, 2001), 208.

pillaging their own people. They did give receipts, which were as worthless as the scrip.

In August 1777, John Adams addressed the specter of scrip-driven inflation in a letter to his wife, "We are contriving every way we can to redress the evils we feel and fear from too great a quantity of paper. Taxation as deep as possible is the only radical cure. I hope you will pay every tax that is brought you, if you sell my books, or clothes, or oxen, or your cows to pay it." Congress had no answer to problem that they created and if the men of Congress were starting to panic, the people on the streets were beginning to feel it even worse.

By 1781, they had had enough and in the May 12 edition of the Rivington's *New York Gazette* the following story took over the front page.

> The Congress is finally bankrupt! Last Saturday a large body of the inhabitants with paper dollars in their hats by way of cockades, paraded the streets of Philadelphia, carrying colors flying, with a dog tarred, and instead of the usual appendage and ornament of feathers, his back was congress covered with the Congress' paper dollars. This Bankrupt. example of disaffection, immediately under the eyes of the rulers of the revolted provinces, in solemn session at the State House assembled, was directly followed by the jailer, who refused accepting the bills in purchase of a glass of rum, and afterwards by the traders of the city, who shut up their shops, declining to sell any more goods but for gold or silver. It was declared also by the popular voice that if the opposition to Great Britain was not in future carried on by solid money instead of paper bills, all further resistance to the mother country were vain, and must be given up.[18]

This was a telling account of the effect of the poor value of the scrip and the effect that it had on the people. Though this newspaper was published with a loyalist leaning, there is much to be seen from the perspective of one's enemy. This sentiment was felt all across the fledgling nation. Had Congress been able to stop the rampant inflation and build confidence in its own brand, the economy and the war effort would have been stronger.

One attempt that Congress made in order to keep the economy "under control" was price fixing. It was hoped that by attempting to control prices for certain items, everything from foodstuff to clothing, they would be able to stop prices from rising in response to increased demand and low supply. Being part of a colonial system was hurting

18. Moore, *Diary*, 425-6.

the country right out of the gate. Before the war, raw material was sent on to England and finished goods sold back in return. As such, the industrial capacity of the colonies was not that strong, leading to shortages of finished goods.

This led to resolutions from Congress, such as one from October 1775 recommending that since the manufactory of cloth could not keep up with demand, people should supplement their wardrobe with leather, starting to be fair, with members of Congress themselves. The resolution made strong recommendation that "dealers" in the skins continue to sell at the usual rate to avoid inflation.[19]

On May 30 1776, they added salt to the list of items that would be held to a regulated price:

> Whereas it hath been represented to Congress, that avaricious, ill designing men, have taken advantage of the resolve of Congress, passed the 30th of April, for withdrawing, from the committees of inspection, the power of regulating the price of goods, to extort from the people a most exorbitant price for salt: Resolved, That it be recommended to the committees of observation and inspection in the United Colonies, so to regulate the price of salt, as to prevent unreasonable exactions on the part of the seller, having due regard to the difficulty and risqué of importation; subject, however, to such regulations as have been, or shall hereafter be made, by the legislatures of the respective colonies.[20]

During one particular debate over where to purchase supplies for the army, it was pointed out that merchants in Philadelphia had raised their prices fifty percent above the "market rate." A proposal was made to purchase said products in New York to punish Philadelphia for breaking the association. The debate ended with a resolution to try to convince Philadelphia to lower its price, or the items would be purchased elsewhere.[21] It was through methods like this that Congress tried to keep the prices steady.

By 1780, Congress was left with trying to limit the prices of not only goods inside the country, but goods being imported into the country. Then the price of labor started to fall under the price fixing scheme.

> RESOLVED, therefore, that it be recommended to the Legislatures of the respective States to pass laws for limiting the prices of labour and all commodity foreign and domestic (salt and military stores excepted) so as not to exceed twenty prices of what the same article sold for in the

19. *Journals of the Continental Congress*, 2: 293.
20. Ibid, 4: 404.
21. Ibid, 2: 472-3.

> year allowing such additional price for imported articles, for insurance, freight and other charges as the nature of the trade of each State shall justify and allowing also as an encouragement for country manufactures the same price as a foreign commodity of like quality shall sell for, deducting the price of insurance.
>
> RESOLVED that for the more certain limitation of the price of foreign articles and for the encouragement of importations it may be expedient for the several States to open offices for insuring the importations of their respective inhabitants.[22]

The issue with price fixing is that it is normally done with an eye towards limited shortages of goods, and in some cases labor. What usually ends up happening is that if the price of a good is not allowed to increase the shortage of said item does not go away, but in fact it tends to get worse. If the cost of an item is allowed to go up, demand will decrease and cause the price will fall. Trying to short that circuit causes two possible outcomes. One, the shortage get worse because demand only increases. Second, a black market forms around those that are willing to pay more to end-around the shortage. Congress, by turning to price fixing, only made the economy worse, but it was something that they could not control that would bring the economy to its knees.

Counterfeiting was a major issue for Congress and helped to lead the major inflation that threatened to ruin the economy. Not only criminals, but the British themselves took to creating fake Continental scrip that flooded the market. John Adams addressed this in a letter home in 1777. "Their principal dependence is not upon their arms, I believe, so much as upon the failure of our revenue. To think they have taken such measures, by circulating counterfeit bills, to depreciate the currency, that it cannot hold its credit longer than this campaign. But they are mistaken."[23]

The only good thing with the counterfeit money was that it was usually easily uncovered, especially since it was of higher quality than what Congress produced! The paper was usually a higher quality and the engraving was of a much higher quality. The $30 bill that was produced by congressional engravers even misspelled Philadelphia as "Philidelpkia" while the counterfeit version had it spelled correctly.[24]

Even members of Congress personally had to deal with the specter of counterfeit scrip. John Adams admonished his wife: "How could it happen that you should have counterfeit New Hampshire money?

22. Ibid, 16: 57.
23. Adams, *Letters of John Adams*, 1: 263.
24. Bobrick, *Angel in the Whirlwind*, 292.

Can't you recollect who you had it of? Let me entreat you not to take a shilling of any but continental money or Massachusetts, and be very careful of that. There is a counterfeit continental bill abroad sent out of New York, but it will deceive none but fools, for it is copper plate, easily detected"[25]

In 1780 Congress passed a resolution attempting to strike at the heart of the counterfeiters by offering a bounty on them, "two thousand dollars in the present Continental currency to any person or persons who take and prosecute to conviction." It was worth about $10 specie at the time.[26] Even with counterfeiting being a capital offense, by the end of the war almost half of all Continental scrip in circulation was fake.

In the end the war was won, so it would be easy to say that Congress was successful in finding ways to pay for the war. The problem with saying that is that while it may seem that way on the outside, on the inside it just was not true. The new nation started off in deep debt with a shaky economy that would not recover for years. Foreign debts were piled high, and relief was only found eventually by not repaying the French what they had loaned. The Continental soldiers were not paid, or were only paid a fraction of what they were owed. Many held out for the promise of what Congress owed them, only to fall victim to speculators and soaring prices. Some were even forced into outright rebellion when they could no longer afford the very land they fought for. In the end it would take a new government, a new version of Congress, to set the country on the right path economically.

25. Ibid, 232.
26. *Journals of the Continental Congress*, 17: 530.

Patrick Ferguson and His Rifle

MATTHEW MOSS

Major Patrick Ferguson's rifle is one of the most interesting and significant early attempts at a breech-loading service rifle. Coupling a screw breech plug with rifling, Ferguson's rifle was said to be capable of an impressive seven rounds per minute. Most importantly it has the distinction of being the first breech-loading rifle adopted for service and used in action by the British Army. In an age when three or four rounds a minute from a trained infantryman was regarded as an impressive standard six or even seven accurate shots a minute had the potential to be tactically ground breaking.

Born in Aberdeenshire in 1744, at fifteen Ferguson was commissioned as an officer in the Royal North British Dragoons, known as the Scots Greys. Cornet Ferguson then spent two years at the Royal Military Academy at Woolwich, an institution that specialised in training artillery and engineer officers, an indication of the young man's intelligence.[1] He first saw action during the Seven Years War in Europe. In 1768, seeking advancement, Ferguson sold his cornetcy and transferred to the 70th Regiment of Foot, buying a commission as a captain and serving in the Caribbean for several years.

In 1771, the British Army introduced dedicated light infantry companies to each infantry battalion; Captain Ferguson was given command of the 70th Foot's light company. Initially, the British Army's light infantry arm was merely "light" in name with little specialist training given.[2] In 1774, Ferguson and his company spent the summer at Maj. Gen. William Howe's light infantry training camp, learning how to deploy and fight as skirmishers.[3]

1. Marianne M. Gilchrist, *Patrick Ferguson 'A Man of Some Genius'* (Edinburgh: NMS Enterprises Limited, 2003), 5.

2. Matthew H. Spring, *With Zeal and With Bayonets Only: The British Army on Campaign in North America, 1775-1783* (Norman, OK: University of Oklahoma Press, 2010), 246-8.

3. Spring, *With Zeal,* 13.

Ferguson was part of a generation of active, intelligent, professional and ambitious British light infantry officers. The light infantry arm of the British Army in the 1770s and 1780s was arguably one the most able elements of its day. Ferguson was reputedly one of the army's finest marksmen and by the time he arrived in North America he was well versed in the light infantry tactics of the day, including skirmishing, scouting and irregular warfare.

It is believed that Ferguson began developing his rifle shortly after his time at the light infantry training camp. His rifle, however, was not the British Army's first experimentation with a screw plug breech-loader. In 1762, John Hirst had provided the Board of Ordnance with five breech loaders; twenty more were reportedly ordered but they never saw service.[4] Twelve years later, in 1774, Ferguson started working on his rifle, commissioning Durs Egg, a renowned Anglo-Swiss gunmaker, to produce a slightly improved version of Isaac de la Chaumette's screw plug breech loading action. La Chaumette had originally developed his screw breech rifle in the early 1700s, with his "Fusil qui se charge par la culasse" or roughly translated "rifle which is loaded by the breech" first appearing in 1704.[5] La Chaumette came to Britain as a Protestant refugee and patented some of his firearms designs in 1721. Several years later Michael Bidet built a sporting gun for King George II using La Chaumette's screw breech system.[6]

In principle Ferguson's rifle was similar to a number of earlier screw breech rifle designs which preceded it. In addition to La Chaumette's system, numerous British gunmakers produced screw breech guns including John Warsop, Joseph Griffin, John Hirst, Joseph Clarkson and George Payne.[7]

While clearly not unique, Ferguson made a number of improvements to La Chaumette's earlier work, principally by introducing a multi-start perpendicular screw breech plug with ten or eleven threads at one pitch. This meant the breech could be opened by completing just one full revolution of the trigger guard which was attached to the base of the plug, and acted as a lever. While it might be expected that

4. "Flintlock breech-loading rifle—By John Hirst (about 1760)," *Royal Armouries*, collections.royalarmouries.org/object/rac-object-361.html , accessed November 3, 2018.

5. Howard L. Blackmore, *British Military Firearms 1650-1850* (Huntingtdon: Ken Trotman Publishing, 2010), 72.

6. "Flintlock breech-loading gun (1727)," *Royal Armouries*, collections.royalarmouries.org/object/rac-object-15502.html, accessed November 3, 2018.

7. Discussed in William Keith Neal, "The Ferguson Rifle and its Origins", *American Society of Arms Collectors*, Bulletin #24 (Fall, 1971), and De Witt Bailey, *British Military Flintlock Rifles 1740-1840*, (Lincoln: Andrew Mowbray, 2002), 35.

A close up of the Ferguson rifle's breech plug unscrewed to open the breech. (*Author*)

fouling from powder residue or from dust and dirt might quickly seize up the screw breech, Ferguson designed the screw to have a number of recesses and channels to provide a place for fouling to go during use, and while not noted in contemporary sources the plug itself could be lubricated.

Ferguson's breech plug was also tapered at a ten or eleven degree angle, making it less prone to fouling but still able to create an adequate breech seal. Unlike most contemporary rifles pressed into service Ferguson' rifle could mount a bayonet and also had an adjustable rear sight—the first of its kind to see service. In 1775, Ferguson began lobbying senior officers including Lord Townsend, the Master General of Ordnance. He told Townsend in a letter that his rifle "fires with twice the expedition, & five times the certainty, is five pounds lighter and only a fourth part of the powder of a common firelock."[8]

British encounters with rebel militia and especially with riflemen in America during 1775 fuelled interest in the adoption of suitable rifles for British service. In the summer of 1776, American Gen. Charles Lee wrote that "the enemy entertain a most fortunate apprehension of American riflemen."[9] As a result, 1,000 German Jaeger-pattern rifles (described as the Pattern 1776 Infantry Rifle by firearms historian De

8. Gilchrist, *Patrick Ferguson*, 25.

9. Jared Sparks, ed., *Correspondence of the American Revolution Vol. II* (Ithaca: Cornell University Library, 2009), 501-502.

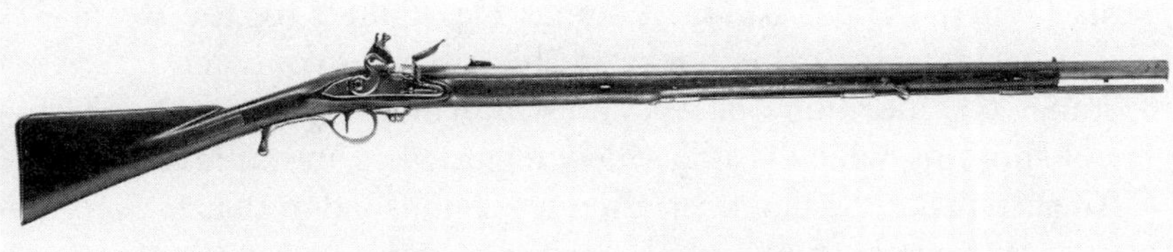

This is one of three prototypes Patrick Ferguson had made in 1776. It is the same rifle Ferguson fired in a demonstration for George III. Ferguson gave the rifle to Frederic De Peyster, a New York loyalist militia officer. (*National Museum of American History/Smithsonian Institutio*n)

Witt Bailey) were ordered in late 1775.[10] In April 1776, Ferguson's attempts to interest to British Army's senior officers in his breechloading rifle began to bear fruit. Ferguson was allowed to demonstrate his gun before senior officers on the April 27, 1776.[11] He fired at targets at 80, 100 and 120 yards away and "put five good shots into a target in the space of a minute."[12] Durs Egg was directed to make improvements and two more rifles were built; Egg appears to have had a close working relationship with Ferguson with several of the surviving rifle's being Egg-made guns.[13]

Ferguson never claimed to have invented the breech system himself, writing that "altho the invention is not entirely my own, yet its application to the only Arm where it can be of use is mine, and moreover there are several original improvements . . . which are entirely mine."[14] As such Ferguson's subsequent patent, filed in December 1776 and granted the following March, is titled "Improvements in Breech-loading Fire-arms."[15]

In the early hours of Saturday, June 1, 1776, Ferguson was advised that Lord Townsend along with Gen. Lord Jeffery Amherst (the Lieutenant-General of the Ordnance), Lt.Gen. Edward Harvey (the Ad-

10. Bailey, *British Military Flintlock Rifles*, 26-29.

11. *The Scots Magazine*, Vol. 38, 1776, 217, books.google.co.uk/books?id=ft4RAAAAYAAJ&dq=%27Captain+Patrick+Ferguson%27+the+king&q=ferguson#v=snippet&q=rifle&f=fa lse , accessed October28, 2018.

12. *The Scots Magazine*, 217.

13. Bailey, *British Military Flintlock Rifles*, 37.

14. Quoted in Bryan Brown and Ricky Roberts, *Every Insult and Indignity: The Life Genius and Legacy of Major Patrick Ferguson*, (CreateSpace Independent Publishing Platform 2011), chapter 3.

15. *The Gentleman's Magazine and Historical Chronicle*, Vol.41, 1776, 575, books.google.co.uk/books?id=cL9NAAAAcAAJ&dq=he+fired+during+four+or+five+minute+at+a+target%2C+at+200+yards+distance%2C+at+the+rate+of+four+shots+each+minute.&q=ferguson#v=snippet&q=ferguson&f=false, accessed October 30, 2018

jutant-General) and Lt. Gen. Thomas Desaguliers (of the Royal Artillery) wished him to demonstrate his rifle at Woolwich later that morning. The morning was wet and windy but Ferguson put on a display of shooting which is still widely regarded as an impressive feat.

An account of the demonstration was published in the *Annual Register,* a yearly almanac of notable events;

> under the disadvantages of heavy rain and a high wind, performed the following four things, none of which had ever been accomplished with any other small arms. 1st, He fired during four or five minute at a target, at 200 yards distance, at the rate of four shots each minute. 2dly, He fired six shots in one minute. 3dly, He fired four times per minute advancing at the same time at the rate of four miles in the hour. 4thly, He poured a bottle of water into the pan and barrel of the piece when loaded, so as to wet every grain of the powder, and in less than half a minute fired her as well as ever, without extracting the ball. He also hit the bull's eye at 100 yards, lying with his back on the ground; and, notwithstanding the unequalness of the wind and wetness of the weather, he only missed the target three times during the whole course of the experiments.[16]

The demonstration had a dramatic effect. Lord Townsend, the Master General of Ordnance, directed that one hundred rifles should be produced and that Ferguson was to oversee their production. Four Birmingham gunmakers were contracted by the Board of Ordnance to produce twenty-five rifles each; these companies were William Grice, Benjamin Willetts, Mathias Barker (in partnership with John Whateley) and Samuel Galton & Son. Birmingham was then the hub of British gun manufacture; in 1788 it was estimated that some 4,000 gunmakers were at work in the area.[17] Each contractor was paid £100 for twenty-five guns, each rifle costing £4. Little is known about the production of the guns and the manufacturing techniques used but the screw plugs would have taken many hours of work using a treadle lathe and lapping techniques to fit them for each rifle.[18]

16. *The Annual Register, or a View of the History, Politics and Literature for the Year 1776*, 148, books.google.co.uk/books?id=JJI-AAAAYAAJ&pg=RA1-PA148&lpg=RA1-PA148&dq=he+fired+during+four+or+five+minute+at+a+target,+at+200+yards+distance&source=bl&ots=KKUtd0ASaK&sig=Ea0az8UUxbhYUzPTzuXg25LPzWo&hl=en&sa=X&ved=2ahUKEwio_NvlvObdAhVKDMAKHQl7CM4Q6AEwCnoECAoQAQ#v=onepage&q=he%20fired%20during%20four%20or%20five%20minute%20at%20a%20target%2C%20at%20200%20yards%20distance&f=false , accessed September 28, 2018.
17. David Williams, *The Birmingham Gun Trade* (Stroud: The History Press, 2009), 37.
18. Richard Keller and Ernest Cowan, "Shooting the Military Ferguson Rifle," *British Military Flintlock Rifles*, edited by Bailey, 219-221.

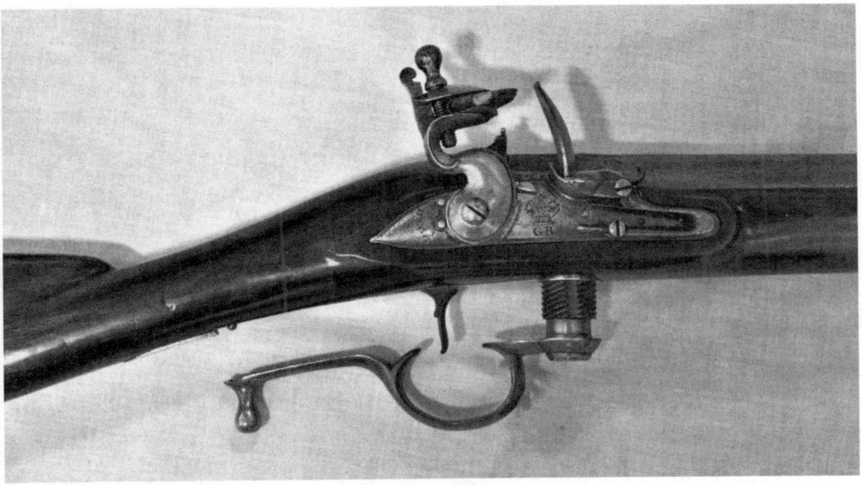

A military pattern Ferguson rifle made by Durs Egg, similar but not identical to the rifles taken to America in 1776. (*Author*)

The rifles were handmade and as a result none of their parts were interchangeable. To ensure the unique breech plugs were matched to the right rifle, engraver William Sharp was paid three pence per rifle to engrave serial numbers in three places on the rifles: the butt plate, trigger guard and the tang.

Keen to experiment, Ferguson was given a small detachment of six men from the 25th Regiment of Foot to train in the use of his rifle and on October 1, he gave a demonstration for King George III at Windsor.[19] With his small detachment Ferguson repeated some of his earlier feats of marksmanship, firing from his back and putting five rounds into the bullseye.

During his meeting with the King, Ferguson also confidently proposed a new practical uniform for light troops. Sources do not confirm the color of these proposed uniforms, but Ferguson's experimental corps did later have green jackets made up when they arrived in America.[20] This was not unusual, during the previous French & Indian War some British light infantry units including Rogers' Rangers and Gage's 80th Regiment of Light-Armed Foot had worn proto-camouflage uniforms just as did some of Ferguson's contemporaries like the Queen's Rangers and Tarleton's British Legion.

19. *The London Magazine, Or, Gentleman's Monthly Intelligencer*, Vol.45, 1776, 557, books.google.co.uk/books?id=DfgRAAAAYAAJ&dq=american+riflemen&q=riflemen#v=snippet&q=riflemen&f=false , accessed October 18, 2018,
20. Gilchrist, *Patrick Ferguson*, 29.

As a result of his demonstrations and petitioning of senior officers Ferguson was authorised to raise an experimental corps of riflemen to test the rifle in the field, composed of 200 men formed into two companies.[21] This plan was temporarily cancelled in late 1776, but early the next year Ferguson was directed to begin forming and training a company of men at Chatham. The men who formed the new corps were drawn from the 6th and 14th Regiments of Foot, Ferguson and 100 riflemen were given orders to sail to sail for America on the March 11, 1777.[22] There they would join Gen. William Howe's imminent campaign to take Philadelphia. With time short, Ferguson scrambled to gather supplies and begin training his men in the use of his rifle.

Captain Ferguson was formally seconded from the 70th Foot and officially given his command on March 6, 1777, his corps authorised for one campaign season after which Ferguson and his men would have to return to their units unless the experimental corps was seen as worthy of maintaining. Ferguson and his men arrived in New York in late May. Interestingly, according to Roberts and Brown's book *Every Insult & Indignity*, Ferguson's report to the Ordnance Store Keeper in New York noted that his corps arrived with only sixty-seven "rifle guns."[23] Correspondence dating from June 1777 from the Master General of Ordnance's secretary shows that a further thirty-three rifles were sent to America along with forty bayonets. It is unclear if these reached Ferguson and his men by the time they embarked for the Philadelphia campaign.[24]

Ferguson's company took part in the fighting in New Jersey in June 1777 before General Howe withdrew his army from that region and regrouped to take a different approach to Philadelphia. In July, Ferguson confirmed that his "small command," which had lost six men in early skirmishing, "never exceeded 90 under arms," a far cry from the 160 to 200 he had hoped to field.[25] Ferguson realised that to grow his corps he would have to take men from other battalions, who were naturally averse to this. If Ferguson did not have enough rifles to equip his entire corps it seems likely that his men were armed with a mixture of rifles and standard issue muskets.

21. Ibid., 32.

22. *The Gentleman's Magazine*, Vol.47, 1777, 144, books.google.co.uk/books?id=bHfPAAAAMAAJ&dq=he+fired+during+four+or+five+minute+at+a+target%2C+at+200+yards+distance%2C+at+the+rate+of+four+shots+each+minute.&q=ferguson#v=snippet&q=riflemen&f=false , accessed October 24, 2018.

23. Roberts & Brown, *Every Insult and Indignity,* Chap. 11, Kindle.

24. Bailey, *British Military Flintlock Rifles,* 44.

25. Gilchrist, *Patrick Ferguson,* 37.

Throughout the Philadelphia campaign Ferguson's experimental force acted as scouts and fought in a number skirmishes and engagements, the largest of these being the Battle of Brandywine. Ferguson and his company were attached to Gen. Wilhelm von Knyphausen's column which was tasked with fixing George Washington's Continental Army in place while General Howe's main force flanked the American position. Ferguson and his men found themselves in some hot fighting at the head of Knyphausen's column with the light infantry vanguard which screened the advance. Alongside the Loyalist light infantry battalion, the Queen's Rangers led by Maj. James Wemyss, Ferguson's riflemen pushed back American light infantry under Brig. Gen. William Maxwell.[26]

During the battle Ferguson and a party of his riflemen supposedly encountered George Washington, chivalrously deciding not to open fire. However, despite Ferguson's own account of the encounter he could not confirm it was Washington and much myth surrounds the story. While the story cannot be proven with any degree of certainty it is definitely a colourful anecdote. Shortly after the alleged encounter Ferguson was badly wounded and his men were forced to fall back. He was shot in the right arm, his elbow shattered by a musket ball.[27] It took a year for Ferguson to recuperate, requiring numerous painful surgeries removing bone fragments to save his arm from amputation.

In the meantime, with well-trained light infantry in short supply, Ferguson's experimental corps was disbanded. His men were returned to their original parent units and while one contemporary source suggest their rifles were placed in store, other evidence suggests the men took their kit back to their parent battalions.[28] Heavy casualties are often described as one of the key reasons for the rifle corps' disbandment.[29] In reality Ferguson's losses were comparatively minor. Wemyss' Rangers suffered heavily, losing fourteen killed along with ten officers and forty-four other ranks wounded, while Ferguson's corps suffered just two killed and six wounded—including Ferguson himself.[30] In a

26. Michael C. Harris, *Brandywine: A Military History of the Battle that Lost Philadelphia but Saved America, September 11, 1777* (El Dorado Hills: Savas Beatie, 2014), 223-238.
27. *The Scots Magazine*, Vol.39, January 1777, 603, books.google.co.uk/books?id=F14AAAAAYAAJ&dq=%27Captain+Patrick+Ferguson%27+the+king&q=ferguson#v=snippet&q=ferguson&f=false , accessed October 29, 2018
28. Bailey, *British Military Flintlock Rifles*, 54.
29. Blackmoore, *British Military Firearms*, 85.
30. *The Westminster Magazine or the Pantheon of Taste for June, 1777*, Vol.5, Issue 2, 645, books.google.co.uk/books?id=NAQwAAAAYAAJ&pg=PA645&dq=Ferguson%27s+corps+of+riflemen&hl=en&sa=X&ved=0ahUKEwj4vrSXv4zeAhUKLMAKHf6bA58Q6AEIPDAE#v=onepage&q=Ferguson's%20corps%20of%20riflemen&f=false, accessed October 27, 2018.

letter home to his brother George, Ferguson attributed this relatively low casualty rate to "the great advantage of the Arm [his rifle] that will admit of being loaded and fired on the ground without exposing the men."[31]

Xavier della Gatta's 1784 painting of the Battle of Paoli shows what is believed to be some of Ferguson's men, in their green jackets with their long sword bayonets fixed, over a week after Brandywine.[32] De Witt Bailey also notes that a February 1778 entry in the orderly book of the Guards brigade calls for an inventory of the rifles still in use with various battalions.[33] If this was the case then attrition of the remaining guns from use in the field partially explains why so few survive today. In July 1778, an order was issued to the army for the return of all Ferguson rifles still in use to the Ordnance Office for repair and probably storage.[34]

Recovered but with a largely lame right arm, Ferguson returned to duty in late 1778, leading a number of scouting expeditions and raids on American bases at Chestnut Neck and Little Egg Harbour, in New Jersey.[35] He was subsequently made a brevet lieutenant colonel and appointed commanding officer of a Loyalist militia force, the Loyal American Volunteers, and later was made Inspector of Militia in the Carolinas.[36] During 1779 and 1780, Ferguson led his Loyalist volunteer forces in the Carolinas.[37] Interestingly, a Commissary of Artillery ordnance stores return from November 1779 to May 1781, found in the Sir Henry Clinton Papers, notes that 200 "serviceable" rifles were issued to a "Capt. Pat. Ferguson" on December 16, 1779.[38] It does not state whether any of these rifles were of his pattern or if they were all muz-

31. Gilchrist, *Patrick Ferguson,* 39-40.

32. S.R. Gilbert, "An Analysis of the Xavier della Gatta Paintings of the Battles of Paoli and Germantown, 1777: Part 1," *The Military Collector & Historian*, 46, (1994), 98-108.

33. "Orderly Book of Composite Guards Brigade, 21 Feb. 1778," William L. Clements Library, Ann Arbor, Michigan, quoted in Bailey, *British Military Flintlock Rifles,* 54.

34. Bailey, *British Military Flintlock Rifles,* 54.

35. *The London Gazette, November 28, 1778, Issue: 11931*, 2, www.thegazette.co.uk/London/issue/11931/page/2, accessed November 2, 2018.

36. *The Scots Magazine, Vol.42, 1780*, 425, books.google.co.uk/books?id=uV4AAAAAYAAJ&pg=PA425&dq=Ferguson+71+major&hl=en&sa=X&ved=0ahUKEwjjrfbb-wozeAhVNasAKHUS1BIUQ6AEIKTAA#v=onepage&q=Ferguson%2071%20major&f=false, accessed November 6, 2018.

37. "Col. Ferguson's defeat," *The Scots Magazine, Vol.42, 1780*, 688, books.google.co.uk/books?id=wEc2AAAAMAAJ&dq=%27Captain+Patrick+Ferguson%27+the+king&q=ferguson#v=snippet&q=ferguson&f=false, accessed November 3.

38. "Return of Small Arms in Ordnance Stores, New York, Nov. 30, 1779—May 8, 1781," Sir Henry Clinton Papers 155: 7, W. L. Clements Library, University of Michigan.

zleloaders. While commanding the Loyalist militia force Ferguson was killed during the Battle of Kings Mountain in South Carolina, in October 1780.[39]

Opinions of Ferguson from historians is somewhat divided. Andrew O'Shaughnessy describes him as an example of "ambition, motivation, professional dedication and courage."[40] Ian Saberton describes Ferguson as "a humane, benevolent officer who, despite trying circumstances, applied his best endeavours."[41] Wayne Lynch is more critical of his strategic skill, suggesting that despite being "an active and enthusiastic soldier, I do not see military genius . . . he was a probably a good officer at times but not really the stuff of independent command."[42] Despite his debated ability as a soldier and tactician, Ferguson's true legacy lies with his innovative rifle, his belief in his design and the limited but intriguing service it saw.

FERGUSON'S RIFLE

For the purposes of this article we will confine our discussion to the military-pattern Ferguson rifles, excluding later hunting pieces. There is a great deal of variation amongst the few surviving Ferguson Rifles, in terms of minor differences such as wood or steel ramrods or the type of rear sight, but also more fundamental differences such as the use of brass or bronze plugs or the number of breech screw threads and the presence and positioning of fouling grooves. This is the result not just of eighteenth century manufacturing processes but also due to choices made by individual gunmakers and evolution of the design itself.

Typically, the surviving rifles have a number of common features including the multi-start breech plug, trigger guard lever, the presence of one of two unusual patterns of rear sight and a bayonet lug beneath the barrel. While there is some slight variation in barrel length and bore

39. *The Scots Magazine*, Vol.32, 1780, 29, books.google.co.uk/books?id=lOERAAAAYAAJ&pg=PA29&dq=scots+magazine+captain+patrick+ferguson++king&hl=en&sa=X&ved=0ahUKEwiuutvo1ubdAhVkK8AKHZd_DUsQ6AEIKTAA#v=onepage&q=scots%20magazine%20captain%20patrick%20ferguson%20%20king&f=false, accessed November 6, 2018.

40. Andrew O'Shaughnessy, *The Men Who Lost America* (London: Oneworld Publications 2013), 263.

41. Ian Saberton "The Revolutionary War in the South: Re-Evaluations of Certain British & British American Actors," *Journal of The American Revolution,* allthingsliberty.com/2016/11/revolutionary-war-south-re-evaluations-certain-british-british-american-actors/ , accessed October20, 2018,

42. Wayne Lynch, "A Fresh Look at Major Patrick Ferguson," *Journal of The American Revolution,* allthingsliberty.com/2017/09/fresh-look-major-patrick-ferguson/ , accessed October 17, 2018.

diameter, the style of stock seen on the rifles is fairly uniform. The Board of Ordnance rifles had .65 calibre bores and used the same eight-groove rifling as the Jaeger-pattern 1776 muzzle-loading rifles, not the four-groove rifling that Ferguson patented, presumably for ease of manufacture.

Markings on the rifles vary with the manufacturer. The guns made for the Board of Ordnance have marker's stamps on the barrel, various proof markings and a serial number at the tang while the locks were marked with "Tower" and "GR." The non-Board of Ordnance guns have commercial gunmaker's marks on both lock and barrel. Most of the surviving military pattern rifles have wooden rather than steel ramrods. There is some slight variation in the brass pipes which hold the ramrod as well as some differences in the position and width of the bass nose cap. The ramrod could be used to muzzle-load the rifle if the screw plug became jammed or so fouled it could not be opened. Provided the plug was in place the rifle could still be loaded from the muzzle, but without the plug the rifle was useless.

Two patterns of rear sight are seen, the Board of Ordnance guns having a rear notch post sighted at 200 yards, a folding leaf sight with an aperture sighted at 300 yards, and a further notch cut above the aperture likely sighted for 350 yards. The other pattern of sight, not seen on the Ordnance contract guns, is a brass rear sight located behind the breech, just in front of the tang, which slides up and down. This sight is on two Durs Egg-made rifles as well as an example produced by Hunt dating from 1780 held by the National Army Museum.[43]

The two surviving rifles believed to be original Board of Ordnance guns, held at the Morristown National Historical Park and the Milwaukee Public Museum, have eleven-thread breech plugs; other surviving rifles have ten.[44] Not all of the surviving Ferguson rifles appear to have the anti-fouling cuts described in the 1776 patent. The style of trigger guard varies with most being made from iron, but all appear to be held in the closed position by a similar detent projecting from the rifle's wrist. Damage to the guns is common as the stocks proved to be somewhat fragile. The two of the surviving rifles believed to have been used by Ferguson's experimental corps have a number of cracks and breaks in their stocks; whether these occurred during service or in the

43. "Ferguson flintlock breech-loading rifle, 1780," National Army Museum, collection.nam.ac.uk/detail.php?acc=1976-11-74-1, accessed November 2, 2018.
44. "Ferguson Rifle," American Revolutionary War Morristown National Historical Park, www.nps.gov/museum/exhibits/revwar/image_gal/morrimg/fergusonmusket.html, accessed October 12, 2018; and "Ferguson Breech Loading Rifle," Milwaukee Public Museum, www.mpm.edu/node/27076 , accessed October 12, 2018.

Top, a view into the open breech from above the Ferguson rifle; the maker's mark on the barrel is also visible. Bottom, a close up view into the breech of the Ferguson, where the chamber that held the powder and ball can be seen; note the adjustable brass rear sight. (*Author*)

years afterwards is unknown but the wrists and wood surrounding the breech and lock are fragile.

Some of the improvements that Ferguson made to La Chaumette's earlier system are discussed above. According to Ferguson's patent the breech plug was designed to be cleaned without having to be fully removed from the rifle; the lower section of the plug on some guns was smooth and allowed fouling to be pushed out of the threads as the action was worked. The plug was not retained in the gun by any mechanical means, however, and if unscrewed too far could come free. Additionally, according to Ferguson's patent, the threads cut into the plug directed fouling away from the breech and were intended to spread powder gases evenly.[45] A "hollow or reservoir" behind the plug also helped direct fouling out of the action; not all surviving examples have this. The chamber and ball had a larger diameter than the barrel to ensure the ball remained seated until fired and to make sure it engaged the barrel's rifling.

FIRING THE FERGUSON

The loading procedure prescribed by Ferguson for his rifle is uncertain as no instructions have survived. The rifle used the British Army's standard .615 calibre carbine ball, rather than a full sized .71 musket ball. Like the British 1776 Jaeger-pattern rifles, Ferguson's rifle used special double-strength or "double glazed" rifle powder. De Witt Bailey notes that five 100-pound barrels of this powder were ordered for Ferguson's corps before they embarked for America, each barrel costing £7 and 10 shillings, roughly six times more expensive than regular issue powder.[46]

Riflemen likely carried both paper cartridges and a powder flask and ball bag. To load, the rifleman would first place the rifle on half cock (a safety position where the trigger cannot be pulled) and then unscrew the breech. He would then place a ball into the breech, where it was held in place by the narrower bore. Then he would pour in powder behind the ball either from his flask or from a cartridge, before screwing the breech plug back into place. He then primed his pan from either his flask, the remains of the cartridge, or by pushing excess powder from the top of the breech across into the pan. He was then ready to fire.

The Ferguson had the advantage of much quicker and easier loading than contemporary muzzle-loading rifles. A muzzle-loading rifle takes longer to load as the ball has to be forced down the rifled bore, mating it with the grooves, which becomes more difficult as the barrel fouls with black powder residue. The Ferguson also had the distinct advantage of allowing the rifleman to rapidly load and fire in almost any position, or even while on the move, enabling him to make best use of cover—a tactic favoured by the light infantry.

The all-important question is, how good of a weapon was the Ferguson? The two greatest advantages of Ferguson's design were the ease and speed with which it could be loaded, and its accuracy. While speed was not Ferguson's primary focus his impressive demonstrations showed that it could be fired far more rapidly than a muzzle-loading musket. During the 1777 campaign, and specifically during the Battle

45. Patrick Ferguson, Patent No. 1139 December 2, 1776, UK National Archives.
46. Bailey, *British Military Flintlock Rifles,* 43.

of Brandywine Creek, Ferguson found that the weapon's ability to be loaded from cover was a significant advantage. At just over thirty-two inches long the barrels of Ferguson's 1776 rifles were ten inches shorter than the Short Land Pattern musket (today commonly called the Brown Bess) then in service. It was substantially lighter, weighing around 7.5 pounds to the musket's 10.5 pounds.[47] This made the rifle a handier weapon, one ideal for use by light infantry. The Ferguson was also far more accurate than the Short Land Pattern muskets.[48] But while the rifle was light, accurate and reliable it did have several weaknesses.

The first weakness stemmed from its construction. The rifles' slender, lightweight stocks were prone to cracking at the lock mortice where the wood was thinnest. As a result an iron horseshoe-shaped repair beneath the lock surrounding the breech screw was added to the rifle held at the Morristown National Historic Park, but it is unclear when this reinforcement was added. While not as robust as a standard issue musket, it is important to remember that the first batch of Ferguson rifles were still prototypes and the design could have been improved.

The cost of the rifles was also a disadvantage, as they were markedly more expensive than a smoothbore musket or even the Jaeger-pattern muzzle-loading rifles, which were around seventeen shillings cheaper. The cost of producing one Ferguson Rifle during the first production run of one hundred was in £4, double the cost of the Short Land Pattern musket, although economies of scale may have made the rifle cheaper had it gone into large-scale production. This and the slower rate at which the rifle was able to be produced meant that it could not be produced in the numbers necessary to challenge the dominance of the musket as the primary light infantry weapon.

Only one hundred rifles were officially made for the army, and the fate of most of them is unknown. A handful of original Ferguson rifles survive in private and public collections. After his death some of London and Birmingham's finest gunsmiths, including Egg, Henry Nock and Joseph Hunt, made Ferguson-pattern rifles in relatively small numbers for both military and hunting purposes.

Ernie Cowan and Richard Keller, who have built replicas of the rifle, describe it as "one of the finest rifles built during the eighteenth century."[49] But Bailey describes it as "virtually useless as a military weapon"

47. Ibid., 201.
48. De Witt Bailey, "British Military Small Arms In North America 1755-1783," *American Society of Arms Collectors*, Bulletin #71 (Fall, 1994), americansocietyofarmscollectors.org/wp-content/uploads/2015/05/British-military-small-arms-in-North-America-1755-to-1783-B071_Bailey.pdf , accessed October 20, 2018.
49. Bailey, *British Military Flintlock Rifles*, 219.

because the weakness of the rifle's stock and the potential for fouling of the breech and bore.[50] In these criticisms I believe Bailey is too harsh. It must be remembered that these were prototype rifles being used by an experimental corps; the strength of the rifle's wooden furniture could have been improved relatively easily and the impact of fouling is debated by those who have experience with modern black powder replicas.

While some erroneously believe the rifle was destined to replace the Short Land Pattern musket in general service, this is not the case. The Master General of Ordnance had initially directed the future focus of rifle production should be on the Ferguson breech-loader rather than the Jaeger-pattern, however, if larger scale production had begun, the rifles would only have been destined for light troops, the elite, disciplined well trained, skirmishers who were best suited to their use. Ferguson himself was a proponent of light infantry, even suggesting that half the army in America should be light infantry, but I do not believe he intended his rifle to be issued to every soldier.

Ferguson's riflemen never really had the chance to make the impact their commander desired. Sir William Howe made no mention of him or his men during his official report on the Battle of Brandywine.[51] The experimental corps was simply too small to do anything more than prove their concept. By the late 1770s the conventional British light infantry were more than a match for their American counterparts. Ferguson himself wrote Gen. Clinton in August 1778, noting that British light troops had gained "that superiority in the woods over the rebels which they once claimed."[52]

The Ferguson Rifle has the distinction of being the first breech-loading rifle adopted for service by the British Army. Its service life, however, was short, especially compared to the 1,000 Board of Ordnance 1776 Jaeger-pattern rifles used throughout the war. Sadly, with so few made and with the wounding and later death of its inventor, the rifle did not have the opportunity to fully prove itself. It would be another twenty-two years, during the Napoleonic Wars, before the British Army experimented with a green-coated, rifle-armed unit again—what would become the 95th Rifles.

50. Ibid., 220.

51. *The Gentleman's Magazine, Vol.47, 1777*, books.google.co.uk/books?id=bHfPAAAAMAAJ&dq=he+fired+during+four+or+five+minute+at+a+target%2C+at+200+yards+distance%2C+at+the+rate+of+four+shots+each+minute.&q=brandy#v=snippet&q=brandywine&f=false , accessed October 21, 2018.

52. Howard Peckham, ed., *Sources of American Independence* (Chicago: Chicago University Press, 1978), 2307.

A Chink in Britain's Armor: John Paul Jones's 1778 Raid on Whitehaven

ANDREW A. ZELLERS-FREDERICK

John Paul Jones has earned enduring fame in American history for his sailing and fighting exploits during the American Revolution. His influence on the war, however, went far beyond his alleged immortal words while engaging the HMS *Serapis* with his vessel, the *Bonhomme Richard.* For a period in 1778, the mere mention of his name caused terror within the very consciousness of the British nation. Jones's successful employment of psychological warfare influenced many future commanders. He calculated that as Great Britain became more and more overextended by a global conflict there would be fewer military resources to defend the home island.

For the first three years of the American Revolution, as James Thomson's 1740 patriotic poem proclaimed, Britannia literally did rule the waves with its vast Royal Navy. The British Isles felt firmly secure behind their fleet's "wood walls" of protection. The last time any foreign power had mounted a victorious amphibious landing on English soil was over a century before. During the Second Anglo-Dutch War, in 1667 the Dutch raided and burned the fortifications at the Southeastern Kentish port of Sheerness on the river Medway, including the humiliating capture of the mighty British eighty-gun warship *Royal Charles*. In 1778 a daring young transplanted Scotsman named John Paul Jones wanted to carry America's struggling war effort to the very doorstep of King George III.

Jones's vision for innovative use of the fledgling American navy won the endorsement of influential members of the Continental Congress. After meeting Jones in France, John Adams recorded in his diary that

> This is the most ambitious and intriguing Officer in the American

> Navy. Jones has Art, and Secrecy, and aspires very high. You see the Character of the Man in his uniform, and that of his officers and Marines, variant from the Uniforms established by Congress. Golden Button holes, for himself - two Epauletts - Marines in red and white instead of Green. Excentricities and Irregularities are to be expected from him — they are all his Character, they are visible in his Eyes. His Voice is soft and still and small, his Eye has keenness, and Wildness and Softness in it.[1]

Jones had developed a clever strategy that he believed would prove that the British homeland was not impregnable. In a later memorandum to the American Plenipotentiaries and to the French Minister of Marine, Antoine de Sartine, he outlined his ongoing "Plans for expeditions," a template for future actions that would carry America's war effort directly to the shore of its enemy. One proposal was that, "Three fast frigates with tenders might burn Whitehaven and its fleet, rendering it nearly impossible to supply Ireland with coal next winter." He believed he could bring "inconceivable panic in England. It would convince the world of her vulnerability, and hurt her public credit." Benjamin Franklin, who was well aware of unrest in Ireland, fully agreed with Jones that a disruption of its coal supply would further increase problems with the Crown's administration of Ireland. Franklin also concurred that such a raid would cause Britain to divert military power to protect the homeland; however, as a cunning politician, Franklin no doubt understood that it would not be a good idea to be openly associated with an act that in modern terminology might be considered terrorism. Nevertheless, Jones proposed at least half a dozen similar plans and projects; but the 1778 Whitehaven proposal was the one brought to fruition.[2]

Jones, among others, realized the impossibility of America building large warships to confront the Royal Navy.[3] He placed his conclusions in an April 1776 letter to America's commissioners in France, wrting, "We cannot yet Fight their Navy, as their numbers and Force is far Superiour to ours," and attempts to face them on their own terms would be ruinous. He felt that it would be America's "most natural Province

1. L.H. Butterfield, ed.. *Diary and Autobiography of John Adams, May 13, 1779*, Series 1 (Cambridge: The Belknap Press, 1962-66), 2: 370-371.
2. John Paul Jones, "Memorandum, July 4-5, 1778," *The Papers of Benjamin Franklin,* Claude A. Lopez et al., eds. (New Haven: Yale University Press, 1959 - 2014), 27: 45.
3. Jonathan Feld, *John Paul Jones' Locker: The Mutinous Men of the Continental Ship Ranger and the Confinement of Lieutenant Thomas Simpson* (Washington: Naval History and Heritage Command, 2017), 13-14.

to surprize their defenceless places and thereby divide their attention and draw it off from our Coasts."[4]

Jones was not a novice at taking offensive measures to bring the war to the doorstep of the British. On September 22, 1776, as the captain of the twelve-gun sloop-of-war *Providence*, Jones raided the Nova Scotian town of Canso and its surrounding fishing villages. His attack destroyed fifteen vessels and considerable property on shore. He returned later in November, striking the communities of Petit-de-Grat and Arichat on Isle Madame. On this occasion, nine ships were taken and their captured crews were used to man the seized prizes. Jones's repeated raids vastly contributed to the devastation of the Nova Scotian maritime economy. As an example, Jones obliterated the fishing storehouses and other supporting structures owned by John Robin on Jerseyman's Island in Arichat Harbor. Robin did not feel it was safe to take a chance to re-establish his business until the end of the war. Jones reported that, "The fishery at Canso and Madame is effectively destroyed." He concluded that if the raid had gone further with additional devastation and imprisonment of sailors, "I should have stood chargeable with inhumanity."[5] Other continual American threats to this area cost the British tens of thousands of pounds and forced them to deploy urgently-needed warships and troops. Jones's raids essentially shattered the Nova Scotian fishing industry and caused an economic panic that was felt in Great Britain. Hitting the enemy on their own loyal territory was not merely an opportunity to seek revenge for destroying American New England seaports, it was policy Jones followed in order to have deep commercial and military consequences for the British, which eventually and significantly aided America's military efforts.[6]

Jones may have learned from French governmental sources of an official British policy to burn and destroy American seaports. In March 1778, the British Secretary of State for the American Colonies, Lord George Germain, ordered Gen. Sir Henry Clinton, commanding in New York, "to endeavor without delay to bring Mr. Washington to a general action. And, if that could not be accomplished, to give up every idea of offensive operation within land and employ the troops under my command only in desultory expeditions in conjunction with the

4. "John Paul Jones to the American Commissioners, December 5, 1777," *The Papers of Benjamin Franklin,* 5: 248.

5. "John Paul Jones to Esek Hopkins, September 30, 1776," Mrs. Reginald de Koven, *The Life and Letters of John Paul Jones* (New York: Charles Scribner's Sons, 1913), 1: 116.

6. *Raid on Canso.* www/revolvy.com/page/Raid-on-Canson-%281776%29, accessed January 16, 2019.

King's ships of war, for the purposes of attacking the rebel seaports between New York and Nova Scotia and seizing or destroying all their vessels, wharves, docks, and naval and military stores along the coast."[7] Jones's proposed a plan of retribution consisting of: raiding an English mainland port in retaliation for the British burning of Norfolk, Virginia, Charlestown and Falmouth, Massachusetts, and Fairfield, Connecticut; destruction of commercial and military shipping; and seizure of individuals highly regarded and politically connected as hostages to compel the British government to exchange captured American sailors languishing in British captivity. In a letter to Continental Congressman Robert Morris, Jones was particularly incensed with the treatment of imprisoned American Sailors in "English dungeons, not as Prisoners of War, but under the complicated appellations of Traitor, Pirates and Felons whose necks they wish to destine to the cord, and whose hearts they wish to destine to the flames.[8]

The plan had the backing of many influential men who fully agreed with this concept of warfare. Morris had told Jones,

> It has always been clear to me that our infant Fleet cannot protect our own coasts & that the only effectual relief it can afford us is to attack the Enemies' defenseless places & thereby oblige them to Station more of their Ships in their own Countries or to keep them employed in following ours and either way we are relieved so far as they do it.[9]

Early in the war, members of the Continental Congress's Marine Committee had refrained from ordering total warfare on the English populace; but as the brutality of the fighting increased, it became apparent that within this struggle all previous restrictions were off and Jones's views fully prevailed. In a never-sent draft, it was urged that "open and hostile operations" be utilized on any of "the Towns of Great Britain or the West Indies." These targets, which included the important ports of "London, Bristol, Liverpool, Glasgow and Edinburgh," were "to be considered as the first objects of national retaliating resentment." In particular, the war should be carried to, "London, the Seat of royal Residence and vindictive rage and the quarter from which have

7. William B. Wilcox, *The American Rebellion: Sir Henry Clinton's Narrative of His Campaigns, 1775-1782* (New Haven: Yale University Press, 1954), 87.

8. "John Paul Jones to Robert Morris, December 11, 1777," de Koven, *The Life and Letters of John Paul Jones*, 1: 237.

9. "Marine Committee to John Paul Jones, February 5, 1777," *Letters of Delegates to Congress 1774-1783*, Paul H. Smith, et al, eds. (Washington: Library of Congress, 1976-2000), 6: 222.

issued orders for the conflagrations which have by the Enemy been lighted up in these United States."[10]

Jones had at his disposal the American-built sloop-of-war USS *Ranger*. Jones possessed tremendous talents as an ocean-going sailor and acquired detailed technical knowledge of each vessel he commanded, and went to extraordinary efforts to enhance the effectiveness of the *Ranger*. For example, he determined the warship was too lightly constructed to successfully bear its original twenty cannon and decreased the armament to a more efficient eighteen six-pound guns. This new distribution of weapons lowered the vessel's center of gravity. Jones also believed the *Ranger* was over-sparred and had the sails shortened and recut, and added thirty tons of lead ballast. During the ship's refit in the French port of Brest, the crew scraped and cleaned the *Ranger's* bottom to maximize its speed and handling. Jones's accomplishments as an effective warship commander owed as much to his pre-campaign preparations as to his talented and decisive tactical judgements made during the heat of battle.[11]

On April 10, Jones and his crew of the *Ranger* sailed from Brest for the Irish Sea and in quick succession seized many British merchantmen, culminating on April 18 with a minor engagement against the revenue wherry *Hussar*. The *Hussar* managed to escape, and the boat's captain reported that the *Ranger's* commanding officer was "dressed in white with a large Hat Cocked" which puzzled him as white was neither the dress of the French Navy nor that of any merchantman, but of the French Army.[12] It is possible that Jones dressed in this manner for mere bravado.

Jones was prepared to teach Britannia a major lesson, "with every intention to make a descent at Whitehaven," including "everything in readiness to land" accompanied by "a party of volunteers." But, "the unpredictability of nature" delayed the attack as "the Wind greatly increased" along with "the Sea" making it "impossible to effect a landing."[13]

10. "From the Marine Committee to John Paul Jones: Proposed Letter, July 19, 1779," *The Papers of Benjamin Franklin,* 30: 115-116; Franklin had previously ordered Jones to desist from destroying unprotected communities, although he was permitted to do so if ransom was declined and if he provided satisfactory warning for the sick, aged, women, and children for evacuation.

11. E. Gordon Bowen-Hassell, Dennis M. Conrad and Mark L. Hayes, *Sea Raiders of the American Revolution: The Continental Navy if European Waters* (Washington: Naval Historical Center, 2003), 58-59.

12. Samuel Eliot Morison, *John Paul Jones: A Sailor's Biography* (Boston: Little, Brown and Company, 1959), 135-137.

13. "To American Commissioners, May 27, 1778," *John Paul Jones and the Ranger*, Joseph G. Sawtelle, ed. (Portsmouth, NH: Peter E. Randall, 1994), 160.

That soon changed. A British report from Whitehaven on April 23 said, "The Ship *Ranger* an American privateer, John Paul Jones Master Carrying Eighteen Six pounders pierced for 20–150 men landed 30 Men at this Port between two and three o'clock this Morning with an intent to set fire to the Shipping."[14] Jones's account was that with the advent of "fair Weather" on April 22,

> At Midnight I left the Ship with two boats and 31 Volunteers: When we reached the outer Peir the day began to dawn; I would not however abandon my Enterprize, but dispatched One boat under the direction of Mr. Hill and Lieutenant with the necessary combustables to set fire to the Shipping on the North side of the Harbour; while I went with the other party to attempt the South side. I was successful in scaling the Walls and Spiking all of the canon on the first Fort; finding the Sentinals shut up in the Guard house they were secured without being hurted; having fixed Sentinals, I now took with me one Many only (Mr. Green) and spiked up all the Cannon on the Southern Fort, distant from the other a Quarter of a Mile.
>
> On my return from this Business, I naturally expected to see the Fire of the Ships on the North side as well as to find my own party with everything in readiness to set Fire to the Shipping on the South. Instead of this I found the Boat under the direction of Mr. Hill and Lt. Wallingford returned, and the party in some confusion, their Light having burnt out at the instant when it became necessary. By the strangest Fatallity my own Party were in the same situation, the Candles being all burnt out: The day too came on apace yet I by no means retreat while my hopes of Success remained. Having again placed Sentinals a light was obtained at a House disjoined from the Town; and Fire was kindled in the Steerage of a large Ship [a collier named the Thompson] which was surrounded by at least an Hundred and Fifty others, chiefly from Two to Four hundred Tons burthen, and laying side by side aground, unsurrounded by the Water.[15]

Realizing the element of surprise was gone as Whitehaven's "Inhabitants began to appear in Thousands and Individuals ran hastily towards us," Jones "stood between them and the Ship on Fire with a pistol in my hand and ordered them to retire which they did with precipita-

14. "Port Captain John Botterell, R.N., To Philip Stephens, Secretary of The Lords Commissioners Of The Admiralty, April 23, 1778," Michael J. Crawford, et. al.,eds., *Naval Documents of the American Revolution* (Washington: Naval History and Heritage Command, 1962-), 12: 592.

15. "John Paul Jones to the Commissioners, May 27, 1778," *Papers of John Adams*, Robert J. Taylor, ed,, (Cambridge: Belknap Press, 1977-), 6: 161-162.

tion"[16] He later learned that the outpouring of people into the streets was due to a member of his crew. The sailor was an Irishman and former British soldier named David Freeman who had originally enlisted under the sobriquet of David Smith with the hope of returning to the British Isles by seizing any opportunity that might present itself. He had turned traitor and aroused the seaport as a sort of horseless Paul Revere, warning the residents house-to-house to arise and save their ships. The townspeople and the crews of the harbor's anchored ships poured into Whitehaven's streets and advanced towards Jones's position on the quay armed with everything from muskets to carving knives.

Jones frantically urged his men to join him in torching as many stranded British vessels as possible, with the hope that their closeness and highly flammable combinations of wood, tar, and canvas would cause a vast conflagration. Some of his crew appeared listless or staggered about as his commands seemed to go unheeded or even uncomprehended. Apparently, some of the sailors had discovered a nearby tavern and appropriated its inventory of ale and whiskey for their personal consumption. These rebellious sailors had even planned to abandon their captain on Whitehaven's quay and proceed back to the ship. Fortunately, Swedish volunteer Lt. Jean Meijer, the one officer who had consistently proven his loyalty to Jones during the cruise, prevented this action by wisely posting a trustworthy armed midshipman to guard the *Ranger's* small boats.

As the greatly outnumbered Americans backed into their boats, Jones continued to indicate he would shoot if Whitehaven's inhabitants did not withdraw. As insurance, he had seized several local citizens as hostages, but all but three were released once the small boats were underway back to the *Ranger*. The freed garrison and the townspeople tried to halt Jones, but soon discovered their cannon were useless because of his previous sabotage. After much difficulty, a few cannon were repaired and rearmed, but their fire went wild and fell harmlessly into the harbor. As a mock salute, Jones and his men fired a swivel gun and pistols into the air. By half past six, the action was over and all were safely back onboard the *Ranger*.

The next day Jones tried another facet of his strategy, attempting to kidnap a person of consequence. This effort was even less successful than the Whitehaven raid, even though he did manage to get into the home of a Member of Parliament.

The consequences of Jones's actions went much farther than the burning of a single ship, the humiliation inflicted on the town's garrison

16. Ibid, 6: 162.

by locking them in their own guardhouse, or the spiking some artillery. Jones wanted to bring the war home to the English and he accomplished this far beyond his expectations. His actions created a panic in the British Isles. As word spread throughout the kingdom, troops were summoned to protect Great Britain's seaports and coastal towns against future retribution by Jones. For example, the Isle of Man's Lt. Gov. Richard Dawson summoned the local Manx Fencibles, requested gentlemen to volunteer to serve, and required these resident forces to provide a twenty-man guard to protect his official residence every evening until further notice.[17] For Whitehaven itself, the spirited Penrith Fencibles were immediately dispatched and arrived in the seaport the day following Jones's assault.[18] Two local justices of the peace reported that "There are now three Companies of Militia marched into the Town, and a Watch of Seamen established for Security of the Harbour; so that such attempts will not be easily carried into execution for the future."[19] The citizens of Whitehaven, along with many other communities, petitioned the government "to order such protection to this place"[20] A Whitehaven resident wrote that, "We are all in a bustle here, from the late insolate attack of the provincial privateer's men. I hope it will rouse us all from our lethargy."[21]

Eventually, troops were garrisoned at almost every potential target in Great Britain that might tempt Jones. Although these were militia and fencibles whose purpose was to defend the homeland anyway, recruiting and sustaining these numerous defense forces further strained Britain's already thinly deployed military forces throughout the globe. Additionally, there were major expenditures of public funds for almost every seaport and coastal community as an intense rebuilding and strengthening campaign of previously neglected defenses was implemented. Throughout the Kingdom, rumors spread that Jones would make another cruise. There was high anxiety that another such "visit" might occur in the Clyde to disrupt vital shipping with Greenock and the anchorages of the upper Firth as a prime target. At enormous gov-

17. Samuel Eliot Morison, *John Paul Jones: A Sailor's Biography* (Boston: Little, Brown and Company, 1959), 142.
18. J. Bennett Nolan, "A British Editor Reports the Revolution," *The Pennsylvania Magazine of History and Biography* 80 (1956): 109.
19. "Sequel Of The Proceedings of Captain Paul Jones And His Crew at Whitehaven—Henry Ellison and William Brownrigg to Earl of Suffolk, April 24, 1778, *Naval Documents,* 12: 597.
20."Principal Inhabitants of Whitehaven, England to Earl of Suffolk, April 28, 1778," Ibid, 12: 592.
21."Gazetteer and New Daily Advertiser, May 1, 1778," Don C. Seitz, *Paul Jones: His Exploits in English Seas During 1778-1780* (New York: E.P. Dutton and Company, 1917), 11.

ernmental expense, coastal batteries were placed at Greenlock (Fort Jarvis), at the Tan between the two Cumbraes in order to defend the Auchenharvie coalfield from potential naval bombardment. These valuable military assets waited for additional raids and a possible invasion that would never come.[22]

An early nineteenth-century British illustration of John Paul Jones as a pirate. (*Library of Congress*)

Among the general populace, the concept that an "Englishman's home" could be violated caused irrational thinking and feverish horror. The American "rebellion" had been a conflict out-of-sight and in some ways out-of-mind, but when shipping could be attacked in home waters, unprotected ports raided, warships defeated off of the coastlines, and citizens put in danger of capture in their very homes, the war now became a completely different matter. People living on the coast prepared to remove their valuables to locations of relative safety and banks had their gold assets transferred further inland for protection. Wagonloads of personal and business treasures, moved from coastal areas, restricted the availability of valuable resources, triggered widespread confusion, and caused great expense to the nation.

The overall apprehension was that the invasion at Whitehaven could occur at any coastal community and the next raider, almost positively, would not be hindered by an inept and mutinous crew. Printed colored chapbooks listing Jones's depredations portrayed him as a bloody pirate armed to the teeth, further fanning the flames of fear. Parents terrified their children with the mention of his name as Jones was immortalized in songs, replacing the infamous Captain Kidd as the foremost buccaneer in their history. To these people, Jones was well-qualified to bear the title of "pirate" as he commanded a vessel disguised as a merchantman, made unexpected and secretive midnight attacks on ships and

22. Gerald Johnson, *The First Captain: The Story of John Paul Jones* (New York: Cowards-McCann, Inc., 1947), 203; Eric J. Graham, *The Shipping Trade of Ayrshire 1689-1791* (Darvel, Ayrshire: Walker & Connell ltd, 1991), 32.

seaports, and in their eyes had a cold-blooded ruthlessness reminiscent of the savage Vikings immortalized in literature.[23] The general panic grew to such a point of ridiculousness that the press satirized it. One of their favorite jests was that the faculty of an Edinburgh medical school had moved completely into the town to attempt to restore the citizens to rationality and composure.[24]

The Whitehaven Raid hit Britain at its inner core, the empire's economy. Jones had predicted that this project "would convince the world of her vulnerability, and her public credit."[25] Almost immediately following the attack, the cost of war-risk insurance carried by private underwriters and not by the government rose to unprecedented levels. Beforehand, insurance underwriters had calculated that their risk started only when an indemnified vessel departed from home waters and ended when she returned to them. Now their shocking realization was that ships were in jeopardy when docked at the wharves in British ports, which caused them to quickly revise all of their rates abruptly higher. For example, the premium on a cargo to Ireland jumped from one-and-a-half percent of the cargo's value to five percent. This alone cost British merchants more than the value of Jones's destruction in Whitehaven. In addition, there was an instant interruption of business and trade as defensive measures for merchant ships, such armaments and convoying, were developed and implemented.[26]

Jones himself was distressed that his raid had not caused more destruction to the seaport where he had spent some of his formative preteenage years before immigrating to America.[27] He informed the American commissioners in France that his men landed "at Whitehaven and burned shipping; if we could have arrived earlier we should have destroyed the town, but we did show the enemy that what they have done in America can happen to them."[28] Jones did admit he "was pleased that in this business we neither killed nor wounded any person." He further believed that, "What was done however is sufficient to shew that not all their boasted Navy can protect their own Coasts - and the Scenes of distress which they have occasioned in America may be soon brought home to their own door."[29]

23. de Koven, *The Life and Letters of John Paul Jones*, 1: 291-293.

24.Johnson, *First Captain*, 203.

25."Memorandum," *The Papers of Benjamin Franklin*, 27: 45.

26. Ibid, 27: 202-203.

27. British estimates ran from 250 to 1250 pounds. Morison, *Jones*, 142.

28. "John Paul Jones to the American Commissioners, May 27, 1778," *Papers of Benjamin Franklin*, 26: 535.

29."Jones to the Commissioners, May 28, 1778," *Papers of John Adams*, 6: 162-163.

Once the news reached America, the destruction was exaggerated as Jones's exploits spread throughout the states. Congressman Elias Boudinot wrote to his wife that once the *Ranger's* marines and sailors landed in Whitehaven, they "burned all the Ships in the Harbour, and spiked up about 30 Cannon in the fort & came off."[30] Also in Congress, Richard Henry Lee continued the embellishment: "He landed at Whitehaven & fired the shipping in the Harbour, and did them other damage, where he also spiked 30 or 40 pieces of cannon."[31] American newspapers repeated British news reports on the *Ranger's* escapades, saying that as a "large column of smoke has been seen on the Scotch shore, this afternoon, it is feared she has done some mischief there."[32] In actuality, a preliminary report to the British Admiralty confirmed Jones's original assessment that "One ship was in a blaze, and as the Harbor was then dry, it might soon have spread and burnt the whole which are numerous but providentialy it was got the better of by about Six and no other damage happened but to this Single Ship."[33]

As the news spread across Britain, newspaper accounts played into Jones's hands as they heightened the feelings of dread and panic amongst the populace. Whitehaven's *Cumberland Chronicle* presented quite a different view than the heroics of Jones's later biographies and American naval histories. The newspaper told of a half-drunken rabble of ill-disciplined pirates who headed for the town's alehouses instead of accomplishing their mission. There was no reluctant recognition of Jones's bravery as he stood alone on the pier, armed only with a pistol, to protect the retreat of his men. Instead, he was remembered as a gangly youth who was found around the local taverns with a discernible talent for quarreling and insubordination. It was mentioned that he previously "went by the name of John Paul" and "was found guilty" in a London court for the murder of a ship's carpenter while he was "the Master of a vessel, called the John," but "made his escape" from justice to America. The editor bitterly continued that

> Every possible means is now put in practice to secure this harbor from future attempts of such daring wretches who having lost all feeling for their native country scruple not, under the sanction of a Congress commission to sharpen the sword of America in order to lacerate the bowels of their fellow countrymen.

30. "Elias Boudinot to Hannah Boudinot, July 14, 1778." Smith, *Letters*, 10: 276.
31. "Richard Henry Lee to Francis Lightfoot Lee, July 12, 1778," Ibid, 267.
32. *The Pennsylvania Evening Post*, July 28, 1778.
33. "Botterell to Stephens," *Naval Documents*, 12: 592.

The article also published a copy of an affidavit by David Freeman, which was reprinted by many other newspapers, attesting to Jones's mission to destroy Whitehaven's shipping. Later, as Jones enhanced his perceived nefarious reputation, the *Cumberland Chronicle* would carry a front-page headline in the largest type in their possession: "Unparalleled Imprudence!"[34] Newspapers also contributed to the public's general nervousness, occasionally to the point of hysteria, with accounts, real or concocted, of American spies throughout Great Britain. It is inconceivable how the Continental Congress, with little funds at its command, could have set-up a spy or sabotage network as terrifying as was intimated by the press.

On a worldwide perspective, the Whitehaven raid, the subsequent failed attempt to capture a nobleman, and the overwhelming naval defeat of the fourteen-gun *Drake* off Carrickfergus within Irish home waters, gave the impression of negligence and unpreparedness on all levels by the Royal Navy. If this was true, then the Dutch nation might have an opportunity if they allied with the Americans and the French. It is entirely possible that Jones's against-all-odds victories, albeit small in scale, helped bring the Dutch into the war.[35]

Historically, one of the raid's other repercussions was the effect it had on British politics and the government of Lord North. Up until now, little public attention was paid to the anti-war views of Edmund Burke, William Pitt, Charles Fox and other liberals who had asserted the conflict was unwarranted and pointless; although the very spirit of the British constitution was on their side, their opinions had been quietly disregarded. A letter to the *London Courant,* published more than eighteen months after Whitehaven, said that Jones "hath stripped you [Lord North] naked, and driven you from every subterfuge, and exposed your negligence and incapacity, more generally, if possible, than they were before exposed." If North and his government could not defend "our coasts from the long-continued depredations of a daring freebooter," how could they "be fit to direct the naval force of this nation against the united efforts of the House of Bourbon."[36] Now many Englishmen thought that self-preservation required serious attention. The viewpoint spread that if the American war was unjust from its beginning, it was now menacing enough to develop to become extremely dangerous to the home-front. The newspapers reported that an unjust

34. *Cumberland Chronicle*, April 25, 1778, Nolan, "A British Editor," 109-110.

35. Johnson, *First Captain*, 200.

36."London Courant, November 26, 1779". Troy Bickham, *Making Headlines: The American Revolution as Seen through the British Press* (DeKalb, IL: Northern Illinois University Press, 2009), 129.

war was bad, but if it threatened to bring retaliations to Great Britain's shores it was more than dangerous, it was insufferable.[37]

The shadow of Jones's landing on English soil and the threat of future expeditions kept the British populace in a heightened state of worry and alarm into the next year. Their fears were realized when, in August 1779, a combined Franco-Spanish fleet of approximately sixty-six warships anchored off of Plymouth with the aim of invasion. This time the British were better prepared and their adversaries, because of inept scouting, had no idea of the British channel fleet's whereabouts. As civilians on the coast relocated inland, the various militias took to arms. Plymouth dockyard workers were furnished with weapons, and tin-miners from Cornwall marched by the thousands to offer support. The Admiralty sent orders for the British naval forces anchored at the Downs and the Nore to block the eastern end of the Channel. To further confuse the enemy, all helpful navigational aids were removed and all horses were taken inward from the coast to prevent their seizure. In addition, naval officers were posted in high places, such as Cornwall's Maker Church, to monitor the enemy fleet and issue warning if necessary. In the end, the Franco-Spanish expedition achieved nothing because they neglected to take proper scouting measures and never obtained any pilots familiar with England's south coast.[38]

In September 1779, Jones's fame and persona grew exponentially with the epic engagement and subsequent victory over the forty-four-gun frigate HMS *Serapis* off of Britain's Flamborough Head; characterized by historians as "one of the most desperate sea-fights in naval history involving an American vessel during the American Revolution."[39] The tangible effects of Jones's exploits continued to receive notoriety and reached farther than anyone could ever have hoped. Ultimately, during the eighteenth century, John Paul Jones proved to be one of the most formidable opponents England faced on the high seas, due to his extraordinary foresight, experience with the English coastline, and unparalleled fighting abilities; however, what sets him apart from other American naval commanders was his concept of attacking the British mind rather than their navy. The psychological shockwave Jones dispensed to the British Empire, and the repeat performance by him the following year, was tremendous. The overall destruction Jones caused to the Royal Navy was insignificant compared to the immense harm he exacted upon Great Britain's will to fight.

37. Ibid, 204.
38. Willis, *Struggle for Sea Power*, 290-291.
39. Bowen-Hassell, *Sea Raiders*, 42.

The Treaty of Fort Pitt, 1778: The First U.S.–American Indian Treaty

ERIC STERNER

In June 1777, Henry Hamilton, the British lieutenant governor for Quebec and Superintendent for Indian Affairs at Detroit, held a council at Detroit with all who would attend. His goal was simple: mobilize the western Indian nations to attack Americans all along the Ohio frontier, just as the Six Nations were doing along the northern frontier in Pennsylvania and New York. In addition to the local militia and Frenchmen who called Detroit home, senior leaders from the Ottawa, Chippewa, Miami, Shawnee, Potawatomis, Delaware, and Huron/Wyandot nations all attended.[1] Many Indians took up Hamilton's call. The lieutenant governor then issued a general proclamation, calling on all who read it to abandon the American cause, offering shelter to those who came within the control of British authorities, and enjoining those so inclined to take up arms against the rebel cause by promising two hundred acres of land as a bounty.[2] Together, the council and proclamation represented a change in British strategy north and west of the Ohio River, moving from a defensive crouch to a more aggressive stance. It had some effect, both on the Native Americans and whites living along the frontier. By September, Brig. Gen. Edward Hand, commanding at Fort Pitt, could report to Washington, "the western Indians are United against us. Gouvernor Hamilton's Proclamation together with his Agents have gaind many of the Infatuated Inhabitants even of this remote Corner to the British Interest."[3]

1. "Council at Detroit, Official Report of Hamilton, June 17th, 1777," in Reuben Gold Thwaites and Louise Phelps Kellogg, eds., *Frontier Defense on the Upper Ohio, 1777-1778*, Draper Series, Vol. III (Madison: Wisconsin Historical Society, 1912), 7-13.
2. "Hamilton's Proclamation, Detroit, 24th June, 1777," in Thwaites and Louise Phelps Kellogg, eds., *Frontier Defense on the Upper Ohio, 1777-1778*, Draper Series, Vol. III, 14.
3. Edward Hand to George Washington, September 15, 1777, *Founders Online*, founders.archives.gov/?q=Ohio%20Period%3A%22Revolutionary%20War%22&s=111131 1111&sa=&r=67&sr=, accessed November 13, 2018.

Congress formed a committee in the fall of 1777 to look into the state of affairs. On November 20, it took up the committee's report, which accurately noted, "the Shawanese and Delaware Indians continue well affected and disposed to preserve the league of peace and amity entered into with us; for which reason they are threatened with an attack by their hostile neighbours who have invaded us, and are at the same time exposed to danger from the attempts of ill-disposed or ill-advised persons among ourselves."[4] With that in mind, the committee recommended appointing three commissioners and dispatching them to Fort Pitt to: 1) further investigate the sources of the "spirit of disaffection" on the frontier and determine those steps needed to rectify the situation; 2) remove and replace any American officers for misconduct; 3) imprison those acting against the "rights and liberties of America" given sufficient evidence of misbehavior; 4) cultivate the friendship of the Shawnee and Delaware; 5) engage individuals of the Shawnee and Delaware tribes in American service; and 6) cooperate with the Continental commander, Gen. Edward Hand, to carry the war into territory controlled by the British, particularly Detroit. It also recommended that the legislatures of Virginia and Pennsylvania invest the commissioners with additional power over the local militia and citizens of their respective states to carry out the aforementioned mission. Congress adopted the report, with the additional provisos to prevail upon General Washington to send Col. William Crawford to Pittsburgh to assume command over the Continental and militia troops there and that the commissioners look into reports of misbehavior by Col. George Morgan, the Continental Indian agent at Pittsburgh.[5]

The Commissioners arrived with their plenipotentiary authorities in March 1778, just after the Continental commander, Brig. Gen. Edward Hand, aborted his foray against a rumored British supply depot on the Cuyahoga River, near where it emptied into Lake Erie. Hand's campaign, known derisively as "The Squaw Campaign" for its desultory results, had likely set back the commissioners' goal of building con-

4. Library of Congress, *Journals of the Continental Congress, 1774–1789, Volume IX, 1777*, October 3-December 31 (Washington, DC: Government Printing Office, 1907), 943, memory.loc.gov/cgi-bin/ampage?collId=lljc&fileName=009/lljc009.db&recNum=7&itemLink=r%3Fammem%2Fhlaw%3A%40field%28DOCID%2B%40lit%28jc0092%29%29%230090008&linkText=1, accessed November 3, 2018.

5. Ibid., 944. Loyalties were constantly changing on the frontier and it was common practice to accuse one's personal, business, or political adversaries of disloyalty or misbehavior to advance an individual's self-interest. In the eyes of many frontier settlers, Morgan's greatest crime was to differentiate among Indian tribes and find sympathy with those earnestly seeking peace and justice. Crawford was a local landowner and long-time business associate of George Washington who had done extensive service with the Continental Army on the Atlantic seaboard.

structive relationships with the Shawnee and Delaware nations by killing and capturing members of the latter tribe. Hand never came close to the Cuyahoga, aborting his march without proceeding much beyond the Beaver River.

Almost simultaneous with the commission's arrival, Pittsburgh erupted in a round of the disaffection that had helped prompt its visit in the first place. On March 25, Alexander McKee, Simon Girty, Matthew Elliott and four other men slipped out of Pittsburgh bound for the Ohio country and, eventually, Detroit, where all would join the British cause. Girty, who had served the American militia and Continental Army as a messenger, scout, and interpreter on the frontier, only recently returned with Hand's force. McKee was a former British Indian agent on parole. Elliott was a trader and close associate of McKee's. All three were well-traveled, closely connected to Native American nations across the Iroquois Confederacy and the Ohio tribes, and had intimate knowledge of American military forces and capabilities from Kentucky County, Virginia to Lake Erie. Collectively, their defection represented a significant threat to American interests on the Ohio frontier.[6] John Heckewelder, a missionary from the Church of the United Brethren well-liked by various Delaware leaders, and some colleagues were then returning to their mission on the Muskingum River and described the state of affairs, "as we drew nearer to Pittsburg, the unfavourable account of the elopement of M'Kee, Elliot, Girty, and Others, from the latter place to the Indian country, for the purpose of instigating the Indians to murder, as was generally expected. Indeed the gloomy countenances of all men, women and children, that we passed, bespoke fear—nay, some families even spoke of leaving their farms and moving off."[7] The missionaries routinely passed abandoned farms and houses on the journey.

The commissioners quickly reviewed Morgan's case and reported, "after the clearest and most satisfactory testimonies, [we] wholly acquit the said Colonel George Morgan of the charges against him, of infidelity to his public trust, and disaffection to the American cause; and we testify that we are possessed of the knowledge of various facts and circumstances, evincing not only his attachment to that cause, but also

6. For excellent biographies of McKee and Girty, see Larry L. Nelson, *A Man of Distinction among Them: Alexander McKee and the Ohio Country Frontier, 1754-1799* (Kent, OH: The Kent State University Press, 1999) and Phillip W. Hoffman, *Simon Girty: Turncoat Hero* (Franklin, TN: Flying Camp Press, 2008).

7. Paul A.W. Wallace, ed., *The Travels of John Heckewelder in Frontier America* (Pittsburgh: University of Pittsburgh Press, 1958), 146. Wallace strung together entries from Heckewelder's journals, letters, and diaries to create a continuous narrative.

an uncommon degree of diligence in discharging the duties of his employment, and of attention to the interests of the United States."[8] While clearing their own Indian agent, who had good relations with the Delaware nation, might have given the Americans a firm foundation to pursue the diplomatic initiative, the McKee, Girty, and Elliott defection threatened to set it back. They made a beeline for the center of Delaware power on the Muskingum River.

On their flight from Pittsburgh, Girty, McKee and Elliott spread stories that the Americans meant to exterminate the

> whole Indian race, be they friends or foes, and possess themselves of their country; and that, at this time, while they were embodying themselves for the purpose they were preparing fine sounding speeches to deceive them, that they might with the more safety fall upon and murder them. That now was the time, and the only time, for all nations to rise, and turn out to a man against those intruders, and not even suffer them to cross the Ohio, but fall upon them where they should find them; which if not done without delay, their country would be lost to them forever![9]

McKee and Girty, at least, knew that story was exaggerated and that a major offensive from the Americans was not imminent that spring, which McKee reported to the British.[10]

The message exacerbated internal splits among the Delaware with a pro-peace faction led by Koquethaqechton, known as White Eyes, and anti-American clans led by Hopocan, known as Captain Pipe. Rather than let Captain Pipe use the exaggerations from McKee et. al. to stampede the tribe into war, White Eyes and his allies called for a national council. There, he put the question of joining the war against the Americans on the table, but proposed delaying a decision ten days while the Delaware collected additional information, including a hoped-for message from the American Indian agent at Pittsburgh,

8. Library of Congress, *Journals of the Continental Congress*, 1774-1789, Volume X, 1778, April 7, 1778 (Washington, DC: Government Printing Office, 1908), 313.

9. John Heckewelder, *A Narrative of the Mission of the United Brethren among the Delaware and Mohegan Indians, from its Commencement, in the Year 1740 to the Close of the Year 1808* (Philadelphia: McCarty & Davis, 1820), 170-171. Heckewelder was well known and well-liked by the peace factions among the Delaware, although he was still in Pennsylvania when Girty and company fled Pittsburgh. This is likely a summary of the main points McKee made, which Heckewelder would have been told second-hand not long after the event. That said, he had a clear dislike for Girty, who became notorious on the frontier for leading Indian raids against American forts and settlements.

10. Nelson, *A Man of Distinction among Them*, Kindle ed., loc 2034.

George Morgan.[11] Captain Pipe agreed, but the chief also proposed to his clan that it declare any Delaware opposed to making war on the Americans as enemies of the people. One way or the other, he planned to bring the internal debate to an end and neutralize White Eyes once and for all. White Eyes responded by telling his own clansmen that if they were resolved to ignore his judgment and go to war, he would lead them and be the first to fall, rather than sending others to do his bidding, for he believed that war against the Americans would mean the end of the Delaware and he had no desire to outlive his nation.[12] Among the Delaware, the die was cast, or appeared so.

Back in Pittsburgh, George Morgan was already desperate to counteract McKee but getting word to the Delaware that the Americans wanted peace and a council meeting at Fort Pitt was proving difficult. Most of the scouts and messengers usually in the Pittsburgh area were already out on missions. Fortunately, Heckewelder and another missionary arrived about this time and resolved that the safety of the Delaware nation and, perhaps more importantly to the missionaries, the fates of their mission villages, depended on the continued neutrality of the Delaware.[13]

Heckewelder and a colleague promptly set out for the mission village of Gnadenhutten, traveling day and night while avoiding several war parties. After a few hours rest, Heckewelder proceeded to White Eyes' village, where he received a cold welcome.[14] White Eyes pointedly asked Heckewelder several factual questions, suggesting he was counteracting some of the stories McKee had spread: were the Americans defeated everywhere east of the Alleghenies? Was Washington dead? Had Congress been dissolved and some of its members hanged? Were there but a few undefeated Americans now west of the Alleghenies intent on exterminating all Indians? Heckewelder assured him that the stories were false and asked if the Delaware would hold a council meeting at which he might address them. Tribal leaders agreed and Heckewelder delivered Morgan's message, as well as a newspaper describing Burgoyne's surrender. White Eyes took the opportunity to remind his fellow Delaware that the Americans had not attacked the Delaware and that the tribe had avoided the war's destructive effects. For the mo-

11. Heckewelder, *A Narrative of the Mission of the United Brethren*, 172.

12. Ibid. White Eyes was increasingly isolated within his own tribe, or so he reported to the Moravian missionaries working among the Delaware. Herman Wellenreuther and Carola Wessel, eds., *The Moravian Mission Diaries of David Zeisberger, 1772-1781* (University Park, PA: The Pennsylvania State University Press, 2005), 440-441.

13. Paul A.W. Wallace, ed., *The Travels of John Heckewelder in Frontier America*, 147.

14. Ibid., 148.

ment, he had neutralized Hopocan's efforts to drag the Delaware into the war on the British side.[15]

The commissioners had set April 25 as a deadline for responding to Morgan's message, which made its way to the Delaware nation with Heckewelder and through correspondence with other missionaries residing in the mission villages along the Muskingum. White Eyes made a brief trip to consult with authorities at Fort Pitt, then returned to the Muskingum, satisfied that McKee had lied, but also understanding that the militia still looked askance at the Delaware.[16]

With Heckewelder's delivery of his message and White Eyes' visit to Pittsburgh, the Congressional Commissioners and George Morgan appeared to succeed in at least neutralizing Henry Hamilton and Alexander McKee's efforts to enlist the Delaware nation in the tribe by the early summer of 1778. The militia and military officers, however, still thought it necessary to carry the war into the Ohio territory, launching their own offensives against the Indians and Detroit. George Rogers Clark of Kentucky County, Virginia was one of the first to act, proposing to Virginia Gov. Patrick Henry an expedition against the Illinois Territory. For his part, General Hand reported to Washington that the militia around Pittsburgh were of the same mind.[17] His own attempts at an offensive against Detroit in 1777 had been aborted due to insufficient supplies and manpower, followed by the similarly aborted "Squaw Campaign."[18] In coming years, both Clark and Hand's successors at Fort Pitt would return to the idea of an offensive against Detroit, which they erroneously thought the source of many of their problems. (The Native Americans in the Ohio region had their own reasons to wage war on the Americans, as they would do after the war.)

Morgan, Hand and his successor, Brig. Gen. Lachlan McIntosh, realized that a direct campaign against Detroit would pass through Delaware country on the Muskingum. To sustain such an offensive in the spring of 1779, it would be necessary to build a series of forts capable of accumulating supplies. Such forts could also shield the Pittsburgh frontier from tribes raiding eastward and ease pressure against the Delaware from the warring tribes in western Ohio, namely the

15. Ibid., 149.

16. Wellenreuther and Wessel, eds., *The Moravian Mission Diaries of David Zeisberger, 1772-1781*, 446-447.

17. Hand to Washington, September 15, 1777, *Founders Online.*

18. Hand to Washington, November 9, 1777," *Founders Online*, founders.archives.gov/?q=Ohio%20Period%3A%22Revolutionary%20War%22&s=1111311111&sa=&r=69&sr=, accessed November 13, 2018.

Wyandot.[19] Thus, they would satisfy several of the goals Congress had established when dispatching its commissioners to Pittsburgh. Preparations got underway, but logistical and political difficulties in 1778 created continual delays. Still, throughout the summer, McIntosh scrambled to assemble an army with which to campaign against Detroit.

With all that in mind, Morgan set out to reach a new agreement with the Delaware. The Ohio Indian nations met frontier whites at Fort Pitt annually, but their numbers had declined as an ever-growing number of western tribes joined the British. In September 1778, only the Delaware attended. Since militia were to make up a substantial portion of the American force, commissioners from Virginia and Pennsylvania were to be appointed. Gov. Patrick Henry appointed Andrew and Thomas Lewis, experienced soldiers and frontiersman; Pennsylvania rather typically never got around to appointing its representatives. The Continental government was represented by George Morgan and Brigadier General McIntosh. Several officers from the 8th Pennsylvania and 13th Virginia Regiments were also present. The Delaware were principally represented by White Eyes, Gelelemend (known to whites as John Killbuck, Jr.) and Captain Pipe.[20] Discussions began on September 17. Eventually, White Eyes, John Killbuck, Jr., and Captain Pipe signed the Treaty of Fort Pitt on behalf of the Delaware. Andrew and Thomas Lewis signed the Treaty on behalf of the United States.

The Treaty, generally thought to be the first between an Indian nation and the new United States, contained six articles, beginning with a mutual pledge to forgive and forget past transgressions against one another and pledges of perpetual peace.[21] The treaty created a lopsided relationship, giving the Americans permission to pass through Delaware territory when conducting military operations against the British, requiring Delaware warriors to assist the Americans when possible, and establishing an asymmetrical economic relationship, the

19. Randolph C. Downes, *Council Fires on the Upper Ohio* (Pittsburgh: University of Pittsburgh Press, 1969), 212-214; Thomas L. Pieper & James B. Gidney, *Fort Laurens, 1778-1779: The Revolutionary War in Ohio* (Kent, OH: The Kent State University Press, 1976), 12-14. According to Pieper and Gidney, the idea originated with Morgan before Congress adopted it as policy.

20. Gelelemend was the son of Benino, known among whites as Killbuck. Whites added the "John" and "Jr." to distinguish the son from the father. Influenced by the Moravian missionaries on the Muskingum, Gelelemend eventually adopted Christianity and was baptized as William Henry. Like White Eyes, he also joined the Americans in their campaigns on the Ohio frontier, making him a veteran of the American Revolution. His gravesite has three markers listing all three names and noting his service as a scout to Col, John Gibson, who was second in command at Fort Pitt during the war's later years.

21. C.A. Weslager, *The Delaware Indians: A History* (New Brunswick, NJ: Rutgers University Press, 1972), 304; Colin G. Calloway, *The Indian World of George Washington* (Ox-

terms of which were to be left to Congress with the "advice and concurrence" of Delaware representatives. The United States also agreed to provide goods to the Delaware and to build and garrison a fort to provide for better security while the Delaware Nation's warriors were away. It sought to replace revenge killings with trials when crimes were committed against either the Americans or the Delaware. The Americans guaranteed the integrity of Delaware territory, so long as the Delaware "shall abide by, and hold fast the chain of friendship now entered into." Most interesting, and perhaps surprising, the contracting parties undertook "to invite any other tribes who have been friends to the interest of the United States, to join the present confederation, and to form a state whereof the Delaware nation shall be the head, and have representation in Congress." In other words, the American commissioners, White Eyes, Killbuck, and Captain Pipe intended to create a fourteenth state populated by Indians and led by the Delaware! Such a development was subject to the approval of Congress, which never agreed to the treaty.

In the moment, the Treaty of Fort Pitt augured well for White Eyes and his attempts to maintain Delaware neutrality in the face of constant provocations from the western Indian nations allied with the British. On paper, it would guarantee Delaware independence from those tribes and held out the possibility of joining the United States as an equal, sovereign state on par with Virginia, Pennsylvania, New York. etc. Even more, Captain Pipe, the strongest advocate for war in the tribe, had signed it. Unfortunately, the paper signed at the negotiating table would not survive the harsh reality of the American Revolution on the frontier.

On September 26, at least some of the chiefs at Fort Pitt arrived back on the Muskingum. David Zeisberger, the Moravian missionary and diarist who lived close by with a growing number of Delaware who had embraced Christianity, recorded that the chiefs had "been informed" that they were now allies after first seeing a 900-man army poised to invade Indian territory, suggesting more of an intimidating affair.[22] This was the army McIntosh had been slowly assembling all summer for his campaign against Detroit, before the Treaty of Fort Pitt

ford: Oxford University Press, 2018), 267. The Delaware had been party to informal agreements between July 4, 1776 and September 1778, but the 1778 Treaty was formal, which distinguishes it from the others. The Treaty text is available at Yale Law School Library's Avalon Project. "Treaty with the Delawares: 1778," The Avalon Project, Lillian Goldman Law Library, Yale Law School, avalon.law.yale.edu/18th_century/del1778.asp, accessed November 14, 2018.

22. Wellenreuther and Wessel, eds., *The Moravian Mission Diaries of David Zeisberger, 1772*-1781, 469.

was signed. White Eyes, Killbuck, and Captain Pipe had a figurative gun pointed at their heads when they made their marks, even if the Treaty helped White Eyes achieve many of the goals he had for his nation. Subsequent historians argued that the Treaty had been misrepresented to the Delaware as securing their neutrality, rather than enlisting them in the American cause to facilitate McIntosh's campaign. Killbuck later proclaimed the treaty he signed did not, in fact, say what he had been told it said: "I have now looked over the Articles of the Treaty again & find they are wrote down false."[23] Morgan himself later proclaimed, "There never was a Conference with the Indians so improperly or villainously conducted."[24] Liquor apparently flowed freely.

With the Treaty of Fort Pitt signed and the chiefs returned home to deliver the news, McIntosh finally launched a campaign against Detroit in October 1778. White Eyes joined him as a scout, suggesting he, at least, understood the new alliance between the Delaware and the United States, but he died on the march. His tribe was informed that smallpox took him, but Morgan believed he was assassinated.[25] Leadership fell to Killbuck and Captain Pipe, but others stepped up as well. Without White Eyes, however, Killbuck was not strong enough to keep the tribe from fragmenting and by the late spring of 1779, Captain Pipe had moved a large faction westward, from where he would wage war on the Americans. Killbuck eventually ended up sheltering under the less-than-secure walls of Fort Pitt, where he and members of his tribe were under as much threat from the locals as they were from warring western Indians. McIntosh got a little further than General Hand, eventually reaching the eastern tributary of the Muskingum, known today as the Tuscarawas River, where he built Fort Laurens. It was too far north to protect the Delaware and too far east to serve as a staging base against Detroit. After a failed siege by the western tribes in the first months of 1779, McIntosh's replacement, Col. Daniel Brodhead abandoned the fort. Less than a year after it was signed, neither the Americans or the Delaware had much to show for the Treaty of Fort Pitt.

23. Downes, *Council Fires on the Upper Ohio*, 216-217.

24. Morgan, quoted in Downes, *Council Fires on the Upper Ohio*, 216; Killbuck, quoted in Weslager, *The Delaware Indians*, 305.

25. Weslager, *The Delaware Indians*, 306. Many had motives to kill White Eyes: whites who coveted Indian lands and opposed statehood; pro-war factions among the Delaware who felt betrayed by the Treaty of Fort Pitt; the British and western tribes that wanted to enlist the Delaware in the war on the Americans; or even internal Delaware leaders seeking to displace the elder statesman. It was also common for individual settlers on the frontier to kill Indians at the first opportunity, either out of blind revenge for raids on their families or neighbors, or simple reasons of greed. Morgan had his suspicions, but did not name the perpetrator[s], which suggests they were whites.

The Last Vestiges of the Clove Road

GABRIEL NEVILLE

With no actionable intelligence, General George Washington had to guess where British major general William Howe was taking his army. So in July 1777, Washington led the Continental Army north from New Jersey into what was then a rough, dangerous, and little-known pass through New York's Ramapo Mountains. He guessed incorrectly, however, and they were soon racing south again. Two hundred and forty-two years later, one of the last vestiges of this frantic Revolutionary detour may fall to a bulldozer.

After wasting much of the spring of 1777 trying to lure Washington's army out of the Watchung Mountains, General Howe moved his army out of New Jersey and back to Staten Island. The preceding twelve months included the battles of Long Island, Harlem Heights, White Plains, Trenton, Assunpink Creek, Princeton, and Short Hills, but Howe was now literally back where he had begun. Together, the eight battles had earned the British little more than possession of Manhattan.

In July, Howe's soldiers began to board ships. This was big news, but not actionable intelligence. Washington needed to know where the enemy planned to go. Howe's ships could take the Crown troops any place near navigable water. The Continentals, on the other hand, would have to race on foot to meet Howe's Anglo-German army, planning their first movements on nothing more than an educated guess. This was an extreme disadvantage for the Americans. Washington reported to congressional President John Hancock, "The amazing advantage the Enemy derive from their Ships and the Command of the Water, keeps us in a State of constant perplexity and the most anxious conjecture."[1]

Conjecture focused on two primary possibilities: Howe might move up the Hudson River and seize the Hudson Highlands, a strategic

1. George Washington to John Hancock, July 25, 1777," *Founders Online,* National Archives, founders.archives.gov/documents/Washington/03-10-02-0402 , accessed April 11, 2019.

choke point on the river next to the site where the United States Military Academy was later built and sixty miles upriver from New York City. With Gen. John Burgoyne's forces moving south from Canada, this maneuver would complete the British plan of achieving control of the critically important Hudson-Lake Champlain corridor. The other scenario was an attack on Philadelphia, the target Howe had seemed intent on taking through the spring. If the seat of Congress was in fact his target, a landing on the west bank of the Delaware River now seemed most likely.

The American troops began to congregate at Morristown. When news arrived that General Burgoyne had taken Fort Ticonderoga, the Hudson Valley scenario suddenly seemed to be unfolding. American Gen. John Sullivan was sent racing north with an advance force. The rest of the army followed as far as Pompton Plains, where it was bogged down by rain, and then continued on to the "Clove."[2]

The Clove—known also as the Ramapo Pass, the Ramapo Valley, Sidman's Pass, Smith's Clove, and other names—was a pass through New York's Ramapo Mountains that followed the river of the same name.[3] In the words of a local historian, the Clove "was of ample width and broad enough in the mid-valley to allow extensive tillage, but at two points—at Woodbury Falls within the northern mouth and at Ramapo within the southern—it narrowed to funnel-like defiles barely wide enough to allow the passage of both a road and a narrow waterway." The name comes from the Dutch word *kloof,* which means "chasm" or "gap." The Clove Road was the primary overland route from points south to the Highlands. The critical strategic importance of the Highlands made the pass an important military thoroughfare. Maj. Gen. Charles Lee—after declaring, "I am going into the Jerseys for the

2. Octavius Pickering, *The Life of Timothy Pickering* (Boston: Little, Brown, and Co., 1867), 1: 145-146; Jonathan Clark, *Diary,* Filson Historical Society manuscript collection, Louisville, KY, July 6, 1777; Michael C. Harris, *Brandywine: A Military History of the Battle That Lost Philadelphia but Saved America, September 11, 1777* (El Dorado Hills, Cal: Savas Beatie, 2014), 63.

3. Sources in this paragraph are from: Richard J. Koke, "Corridor Through the Mountains," orangecountyhistoricalsociety.org/ Koke_Part_1_Chapter_1.html, Part 2, Chapter 5, accessed April 14, 2019; "Sloatsburg's Original Watering Hole," *Sloatsburg Village: Local News & Community Life,* April 3, 2019, www.sloatsburgvillage.com/sloatsburgs-original-watering-hole , accessed April 7, 2019; William Heath, *Health's Memoirs of the American War Reprinted from the Original Edition of 1798,* Rufus Rockwell Wilson, ed. (New York: A. Wessels Company, 1904), 105-108; Dominick Mazzagetti, *Charles Lee: Self Before Country* (New Brunswick: Rutgers University Press, 2013), 134-135; J. Bogart Suffern, "The Ramapo Valley During the American Revolution," in Historical Society of Newburgh Bay and the Highlands *Historical Papers,* 13 (1906): 185-190.

Romopogh (Ramapo), center, is the site of Suffern's Clove/Suffern's Tavern. The northern terminus of the Clove is more or less where the three ponds feed the Romopogh (Ramapo) River. Fort Montgomery is just to the east of the ponds. (*Library of Congress*)

salvation of America," led troops through the Clove in December 1776 shortly before he was captured by the British. Reinforcements from Gen. Horatio Gates' northern command also came through the Clove to join Washington before the Battle of Trenton.

The route from Morristown to Pompton and through the Clove was fairly direct. From the northern end of the passage one could continue on toward Albany or hook east to the Highlands. For most purposes, the Hudson River was a better transportation artery, but the lower part of the river was now controlled by the enemy. Though newly important, the Clove Road was still a rough way to go. Over the years it had been progressively described as an "Indian path," a "horse path," and "very stony and narrow" road. As late as 1779 an American officer dramatically described the valley as "most villainous country, Rough, Rocky and a bad climate. Rattle snakes & Robbers are plenty. It was an infringement on the rights of the wild Beasts for man ever to enter this Clove, it ought to have remained as Nature certainly intended for it for the sole use of snakes, adders, & Beasts of prey." Among those beasts of prey was a group of Loyalist outlaws known as Claudius Smith and the Cowboys, whose tactics approximated modern definitions of terrorism.[4]

The southern entrance to the pass was known as "Suffern's Clove," aligning with the name of a tavern that was open for business there. "Smith's Clove" was the name for the northern defile and a name that was sometimes used to refer to the entire pass. There were seven taverns and houses available to travelers coming and going along the twenty-mile length of the Clove Road. The southernmost was Suffern's Tavern. From Suffern's, a north-bound traveler would encounter Sidman's, Sloat's, Galloway's, June's, Smith's, and Earl's taverns. They varied significantly in size and in the quality of their accommodations. Suffern's sat at an important spot where roads converged to enter the Clove. Smith's, near the north end, also offered quality accommodations. Earl's was described as "a rather poor inn" and Galloway's was nothing more than "an old log house."[5]

4. J. Wadsworth to Samuel B. Webb, June 17, 1779, in J. Watson Webb, ed., *Reminiscences of Gen'l Samuel B. Webb of the Revolutionary Army* (New York: Globe Stationery and Printing, 1882), 309; Koke, "Corridor Through the Mountains," Part 1, Chapter 3; orangecountyhistoricalsociety.org/Koke_Part_1_Chapter_1.html and orangecountyhistoricalsociety.org/Koke_Part_1_Chapter_3.html , accessed April 8, 2019; Charles Dewey, "Terror in the Ramapos," *Journal of the American Revolution*, March 25, 2019, allthingsliberty.com/2019/03/terror-in-the-ramapos/.

5. Koke, "Corridor Through the Mountains," Part 1, Chapter 5.

The army set up camp near Suffern's Clove on July 15, still wondering where Howe was going. It was unfamiliar territory for most of Washington's men, some of whom mistook the name of it as "Sovereign's Clove." Morale was high. The army had been resupplied and the enemy had abandoned New Jersey.[6]

After five days, Washington received intelligence that Howe was indeed headed up the Hudson. He took the Continentals into the Clove. "We marched over a very difficult and rugged Road till Night," he reported to Congress. Gen. William Maxwell's New Jersey Brigade took the van and Gen. Peter Muhlenberg's brigade of Virginians took the rear. They camped again around Galloway's for two rainy days. Little is known about this place. Though contrary to local histories, it is plausible to think that Galloway's was not a tavern at all but rather a private residence. Here, Washington slept in a bed with his *aides de camp* on the floor around him.[7]

On July 22, the army arrived at Smith's Tavern, just eleven miles from the Hudson. New intelligence, however, contravened the earlier report: it was still unclear where Howe was going. Washington was forced to hedge. Lord Stirling's brigade was already positioned on the east side of the Hudson at Peekskill. Two divisions under generals Adam Stephen and Benjamin Lincoln were sent west to the village of Chester, from where they could rush to Philadelphia or to the Hudson Highlands as events might warrant. Jonathan Clark, a captain in the 8th Virginia Regiment, noted in his always terse diary that he "march'd as far as Smith's Tavern about eleven miles from the N[orth, or Hudson] River and turned towards Philadelphia, march'd thro Chester [New York] and encamped near ditto. Lay 13 miles from Smiths."[8]

Definitive intelligence finally arrived: Howe had taken his seaborne army south on July 23. He tried to misdirect the Americans with false information, but Washington didn't fall for it. On July 25, Captain Clark wrote that he, in Stephen's Division, marched sixteen miles south past the village of Warwick, New York and on the following days into New Jersey: twenty miles to Andover Furnace, twenty-three miles to

6. Jonathan Clark, *Diary*, July 15, 1777; Pickering, *Life of Timothy Pickering*, 147; Persifor Frazer to Polly Frazer, July 18, 1777 in Persifor Frazer, *General Persifor Frazer: A Memoir Compiled Principally from His Own Papers by His Great-Grandson* (Philadelphia: privately published, 1907), 164, quoted in Thomas J. McGuire, *Philadelphia Campaign,* (Mechanicsburg: Stackpole Books, 2006), 1: 78.
7. General Orders, July 19, 1777; Washington to Hancock, July 25, 1777; Clark, *Diary,* July 20, 1777; Pickering, *Life of Timothy Pickering,* 1: 147.
8. Clark, *Diary,* July 23, 1777; Washington to Hancock, July 25, 1777.

The west front of Sidman's Tavern in 2019. (*Courtesy Aidan Hand*)

Hacketts Town, seventeen miles to Pittstown, and so on. Another soldier in Stephen's Division, Sgt. William Grant of the 12th Virginia, described this as a "very hard and fatiguing" forced march. After he defected to the British in September, he claimed that during this movement they were "marching at the rate of thirty miles per day, which killed a number of the men. It was no uncommon thing for the rear guard to see 10 or 11 men dead on the road in one day occasioned by the insufferable heat and thirst; likewise in almost every town we marched through, their Churches were converted into hospitals."[9]

The two armies finally clashed in a skirmish at Cooch's Bridge on September 4 and in a major battle at Brandywine on September 11. Given the importance of holding the pass through the Ramapo Mountains, however, other troops were kept stationed at the Clove. Col. William Malcolm's Additional Continental Regiment, most often under the actual command of Lt. Col. Aaron Burr, was stationed at Suffern's in September. A year later, an alarmed General Washington emphasized the importance of the road in a letter to Gen. William Woodford. "I am in hopes," he wrote, "there is no foundation for the

9. Clark, *Diary*, July 23-31, 1777; "Narrative of Sergeant William Grant," in *Documents Relative to the Colonial History of the State of New-York; Procured in Holland, England and France,* E.B. O'Callaghan, ed. (Albany: Weed, Parsons and Company, 1857), 728-734. While Grant's narrative is generally correct, he appears to be exaggerating here, at least with regard to distances, and may have been under pressure to please his interrogators and to give detail he couldn't accurately provide.

report you mention of the Enemy's being at the Clove. That pass is so exceedingly important that they should never be suffered to possess it, and whatever position you take should be calculated to give it perfect security."[10] Iron for the Great Hudson River Chain was transported through the pass in 1778. Late in the war, part of the Continental Army coming from Newburgh used the pass on their way to Yorktown. In his 1886 history of Rockland County, New York, Frank Bertangue Green summarized:

> The Ramapo valley, or Sidman's Pass, was the great pathway from West Point and New Windsor to the country south of the Highlands, and was in almost constant use by some portions of the army from 1776 till the close of the war. Through its narrow defile Burgoyne's army passed as prisoners, on their long march from New England to Virginia in the autumn of 1778. In June, 1779, it was again the camping place of the Continental Army, and was strongly intrenched at that time. The remains of the intrenchments are still visible, and the relics of its military occupation are not few.[11]

While the relics of the Clove's military use may have been plentiful in 1886, that is no longer true. Of the seven taverns only two remain: Sloat's and Sidman's. Sloat's stayed in the possession of the Sloat Family until 1905 and is still a private residence. Sidman's Tavern is just a mile south of Sloat's and is better known today as the Smith House. Parts of the house may be more than three hundred years old. Elements of a tavern built about 1714 were incorporated into the current structure by Stephen Sloat around 1753-1755. The Rockland County Historical Society believes that General Lee, Gen. George Clinton, Gen. James Clinton and other notable figures including Lord Jeffrey Amherst were guests at Sidman's Tavern.[12]

The last residents of the Smith House were the Pierson Mapes family, who moved out two decades ago. In 2014, the Town of Ramapo approved the construction of a large apartment building on the property, to be known as the Ramapo Woodmont Apartments. The village of Sloatsburg fought the development, but lost. The woods that once concealed the house have been cut down and the deteriorating house now stands exposed. Notably, the house is not the only thing of historic value

10. "To Brigadier General William Woodford," September 30, 1778, Papers of Washington, 17:212-213.

11. Frank Bertangue Green, *The History of Rockland County* (New York: A.S. Barned & Co., 1886), 82.

12. Sloat House, National Registry of Historic Places Inventory Nomination Form, November 5, 1974, catalog.archives.gov/id/75321502 , accessed April 14, 2019.

on the property. There is also a cemetery that dates to before the Revolution. It may contain military graves. The last unaltered stretch of the original Clove Road also runs by the house. The tree removal has, however, made the dirt road almost indistinguishable from the dirt around it. Woodmont Properties agreed in 2014 to give the house to Ramapo, but it is unclear if that will save it. The town has reportedly "been trying to reduce it's [*sic*] historical property portfolio, leaving Woodmont in a sort of limbo about what to do with the Smith House/Sidman's Tavern." The developer has said it plans to preserve the cemetery and wants to erect a historic marker to memorialize the road.[13]

It seems that Sidman's Tavern and the last preserved stretch of the road may soon be gone. Though Sloat's Tavern would also remain, a preserved cemetery and a historic marker would be paltry reminders of the significant events that occurred along the Clove Road during the Revolutionary War.

Update: The Woodmont Hills apartment complex opened in October of 2019. Sidman's Tavern and the cemetery were left intact by the developer. As of that date, the Historical Society of Rockland County was seeking to have the property designated as part of the Preservation League of New York's list of "Seven to Save" historic properties.[14]

13. "Sloatsburg's Original Watering Hole;" "Where Sloatsburg Started," Rockland County Historical Society, www.sloatsburgvillage.com/wp-content/uploads/2019/04/Smith-House-Pamphlet-PDF.pdf , accessed April 14, 2019.

14. "Move In Day at Woodmont Hills Ramapo Shines a Light on Historic Preservation," Sloatsburg Village Local News and Community Life, October 14, 2019, https://www.sloatsburgvillage.com/move-in-day-at-woodmont-hills-ramapo-shines-a-light-on-historic-preservation/.

Misadventures in the Countryside: Escape from a British Prison Ship

KATIE TURNER GETTY

Thomas Painter inhaled sea water. As he struggled to recover from the "draft of Salt Water" that flooded his mouth and throat, he was inundated by another wave. Unable to catch his breath, he floundered in the darkness as waves crashed around him. As he fought to keep his head above the "heavy tide ripple", his legs hung straight down below him, his feet pointed downward into the depths that threatened to swallow him.[1]

Painter, of West Haven, Connecticut, had just embarked on a daring nighttime escape from the British prison ship *Good Hope*, moored between New York City and Paulus Hook at the mouth of the North (Hudson) River. Painter had been serving on a whaleboat commanded by Capt. Elisha Elderkin in Long Island sound. Captured by the Royal Navy while trying to take a sloop, both men had been confined on the *Good Hope*. Realizing he risked contracting smallpox while on board—as the deadly disease was notoriously rife on prison ships—Painter immediately conjured an escape plan and enlisted Captain Elderkin to help execute it.[2]

Together, Painter and Captain Elderkin saved their daily allowance of rum until they had managed to fill a bottle. Permitted on deck one night at about 10:00 p.m. to fill their cups with water, the two men instead filled their cups with the hoarded rum. In his memoir written decades after the war, Painter recalled that he and Captain Elderkin generously "invited the Sentinels to partake with us." The guards "read-

1. Thomas Painter, *Autobiography of Thomas Painter: Relating His Experiences During the War of the Revolution* (Washington, D.C.: privately printed by Mrs. Lewis Clephane, 1910), 25 archive.org/details/autobiographyoft00pain.
2. Ibid., 22-23.

ily accepted, and repeated their drinks, until they became so happy as to wholly neglect their duty."[3]

The alcohol so impaired the guards' judgment that they released all of the prisoners from the *Good Hope*'s hold and allowed them on deck "without any Restraint, which caused much noise and confusion. Some were about making their Escape by swimming on Shore."[4]

Having not anticipated this uproar, Painter fretted that his moment to escape would be lost. Soon, the guards had called an alarm and were chasing down prisoners "a part of the way down the Cable, and some in the Water, some on the Wales and some Elsewhere."[5] Unable to find Captain Elderkin in the tumult, Painter could wait no longer—cloaked by the dark of night, he shimmied down the *Good Hope*'s cables and plunged unseen into the turbulent waters of the Hudson River.

Thrashing frantically and starting to slip beneath the surface, Painter finally remembered the oar. Having planned to steal a boat during the escape attempt, Painter had tossed an oar to a prisoner who, having also seized the moment to escape, was already in the water. But in his urgency, Painter had neglected to grab an oar for himself. Now "in a drowning state" Painter called for the other prisoner to pass him the oar. Painter clung to it, steadying himself until he was able to continue swimming. Eventually, the two men separated. Painter recalled swimming alone to the New York shore and lying down to rest by "an Old Breast work, which had been built by our people, and partially covered myself with bushes, clods, &c to keep off the mosquitoes."[6]

Thomas Painter had defied the odds - he had successfully escaped from a prison ship. Of the thousands of American prisoners confined on British prison ships in the New York area during the war, only a small number managed to break free of the confines of the filthy hulks.

From the Horrors of Imprisonment to Freedom

The prison ships churned through prisoners like grist mills—devouring men who once enjoyed the warm sun on their backs and felt the fresh sea breeze on their faces—and spit their corpses from the hold every morning. Sewn into blankets, the bodies would be tossed in a pit on shore and carelessly covered with a few shovelfuls of sand.

Men's bodies and spirits withered as the rancid, scant food allowances on board reduced them to "walking skeletons."[7] They sub-

3. Thomas Painter, *Autobiography of Thomas Painter*, 23.
4. Ibid.
5. Ibid., 24.
6. Ibid., 25-26.
7. Danske Dandridge, "The Narrative of Captain Alexander Coffin," in *American Prisoners of the Revolution* (Charlottesville: The Michie Company, Printers, 1911), 313.

sisted on starvation rations, eating raw, spoiled pork, wormy bread, foul water—and even the lice on their shirts[8] - in a desperate effort to stay alive. Smallpox and other dread diseases festered in the close confines of the ships, felling men with the efficiency of a scythe through a wheat field. Locked overnight in the hold, prisoners suffering from the bloody flux lost control of their bowels and evacuated where they stood, soiling themselves, the floors and even fellow prisoners with waste.

Escape from the hellish confines of a prison ship must have felt exhilarating—at first. While he swam northward away from the *Good Hope*, the salty waters of the Hudson would have cleansed Painter's body of the prison ship's filth. Painter could inhale the pure air of the countryside rather than the noisome stench of the hold. He could luxuriate in the sensation of fresh earth under his feet and drink in the sweet fragrance of grass. During their imprisonment on the rotten and stinking prison ships, men yearned for such simple, natural indulgences.

Imprisoned on HMS *Jersey* in 1782, Capt. Thomas Dring of Rhode Island described returning to the ship after a brief excursion on shore to bury fellow prisoners.

> A return to our pestilential confinement was truly distressing to us, particularly as we had experienced . . . the exquisite pleasure of breathing the sweet air of our native soil . . . we implored permission of our guards to permit us to bathe or wash ourselves for a moment, but it would not be complied with. . . . I believe I was the only one among the prisoners who had at this time a pair of shoes on. I well recollect the circumstance of my taking them off my feet that I might have the pleasure of feeling the earth, or rather the sand. . . And when we reached a spot where there was some sod, we tore up pieces of it and by permission were allowed to take it on board for our comrades to smell of. It was . . . passed around like a fragrant rose among them.[9]

Yet despite the great triumph of escape and the delicious abundance of fresh air, earth and water, Painter's travails were far from over. From the moment of escape onward, a prisoner's journey home was fraught with danger as he faced a whole new set of problems.

Though free from the stench and starvation of the prison ships, an escaped prisoner had to traverse miles of unknown, possibly hostile countryside as he made his way home. Some wore only rags—Painter wore little more than the collar and shoulders of his shirt and the waist-

8. Christopher Hawkins, *The Adventures of Christopher Hawkins* (New York: Privately Printed, 1864), 71, archive.org/details/adventureschris00bushgoog/page/n90.
9. Thomas Dring, *Recollections of Life on the Prison Ship Jersey*, ed. David Swain (Yardley, PA: Westholme Publishing, 2010), 52-53.

band of his trousers.[10] His near-nakedness necessitated he stay completely out of sight while he traveled.

Hour after hour, minute by minute, an escaped prisoner endured the fear of parties of British soldiers around every bend in the road and the constant dread of re-capture. Lacking in provisions and attire, men were forced to call at unfamiliar houses to ask for food and clothing, throwing themselves upon the mercy of unknown occupants of unclear political allegiance. The escapees navigated unfamiliar territory, sized up situations and people instantly, and made split-second decisions. A single error in judgment or an unlucky break could send a man back to the disease, squalor and starvation of the prison ships.

THOMAS PAINTER'S FIRST DAYS OF FREEDOM

After spending his first night of freedom on the New York shore sleeping against the abandoned breastwork that had been built by American soldiers before the island came under British control, Painter set out the next morning to find a safe place to spend the day. He finally found a large bramble bush and hid beneath it.[11]

Later that night, after leaving the bramble bush, Painter contemplated swimming out into the Hudson River until a boat picked him up, but the wind was forbidding and he decided against it. "Went down to the River, in order to swim off and try to obtain a boat among the shipping. But the wind being fresh from South West, and considerable sea, I became discouraged." He ended up back at American breastwork, and spent another night "without tasting any food or Drink Since leaving the Ship."[12]

The next day, Painter tried to walk to Harlem with a design to reach Connecticut. But he encountered British soldiers' encampments along the way and was forced to turn back.[13] He spent the remainder of the day hiding among brush wood on a hilltop, and then slept on a heap of hay.

He spent the entirety of his third day of freedom in hiding. "Here, I seemed to feel tolerably safe from my Enemies. But, Oh! Hunger, and Thirst, they would find me, and it seemed as though I must perish by starvation, having had no food since leaving the Ship."[14] Formerly imprisoned on the *Good Hope* subsisting on prisoner rations, Painter was now imprisoned in New York with no provisions at all.

10. Painter, *Autobiography*, 38.
11. Ibid., 28.
12. Ibid., 29-30.
13. Ibid.
14. Ibid., 31.

Thomas Painter's triumphant escape from the ship was rapidly devolving into an "awful situation." He had not managed to put any appreciable distance between himself and the *Good Hope*. He sank into despair and recalled that he spent the entirety of the next day sitting in the hot July sun, "diligently Employed, in thinking of my present situation, of my willingness to meet Death, and whether I was prepared to meet my Judge in peace." That night he lay down on the ground to sleep. His mind worked feverishly, formulating then dismissing various avenues of escape from New York. "But finally I could see no possible way, unless I could swim the North River, and reach the Jersey Shore."[15]

Daunted by the prospect of swimming the Hudson River, Painter lamented, "But Oh! miserable Employment for me, to think of my Empty Stomach, my pinched up frame . . . then to look at the distance to the Jersey Shore, and the yawning gulph between that and me, and then to think of gaining the other side by swimming." But he had no choice. In order to escape New York, he knew that he must swim the Hudson. "I began to blame myself, for not having made the attempt before, as I had now been without food, for such a length of time, I thought my strength must be nearly gone."[16]

Summoning all of the strength his "pinched up frame" could muster, Painter beat the odds again. In a feat of herculean endurance, he swam across the Hudson River and reached the New Jersey shore. He had set out shortly after sunset and to his "unspeakable joy" his feet struck sand at two or three in the morning. He climbed a hill and "took a last look at the little city of New York." Close to one week after escaping, he was still within eyeshot of the *Good Hope*. Now headed for the safety of the American lines, he turned and "set out on a quick pace, through the Woods and bushes, Endeavoring to avoid all roads and highways."[17]

After his surge of superhuman strength had carried him across the Hudson, Painter's body finally began to fail. He felt himself succumbing to the physical punishment of the journey and lack of food.

> All at once I began to feel my feet and legs to be very sore, and when I came to search them, I found they were much cut with Scratch Grass and Briars. My strength also began to fail me, and my back, to smart, by the Blisters, which had been made by the Sun as my clothing was little more than the collar, and Shoulder Straps of my Frock, and the Waistbands of my trousers . . . I seemed to be gone in Every part, and was obliged to lie down by the Fence, and it seemed as though I never

15. Ibid., 31-32.
16. Ibid., 32-33.
17. Ibid., 34-35.

> could get to a house, although there was a number in sight . . . So I tried to get along by walking a little way, and then lying down, to try and gain strength, and then walking again &c.[18]

Finally, he glimpsed a man and his two sons "cradling grain"[19] in a field and made his way toward them.

THE MAN AND HIS SCYTHE

Escaped prisoners traveled in a constant state of heightened awareness, forever on the alert and unsure who to trust. Surveilled by unfriendly eyes from the doorways and windows of houses along the road, escapees had no way of knowing who would prove hostile and turn them in to the British. But driven by hunger and thirst, escaped prisoners approached strangers out of sheer desperation. Trusting that he had traveled far enough away from British lines to enjoy a friendly reception, Painter approached the father and sons in the field. "[The father] immediately looked at me with a stern, and unfriendly look, and demanded to know where I came from."[20] Painter answered that he had recently escaped from a prison ship and had swam ashore.

The man advanced toward Painter, still holding his scythe, with a "much more angry countenance than before," and stated that he did not believe Painter. The man again demanded to know where Painter came from, "with a severe caution to tell the truth."[21]

Mere moments before, Painter had been staggering along the highway, sinking with exhaustion. But he recounted that, "as my fright increased, by the appearance of danger, my strength and activity increased also, so that I felt no more of my late weakness, and sores but perfectly able, for almost any contest, be it ever so formidable, and fully determined never to be taken alive."[22] Now electrified by fear, Painter retreated from the man and his scythe and ran back to the highway.

Upon seeing Painter's panic, the man's tone of voice and face instantly changed. He called to Painter that he was a "friend" and claimed that he had been afraid that Painter was a spy for the British, sent to "deceive and Ensnare him." The man explained to Painter that if he was seen assisting him, "it might serve as an Excuse for the British who were his neighbors to come, and strip him of Every thing he had." Painter stopped retreating, but remained wary. Despite the man's as-

18. Painter, *Autobiography*, 38-39.
19. Ibid., 39.
20. Ibid.
21. Ibid.
22. Ibid., 40.

surances that he was a friend, Painter recalled that he "could not get rid of the fright he had given me."[23]

The man offered Painter a drink and invited him to his house for some food. Still cautious, Painter asked which house was his. "He pointed me right towards the Enemy's lines, and I refused to go that way." The man told him that he would walk with him to the house. Unsettled, Painter reluctantly walked with him. "On our way, he asked me if I could talk Dutch. I told him, I could not. As soon as we got to the House, he, and his Wife began to gabber away in Dutch, at a great rate. This again, made me more fearful, that I might soon see the Enemy Enter the Door."[24]

Although still skittish and unsure if he should trust the man, Painter stayed in the house. The man provided him with some suppaun (a bland boiled milk and cornmeal dish), explaining that more substantial fare would probably kill him due to the starvation he had endured. After Painter finished eating, the man gave him a new shirt, waistcoat, and trousers which Painter changed into, throwing away his lice-ridden "collar and waistband." Packing bread and cheese in a bundle for Painter's journey and giving him two dollars, the man intimated that the area had "an abundance of Tories [and] horse thieves." He cautioned Painter that he was "in great danger of being taken up and carried back." Painter still felt wary of the man. "For strange as it may appear, after all this kindness, I could not get entirely clear of the fright he had first given me, and I felt very anxious to be on my way."[25]

Painter's fears that the British would crash through the man's door at any moment[26] and force him back to the prison ship proved unfounded. Painter was soon on his way again. "I then proceeded . . . keeping the highway and carrying a substantial Hickory Cane, or Club, for my staff, meaning to use it if I was seriously interrupted."[27] Although initially giving Painter a fright, the man proved to be trustworthy - providing aid and fortifying Painter for the continuation of his journey. Not everyone that Painter encountered on the road, however, would prove to be so friendly.

TWO VERY INQUISITIVE MEN

Much later that day, toward nightfall, two "very inquisitive" men fell

23. Ibid.
24. Ibid., 41.
25. Ibid., 42.
26. Ibid., 41.
27. Ibid., 43.

into step alongside Painter on the road. One of the men walked disconcertingly close to him, almost up against his left side. The other man hung back and walked behind them. The man on Painter's left asked where he was headed. Painter confessed that he was an escaped prisoner and was heading toward the American lines. The man said that they would accompany him as they were headed that way, too, and that the quickest way to get there was by leaving the road and cutting across some lots. Painter acquiesced and the three started making their way across a lot.[28]

After walking with the two men just a short distance, Painter stopped and told them that he preferred to walk on the highway due to his sore feet. He turned and headed back to the road. The men followed him, and said that as he was a "stranger," they would be his "Company round."[29] But by this time, Painter had started to feel a vague sense of alarm about the two men and their insistence on remaining so close to him. The three were back on the road, walking in the same formation as before—the talkative one very close to Painter on his left, the other trailing behind. Painter was carrying his hickory walking stick in his right hand when the man on his left asked to have it. Painter refused.

"On my refusal, he told me, he must take me up, and that I must go no farther, and on my Stepping a little farther off, he caught a stake out of the fence as handily as appeared to me, as if it had been put there on purpose, and ordered me to stop, or, he would knock me down. The other man (his companion,) singing out to him all the while "Knock him down! Knock him down!"[30]

Painter made the lightning-quick calculation that he was just out of the reach of the fence stake and took off with blazing speed, racing away from the two men on sore, scratched, road-weary feet. The two men instantly gave chase, "one crying out, Stop! Or, I'll knock you down; the other saying Knock him down; Knock him down."[31]

Sprinting away, Painter left the two men in his wake. Now on high ground, he spied a swamp in the distance, with woods beyond it. Hoping to reach the woods, he crashed into the swamp, and was trying to make his way across it when exhaustion forced him to stop and rest. After calming his ragged breaths, he continued across the swamp. As he got close to the other side, he had a disturbing thought. What if the

28. Painter, *Autobiography*, 43.
29. Ibid.
30. Ibid., 44.
31. Ibid.

two men had been able to close the distance between them while he rested, and were, at this moment, on the other side of the swamp, waiting for him to come out?[32]

He stealthily emerged from the swamp. "I therefore came out very still, looking carefully Each way, to see if I could discover them." Suddenly his eyes lit upon the two men "standing still, by the side of the swamp, a listening."[33] Like predators stalking prey, the two men stood silently surveying the swamp and waiting for him. Without a sound, he turned and slipped back into the swamp. Evading the two men, he headed back to the road. They never caught sight of him again.

In addition to the relentless physical demands of the journey from prison ship to freedom, an escaped prisoner was accompanied by an ever-present, gnawing uncertainty—who could he trust? The father in the field had acted threatening at first, but proved to be a friend. The two men in the road had acted helpful at first, but proved to be dangerous. Luckily, Painter did not have to grapple with the anxiety of not knowing who to trust for much longer. That night, he reached the American lines. He set out for his hometown of West Haven the next morning.

"My friends, on my arrival, appeared almost as much surprised, as if one had rose from the dead, as they supposed my Escape to be next to, utterly impossible."[34] Finally, Thomas Painter was among friends again. He knew exactly whom he could trust.

32. Ibid., 45.
33. Ibid.
34. Ibid., 46.

George Farragut: The Epitome of an American Colonial

JAUME SASTRE MOLL

Jordi Ferragut Mesquida, better known by his anglicized name George Farragut, was the only known Spanish volunteer who fought under the American flag in the War of American Independence. Over one hundred thousand Spanish soldiers and sailors fought against Britain during that war, such as Bernardo de Gálvez in the Gulf Coast, as well as overseas at the Great Siege of Gibraltar. An equal number of French soldiers and sailors also fought Britain during the war, including thousands of volunteers who fought under the American flag, like Lafayette and Fleury. But Farragut's name, now most closely associated with his son, the Civil War admiral David Farragut, also deserves its place in the pantheon of émigré volunteers who fought side by side with their fellow America colonials, and epitomized the spirit of independence.

Farragut was a native of Minorca, one of the Balearic Islands in the Mediterranean (along with its better-known neighbor Majorca) which has had a long and complicated history with Spain. The island had been an Islamic territory from the earliest days of Muslim rule in Iberia until January 17, 1287 when it was conquered by the Spanish Christian state of Aragón y Valencia (January 17 is the island's *Día de Menorca*, celebrated much like July 4 in the USA). It remained under Spanish rule until Britain conquered it in 1708 during the War of the Spanish Succession, and remained in British hands despite a brief French occupation during the Seven Years' War. Minorca was re-taken in 1782 by Spain during the War of American Independence, ceded to Spain in the Peace of Paris in 1783, and became a permanent Spanish possession under the terms of the Treaty of Amiens in 1802.

This article was translated from the original Spanish by Larrie D. Ferreiro.

Under the British regime, Minorca had a mixed Spanish-British governing system with two capital cities: Ciudadela (today Ciutadella) in the west, home to the university and the local assembly, and Mahón, the center of British political power and site of its naval base at Port Mahón and military base at Fort San Félipe. The majority of the island's population were farmers, mostly sharecroppers beholden to a few hundred ruling families. But Minorca's position in the Mediterranean also meant it had a booming economy in trade, with both Ciudadella and Máhon having a very cosmopolitan flair and filled with craftsmen, lawyers, lawyers, notaries, scribes, doctors, apothecaries, etc. There was also a great deal of migration to and from the island, with inhabitants closely connected to other urban centers in Majorca, Barcelona and Valencia.[1]

Farragut's family originated in Sineu, Majorca, at least as far back as the mid-seventeenth century, and like many Majorcans, were of Catalan origin (which is why the family name was spelled Ferragut). The family founder was Juan Ferragut Florit, who married Antonia Besset in 1632. The line of descendants went through Antonio Ferragut Besset (married to Magdalena Riutort), then Jordi Ferragut Riutort (married to Ursula Guitard Rossinyol), and then to Antonio Ferragut Guitard. Antonio was of the many émigrés who moved from Majorca to Minorca, marrying Juana Mesquida Bagur in Ciudadela in 1750, and subsequently became a sailor. Their son Jordi Ferragut Mesquida was born in that city on September 29, 1755.[2]

Antonio and Jordi (then barely fifteen years old, although he had been a sailor since age ten) enlisted in 1770 aboard a British privateer which fought in the Russo-Turkish War of 1768-1774, in support of the fleet of Catherine II ("The Great") of Russia. They fought in the naval battle at Chesma on July 5-7, 1770 in the waters around the Greek island of Chios. This battle led to a defeat for the Turkish navy squadron in the Mediterranean and the beginning of the end of the great Ottoman Empire. After this battle, at seventeen years of age, Jordi Ferragut left the island of Minorca to move to Barcelona, with the in-

1. John Armstrong, *The history of the island of Minorca* (London: C. Davis, 1752); Juan Llabrés Bernal, *De la marina de antaño: Notas para la historia de Menorca*, 2 vols. (Palma de Mallorca: Antigua Imprenta Soler / Imprenta Alfa, 1955/1967); Llabrés Bernal, *La estación naval norteamericana en Mahón. 1815-1826: Durante los mandos de los comodoros John Shaw, Isaac Chauncey, Charles Stewart, William Bainbridge, y John Rodgers* (Palma de Mallorca: Imprenta Bristol, 1969); Llabrés Bernal, *Menorca y la escuadra norteamericana en el siglo pasado 1825 – 1830* (Palma de Mallorca: Imprenta Bristol, 1971).

2. Archivo Diocesano de Ciudadela: Llibre de baptismes de la parroquia de Ciudadela, D. L. 039 (Cuidadela, Minorca).

tention of beginning his nautical studies. We cannot say with any certainty which studies Jordi undertook while in the Catalonian city, although they presumably included some instruction in shipbuilding and navigation.

Two years later, on April 2, 1772, he followed his adventurous spirit and emigrated from Minorca to North America via Barcelona. At that time, Barcelona was one of the Spanish ports on the Mediterranean that was directly linked to Cádiz on the Atlantic coast, from where most of the ocean vessels departed for the Caribbean ports in the Spanish American empire. Being a young man of twenty, with nautical knowledge, allowed him the opportunity, in 1773, to be appointed captain of a small cargo ship which periodically would make the voyage between Havana and Veracruz, where his name is recorded in port registry books as captain of a merchant ship. This experience allowed him to gain accurate knowledge of sailing the Caribbean Sea. At some point he dropped "Jordi" and began calling himself Jeorge (Jordi is Catalan; he did not call himself Jorge, which is Castilian); over time, "Jeorge" became "George," and "Ferragut" became "Farragut."[3]

Farragut first came to New Orleans, the capital of Spanish Louisiana, in 1775. His arrival on the American coast coincided with the outbreak of the American Revolution. There, Farragut learned of this brewing conflict, for that port city had become the center of American espionage for the Spanish Empire. "For the first time" Farragut later wrote, referring to himself in the third person, "he heard of the difficulties between England and her colonies, and immediately determined to assist with his life and his fortune in the struggle for American Independence." It is not clear what led him to participate in The Cause (as the Americans called the fight), but it is possible that Farragut saw it as a way to launch a blow against the British occupation of his own home island. He sailed from New Orleans to Port-au-Prince, Saint Domingue (notorious for smuggling French-made arms to American colonists) where he traded his cargo for "cannon, arms, powder and ball." He brought these munitions to Charleston, South Carolina in March 1776, where he presumably sold them to the Americans preparing their defenses against the forthcoming British siege (later known as the Battle of Sullivan's Island). His seafaring experience proved valuable to the colonists, for he was soon commissioned as lieutenant aboard the 12-gun sloop *Vixen*, commanded by Downham Newton. He "gave much satisfaction to his captain," for *Vixen* had a

3. Jaime Sastre Moll, "David Glasgow Ferragut," in Francesc Riera i Montserrat (ed.), *América, l'altra història de les Balears* (Palma de Mallorca: Gràficas Miramar, 1992).

"George Farragut, Father of David G. Farragut," by William Swain. (*Naval History and Heritage Command/National Portrait Gallery*)

particularly successful cruise in the summer of 1777, capturing several prizes and giving a poke in the eye to a larger British squadron.[4]

At the recommendation of Captain Newton, Farragut was appointed as a first lieutenant of the South Carolina navy. There he played a dual role; first, as a builder of shallow-draft oared galleys in Charleston, designed to defend ports; and second, and as a commander of these galleys, notably *Revenge*, during the Capture of Savannah (1778) where "he fought a severe action … and did not quit the deck of his vessel until it was covered with the dead and the dying." The battle resulted in an overwhelming defeat for the defending American forces, so Farragut was obliged to bring his galley far up the Sampit River above Georgetown to hide it from the roving British forces. Farragut also participated in the unsuccessful siege of Savannah a year later by American and French forces.[5]

4. The information on the service of George Farragut in the United States is from: George Farragut, Letter to Secretary of the Navy William Jones, New Orleans, May 20, 1814, Naval History and Heritage Command (Washington, DC), Navy Department Library, Personnel files ZB-F Box 095; Marshall DeLancey Haywood, "Major George Farragut," *The Gulf States Historical Magazine* 2/2 (September 1903), 90-98; Moll, "David Glasgow Farragut," 1992; Robert L. Caleo, "'A Most Serious Wound': The Memorial of George Farragut," *The Journal of East Tennessee History* 79 (2007), 63-79; Robert L. Caleo, *Farragut and Family: The Making of an Elder Hero* (Bloomington, IN: Xlibris, 2015), 27-39.
5. John J. Sayen Jr., "Oared Fighting Ships of the South Carolina Navy, 1776-1780," *The South Carolina Historical Magazine* 87/4 (October 1986), 213-237.

The Battle of Charleston in 1780 was by far a more important strategic loss for the Americans. The amphibious British assault easily penetrated the port of Charleston, in spite of the suicide strategy employed by the Americans. In an attempt to prevent the city from being bombed, they sank eleven available galleys, one of which was commanded by Farragut, with the objective of forming a barricade at the mouth of the river. Meanwhile, the galleys' cannon were unshipped and were placed with their crews on each side of the port, to reinforce the ground troops. Although a man of the sea, George Farragut exchanged his role for that of a foot soldier. He was assigned to command one of the batteries, defending the position with the same patriotic fervor as any other American officer. During one of the engagements, Col. Richard Parker of Virginia "died in [my] arms," Farragut later reported. The resistance in Charleston lasted for a month. Even so, the British took the city and captured around 5,000 men. The higher-ranking officers were taken north, to Philadelphia, where a prisoner exchange took place between the two sides. Farragut's name appears on that list.

Once exchanged, George Farragut returned to the war in South Carolina, but on the return trip aboard a privateer bound for Charleston, his right arm was shattered during an "engagement" by a musket ball (Farragut did not reveal the circumstances of the "engagement"); the arm was set by Doctor Frederick Ridgely. From then on, his arm was largely useless except as a weather barometer, and he could not serve as a fighting sailor; instead, he offered his services to Francis Marion (the Swamp Fox). In January 1781, Farragut joined a rifle militia in South Carolina that was active in the wooded area of Cowpens on the border between the two Carolinas, commanded by Andrew Pickens, positioned to head off the British infantry. There, the British and American armies fought a decisive battle, in which both the infantry and cavalry intervened. The battle ended up being a turning point for the war. If prior to the Battle of Cowpens the advantage had leaned toward the British, now the war was leaning toward the side of the colonies. After this battle, the army of General Cornwallis was left in a very weakened state due to the number of casualties.

The day after the Battle of Cowpens, George Farragut headed to Wilmington, North Carolina, following the course of the war as an artillery gunner, where he was engaged in a minor skirmish at Beaufort's Bridge across the North East Cape Fear River. He then raised a volunteer company of cavalry, charged with capturing stragglers from Cornwallis's army as they advanced towards Virginia. Those initiatives earned him the command of a newly formed cavalry unit with the rank of captain, supporting the military operations of Francis Marion.

For George Farragut, the war ended there as the peace negotiations dragged on from 1782 through 1783. Now back in North Carolina, with hardly a penny to his name, he found himself in a precarious situation, which he protested to the authorities. Nevertheless, the state was nearly broke and could not pay even a portion of his arrears for several years. In light of this, Farragut returned to his prior occupation as a seaman for a decade, coming home to North Carolina in 1792 and engaging in surveying and farming in the newly-formed Southwest Territory (now Tennessee). The Territory's governor William Blount appointed him as a major of the militia in 1793, during which time he fought against the Cherokee nation. Farragut continued to serve the nation he helped create, being appointed a sailing master of a gun boat in New Orleans in 1807, and again fighting the British during the War of 1812.

George Farragut also started a family in his adopted land. He married Elizabeth Shine in 1795, and together they had five children before she died in 1808. The most famous of his sons was James Glasgow Farragut, who was only seven years old when his mother died. George Farragut had befriended a naval officer, David Porter, who died the same day as Farragut's wife. Bereft and broke, George Farragut agreed to let David Porter's son, David Porter Jr. (also a naval officer), take young James into his charge. James Farragut soon changed his first name to David in honor of his adopted father, and David Glasgow Farragut went on to become one of the most effective admirals in the Union Navy during the Civil War.

George Farragut continued to serve the United States after the War of 1812 was over. Rejected from further service the navy, he enlisted as a volunteer companion to Gen. Andrew Jackson's troops, defending the coast around New Orleans from any possible British incursion. But within a few years, the toll of his service caught up with him and on June 4, 1817, George Farragut passed away at age fifty-six in Pascagoula, Mississippi. Like many soldiers and sailors, he was interred in an unmarked grave. His son David, who did not see his father again after he left home in 1808, returned to his father's home island of Minorca in 1815 as a midshipman, and again in 1868 as commander of the European Squadron, the first American naval officer with the rank of full admiral.[6] It is has often been remarked that the Civil War achieved the unification that the Revolutionary War had begun; so it is perhaps fitting that the father George Farragut, who helped create the United States, was followed by the son David Farragut who helped to make it one nation.

6. Eva M. García, ed., *Farragut y Menorca: el legado español en la U.S. Navy: the Spanish legacy* (Madrid: Ministerio de Defensa, 2017).

Donald McCraw of the 42nd Regiment Wields His Broadsword

DON N. HAGIST

In March and April 1780, there was a string of home invasions and robberies around the villages of Jamaica and Flushing on Long Island, New York. The farming region had been a British army garrison since the autumn of 1776, and was teeming with residents, soldiers, sailors, prisoners of war, refugees, and an assortment of itinerant and displaced people. Crimes were bound to occur in such crowded conditions, with many opportunistic and desperate people, but this early 1780 spree was particularly disturbing. Residents heard a knock on the door in the middle of the night; if they didn't answer, doors were broken open and men with blackened faces burst in, demanding money, guns, wearing apparel, watches and other valuables. Sometimes they compelled the homeowners to light candles and lead them to goods, other times they forced their victims to cower under bedding while they ransacked the home, threatening to kill those who didn't comply. Residents were tied up, knocked down, blindfolded, belittled and overpowered. No one was sure exactly how many perpetrators there were - three, four, five – faces blackened, wrapped in greatcoats, at least one carrying a gun – but they all had the appearance of soldiers, particularly one who wore a light infantry cap.

On May 8 they struck again, for at least the fifth time, at a farmhouse occupied by William Creed and his adult son. In the middle of the night, there was noise as people attempted to enter the front door. Failing to break it open, they went to the kitchen door. Four men, one wielding a musket with fixed bayonet, burst through and rushed on the elder Creed, demanding his watch and purse. After threatening to kill him if he didn't comply and demanding a candle, they forced him to hide in his bed under his blankets. But there was something the robbers hadn't counted on. There was another person in the house, Sgt. Donald

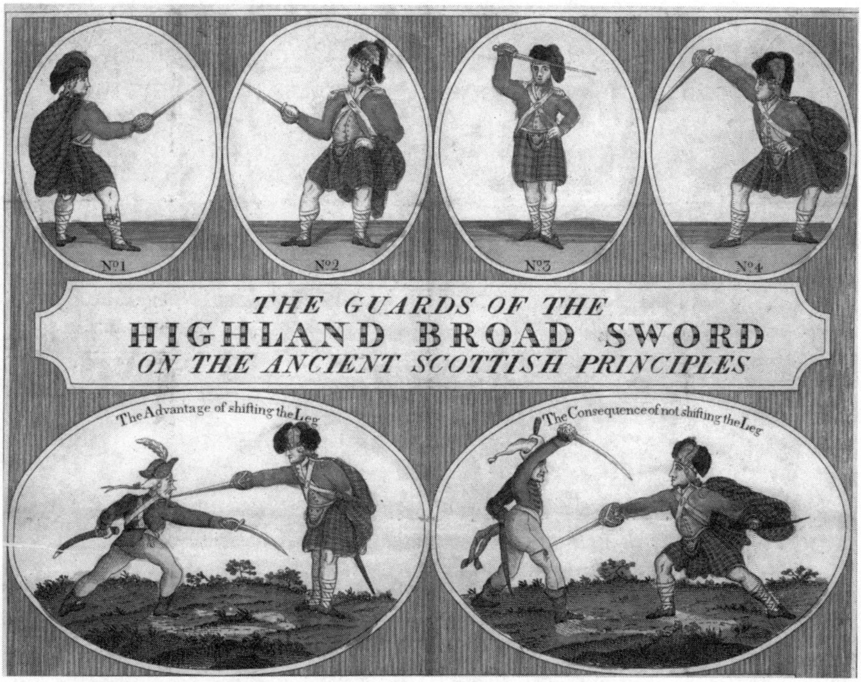

"The Guards of the Highland Broad Sword on the ancient Scottish principles," 1798, detail. (*Anne S.K. Brown Military Collection, Brown University*)

McCraw of the 42nd Regiment of Foot, the Royal Highlanders, a seasoned veteran soldier wielding a broadsword.[1]

McCraw, from the village of Dunkeld about fifteen miles north of Perth in the middle of Scotland, had enlisted in the regiment in 1756 at the age of twenty-two.[2] Over the next twenty-four years his regiment had been through some scrapes, in particular the disastrous assault on Fort Ticonderoga during the French and Indian War. By the time the 42nd returned to America in 1776, McCraw was a corporal in the regiment's grenadier company, and within two years was appointed sergeant;[3] detached from the regiment and placed in a grenadier battalion, it was in the forefront of the difficult and dangerous campaign in New York and New Jersey in 1776 and 1777, battles like Brandywine and

1. Court martial of nine soldiers of the Kings American Regiment, WO 71-92, 227 – 238, National Archives of Great Britain. All other details about the trial come from this document.
2. Out-pension admission book, WO 116/7, examinations for November 10, 1780, National Archives of Great Britain.
3. Muster rolls, 42nd Regiment of Foot, WO 12/5479, National Archives of Great Britain.

Monmouth, and countless actions that were smaller in scale but every bit as harrowing for the individual soldiers. There were also the dangers imposed by long sea voyages, harsh wilderness campaigns, and even civil unrest in Ireland.

By 1779, McCraw had contracted an abdominal hernia which limited his ability to march and exercise with the regiment. Instead, he and his wife worked for his commanding officer, Capt. John Peebles, procuring provisions, cooking, handling laundry and other chores. In December 1779 the grenadier battalion, quartered in Long Island, was ordered to prepare for the expedition to Charleston, South Carolina. Capt. Peebles sent McCraw to Brooklyn to sell a horse, which the sergeant dutifully did, returning with ten guineas (gold coins worth twenty-one shillings, or one pound 1 shilling).[4] When it came time for the battalion to embark, McCraw, his wife and son remained behind in Long Island. He took quarters at the house of William Creed, whose family treated him well enough that he felt a responsibility to protect them. He wasn't about to let a band of ruffians bring them harm.

The troops of the 42nd Regiment had been issued broadswords, traditional weapons of highland soldiers, but it's not clear whether they were routinely carried in America. It is clear that McCraw had his, and had it handy. Hearing the commotion, he stormed out of his room sword in hand to confront the invaders. The gunman pushed at McCraw with his bayonet, but the Scotsman parried the thrust with his bare hand; with the other hand he swung his sword at his assailant, then seized the musket. McCraw then turned on another robber who was at the fireplace attempting to light a candle, and ran him through with his sword. The invaders attempted to regroup and seize the elder Creed, but McCraw and the younger Creed rescued him, cutting one on the head in the process, upon which three of the attackers dragged their stabbed comrade out of the house and fled. McCraw received two wounds in the scuffle.

The following morning, McCraw and the younger Creed found a wounded man outside sitting by the well. He had been stabbed, not by McCraw, but by the band of robbers; he had been with them, but when he refused to help break down the Creeds' door, they ran him through.

They took the wounded man inside, and learned that although he was wearing "a Countrymans Coat," he was a soldier in the King's American Regiment, a Loyalist corps composed of men enlisted in America to fight with the British army. They sent word to his regiment

4. Ira D. Gruber, ed., *John Peebles' American War: Diary of a Scottish Grenadier* (Mechanicsburg, PA: Stackpole Books, 1998), 316.

and two officers came. To the officers, the soldier confessed having participated in three other robberies, giving the names of several fellow soldiers of his regiment who had been involved including a sergeant and a corporal. Then he died.[5]

The fight with the marauding soldiers was Sergeant McCraw's last battle. In June, the grenadier battalion returned from South Carolina and encamped on Long Island. In consideration of McCraw's health issues, Captain Peebles deemed him eligible for discharge, noting in his diary on July 2, "presented Sergt. McCraw to the board of Physicians & got him Invalided he fought well last winter in suppressing a gang of Robbers at Jamaica, he killed one & wounded two, & recd two wounds." Being invalided meant that McCraw could return to Great Britain and apply for a pension. On July 4 Peebles wrote, "saw Sergt. McCraw & his wife & child told them to get ready to go home in the fleet, & gave the Boy 2 guineas." The money was quite a generous gesture, over a month's worth of a sergeant's shilling-a-day base pay, a tribute to the great esteem the officer had for the long-serving soldier and his family.[6]

Before he sailed, though, McCraw had one more piece of military business to attend. He testified at the court martial of nine King's American Regiment soldiers implicated in the string of robberies a few months before. Several Jamaica and Flushing residents also testified, the dead man's confession was read, the court deliberated and announced its verdict: three of the perpetrators were sentenced to death, the others to lashes.[7]

The trial ended on July 22, and the McCraw family sailed from New York soon after. The muster rolls of the 42nd Regiment of Foot indicate that he was discharged on October 1, but this is the date through which he was paid rather than the date that he left the regiment. In typical fashion, he was given several weeks' pay to subsist him on his journey back to Great Britain.[8] He went before the pension board in Chelsea outside of London on November 10.[9] Forty-six years old, after twenty-four years of service in the 42nd Regiment, the brave veteran of two wars was granted a pension to subsist him for the rest of his days.

5. Court martial of nine soldiers of the Kings American Regiment, WO 71-92, 227 – 238.
6. Ibid., 392-393.
7. Court martial of nine soldiers of the Kings American Regiment, WO 71-92, 227 – 238.
8. Gruber, *John Peebles' American War*, 393.
9. Out-pension admission book, WO 116/7, examinations for November 10, 1780.

Augustine Barrett, Escaped Prisoner of War, Pleads His Case

DON N. HAGIST

"About five weeks after he made his escape from Prospect hill," Augustine Barrett told the board of inquiry, "he was confined in the Prison Ship at Boston where he continued between 5 & six Months." Barrett was stating his case to a board of officers convened to settle claims of British soldiers owed paid and other entitlements. It was January 1783, the eighth year of a conflict in America that had seen many British soldiers displaced from their regiments for extended periods due to the fortunes of war.[1]

The most common form of displacement was captivity. From the day hostilities broke out on April 19, 1775, soldiers on both sides had been captured here and there, separated from their own ranks and swept up by their enemies, wounded and left on the battlefield, captured at sea, and taken in an assortment of other circumstances. Sometimes large numbers were captured at one time—two British regiments garrisoning forts along the route from Lake Champlain to Quebec in 1775, several thousand Continental and militia troops on Long Island in August 1776 and again at Fort Washington that November, and almost six thousand British and German soldiers at Saratoga in October 1777. Those captives were marched across Massachusetts to barracks on Prospect Hill (for the British soldiers) and Winter Hill (for the Germans) outside of Boston.

Among the tenants of the hastily-constructed barracks was Augustine Barrett, a twenty-four-year-old member of the 24th Regiment of Foot's light infantry company. Born in Leeds, England, he had been a bricklayer before enlisting in the regiment in 1771; his first name is recorded sometimes as Augustus, sometimes as Augustine. Barrett probably was enlisted by a recruiting party somewhere in England before

1. Proceedings of a Board of Enquiry held at New York, PRO 30/55/6884, The National Archives of Great Britain (TNA).

being sent to his regiment that was on service in Ireland. Soon after he joined, light infantry companies were added to the establishment of British regiments, and the 5' 6" tall Barrett was put into this organization of young, active men. The regiment's muster rolls record that he deserted with another soldier in December 1774 but returned less than a month later, an incident about which no further details are known.[2]

The 24th Regiment was part of the relief force sent to Quebec in 1776 to drive away besieging American forces. The following year, they formed part of Gen. John Burgoyne's army on the expedition that seized Fort Ticonderoga but stalled at Saratoga in its attempt to reach Albany. Interned and put into the barracks on Prospect Hill, Augustine Barrett had other ideas than waiting for an exchange that would never come. He made his escape on November 13, 1777, among the first of hundreds of British soldiers to do so.[3]

Three years later, on September 14, 1780, the brown-haired, dark-complexioned Barrett came into the British garrison in New York City with another escapee from Burgoyne's army, an Irish barber named James Cuffe from the 62nd Regiment of Foot. The two had pulled off a trick used by many captive British soldiers: they enlisted in an American regiment, then deserted when they were close to the front lines. In this case, it was Col. Henry Jackson's regiment, the 16th Massachusetts, posted in Bergen County, New Jersey. Given passes to go into the country to seek provisions in the area between Paramus and New Bridge, Barrett and Cuffe absconded on September 11 and were in New York three days later.[4] Both were put back into active service in the 22nd Regiment of Foot.[5]

Part of a British soldier's enlistment contract was the promise of pay and clothing in exchange for service to the army. As the war wound down, Barrett an others with similar experiences were allowed to claim the pay and clothing—or the value thereof—due to them for the time they were prisoners and escapees; they were, after all, still British soldiers during this time, and had risked life and limb to rejoin the fight rather than remaining in captivity. A board of inquiry convened in New York to hear their claims, and Barrett made his in January 1783. He told the court the date that he had left the 24th Regiment at Prospect Hill, that he had been put on a prison ship in Boston for half a year,

2. Muster rolls, 24th Regiment of Foot, WO 12/4059, TNA. British muster rolls record his enlistment and British service; his age, trade, place of birth, height, hair and skin color are recorded on several American rolls cited below.

3. Proceedings of a Board of Enquiry.

4. Intelligence from Deserters and Others, Emmett Collection, EM, C*, New York Public Library.

5. Muster rolls, 22nd Regiment of Foot, WO 12/3872, TNA.

and then enlisted in Colonel Jackson's regiment where he spent eighteen months before having an opportunity to desert. He explained that he was paid and clothed while in Continental service, but claimed pay for the remaining time as an escapee. His story was like many others the board heard, of escapes and recaptures, suffering on prison ships and in jails, working in the countryside to earn money while on the lam, making connections with sympathetic inhabitants who helped them get to British lines, and many enlistments into rebel service in hopes of finding an opportunity to desert.

What the board of inquiry did not know was that Barrett's story was only partly true. Returns for Col. David Henley's Additional Massachusetts Regiment record that Barrett enlisted in November 1777 within days of leaving the barracks at Prospect Hill.[6] One year later he was appointed corporal in the regiment. In 1779, the organization of the army changed, and enlisted in the 16th Massachusetts Regiment under Col. Henry Jackson. He deserted in August of that year, but returned that October, although he was reduced back to a private soldier for the infraction. A return from that month also indicates that had his "family in camp," suggesting that he had married an American woman after his escape. The rolls record his desertion from the regiment on September 14, 1780.[7]

Augustine Barrett clearly knew how to take advantage of a situation to suit his own needs. He left the bleak conditions of a prisoner of war barracks to enlist in Continental service, took some unauthorized time off from that service, married somewhere along the way, then abandoned the Continental army to rejoin the his former army. Six months after stating his case to the board of inquiry, on June 7, 1783, as the British army was reorganizing and downsizing after the end of hostilities, Barrett deserted one more time.[8] Perhaps he wanted to return to that wife he had in 1779. Or perhaps he sought some new opportunity. His fate has not been discovered.

6. Roll of the Officers of Col. David Henley's Regt & all of the men which has been Inlisted in said Regt, April 18, 1778, Revolutionary War Rolls, National Archives and Records Administration, Washington, DC. Dates of Barrett's enlistment are given as November 14 and November 20 on different rolls for the 16th Massachusetts Regiment. See: Descriptive list of the Non-Commission'd Officer and Privates, Deserters, from the late 16th Masstts. Regt., Revolutionary War Rolls; Muster roll of the 5th Company in the Battalion of Massachusetts Forces, in the Service of the United States, Commanded by Col. Hy. Jackson, Revolutionary War Rolls; Return of the Non Commiss'd Officers & Soldiers Inlisted for the War in the Cols Compy, Muster rolls, 16th Massachusetts Regiment, Henry Jackson Papers, Library of Congress.

7. *Massachusetts soldiers and sailors of the revolutionary war* (Boston: Wright and Potter Printing Co., 1896), 677.

8. Muster rolls, 22nd Regiment of Foot.

Bernard E. Griffiths: Trumpeter Barney of the Queen's Rangers, Chelsea Pensioner—and Freed Slave

TODD W. BRAISTED

The period of the American Revolution does not afford many accounts of individual rank and file soldiers' exploits, particularly on the side British side. The filing of some 80,000 pension applications in the United States makes it much easier to learn of a soldier's activities during the war, whether it be the mundane task of guard duty or the dangers of battle. There was no equivalent pension for British or Provincial veterans. The British method of reward was meant for long-serving or wounded soldiers of the army. Those so "recommended" received the benefit of the Chelsea Hospital in London, where a veteran could be an out-pensioner and simply receive a stipend living somewhere on his own, or an in-pensioner, residing at the hospital, complete with rations, clothing and lodging. Pensioners could also be called upon again for military service, typically in "invalid companies" serving in a fortress or garrison town somewhere in Great Britain, and typically for a limited duration.

In addition to soldiers of the established regiments of the British Army, Chelsea also admitted militia, new-raised British corps (regiments raised after the start of the war and disbanded at its conclusion) and in some cases Provincials (regiments raised in America consisting primarily of Loyalists). Between the years 1778 and 1784, some 10,834 soldiers were admitted as out-pensioners, the vast majority at the end of the war, when there was a general reduction in the size of the army.[1] Scattered among the pensioners were a small number of Provincial sol-

1. "Numbers of Men Admitted Out Pensioners of Chelsea Hospital" for the years 1778, 1779, 1780, 1781, 1782, 1783 and 1784. War Office, Class 245, Volume 2, Great Britain, The National Archives (TNA).

diers, including twenty-two men of the Queen's Rangers. Ten more of the Rangers were admitted over the next five years.

The Queen's Rangers was one of the first Provincial regiments raised in the New York City area upon the arrival of the British forces there in July 1776. The corps was initially commanded by Lt. Col. Robert Rogers, the famed ranger commander from the French and Indian War.[2] Rogers gathered a number of diverse characters together to raise the companies that would compose the corps, including Robert Cook, a Loyalist from Wrentham, Massachusetts who found himself (briefly) a prisoner of the rebels just three days after hostilities commenced at Lexington and Concord.[3]

The Provincial Forces were soon after put under the supervision of Inspector General Alexander Innes, former secretary to Lord William Campbell, the royal governor of South Carolina. Innes had the unenviable task of regulating what amounted to a small army of amateurs, both soldiers and officers, into something approaching the quality of the British Army. The Provincials were to be paid, armed, clothed, fed and disciplined in the same manner as the Regulars, which led Innes to observe on March 14, 1777: "Negroes, Mulattoes, Indians and Sailors, have been enlisted, shall they be discharged, and orders given none in future be admitted?" The answer was an unequivocal yes, commanding they "be discharged and none to be hereafter enlisted on any account."[4]

For the Queen's Rangers, this was just one in a series of events that completely altered the corps late that winter. Unhappy with Robert Rogers and the bulk of his officers, Alexander Innes, with the blessing of the commander in chief of the British Army in America, Sir William Howe, set about replacing Rogers and his officers.[5] Among those affected was Capt. Robert Cook, one of the ousted officers, and his men, apparently all black. The point may have been virtually moot, if a deserter's description from March 2, 1777 was accurate: "Captn. Cook's Company of Negroes are (all but three or four) dead."[6]

2. Rogers' warrant from Howe to raise the Queen's Rangers is undated, but appears to be from about August 1, 1776. Simcoe Family Papers, F 47-3-1-1, Correspondence 1768-1776, Archives of Ontario.

3. Petition of Robert Cook to the Commissioners for American Claims, Saint John, New Brunswick, March 17, 1786. Audit Office, Class 13, Volume 21, folios 120-121, TNA.

4. "Inspectors Report to the Adjutant General 14th March 1777." Headquarters Papers of the British Army in America, PRO 30/55/441, TNA.

5. Regimental Orders for the Queen's Rangers, March 30, 1777. Colonial Office, Class 5, Volume 98, page 87, TNA.

6. Deserter interview of William Fennell, March 2, 1777. George Washington Papers, Series 4, General Correspondence, 1697-1799, MSS 44693, Reel 040, Library of Congress.

The changes led to a series of new commanders for the Rangers, all British Army officers, culminating in October 1777 when John Graves Simcoe, an officer "with Confessed Ability, & very distinguished Honor" was appointed commandant.[7] Simcoe, only twenty-five years old when he took command, had arrived in America in 1775 as a lieutenant in the 35th Regiment before being promoted to a captaincy in the 40th Regiment. By the summer of 1778, the new British commander in chief had promoted him to lieutenant colonel, back-dating his commission to July 1, 1776 so as to give seniority over all other Provincial officers of that rank.[8] Simcoe was clearly a rising star in the British Army.

Under Simcoe's command and active leadership, the Queen's Rangers would see extensive service on the outposts of the British Army, particularly in Westchester County, New York and in New Jersey. The corps also grew and expanded in scope, adding a troop of cavalry along with light artillery and riflemen, making it a formidable corps of light infantry. The Rangers under Simcoe took part in such actions as the Battle of Monmouth and in repelling General Lord Stirling's attack on Staten Island; they set sail in April 1780 to take part in the final stages of the Siege of Charleston, South Carolina.[9]

Arriving towards the end of operations (the city surrendered to the British on May 12, 1780), there was little for Simcoe and his men to do but await further orders and explore the countryside. Simcoe wrote to his friend John André, "We hunt & barbecú in a grove of laurels to morrow, I wish business would permit you to partake of what I expect a novel Pleasure."[10] In addition to fine dining, Simcoe and his men secured several black slaves from the plantations and ranks of the enemy. "I understand Mrs. Elliot is to apply to the Comr. in Chief for four Negro boys now with the Queens Rangers, & I think it necessary to explain to this matter," Simcoe once again wrote to André, continuing

7. Sir Henry Clinton to Lord George Germain, New York, November 8, 1781. Simcoe Papers, 1774-1824, University of Michigan, William L. Clements Library (CL).
8. Orders by Adjutant General Francis Lord Rawdon, New York, July 20, 1778. Simcoe Papers, CL.
9. The initial expedition to take Charleston sailed from New York in late December 1779. The Queen's Rangers had been left behind on Staten Island primarily because Simcoe was a prisoner at the time, having been taken on the raid on Somerset Court House, New Jersey, October 26, 1779. He returned to the British in January 1780 and immediately solicited to have the corps join the troops to the southward. The Queen's Rangers were one of five battalions sent as a reinforcement on April 1, 1780. Simcoe to Deputy Adjutant General John André, New York, February 23, 1780. Sir Henry Clinton Papers, Volume 86, item 26, CL.
10. Simcoe to André, no date, c–May 1780. Sir Henry Clinton Papers, Volume 95, item 57, CL.

"The Boys are Taylors & Musicians, & are at this time clothed in the Rebel Artillery Uniform, which her Husband commanded."[11] This was no doubt a reference to the late Lt. Col. Barnard Elliott, commander of the 4th South Carolina Regiment, an artillery unit.

Simcoe found use in other former slaves as well, most notably for intelligence gathering. One unnamed young black was sent by Simcoe to André to be de-briefed; Simcoe wrote to André, the deputy adjutant general, "I send you a very intelligent Negro Boy, within the Circle of his knowledge—When you dismiss him I will be obliged to you to pass him to the Quarter House, as I mean to keep him."[12]

So who were these young former slaves collecting around Simcoe, and what role could they play in an organization like the Queen's Rangers that was officially barred from enlisting blacks as soldiers? The muster rolls of the regiment may provide some answers. In the Provincial Forces, muster rolls were made out once every sixty-one days and were created for the purpose of paying soldiers. The rolls themselves listed all the soldiers by company, noting things such as dates of enlistment and casualties (deaths, desertions and discharges) over that period. Regrettably, the muster period covering the return of the corps to New York, April 25 to June 24, 1780, does not appear to exist. The one immediately after, however, seems to include some of the men alluded to by Simcoe. While blacks were not allowed to bear arms, some few did serve in other capacities: principally as pioneers (unarmed military laborers) and as drummers or musicians. Each company of men had at least one drummer, often two, with perhaps some fifers. Their job was to communicate signals to the troops in camp, on the march and in battle. Comparing the rolls from before and after the siege, new drummers appear on the rolls with names that suggest they may be among the men Simcoe mentioned to André.

One new drummer appeared in Capt. John Saunders' company, listed as "John Carolina." Other than an annotation that he was born in America, no personal information was listed.[13] Capt. McCrea's company had two new drummers, both Americans, Richard Lockerman and Barney Hartley.[14] The company commanded by Capt. James Kerr had one as well, but being absent sick and not mustered, was listed sim-

11. Simcoe to André, no date, c–May 1780. Sir Henry Clinton Papers, Volume 95, item 56., CL.
12. Simcoe to André, no date, c–May 1780. Sir Henry Clinton Papers, Volume 95, item 58, CL.
13. Muster Roll of Captain John Saunders' Company, June 24 to August 24, 1780. RG 8, "C" Series, Volume 1863, page 35, Library and Archives Canada. Hereafter cited as LAC.
14. Muster Roll of Capt. Robert McCrea's Company, June 24 to August 24, 1780. RG 8, "C" Series, Volume 1863, page 39, LAC.

ply as "A Black Musician Name Not remembered."[15] Andrew Ellis, another American-born drummer, was listed in Capt. Stair Agnew's company.[16] Perhaps most interesting was the Highland Company under Capt. John Mackay, who added a hornsman or "clarinet" by the name of Sampson.[17] Were all these drummers black? Perhaps, perhaps not. They do appear to have included the captured slaves of the Ellis family, not all of whom worked out in their new capacity. Captain Kerr eventually remembered that his drummer's name was Hector Young, "A Black boy intended for the Musick; but found unfit & taken from the Strength 16 Sept. 1780." Were these all of them? Apparently not.

A 1789 certificate from Lieutenant Colonel Simcoe sheds light on the subject, but also some confusion: "That the negroes Barney and Andrew served as Bugle Horns in the Queen's Rangers, from the Siege of Charlestown to the disbanding of that Corps. That Andrew is in Nova Scotia & Barney in London & upon Col. Simcoe's Enquiry of him, he said, that both Andrew & himself belonged to Mr. [John] Izard, who at the Time they joined the Queen's Rangers, was aid du Camp to the Rebel General [Isaac] Huger."[18] Andrew was indeed Andrew Ellis, who at the end of the war was a trumpeter in Capt. David Shank's troop of light dragoons in the Queen's Rangers.[19] The corps had undergone a major expansion starting in 1780, with new troops of light dragoons (cavalry) being raised by Captains John Saunders, David Shank, and Thomas Ives Cooke; later they added a troop of hussars formerly commanded by Capt. Frederick de Diemar.[20] If what Simcoe stated was accurate, that Ellis and Barney had been the property of John Izard and not the Elliotts, they could not have been among the four boys mentioned to André as being used as musicians. And who was Barney?

The certificate referenced above, dated February 25, 1789, appears to coincide with a request made by Simcoe to the War Office on March 20 following. The Queen's Rangers, along with four other Provincial

15. Muster Roll of Capt. James Kerr's Company, June 25 to August 24, 1780. RG 8, "C" Series, Volume 1863, page 32, LAC.

16. Muster Roll of Capt. Stair Agnew's Company, June 24 to August 24, 1780. RG 8, "C' Series, Volume 1863, page 31, LAC.

17. Muster Roll of Capt. John Mackay's Company, August 24, 1780. RG 8, "C' Series, Volume 1863, page 42, LAC.

18. "Certificate of Col. Simcoe dated 25th Feby. 1789." Audit Office, Class 13, Volume 5, folio 30, TNA.

19. Muster Roll of Capt. David Shank's Troop, Camp near Newtown, September 2, 1783. War Office, Class 12, Volume 11035, TNA.

20. Queen's Rangers Abstract of Pay, April 25 to June 24, 1781. RG 8, "C" Series, Volume 1864, page 17, LAC.

battalions, were made regular regiments of the British Army on December 25, 1782, so there was no question that, as British soldiers, men of the Queen's Rangers were eligible for Chelsea pensions provided they met the accepted criteria.[21]

Determining the identity of Barney took some sleuthing, aided by Simcoe's letter to the War Office recommending the young black trumpeter:

> Sir,
>
> B E Griffiths has applied to me for his Discharge from the Queens Rangers. The Particulars of his Situation I take the Liberty of Submitting to you, & entreating the Protection of the War Office on his behalf.
>
> He joined the Queens Rangers at The Siege of Charles Town, & was very useful as a Guide; He served as a Dragoon & was frequently distinguished for his Bravery & Activity—in particular at the action near Spencer's Ordinary, by his presence of mind when sentinel, He was principally concerned in betraying the Enemy into an unfavourable [situation], & in the consequent Charge of Cavalry was distinguished by Fighting hand to hand with a French Officer who commanded a Squadron of the Enemy & taking him Prisoner. When the Cavalry afterwards charged the Rebel Infantry, He by his gallantry preserved the Life of his Captain & was severely wounded. His Activity had made him so remarkable That I personally interfered with The Baron Steuben at the Surrender of York Town to obtain that He might not risk the Hazard of being sent Prisoner into the Country—& had I been with The Regiment when it was disbanded, I should have felt it my Duty to have recommended him as a proper Object for his Majesty's Bounty of Chelsea, not having that Power, I humbly hope that you will direct him to be examined; in particular, as being a Loyal Negro, He has no other means of reaping the Protection his Services in The Opinion of Every Officer of the Corps as well as mine most amply merit.
>
> I have the honor to be Sir, your most obt.
>
> & most Humble St.
>
> J G Simcoe
>
> Lt. Coll. Comdt. (late) Q Rangers[22]

21. "Establishment of the Queen's Rangers Commanded by Lieut. Colonel Simcoe, consisting of Five Troops of Dragoons, and Eleven Companies of Foot, from 25th December 1782 inclusive." Headquarters Papers of the British Army in America, PRO 30/55/6547, TNA.
22. Simcoe to Secretary at War George Yonge, March 20, 1789. War Office, Class 121, Volume 6, No. 420, TNA.

By Simcoe's statement above, this young man had clearly joined the Rangers at the Siege of Charleston, which coincides nicely with his correspondence with André and certificate from the previous month. But was "B E Griffiths" actually Barney? Simcoe himself provided the answer, by writing both this certificate and his book, *A Journal of the Operations of a Partizan Corps called the Queen's Rangers*, in which he described in detail the terrific fighting that took place on June 26, 1781 at the Battle of Spencer's Ordinary, Virginia. If the actions mentioned in Simcoe's letter to the War Office were indeed that conspicuous, the accounts should likewise be in his published account of the battle. And they were.

While Simcoe's narrative of the battle is quite lengthy, as the bloody action that day was quite complicated, it is necessary here to only cover the relevant passages. At this point in the war, the Queen's Rangers were a part of the army serving under Lieutenant General Lord Cornwallis, which was just then occupying Williamsburg, Virginia. The Queen's Rangers, along with a small number of New York Volunteers, North Carolinians and Hessian Jägers, had lagged behind the main army to collect some cattle, giving the main Continental force in Virginia under Maj. Gen. the Marquis de Lafayette an opportunity to attack:

> The highland Company of the Queen's Rangers had been posted in the wood, by the side of the road, as a piquet: a shot or two from their sentinels gave an alarm, and Lt. Col. Simcoe gallopping across the field, towards the wood, saw Capt. Shank in pursuit of the enemy's cavalry. They had passed through the fences which had been pulled down, as before-mentioned, so that, unperceived by the Highlanders, they arrived at Lee's farm, in pursuit of the people who were collecting the cattle. Trumpeter Barney, who had been stationed as a vidette, gave the alarm, and gallopped off so as not to lead the enemy directly to where the cavalry were collecting their forage and watering, and, with great address, got to them unperceived by the enemy, calling out "draw your swords Rangers, the rebels are coming." Capt. Shank, who was at Lee's farm waiting the return of the troops with their forage, in order to post them, immediately joined, and led them to the charge on the enemy's flank, which was somewhat exposed, while some of them were engaged in securing the bat-horses at the back of Lee's farm: he broke them entirely. Serjeant Wright dashed Major Macpherson, who commanded them, from his horse, but, leaving him in pursuit of others, that officer crept into a swamp, lay there unperceived during the action, and when it was over got off. Trumpeter Barney dismounted and took a French officer, who commanded one of the divisions. The enemy's cavalry were so to-

> tally scattered, that they appeared no more: many of them were dismounted, and the whole would have been taken, had not a heavy fire out of the wood, from whence the Highland company were now driven, protected them . . . Cornet Jones, who led the first division of cavalry, was unfortunately killed: he was an active, sensible, promising officer. The mounted riflemen of the Queen's Rangers charged with Capt. Shank: the gallant Sergeant M'Pherson, who led them, was mortally wounded. Two of the men of this detachment were carried away by their impetuosity so far as to pass beyond the enemy, and their horses were killed: they, however, secreted themselves in the wood under some fallen logs, and, when the enemy fled from that spot, they returned in safety to the corps. By a mistake, scarcely avoidable in the tumult of action, Capt. Shank was not supported, as was intended, by the whole of his cavalry, by which fewer prisoners were taken than might have been: that valuable officer was in the most imminent danger, in fighting his way back through the enemy, who fired upon him, and wounded the Trumpeter Barney and killed some of the huzzars, who attended him.[23]

Without doubt, the person that Simcoe had recommended to the War Office, B E Griffiths, was the same "Trumpeter Barney" described in Simcoe's *Journal.* Denied an opportunity to serve as a full-fledged trooper, the young liberated slave capitalized on what opportunity he had by enabling his troop to escape a situation where they were not in a proper fighting posture, capturing an enemy cavalry officer of the 1st Light Dragoons,[24] and saving the life of his troop's commander, Capt. David Shank.[25]

Did Trumpeter Barney get his pension? Yes indeed. The Chelsea Admission Book for August 5, 1789 records one Barnard E. Griffiths (listed in an earlier entry as "a negro") admitted to Chelsea on the recommendation of a letter from the Secretary at War. It further added that Griffiths was twenty-six years old in 1789, was a laborer from

23. John Graves Simcoe, *Simcoe's Military Journal: Journal of the Operations of a Partizan Corps called the Queen's Rangers* (New York: Bartlett and Welford, 1844), 226-237.

24. According to Heitman, a cavalry officer named "Lieutenant Bresco" was captured at Spencer's Ordinary. The 1st Light Dragoons under Major Call were the cavalry in the battle for Lafayette. "Return of the killed, wounded, and missing of the Light Corps under Col. Butler in the action of the 26th June 1781," Papers of the Continental Congress, M247, reel 176, i156, page 169, National Archives and Records Administration. Thank you to Dr. Robert Selig for this reference. See also Francis B. Heitman, *Historical Register of Officers of the Continental Army during the War of the Revolution* (Washington, DC: Rare Book Shop Publishing, 1914), 118.

25. Trumpeter "Black Barney" was listed on the muster roll of Capt. David Shank's Troop of the Queen's Rangers at the time of the battle. RG 8, "C' Series, Volume 1864, page 21, LAC.

Charleston, South Carolina, and had been wounded. The one incorrect detail listed, not uncommon in the Chelsea records, was years of service, given as ten.[26] This may have stemmed from the fact that Barney had actually accompanied Simcoe back to England in November 1781 on board the *Swallow* packet and had never officially received a discharge, although he no doubt stopped receiving pay when the corps was disbanded on October 10, 1783.[27]

While a number of blacks served as drummers, fifers, trumpeters and pioneers in different Provincial units, no other received the sort of commendation written by their commanding officer as Barney did from Simcoe. What other acts of heroism may have taken place, but were not been passed down to us in the annals of history?

26. Chelsea Admission Book entry for August 5, 1789. War Office, Class 116, Volume 9, TNA.

27. *Diary of Frederick Mackenzie* (Cambridge, MA: Harvard University Press, 1930), 2: 694. Thanks to Lt. Col. Don Londahl-Smidt, USAF (ret) for this reference.

Revisiting Bernard E. Griffiths: Former Slave, Queen's Ranger, and "Son of Africa"

STEPHEN BRUMWELL

In a recent article, Todd Braisted reconstructed the remarkable story of a black Loyalist soldier, "Trumpeter Barney" of the Queen's Rangers.[1] Through meticulous archival work, Braisted established that Barney, a runaway slave who joined the British at the siege of Charleston, South Carolina in 1780, was the same man as Barnard E. Griffiths, who was examined in London at the Royal Hospital, Chelsea on August 5, 1789, to establish whether he qualified for an army pension.[2]

That identification rested upon a range of evidence, but especially telling was a fulsome testimonial on behalf of Griffiths that the former lieutenant-colonel of the Queen's Rangers, John Graves Simcoe, wrote to Britain's Secretary-at-War, Sir George Yonge, on March 20, 1789.[3] Simcoe's letter highlighted the exploits of "B. E. Griffiths" during the fierce skirmish at Spencer's Ordinary, Virginia, on June 26, 1781. By comparing it with the detailed account of the same episode that Simcoe published in his 1787 *Journal of the Operations of the Queen's Rangers*, which praised the vigilance and courage of "Trumpeter Barney", Braisted was able to conclude that Barney was Griffiths.[4]

As a commendation written by an officer on behalf of a black Loyalist fighter, Simcoe's letter is a unique survival. Intriguingly, the his-

1. Todd W. Braisted, "Bernard E. Griffiths: Trumpeter Barney of the Queen's Rangers, Chelsea Pensioner - and Freed Slave," Journal of the American Revolution, February 21, 2019.
2. WO 116/9, The National Archives (TNA).
3. WO 121/6/420 (filed under Board of August 5, 1789), TNA.
4. John Graves Simcoe, *A Journal of the Operations of the Queen's Rangers* (Exeter: privately published, 1787), 160-165.

torical Simcoe's unequivocal support for a former slave was echoed by a story-line in the popular AMC television series *TURN: Washington's Spies*. There, a heavily-fictionalised Simcoe (played with villainous relish by Samuel Roukin) not only grants freedom to a black Queen's Ranger, Jordan (Aldis Hodge), but promotes him to his second-in-command.

Of course, *TURN* is primarily entertainment, not intended as a faithful account of events. But by depicting Simcoe as sympathetic to the plight of slaves, it undoubtedly reflects historical reality. In 1790, during his brief stint as Member of Parliament for the Cornish "rotten borough" of St. Mawes, Simcoe spoke in the House of Commons against Britain's involvement in the slave trade. Three years later, as lieutenant-governor of the province of Upper Canada, he was responsible for introducing a bill banning the importation of slaves into that territory, thereby effectively ensuring that slavery would have no future there.[5]

Simcoe's marked antipathy towards the enslavement of Africans helps to explain his intervention on behalf of his former trumpeter in 1789. It also provides context for a postscript to Braisted's article which reveals how the teenaged Barney's personal fight for freedom during the American Revolutionary War paved the way for his subsequent involvement in the wider struggle to liberate many thousands of others, by campaigning to end slavery itself.

As his 1789 testimonial explained, when the Queen's Rangers were captured with the forces of Lord Charles Cornwallis at Yorktown in October 1781, Simcoe had gone to great lengths to ensure that his trumpeter wouldn't risk being reclaimed as "property" by the victorious Rebels. In his published *Journal*, Simcoe recounted how the sloop HMS *Bonnetta*, which the surrender terms left at the disposal of Cornwallis, was used to smuggle out "as many of the Rangers, and of other corps, [who were] deserters from the enemy, as she could possibly hold." Although *Bonnetta*'s ship's muster for that voyage is not among those now held in the United Kingdom National Archives, given the acute danger he faced, it's highly likely that Barney went aboard with Simcoe. The *Bonnetta* arrived in New York on November 1, 1781; some two weeks later, when the convalescent Simcoe sailed on leave to England aboard the packet *Swallow*, Barney may have gone too.[6]

5. Robin W. Winks, *The Blacks in Canada: A History* (Montreal and New Haven: McGill-Queen's University Press and Yale University Press, 1971), 96-99.

6. Simcoe, *Journal*, 180. See also William H. W. Sabine, ed., *Historical Memoirs from 26 August 1778 to 12 November 1783 of William Smith* (New York: New York Times and Arno Press, 1971), 462-463. I am very grateful to Todd Braisted for sharing information regarding the *Bonnetta's* musters.

Little is known of Barney's life between late 1781 and February 1789, when Simcoe wrote a certificate concerning him and another black Queen's Ranger, Andrew Ellis, for consideration by the Loyalist Claims Commission. This confirms that while Ellis—like many other black Loyalists—had emigrated to Britain's Canadian territory of Nova Scotia, Barney was living in London.[7]

In the capital, Barney became part of an established black community which had increased dramatically owing to an influx of Loyalists refugees at the close of the Revolutionary War. Young Barney would have mingled with other freed slaves, including men who are known to have slipped out of Yorktown on the *Bonnetta*. One of them, "Wat," or Walter Harris, informed the Loyalist Claims Commission that he'd been a house slave of Mrs. Mary Boyd of Westover, Virginia. Taken on as a guide by the renegade Brig. Gen. Benedict Arnold in 1781, Harris subsequently accompanied Cornwallis to Yorktown. He'd spent about a year in New York before sailing to England.[8]

Another black Loyalist, Thomas Johnston, must have known Barney even before that cramped voyage aboard the *Bonnetta*. In his petition to the Loyalist Commissioners, Johnston said he too was born in Charleston, South Carolina, although to free parents. By a remarkable coincidence, Johnston was a servant in the family of John Izard; according to Simcoe's certificate of February 1789, Barney maintained that both he and Andrew Ellis had likewise "belonged to Mr Izard." While on his "Master's business" Johnston had been pressed into service by the British Army. Enrolled as a guide to Col. Banastre Tarleton's British Legion, he was instrumental in the surprise of Lt. Col. William Washington's dragoons at Monck's Corner in April 1780. A marked man when Yorktown fell, Johnston escaped retribution when he was "privately sent on board the Bonetta sloop to New York, by Lord Cornwallis's directions."[9]

As Johnston testified in July 1786, he had come to England "at the peace, and since subsisted poorly." His hard experience reflected reality for many of London's black Loyalists, whose arrival had coincided with a post-war economic slump and a glut of labour resulting from the rapid demobilisation of Britain's army and navy. Growing concern about the plight of the "Black Poor"—and the social problems to which they were

7. "Certificate of Col. Simcoe dated 25th Feby 1789", AO 13/5, fol. 30, TNA.

8. For Harris, see Cassandra Pybus, *Epic Journeys of Freedom: Runaway Slaves of the American Revolution and their Global Quest for Liberty* (Boston: Beacon Press, 2006), 26, 44, 63, 78, 212.

9. AO 13/70B part 1, fols. 301-302, TNA.

believed to contribute—lay behind an initiative to ship them off to establish a settlement in Sierra Leone, West Africa.[10]

Although not closely involved with the Sierra Leone scheme, in 1786 the leading anti-slavery campaigner Granville Sharp had issued a pamphlet suggesting "Temporary Regulations" for the proposed settlement. An undated letter to Sharp, which is associated with this period, was signed by twelve ex-slaves who wished to express their sincere gratitude for his championship of the abolitionist cause. They included "Bernard Elliott." Was this Barney, AKA Barnard (or Bernard) Elliott Griffiths?[11]

Here, it is appropriate to pause and consider when, and why, the man formerly known simply as "Barney" might have assumed the name under which he appeared before the Chelsea commissioners in August 1789. Throughout the era of slavery in the British Empire and its former American colonies, slaves were often given fanciful Christian names inspired by ancient Rome—a society that was itself built upon unfree labour. For example, "Nero," "Caesar," "Pompey" and "Scipio" all feature in the manuscript "Book of Negroes" compiled at British headquarters in New York city in 1783. This lists 3000 men, women and children who'd sought sanctuary with the Crown and were inspected between April 26 and November 30 before embarking for Nova Scotia. The same document also highlights another common practice, by which slaves were allotted their owner's family name. For example, "Prince Wigfall," aged twenty-five, was "formerly slave to Mr Wigfall" of Charleston, and, in a scenario that mirrors Barney's own experience, "left him at ye siege of that place."[12]

In his article, Todd Braisted considered the possibility that Barney might have been one of four former slaves of Lt. Col. Barnard Elliott of the South Carolina artillery, enlisted by the Queen's Rangers in 1780.

10. On London's "Black Poor" and the genesis of the Sierra Leone scheme see Mary Beth Norton, "The Fate of Some Black Loyalists of the American Revolution," *Journal of Negro History*, 58, no 4 (October 1973), 402-426; and Douglas R Egerton, *Death or Liberty: African Americans and Revolutionary America* (New York: Oxford University Press, 2009), 209-212.

11. Originally published in Prince Hoare, *Memoirs of Granville Sharp* (2 vols., London: Henry Colburn & Co, 1828), 2: 114-115, and given in Folarin Shyllon, *Black People in Britain 1553-1833* (Oxford: Oxford University Press, 1977), Appendix II, "Letters of Sons of Africa," 266.

12. PRO 30/55/100, doc. 10427, TNA (for "Prince Wigfall" see pp. 31-32). For a discussion of this important source, see James W. St. G. Walker, *The Black Loyalists: The search for a Promised Land in Nova Scotia and Sierra Leone 1783-1870* (New York: Africana Publishing Company, 1976), 11-12.

This scenario is certainly suggestive of a patriarchal link with "Bernard Elliott." But as Braisted pointed out, when Simcoe wrote his certificate in February 1789, he reported Barney's statement that both he and Andrew Ellis had been the property of John Izard.

There's another possible explanation for the name change. Once free, it was common for former slaves to shed the names previously imposed upon them, and adopt others that better expressed their newfound identity. Among the leaders of London's "Black Poor" in the 1780s was Granville Sharp's protégé, Abraham Elliot Griffiths. As a fellow member of London's close-knit black population, it's hard to conceive that Barney would not have been aware of such a conspicuous and respected figure. It's possible that he took his surname. In 1787, when the poorly-planned expedition to Sierra Leone finally sailed, Abraham Elliot Griffiths went with it; so did Barney's old shipmates from the *Bonnetta*, Walter Harris and Thomas Johnston. There's no evidence that Barney (however he now styled himself) sailed too.[13]

While "Bernard Elliott" is not among them, four of the signatures on the undated letter to Sharp mentioned above also appear on a lengthier "Address of Thanks" dated December 15, 1787, and sent to him by the "Sons of Africa." This was the title adopted by a London-based group of black activists who became vocal in the movement that eventually convinced Parliament to abolish the slave trade within the British Empire in 1807. Key members included Ottobah Cugoano, a servant and friend of the prominent society artist Richard Cosway and author of the anti-slavery tract *Thoughts and Sentiments on the Evil and Wretched Traffic,* and Gustavus Vassa, better known by his African name of Olaudah Equiano. His lively autobiography, *The Interesting Narrative of the Life of Olaudah Equiano,* became an influential best-seller, and a powerful indictment of slavery. Subscribers to the first edition, published in March 1789, included not only "Richard Cosway Esq.," but also "Colonel Simcoe."[14]

In the same month that Equiano's book emerged, Simcoe wrote his detailed testimonial on behalf of "B. E. Griffiths." Sir George Yonge promptly forwarded it to the Commissioners of Chelsea Hospital, along with a covering letter of his own. This revealed that the case of the black veteran had come to the sympathetic attention of a man who never ceased to lament the loss of Britain's prized American colonies, King George III. Sir George wrote:

13. Pybus, *Epic Journeys of Freedom,* 211-212. See also Norton, "Fate of Some Black Loyalists", 417.

14. *The Interesting Narrative of the Life of Olaudah Equiano, or Gustavas Vassa, the African* (London, 1789).

> I have the honor to send you enclosed a Letter from Lieut Col John Graves Simcoe, who commanded a Corps of Provincials ... during the late War in North America stating the Services & Gallant behaviour of B. E. Griffiths, a negroe Man, who joined the said Corps at the siege of Charles Town, and to acq[uain]t you that H. M. having been moved on behalf of this Man, has been graciously pleased to permit that he shall be examined by you, & be placed on the Out Pension of Chelsea Hospital at the usual allowance, if found a proper object, notwithstanding he may not be entitled to this indulgence by the Rules of the Board, not having been regularly recommended for that Bounty.[15]

To qualify for the "Royal Bounty of Chelsea," soldiers disabled by wounds or long service, or who'd served for a minimum of twenty years, needed to present a formal recommendation from their commanding officer, written at the time of their discharge from the Army. Griffiths had been badly wounded at Spencer's Ordinary, but as he was not "recommended" when he left the Queen's Rangers, Simcoe's letter sought to make amends.

Although Chelsea Hospital could accommodate about 500 especially-deserving veterans, the vast majority of men who "passed the board" had to fare for themselves on the "out-pension" of five pence per day.[16] In Griffiths's case, however, there was an alternative: on the same day that Sir George wrote to the Chelsea commissioners, he also sent a shorter note to Capt. Robert McCrea of the Invalids, to acquaint him that he had "authorised the Chelsea Board to examine B. E. Griffiths, late of Lieut-Colo. Commandt. Simcoe's Corps of Provincials for the purpose of getting him the Out Pension, or being sent to Garrison Duty as the Board may think fit."[17]

When the twenty-six-year-old Griffiths came before them the Chelsea Commissioners clearly considered that he was hale enough to serve in the Invalids—companies of veterans deemed unfit for field duty, but still capable of manning static strongpoints. His entry on the Hospital's register includes the annotation "D of G"—the abbreviation for "Duty of Garrison."[18]

15. Yonge to the Right Honourable the Lords and others Commissioners for the affairs of Chelsea Hospital, War Office, March 25, 1789, in WO 4/137, pp. 427-28, TNA.

16. For an overview of the Chelsea Pensioners in the second half of the eighteenth century, see Stephen Brumwell, "Home from the Wars," *History Today*, 52, no 3 (March, 2002), 41-47.

17. Yonge to Captain McCreal [McCrea] of the Invalids, March 25, 1789, in WO/4/137, p. 425, TNA.

18. WO/116/9, TNA.

Previously based on the Channel Island of Guernsey, since March 12, 1789 McCrea had captained one of the two invalid companies at Chester, the fortified town on England's border with Wales where the Roman army had established a legionary fortress some 1700 years before.[19] According to the muster roll for McCrea's company dated at Chester on September 8, 1789, private "Barnard E. Griffith" was "appointed" on May 25, 1789—back-dated from his Chelsea appearance. But the next muster, for May 29, 1790 shows "Bern Elliott Griffiths" on "furlough [by his] Captains Leave." On September 5, he was still on furlough with McCrea's permission. The muster for May 1, 1791 records that Griffiths was "discharged" on December 24, 1790.[20]

From this evidence, if Griffiths even joined the Invalids, his time with them was brief. But if Griffiths wasn't patrolling the ancient ramparts of Chester, where was he? The answer reinforces the impression already clear from Todd Braisted's article that he was a singularly determined young man, and helps to explain why Simcoe took such a strong interest in his fate.

On April 25, 1789, *The Diary; or Woodfall's Register* published a letter from the Sons of Africa, thanking William Dickson, formerly private secretary to the governor of Barbados, for his book *Letters on Slavery*, which exposed "the horrid cruelties practised on the poor sable people in the West Indies, to the disgrace of Christianity." The nine signatories included Olaudah Equiano and Ottobah Cugoano, and, last of all, "Bernard Elliot Griffiths." This, surely, was the man previously known as "Trumpeter Barney."[21]

Unlike the celebrated Equiano, Griffiths left no coherent "Interesting Narrative" of his experiences, and as yet, nothing more is known about him after Christmas Eve 1790. But from the evidence that can be pieced together, his journey from slavery to freedom was scarcely less extraordinary.

19. *Army List*, 1789, 159.
20. Musters of the Invalids, Chester 1783-1802, WO/12/11600, TNA.
21. Given in Shyllon, *Black People in Britain*, Appendix II, 271-72.

Major James Wemyss: Second Most Hated British Officer in the South

RANDY A. PURVIS

No British officer was more reviled by Patriots in the South during the American Revolution than Lt. Col. Banastre Tarleton. Based partly on fact and partly on myth, Tarleton's name became synonymous with brutality to many Americans. Another British officer, although less infamous, earned a similar reputation for his actions in South Carolina in 1780. Maj. James Wemyss is most often remembered for the expedition that he led through the Peedee in September 1780. Dr. Robert Bass, who authored biographies on Francis Marion, Thomas Sumter and Banastre Tarleton, referred to Major Wemyss as "a demon" and declared that "Wemyss became the second most hated man in the British army."[1] Walter Edgar, a former Professor of History at The University of South Carolina and author of *Partisans and Redcoats: The Southern Conflict That Turned the Tide of the American Revolution,* echoed the sentiments of Dr. Bass, declaring that Wemyss, after Tarleton, was the most despised British officer in South Carolina.[2]

The opinion that James Wemyss was a ruthless officer is not merely that of modern era historians, but one also shared by his contemporaries. In a letter from American Brig. Gen. H.W. Harrington to British Lt. Col. George Turnbull, Harrington refers to the British major's raid into the region and cites the "wanton cruelties committed on Peedee by Major Wemyss" and adds that "Major Wemyss here played the petty tyrant."[3] Who was James Wemyss? Was he a rogue of-

1. Robert D. Bass, *The Green Dragoon: The Lives of Banastre Tarleton and Mary Robinson* (Columbia, S.C.: Sandlapper Press, 1973), 105.
2. Walter Edgar, *Partisans and Redcoats: The Southern Conflict That Turned the Tide of the American Revolution* (New York: Perennial, 2003), 61.
3. Harrington to Turnbull, 12th November 1780. Ian Saberton, Editor, *The Cornwallis Papers: The Campaigns of 1780 and 1781 in The Southern Theatre of the American Revolutionary War Volume III* (East Sussex. Naval and Military Press, 2010), 162.

ficer intent on unleashing his own brand of barbarism on the inhabitants of South Carolina who supported the patriot cause or was he simply following orders from his superior officers?

James Wemyss was born in Edinburgh, Scotland in 1748. His military career began at an early age when he was commissioned an ensign in the British Army at the age of seventeen. He had served nine years in the army before arriving in Boston in 1775 as a captain in the 40th Regiment of Foot. Wemyss served in several staff positions and took part in the British campaign on Long Island, New York. In 1777, he was promoted to major and given the command of the Queen's Rangers, a unit more closely associated with his successor, Lt. Col. John Simcoe. He led the Rangers for a little over five months and the unit distinguished itself at the battle Brandywine in September and at the battle of Germantown the following month, where Wemyss was slightly wounded. Under his command, the Rangers earned a reputation for gallantry, as a notice printed in *The Pennsylvania Ledger* of December 3, 1777 proclaimed: "No regiment in the army has gained more honour this campaign than Major Wemys's [*sic*] (or the Queens) Rangers: they have been engaged in every principal service, and behaved nobly, indeed most of the officers have been wounded since we took the field in Philadelphia."[4]

In 1778, Wemyss became a major of the 63rd Foot and the following year his regiment sailed with Sir Henry Clinton's expedition to South Carolina. After the surrender of the American army at Charleston, he was ordered to march part of the 63rd Regiment sixty miles up the coast to Georgetown to bring order to the Williamsburg district and to help form a regiment of Loyalist militia. Wemyss found few men worthy of leading the Loyalist cause in the surrounding area. Patriot sympathies in the region were strong and their growing militia discouraged the Tories from turning out in sufficient numbers.

While in Georgetown, Wemyss wrote a letter to Gen. Charles Cornwallis in which he referred to the "principal inhabitants" as the most violent and persecuting rebels that now professed a desire to become good subjects only to save their estates.[5] He thought that their motives were suspect and they should be discouraged from being allowed to take an oath of loyalty and suggested more serious punishment for the leaders of the community. He proposed that the paroles of ten

4. J.G. Simcoe, *Simcoe's Military Journal: A History of the Operations of a Partisan Corps., called The Queen's Rangers* (Cranbury, NJ: Scholar's Bookshelf, 2005), 319.

5. Wemyss to Cornwallis, 11th July 1780. Ian Saberton, Editor, *The Cornwallis Papers The Campaigns of 1780 and 1781 in The Southern Theatre of the American Revolutionary War Volume I* (East Sussex. Naval and Military Press, 2010), 304.

or twelve of these men should be altered and instead of being allowed to remain on their estates, they should be sent to the islands. Wemyss believed that this action would encourage those loyal to the Crown to "take every method of carrying on the purposes of the Government."[6]

In his reply to Wemyss, Cornwallis agreed with his proposal: "I would have you by all means seize all violent and persecuting rebels and send them directly on parole to the islands unless there are a few, very notorious for acts of cruelty, who might be sent under a guard of militia to the Provost's at Charleston."[7] Cornwallis added harsher terms: "All those who are thought by our friends worthy to be trusted with arms will of course take the oaths of allegiance on being admitted into the militia. The remainder must be disarmed and put on parole to remain at home, with the most solemn assurance that if they break their parole by committing any act of hostility, they shall instantly be hanged without any form of trial farther than proving the identity of the person."[8]

After being in Georgetown for ten days, Wemyss informed Cornwallis that the longer he remained in the region, the more he discovered "the disaffection of the people" and added "the motions of the rebells [sic] on the frontier will of course add to their audacity."[9] Cornwallis began to have his doubts about Wemyss's mission to Georgetown. He informed the major, "there can be no hopes of peace and quiet untill [sic] we can advance, nor can you in the present situation of things do any good towards forming a militia at Georgetown. I cannot therefore approve of you making any longer stay there."[10] He ordered Wemyss to march his men to the High Hills of Santee.

Wemyss and the 63rd Regiment did not remain in their new position long. On August 16, the British army under Cornwallis defeated the American army under the command of Gen. Horatio Gates at Camden. In the wake of the American defeat, many Americans were taken prisoner. Under the escort of a small force of British and Provincial troops, 150 of those prisoners were marched to Charleston. At Thomas Sumter's old home at Great Savannah near Nelson's Ferry, Patriot partisans under the command of Francis Marion attacked the column as they camped for the night. The Patriots killed or captured twenty-two British troops and set the American prisoners free.

The Patriot victory at Nelson's Ferry alarmed Cornwallis, raising concerns that his supply lines were vulnerable to attack. He ordered

6. Ibid.

7. Saberton, *The Cornwallis Papers. Volume I*, 305.

8. Ibid.

9. Saberton, *The Cornwallis Papers Volume I*, 310.

10. Saberton, *The Cornwallis Papers Volume I*, 320.

Wemyss to march the 63rd Regiment into the region between the Santee and Peedee rivers and sweep the area of enemy resistance. Wemyss led his men to Kingstree, where they were joined by Provincial troops and Tory militia. From Kingstree, they began their march through the Peedee toward Cheraw, systematically burning and pillaging the homes of suspected Patriot sympathizers.

Much of what is known of Wemyss's raid comes from William Dobein James, who wrote a biography of Francis Marion entitled *Swamp Fox: General Francis Marion And His Guerilla Fighters Of The American Revolution.* James joined Marion's militia at the age of fifteen and was the son of one of Marion's most trusted subordinate officers, Maj. John James. William James experienced the wrath of Wemyss's expedition firsthand. During the raid, British and Loyalist troops descended on the James family home. When Wemyss came to the home he was met by the wife of Major James. The British major told her that if her husband would come in and lay down his arms he would receive a pardon, to which Mrs. James informed him that she had no influence over her husband's actions and that he was compelled to take part in the Patriot cause. Unsatisfied with Mrs. James's reply, Wemyss had her and her children locked up in a room of the house for two and a half days.[11]

Capt. John James, the oldest son of the major, was ordered into custody. He was captured during the fall of Charleston and paroled. The young captain was brought in to stand trial to determine whether he had broken the terms of his parole. If found guilty, he would hang. The slaves belonging to the James family were called as witnesses, but no evidence was presented against Captain James and he was released.[12] Wemyss failed to lure Major James to his home and he was unable to find sufficient evidence to warrant the hanging of John James, but he displayed his wrath by ordering the James family home to be burned to the ground.

The torching of the home had such an impact on William James's life that he mentioned it in the preface of his biography of Francis Marion and cites Wemyss's actions as the reason he had not written the account of Marion's exploits earlier. James wrote: "I felt an early inclination to record the events; but Major Wemyss burnt all my stock of paper, and my little classical library, in my father's house; and, for

11. William Dobein James, *Swamp Fox: General Francis Marion and His Guerilla Fighters of the American Revolutionary War* (Columbia, SC, CreateSpace Independent Publishing Platform, 2013), 42.
12. James, *Swamp Fox,* 42-43.

two years and a half afterwards, I had not the common implements of writing or of reading."[13]

William James provided a vivid account of the destruction wrought by the British expedition into the region. "The country through which Wemyss had marched, for seventy miles in length, and at places for fifteen miles in width, exhibited one continued scene of desolation. On most of the plantations every house was burnt to the ground, the negroes were carried off, the inhabitants plundered, the stock, especially sheep, wantonly killed, and all provisions, which could be come at, destroyed."[14] James elaborated on Wemyss's targeting of sheep. "Major Wemyss, in laying waste to the country, was particularly inimical to looms and sheep: no doubt that he might deprive the inhabitants of the means of clothing themselves. What sheep he did not kill for the use of his men, he ordered to be bayoneted."[15] Patriot homes were not the only structures to be put to the torch. Wemyss also ordered the burning of the Presbyterian church at Indiantown, which he claimed was a sedition shop.[16]

As James's account reveals, slaves were seized from plantations whose owners were suspected of supporting the Patriots. The action, however, was intended more for the purpose of confiscating rebel property than it was an act of emancipating enslaved people. On one occasion Wemyss granted Loyalist militia Col. William Mills "one hundred negroes," which he referred to as "rebel property," to indemnify Mills for the losses he had sustained by his attachment to His Majesty's Government.[17] Mills wrote a letter to Cornwallis and included a certificate issued by Wemyss to appropriate slaves. The Tory colonel claimed to have lost fifty-seven negroes. Cornwallis referred to the "gift" offered by Wemyss as a "princely donation" and stated that "whatever Colonel Mill's merits may have been, we cannot yet afford those kind of presents." He declared the offer null and void and left it to Lieutenant Colonel Balfour to award any small proportion that he thought proper.[18]

During his raid, Wemyss ordered the hanging of at least one person, a ferryman named Adam Cusack. There are various spellings of Cusack's name in different accounts. Cusack was believed to have been

13. James, *Swamp Fox,* 4.
14. James, *Swamp Fox,* 31.
15. James, *Swamp Fox,* 42.
16. Ibid.
17. Wemyss to Mills, Certificate to Appropriate Slaves, 26th September 1780, Saberton, *The Cornwallis Papers Volume III,* 398.
18. Cornwallis to Balfour, 12th December 1780, *The Cornwallis Papers Volume III,* 107.

paroled at Charleston and was taken into custody for either refusing to ferry British officers across a creek or for firing at the slave of a Tory militia officer. Cusack's wife and children pleaded for a pardon and prostrated themselves before Wemyss, who was mounted on horseback. James claims that the major would have ridden over them, had it not been for another British officer stopping him.[19] James Wilson, a local doctor, attempted to intercede on Cusack's behalf, but to no avail. The British carried out the execution. In return for interfering in the affair, Dr. Wilson's home was burned, and his wife fled into North Carolina. Afterwards, Dr. Wilson joined Marion's partisan band.[20]

From Cheraw Court House Wemyss penned a letter to Cornwallis on September 20, informing the commanding general of the progress of his detachment. He did not attempt to hide the severity of his tactics from his commanding general. Wemyss informed Cornwallis that every inhabitant had been or was concerned in the rebellion. He reported that his troops burned and laid waste about fifty houses and plantations, who Wemyss said were guilty of breaking their paroles or oath of allegiance and taken up arms against the British. He also informed his commanding general that he had taken about twenty prisoners, one of whom he referred to as a notorious villain that he planned to execute the following day.[21] The "notorious villain" that Wemyss referred to was Adam Cusack.

Upon learning the details of the expedition and the severity in which Wemyss had dealt with Patriot sympathizers, Cornwallis offered no criticism of the major for his tactics. To the contrary, Wemyss's actions were not only sanctioned by Cornwallis, but encouraged by the commanding general. Cornwallis's own correspondence reveals that he had, in fact, instructed Wemyss to deal with the Patriot supporters severely. In his letter of August 28, 1780, Cornwallis issued the following orders to Wemyss:

> I would have you disarm in the most rigid manner all persons who cannot be depended on and punish the concealment of arms and ammunition with total demolition of the plantation. All those who were enrolled voluntarily in Colonel Mills' militia, or by Lt. Colonel Gaillard, and afterwards joined the rebels must be instantly hanged up, unless

19. James, *Swamp Fox*, 32.

20. Hugh F. Rankin, *Francis Marion The Swamp Fox: The Great Guerilla Leader of the American Revolution-His Life and His Campaigns* (New York: Thomas Y. Crowell Co., 1973), 79.

21. Wemyss to Cornwallis, 20th September 1780. Ian Saberton, Editor. *The Cornwallis Papers The Campaigns of 1780 and 1781 in The Southern Theatre of the American Revolutionary War Volume II* (East Sussex. The Naval and Military Press. 2010), 215.

> you should seize a very great number, in which case you will please to select the properest [sic] objects of mercy. All who have either submitted themselves or have lived quietly at their plantations in an apparent acquiescence to the King's Government, and have since joined in this second revolt, must have their property entirely taken from them or destroy'd and themselves be taken prisoners of war.[22]

Cornwallis conveyed the same sentiments to his commanding officer in New York, Sir Henry Clinton. Cornwallis wrote that he had issued the following orders to Wemyss: "to disarm in the most rigid manner the country between Santee and Pedee and to punish severely all those who submitted or pretended to live peaceably under His Majesty's Government since the reduction of Charlestown and have joined in this second revolt; and I ordered him to hang up all those militia men who were concerned in seizing their officers and capturing the sick of the 71st Regiment." Cornwallis added, "I have myself ordered several militia men to be executed who had voluntarily enrolled themselves and borne arms with us and afterwards revolted to the enemy."[23]

Wemyss's mission to the Peedee did not achieve the desired objectives. Most importantly, he failed to eliminate Francis Marion's partisan force. Upon learning of the advancing column from Kingstree and another from Georgetown, Marion marched his small force across the border into North Carolina to seek temporary refuge. Wemyss also failed to establish an effective Loyalist militia to maintain British authority in the region, nor did his brutal tactics subdue the population. Many of those who were subject to the destruction wrought upon them, decided to take a more active role in the resistance. New volunteers wandered into Marion's camp, determined to join the militia.

Following the raid through the Cheraws, Cornwallis ordered Major Wemyss to march the 63rd Regiment to Broad river to patrol both sides of the bank and protect the mills upon which the British heavily relied.[24] While carrying out his latest assignment, Wemyss received information from a local Tory named Sealy that Thomas Sumter had camped his troops at Moore's Mill, about twenty-five miles away from the British encampment. The major met with Cornwallis to brief him on the intelligence he had received and confidently proposed a plan to

22. Cornwallis to Wemyss, 28th August 1780, Saberton, *The Cornwallis Papers Volume II*, 208-209.
23. Cornwallis to Clinton, 29th August 1780, Saberton, *The Cornwallis Papers Volume II*, 41.
24. Cornwallis to Clinton, 3rd December 1780. Saberton, *The Cornwallis Papers Volume III*, 25.

surprise and rout Sumter. Eager at the opportunity to defeat such an elusive foe, Cornwallis approved the major's plan to attack Sumter's camp at daybreak on November 9. Wemyss marched the 63rd regiment out of camp, along with forty dragoons of the British Legion that Cornwallis had committed for support.[25] He assigned Sealy and five dragoons the job of finding and slaying Sumter.[26] During the march Wemyss learned that Sumter had moved his camp to Fishdam Ford, about five miles from Moore's Mill.

The British located Sumter's camp much sooner than they had planned. Wemyss planned to attack the Americans at daybreak but feared that his troops would be discovered by enemy patrols if he waited until dawn. Around 1:00 a.m. he led the dragoons on a charge into the camp, followed by the men of the 63rd regiment. Sumter's men left their campfires burning, which illuminated the attacking British force. The few alert Patriot sentries fired a volley and Wemyss tumbled from his saddle, having been struck in the arm and knee. Meanwhile, a partially clad Sumter barely escaped from his tent, as Sealy and his assassins rushed in.

With Wemyss incapacitated by his wounds, command of the British troops fell to a very young officer who did not know the ground or the major's plans.[27] He left Major Wemyss and about twenty wounded men under a flag of truce and retreated. According to William James, when Wemyss was captured he had a list of homes that he had ordered burned in Williamsborough and Peedee, which he nervously presented to Sumter and pleaded for protection from the militia.[28] According to other accounts, Sumter read the list and tossed it into the fire without divulging the contents to his men.

In a letter to Lieutenant Colonel Balfour following the skirmish, Cornwallis sarcastically remarked that he feared Wemyss forgot he wasn't an infantry soldier, as he had ridden headlong into the American camp. He also expressed his hope to get the wounded major exchanged and noted that although "he was in the late instance a mad trooper, he is certainly in the main a sensible and useful officer."[29]

25. Ibid.

26. Robert D. Bass, *Gamecock: The Life and Campaigns of General Thomas Sumter* (Orangeburg, SC: Sandlapper Publishing Co., 2000), p.97.

27. Cornwallis to Clinton, 3rd December 1780, Saberton, *The Cornwallis Papers Volume III*, 25.

28. James, *Swamp Fox,* 40.

29. Cornwallis to Balfour, 12th December 1780, Saberton, *The Cornwallis Papers Volume III*, 79.

Following his capture, Major Wemyss was paroled and returned to Charleston, before sailing for New York. Wemyss returned to England in 1781. The following year Wemyss returned to New York and then to Charleston, where he served as deputy adjutant general to Gen. Alexander Leslie. In his new role, Wemyss met with his American counterpart to negotiate the conditions of the exchange of prisoners.[30] Following the British evacuation of Charleston, Wemyss returned to New York and then to England once again. After his resignation from the British Army as a lieutenant colonel, Wemyss retired to his native Scotland. A few years later he emigrated to the United States with his second wife and settled on a farm on Long Island, where he died in 1833.

30. General Alexander Leslie to General Nathanael Greene, 18 September 1782, Dennis M. Conrad, editor, *The Papers of General Nathanael Volume Greene XI 7 April–30 September 1782* (Chapel Hill, NC and London: University of North Carolina Press, 2000) 672.

Benedict Arnold and James Wemyss: Similar Experiences, Contrasting Legacies

GENE PROCKNOW

Often, a person's legacy is defined by decisions made at pivotal moments rather than a lifetime of previous accomplishments. The is especially true for two aspiring, highly competent military officers in senior leadership positions during the fractious American Rebellion. Although initially on opposing sides, the wartime and personal experiences of the infamous Maj. Gen. Benedict Arnold of the Continental Army (later the brigadier general in the British Army) and the little-known Maj. James Wemyss of the British Army are uncannily similar. While both possessed a flair for combat leadership and exhibited heroics on the battlefield, their contemporaries' esteem and their historical legacies are vastly different.

James Wemyss purchased an ensign's commission in 1766 at age eighteen and embarked on a promising military career in the British Army. Equally aspiring, Arnold, a self-made man, developed a thriving merchant and shipping business trading throughout North America and the Caribbean. Both men tragically lost their first spouses to an early illness and later remarried for the remainder of their years.

From the earliest days of the Revolution, Arnold and Weymss actively engaged in fierce, close-quarter combat. Placing themselves in exposed, dangerous situations, both officers excelled at aggressively leading their commands on campaign and in directing soldiers on violent, changeable and complex battlefields. Both received severe and crippling wounds while leading their units from the front lines. Arnold suffered dreadful bullet wounds in the same leg at the Battle of Quebec and two years later during a bold assault on British lines at Saratoga. Wemyss was wounded on three occasions, first on a raid led by Gov. William Tryon on Danbury, Connecticut, next slightly wounded while in the heat of the action in the British vanguard at the Battle of Brandywine Creek, and most severely at Fishdam Ford, South Carolina. In the opening moments of this last clash, musket balls penetrated both of his legs and one shoulder. Gravely wounded, Wemyss' command left him on the battlefield to be captured by the Rebels. Both men experienced long, painful periods of convalescence and both walked with a limp for the remainder of their lives.

Given natural proficiency in military operations and highly aggressive battlefield leadership styles, Arnold and Wemyss received independent commands of regimental-size units. Both molded their units into highly effective fighting forces. Well chronicled is Arnold's epic 1775 trek through the Maine wilderness to attack the city of Quebec and his 1777 contributions to the rebel victory at Saratoga. Likewise, Wemyss transformed a poorly-led and inadequately trained provincial unit, the Queens Rangers, into a highly effective light infantry fighting force.[1] Wemyss's leadership and the unit's performance during critical moments of the Brandywine battle earned plaudits from his senior officer, Lt. Gen. Wilhelm Knyphausen, who stated, "it is my duty to mention the merit of Major Wemyss" in a letter to Lord Germain.[2] Even in defeat, fellow officers praised Wemyss following his defeat at the Battle of Fishdam Ford. Lord Cornwallis wrote to Banastre Tarleton stating that Wemyss's 63rd Regiment "behaved vastly well."[3] In addition to his warrior abilities, Wemyss' superiors thought highly of his military strategy insights, stating, "No man knows better what has been done or what may be expected to be done—his reports may safely be relyed on."[4]

Beyond battlefield and strategic proficiency, both developed reputations for unnecessary killing, wanton destructiveness and wholesale confiscation of civilian property. For example, Lt. Gen. Henry Clinton criticized Arnold for "the loss of some excellent officers and rather too many men" in his raid on Groton and New London, Connecticut and

1. Wemyss was replaced to recover from wounds received at the Battle of Brandywine Creek by John Graves Simcoe, the Queens Rangers continued its history of success as a Loyalist light infantry unit throughout the remainder of the war.

2. K. G. Davies, ed., *Documents of the American Revolution, 1770–1783: Colonial Office Series* (Shannon: Irish University Press, 1972), Vol. XIV, 241.

3. Lord Cornwallis to Banastre Tarleton November 9, 1780, in J. Slack, *The History of the Late 63rd, West Suffolk, Regiment* (Army and Navy Co-operative Society, Limited, 1884), 28, books.google.com/books?id=M2FfZQjhADcC.

4. James Robertson to Lord Amherts, New York, May 8, 1781, in James Robertson, Milton M. Klein, and Ronald W. Howard, *The Twilight of British Rule in Revolutionary America: The New York Letter Book of General James Robertson, 1780-1783* (Cooperstown, N.Y: New York State Historical Association, 1983), 196.

Hessian Captain Johann Ewald reported indiscriminate confiscation of property for his personal gain including "forty-two vessels loaded with booty" during his raid into tidewater Virginia.[5] After adjudication by an Admiralty Court, Arnold received only six percent of the total plunder or two thousand pounds. Adding to the six thousand pounds Arnold received for being a turncoat, even this small allotment evoked jealously from other British officers.[6] Likewise, Wemyss vigorously pursued Patriot militias and destroyed Rebel personal property. Under orders "to punish the inhabitants"[7] along the Pee Dee River on one mission, Weymss burned many Rebel homes, especially the houses of Rebels who broke their paroles by resuming fighting the British. In addition, he confiscated horses to provide mounts for his infantry force. However, there is no evidence that Wemyss confiscated property for his own benefit.

Given their aggressively successful military accomplishments, both Arnold and Wemyss believed they should have been promoted faster and higher. Bypassed for promotion to major general in 1776, Arnold vigorously complained to George Washington and Congress on the injustice of their slight, especially given the relatively scant combat experience of the other generals who were promoted.[8] Likewise, Weymss believed his performance in leading the Queens Rangers and his battlefield heroics at Brandywine demonstrated a compelling case for further advancement. Lt. Gen. William Howe wrote to Lord Germain, "the Queen's Rangers commanded by Captain Wemyss of the 40th Regiment distinguished themselves" while in the vanguard of the attacking British forces.[9] Even when both officers eventually received promotions, both Arnold and Weymss felt insufficiently appreciated and recognized for their accomplishments throughout their military careers.

Given their perceived slights, both Wemyss and Arnold heavily criticized fellow officers and in turn received criticism themselves. Later

5. Henry Clinton, *The American Rebellion Sir Henry Clinton's Narrative of His Campaigns, 1775-1782 with an Appendix of Original Documents*, ed. William D Wilcox (New Haven: Yale University Press, 1954), 331. Johann von Ewald, *Diary of the American War: A Hessian Journal* (New Haven: Yale University Press, 1979), 208.

6. Willard Sterne Randall, Benedict Arnold: Patriot and Traitor, 1st, ed. (New York: Morrow,1990), 589-590.

7. Notes on the 1780-1 Southern Campaigns, researchingtheamericanrevolution.com/british-maj-james-wemyss-manuscripts/#_Toc7620871.

8. Benedict Arnold to George Washington, March 11, 1777, *The Papers of George Washington. Revolutionary War Series* (Charlottesville: University Press of Virginia, 1985), 8: 551.

9. William Howe to Lord George Germain, October 10, 1777, Germantown, Pennsylvania in James J. Barnes and Patience P. Barnes, eds., *The American Revolution through British Eyes: A Documentary Collection* (Kent, OH: Kent State University Press, 2013), 503.

in life, Wemyss penned a document harshly disparaging over fifty British officers including the three British Commanders in Chief as well as almost all of their subordinate generals.[10] Most frequently, Weymss described the British General officers as "without abilities," "useless," "vain" and "pompous."[11] Wemyss' views have been widely quoted by historians but exhibit the hallmark of an officer who was bitter at his lack of advancement and insufficient reward for exemplary service.[12] Further, given events later in life, one would have thought that Wemyss would have been more supportive of the British officers who were supposed to have been more lenient towards the Americans, but he found Howe "unequal to the duties of Commander-in-chief" and Clinton "vain . . . open to flattery . . . and too often misled by aid de camps and favorites."[13] Often, fellow officers regarded Wemyss as petty, overly sensitive and a stickler for the honorific prerogatives of command. For example, when peevish court martial charges brought by Wemyss against Capt. Hayes St. Leger were not sustained, Captain John Peebles observed that "it is worse than ridiculous to accuse a man of more than you can make appear."[14] While Arnold did not leave an extensive collection of his observations, Arnold criticized and received criticism from numerous Rebel officers including Generals Horatio Gates and Moses Hazen and Colonels Ethan Allen, John Brown and James Easton.[15]

Both Weymss and Arnold had significant opportunities for personal financial gain in their respective military commands. Arnold took advantage of several opportunities including as the Continental Army commandant of Philadelphia and during his British Army raids into Virginia. Although avoiding a conviction by court martial for the former, Arnold leveraged his authority to live an extravagant life in Philadelphia and to advance his personal fortunes. While there were

10. James Wemyss, "Major Wemy Paper," trans. Jared Sparks (n.d.), MS Sparks 22, Harvard University Library, iiif.lib.harvard.edu/manifests/view/drs:435585116$242i.

11. For a text version of the Sparks transcription of the Wemyss manuscript with editor notations, see researchingtheamericanrevolution.com/british-maj-james-wemyss-manuscripts/. For an assessment of the Wemyss's characterizations of the senior British officers see researchingtheamericanrevolution.com/2019/05/03/the-harshest-critic-british-major-james-weymss/, which includes an analysis of Wemyss's observations.

12. Most recently, Nathaniel Philbrick, *Bunker Hill: A City, a Siege, a Revolution* (New York: Viking, 2013), 317. Others include David Hackett Fisher and Allen French.

13. Wemyss, "Major Wemy Paper," 214–15.

14. John Peebles and Ira D. Gruber, *John Peebles' American War: The Diary of a Scottish Grenadier, 1776-1782* (Mechanicsburg, PA: Stackpole Books, 1998), 371.

15. James Kirby Martin, *Benedict Arnold, Revolutionary Hero: An American Warrior Reconsidered* (New York: New York University Press, 1997), 399.

several similar opportunities for Wemyss while he served as an aide to quartermaster general and latter barracks master general James Robertson, he did not financially benefit from these roles. Wemyss pointed out high levels of dishonesty and embezzlement for personal gain among many British officers, especially those with quartermaster and barracks master roles. In fact, he said the British officers used "the most effectual means of making immense fortunes; by carrying a successful war on the Treasury of their Country."[16] Even Adm. George Rodney, who had his own issues with corruption, called out the quartermasters and barracks master, "all of whom make princely fortunes and laugh at the sleeves of the generals who permit it."[17]

Crossing paths during the later stages of the Rebellion, they both enjoyed the benefits of having a senior commander, Lt. Gen. James Robertson as an active patron. After his defection, Robertson described Arnold as "the boldest and most enterprising of the rebel Generals." Becoming close colleagues while serving together in New York City, Arnold named a son after the British general.[18] Even more supportively, General Robertson, described Wemyss as "one of my best friends" in an advocating dispatch to the British high command.[19]

However, neither Arnold nor Weymss were satisfied with the respect and returns they received from serving in their respective armies. Facing strikingly similar situations, the two officers made diametrically different decisions—Arnold defected to the enemy and Wemyss remained loyal to his country. Most egregiously, Arnold both sought and received pecuniary returns from his military commands. Although Wemyss had several opportunities to engage in war profiteering, he did not.

After the war, both Arnold and Wemyss emigrated to the country of their initial adversaries. However, one lived as a shunned traitor and the other was welcomed as a valued, respected immigrant. Rejected by British society, Arnold never attained his pre-war success as a merchant or businessman even when he attempted a fresh start in Nova Scotia. After the war, Wemyss also did not achieve significant career advancement nor financial success. He rose one rank to lieutenant colonel (without purchase) but retired when further promotion eluded his grasp. Perhaps his views on his fellow officers became an impregnable impediment. Turning to a civilian life, Wemyss bought an agricultural

16. Wemyss, "Major Wemy Paper," 225.

17. R. A. Bowler, "The American Revolution and British Army Administrative Reform," *Journal of the Society for Army Historical Research* 58, no. 234 (1980): 66.

18.Robertson, Klein, and Howard, The Twilight of British Rule in Revolutionary America, 155.

19. Ibid., 196.

estate in Scotland for 10,000 pounds funded solely by his family money and officer's wages accumulated during the war. However, the property proved financially unsuccessful. Sometime during the period 1795-99, Wemyss made a decision to emigrate to a nation that he fought so hard and suffered horrific wounds to prevent coming into existence. For someone viewed as the "second most hated" British officer during the Revolution this was a bold and risky move.[20] Having acquired considerable experience scouting the area during the war, Wemyss chose to live on Long Island and comfortably settled on a small farm. Wemyss successfully transitioned to a new life in his adopted country and became an American while Arnold never became accepted British in society.

However, both Wemyss and Arnold took regrets and "chips on their shoulders" to their graves. Wemyss used his pen to thoroughly excoriate his fellow offices for mismanaging the war. In the end, Wemyss found an outlet to partially replace his frustrations. He gained gained a strong measure of regard from his Long Island neighbors who sought his military services during the War of 1812. Wemyss declined their offers, choosing not to fight against his native country and old comrades. Wemyss lived a full life, passing away on his Long Island farm in 1833. His tombstone reads, "Formerly a distinguished Officer in the service of his Country."[21] In stark contrast, Arnold died a thoroughly embittered and shunned man without financial means, friends, and country. Expressing the thoughts of much of British high society, the prominent politician Horace Walpole described Arnold as "a man of wretched fame." [22] Invisible to most, Arnold's grave site at St. Mary's Church of London is located in a basement room which serves as a kindergarten classroom. Updated in 2004 by an American seeking to burnish Arnold's legacy, the tombstone reads simply, without praise or comment, "Sometime General in the Army of George Washington."[23]

Arnold and Wemyss faced similar situations but created different legacies—Wemyss "served with distinction during the war" but became a footnote in history; Arnold lost the respect of people on all sides of

20. allthingsliberty.com/2018/11/major-james-wemyss-second-most-hated-british-officer-in-the-south/

21. "James Wemyss (1748-1833)," *Find A Grave* (blog), n.d., www.findagrave.com/memorial/104519871/james-wemyss.

22. Horace Walpole to Horace Mann, February 7, 1782, *Letters of Horace Walpole to Horace Mann 1760 - 1785* (Rich Bentley, 1844), 357, books.google.com/books?id=tqlCAAAAcAAJ.

23. John Hanc, "The Curious London Legacy of Benedict Arnold," *The Smithsonian Magazine*, July 8, 2010, www.smithsonianmag.com/history/the-curious-london-legacy-of-benedict-arnold-1737908/.

the Revolution and his name became synonymously linked to treason.[24] In a strange twist of fate, "the second most hated British officer" during the war lived a peaceful life in the land of his most vociferous adversary while the one of the most gifted Continental Army officers spent the last years of his life in ignominy. While there is a tendency for historians to chronicle and for readers to be fascinated with tragically flawed characters, more should be written about people who made good decisions in the face of personal adversity by honorably serving their countries and by respectably switching their allegiances.

24. Assessment of Wemyss' military career by Historian Jared Sparks, Wemyss, "Major Wemy Paper," 231.

Retracing Alexander Hamilton's Steps Through the Remnants of Revolutionary New York

GINA DIMURO

When Alexander Hamilton arrived in New York in the early 1770s, the city was already the one of the largest in the colonies, second only to Philadelphia. Yet Manhattan's 25,000 residents inhabited just a small portion of the island which stretched from the Battery to well below today's 14th street. The rest was sparsely-inhabited farmland, estates, and wilderness.

Over the intervening centuries, New York City expanded into a sprawling metropolis. The farmland was filled with skyscrapers, the estates laid over with bustling streets, and the wilderness illuminated with neon signs. Hidden among the steel and concrete are, however, a few remnants of the New York Hamilton would have known. These traces of the city's earliest days offer an extraordinary glimpse into its history and breathe life into its distant past. "They talk very loud, very fast, and all together . . . If they ask you a question, before you can utter three words of your answer, they will break out upon you again and talk away," wrote John Adams of the New Yorkers he encountered in 1774.[1]

ST. PAUL'S AND THE BOWLING GREEN

In either late 1773 or early 1774, Hamilton enrolled in King's College, which was rechristened Columbia College after the Revolutionary War. Although today Columbia is a massive complex of university buildings in West Harlem, back when Hamilton attended, the college was a simple three-story building situated in an area that is now bordered by West Broadway, Murray, Barclay and Church streets. Students in 1774

1. David McCullough, *John Adams* (New York, Simon & Schuster, 2008).

would have enjoyed an unobstructed view of the river from their pastoral campus, leading one visitor to dub the location the "most beautiful site for a college in the world."[2]

Today, this area bears little resemblance to the idyllic green landscape that would have been familiar to Hamilton. The college's former location is now located in the hub of the city's financial center and in the shadow of its tallest building. However, Manhattan's ultra-modern Financial District also houses some of the city's oldest relics, given that it is the part of the island that was first colonized by Europeans. In fact, not far from the original location of King's College, on the city's most famous street, is a building that has changed quite little since Hamilton was a student.

St. Paul's Chapel has continually served parishioners in the same spot on Fulton and Broadway since 1766. The chapel miraculously survived the Great Fire of 1776 that destroyed many of the city's oldest buildings, including the original Trinity Church located a bit further down Broadway. Two centuries later, St. Paul's had another near brush with destruction during the 9/11 terrorist attacks. It was practically the only building in the vicinity to survive and served as a shelter for rescue workers.[3]

Although the tiny chapel is now surrounded by towering skyscrapers, during the Revolution it would have stood on the outskirts of the city, with only empty land and the river to its rear. In 1775, Hamilton and several other students from King's College joined up with a local militia company dubbed the "Hearts of the Oak" as a response to the battles at Concord and Lexington. Each morning the young volunteers would drill in St. Paul's churchyard before attending class.

St. Paul's churchyard is one of the oldest that has been in continual use in the entire country. Its most ancient tombstone dates all the way back to 1704, while another bearing the name George I. Eacker, connects the location to Hamilton in another, more tragic way. Eacker was buried here in 1804, just three years after fatally shooting Alexander's son Phillip in a duel that eerily foreshadowed the Founding Father's own.

Hamilton himself returned to the chapel long after his studies were over and when he had moved back to New York and was working as a lawyer. One such documented occasion was a Fourth of July celebration in 1789, during which Hamilton delivered a memorial speech in honor of General Nathanael Greene, perhaps from the same pulpit which still stands in the chapel today. "It is an observation as just as it is common that in those great revolutions which occasionally convulse society,

2. Ron Chernow, *Alexander Hamilton* (New York, Penguin Group 2005).
3. "St. Paul's Chapel." Trinity Wall Street, www.trinitywallstreet.org/about/stpaulschapel.

St. Paul's Chapel, left, is one of the oldest surviving buildings in Manhattan. Few people who pass by the Bowling Green fence, right, realize it is almost three-hundred years old. (*Gina Dimuro*)

human nature never fails to be brought forward in its brightest as well as in its blackest colors," he said during his oration.

Although St. Paul's chapel has undergone several restorations and renovations over its 250-year lifespan, it still contains a few other important remnants of its earliest heritage. These other Revolutionary-era items include the altar rail and the personal pew of St. Paul's most famous congregation member, George Washington.

The east side of the chapel also houses a monument dating back to 1776. It was built to honor the Revolutionary War general Richard Montgomery, who was killed in the 1775 Battle of Quebec, and is considered the first monument ever commissioned by the nascent United States.

THE BOWLING GREEN FENCE

A bit further down Broadway is another hidden piece of eighteenth century history that hundreds of people pass by unknowingly each day.

The sprawling Bowling Green just south of King's College had been a site of public gatherings since the Dutch first arrived in the seventeenth century. By the time Hamilton was a student, it had become a hotbed of patriotic activity. On July 9, 1776, the Declaration of Independence was read out loud for the first time in Manhattan at nearby City Hall. Afterwards, a crowd swept up by patriotic enthusiasm and led by the Sons of Liberty rushed to the Bowling Green, where an equestrian statue of King George III stood not far from where the famous Wall Street Bull now crouches. The mob tore down the statue of the British king, but left the surrounding fence (which had been erected in 1771 with precisely the purpose of protecting the statue), relatively unharmed, apart from sawing off the small crowns that topped the posts.[4]

The statue was melted down centuries ago, but the fence still stands close to its original location. A closer inspection will even reveal the saw marks of the patriots on some of the posts.

BROAD STREET

After the war's end, the now-married Hamilton returned to New York to take up his first permanent residence in the United States. When the Hamiltons settled here, the neighborhood was the heart of New York's financial and political activities. Its dominating feature today is the massive Stock Exchange Building, a testament to its historical and modern importance to American finance.

Hamilton, however, would be hard-pressed to recognize the area today. The Stock Exchange Building did not open until 1903; when it first came into being in 1792, the NYSE operated mostly on the street before finally moving to an indoor location in 1817.[5]

Broad Street also contains an impressive reminder of its past position as the nation's capital. The current incarnation of Federal Hall stands on the same spot as the building where George Washington was sworn in as the first President of the United States in 1789. The original structure was, unfortunately, demolished in 1812 and the current one dates from 1842. Alexander and Liza Hamilton actually rented a house at 57/58 Broad Street in 1783, the remnants of which have long since disappeared, along with most of the street's eighteenth century architecture. A bit further down Broad, however, is a building that Hamilton might find a bit more familiar.

FRAUNCES TAVERN

The corner of Broad and Pearl streets has been occupied for nearly as long as the city itself. The original building where Fraunces Tavern now stands was built around 1719-1722.[6] It was bought by innkeeper Samuel Fraunces in 1762, who christened it the "Sign of Queen Charlotte" that same year. Despite taking a cannonball through the roof in

4. "Bowling Green Fence," Landmarks Preservation Commission s-media.nyc.gov/agencies/lpc/lp/0548.pdf.

5. New York Songlines, www.nysonglines.com/.

6. "History," Fraunces Tavern Museum, SRNY Inc., 2019, www.fraunces tavernmuseum.org/history/.

1775, the tavern survived the war and Great Fire more or less intact. Fraunces, a staunch patriot, knew George Washington personally and secretly passed the Continental general information he obtained while serving British officers during their occupation of New York City.

On December 4, 1783, George Washington gathered his Continental Army officers in the tavern's "long room" and bade them farewell in an emotional speech. "With a heart full of love and gratitude," the general said, "I now take leave of you. I most devoutly wish that your latter days may be as prosperous and happy as your former ones have been glorious and honorable." Although Hamilton had served as an officer as well as the general's personal aid during the war, there is no written evidence that he attended, perhaps because he and Washington had had a bit of a falling out. Years later, Hamilton would return to the tavern for a different, yet particularly significant officers' dinner.

In 1804, Alexander Hamilton and Aaron Burr both attended a dinner at Fraunces Tavern hosted by the Society of the Cincinnati, a (somewhat controversial) group of veteran Revolutionary War officers. According to John Trumbull, who was also in attendance, Burr "was silent, gloomy, sour, while Hamilton entered with glee into the gaiety of a convivial party." Unbeknownst to the other guests, the two had reached the apex of their mutual dislike and the dinner was to be their last meeting before their deadly duel just a week later.

Fraunces Tavern suffered substantial damage from fires in 1832, 1837, and 1852, with the result that the proprietors rebuilt and added to the original structure. By 1900, the tavern (which by then would have been unrecognizable to Samuel Fraunces himself) had been slated for destruction in order to make room for newer buildings. Thanks to the intervention of several patriotic and historical preservation societies, the owners instead agreed to sell the property to the Sons of the Revolution of the State of New York. In 1905, Fraunces Tavern was restored to resemble its original colonial structure as best as could be guessed at by the architects, who were somewhat hampered by the fact that there were no contemporary illustrations of the original tavern available.

The tavern re-opened on December 4, 1907, the anniversary of Washington's Farewell Address. Although the current structure contains few remnants of the original, the architects attempted to fill in the missing elements based on other colonial buildings from roughly the same region. The upper floors contain a replica of the famous long room. The tavern's museum hosts multiple Revolutionary War-related events each year, including a reenactment of Washington's Farewell address in the very spot where the original took place.

Broad Street's few remnants of eighteenth century architecture can actually be found right across the street from Fraunces Tavern. Although the Goldman Sachs building that sits at 85 Broad destroyed part of the historic Stone Street, its construction also revealed the foundations of a tavern that predates Fraunces. The Lovelace Tavern was built in 1641 and its foundations can still be viewed through some unique glass windows strategically placed on the street. The building's plaza is also decorated with a recreation of an eighteenth century British map of the area that outlines nearby streets and landmarks, some of which are still there today.

THE MANHATTAN WELL IN SOHO

Before their falling out, Hamilton and Burr found themselves working together in a strange footnote to their famous story.

In January 1801, the body of a young woman named Elma Sands was found at the bottom of a well in an area known as Lispenard's Meadow. Sands's death was swiftly ruled a murder and fingers were quick to point at the man rumored to be her lover: Levi Weeks.

The case became a huge scandal in the city and public opinion (egged on by salacious newspaper headlines) was so set against Weeks that it seemed certain he would be found guilty. Weeks, however, had an extraordinary stroke of good luck. His defense team consisted of two of the best lawyers in New York: none other than Aaron Burr and Alexander Hamilton themselves.

Hamilton and Burr each had a vested interest in clearing Weeks's name. Levi's brother, Ezra, was the architect Hamilton had hired to build his new home in the north of the island and he had promised to cancel some of Hamilton's debts in exchange for defending Levi. The well in which Sands's body had been found belonged to the Manhattan Company, which had in turn been founded by Burr. Burr could not afford further negative publicity surrounding his company after a recent scandal.

Burr and Hamilton presented such a strong case in defense of Weeks that the jury only took five minutes to deliberate before declaring the young man not guilty. Elma Sands's family were disgusted by the verdict, leading her sister Catherine to ominously rage at Hamilton, "If thee dies a natural death, I shall think there is no justice in heaven."[7]

No one else was ever charged with the murder, but Hamilton and Burr both suspected the culprit had been another boarder who resided in the same house as Sands and Weeks. This same man would eventually be forced to flee the country after raping a thirteen-year-old girl

7. McCoullough, *John Adams*, 606.

before eventually being executed in his native England for strangling a woman.

The "Manhattan Well Tragedy" that had caused such an uproar in the city was soon forgotten. Most people have no knowledge about this strange episode in which Hamilton and Burr made a surprisingly successful team. Long after the case had faded from public memory, however, one important relic of the macabre story lingered on.

The once-infamous Manhattan Well still stands in its original location, although the surrounding area is unrecognizable. (*Gina Dimuro*)

At the time of Elma Sands's murder, Lispenard's Meadow was a fairly isolated area well outside the city limits. Over the intervening centuries, it was built up and transformed into SoHo, now one of Manhattan's trendiest neighborhoods. Eighteenth century residents of the island would be hard-pressed to recognize the area today, but somehow during all the construction and remodeling, the once-infamous well survived.

For years, the well had remained hidden in the basement of the Manhattan Bistro at 129 Spring Street. Although most of the staff and clientele knew nothing about the location's history, ghost stories abounded at the restaurant. The staff frequently recounted how glass bottles would fly across the room unaided in the direction male employees. Today, the well is located in the basement-level of the clothing store *COS*. The massive brick structure stands in stark contrast to the pristine modern design. Visitors are free to wander right up to the infamous well and touch the very layer of brick that once entombed poor Elma Sands.

WEEHAWKEN DUELING GROUND

Alexander Hamilton and Aaron Burr's long rivalry culminated with their infamous duel, for which they set out on the morning of July 11, 1804. They had selected a popular dueling ground across the Hudson in Weehawken for their final face-off. Although dueling was illegal in both New York and New Jersey at the time, the Weehawken location's seclusion and accessibility from the river, combined with New Jersey's leniency towards duelists, made it an ideal choice.

Although the actual spot where Hamilton and Burr faced off that July morning was destroyed by railroad tracks in 1870, the scene from over a century is still eerily vivid to visitors. Peering down the steep cliffsides, it's easy to imagine that the greenery might conceal men on a deadly errand. The sun still reflects off the Hudson in the background, just as it did when Hamilton cast one last glance back towards the city he had made his home and "pointed out the beauties of the scenery and spoke of the future greatness of the city."[8]

The city and the river were far from Hamilton's view as he raised his pistol and fired into the air well above Burr's head. Seconds later, he was fatally struck by a bullet from the vice president's own weapon. The seriousness of the wound was immediately apparent and Hamilton just had time to cry out "this is a mortal wound doctor" before sinking to the ground. His second and the doctor who had accompanied the duelists propped the lifeless Hamilton on a nearby boulder as they desperately tried to examine him.

The very boulder upon which Hamilton lay is still there today, albeit some distance from its original location. The first monument commemorating the duel appeared as early as 1806 on the same spot where Hamilton and Burr had stood. After the arrival of the railroad, it was moved higher up on the palisades. Today the site is marked by the boulder and a bust of Hamilton that dates from the 1930s. It stands proudly silhouetted against the river and the skyline that surely would have exceeded even Hamilton's wildest expectations of grandeur.

JANE STREET

After receiving his "mortal wound" at the hands of Burr in Weehawken, Hamilton was ferried back across the Hudson and taken to the house of William Bayard, in an area that's part of today's West Village. He breathed his last there the next afternoon, just after despairing, "If they break this union, they will break my heart."[9]

Bayard's house itself disappeared long ago, but a building at 80-82 Jane street, fairly near to the location where Hamilton died, bears a small plaque commemorating the site.

TRINITY CHURCH

On the morning of July 14, Hamilton's impressive funeral procession made its solemn way through the streets of lower Manhattan that he had once happily traversed as a young student. He was laid to rest in the graveyard of Trinity Church on Broadway, where he had been a parishioner since moving back to New York.

8. Ibid., 700.
9. Ibid., 708.

The second Trinity Church was torn down in 1839, but the tomb of Hamilton still remains, right beside that of his beloved wife, Eliza. Hamilton's son Philip and his sister-in-law Angelica rest in Trinity Churchyard as well, although the location of their graves is unknown.

Visitors still lay flowers at Hamilton's grave. (*Gina Dimuro*)

Most of the graves in Trinity Churchyard are bare, the families of those who once visited having long since also departed. Hamilton's grave, by contrast, is overflowing with flowers, coins, and wreaths left by reverent visitors. Although he died over two centuries ago, these tokens from modern admirers keep his memory very much alive.

Each year, local historical societies host memorial services in the churchyard on the anniversaries of Hamilton's birth and death. The numerous organizations and visitors from all over the country are testaments to the tremendous importance and scope of Hamilton's influence. Representatives from the island of Nevis and descendants of the Founding Father are often in attendance. They are joined by delegations from the Coast Guard (which Hamilton founded) and re-enactors from the Hearts of the Oak militia that used to drill nearby centuries ago.

While Hamilton lived, Trinity Church was among the tallest buildings in the entire city. Today, it is dwarfed by the surrounding skyscrapers that so powerfully demonstrate the might of Manhattan's Financial District, which owes much of its existence to Hamilton and where his memory lives on, in both the structures of modern steel and centuries-old stone.

Putting a Price on Loyalty: Mary Loring's List of Losses

JOHN KNIGHT

The Revolutionary War took a heavy toll on Great Britain. The treaty of Paris in 1783 left her not just bereft of former colonies but militarily humiliated, politically divided and financially straightened. The cost of the eight-year war had averaged £12 million per annum and left the Treasury with a national debt of £250 million.[1] In addition, Britain had suffered the near collapse of many of her most lucrative import markets. It would have been understandable then, if her government had turned its back on North America, reneged on its financial obligations and drawn a line under all its former associations.

It was to the immense credit of King George III that they did not do so. Indeed George, a man for whom loyalty was a dominant personal characteristic, insisted every American who suffered financially in support of the crown should receive compensation. His Ministers, both at and after, the peace of Paris, fully recognised this principle. Frustratingly it proved to be a principle much easier to recognise than to implement.

In 1784 British commissioners were appointed to investigate the nature of Loyalist debts, but after sitting ten years were still unable to make an award, as when a point was pressed on the American commissioners, they retired, "and would not return unless a promise was made them that that point should be abandoned."[2] Finally in 1802, a convention was formed between the British and American governments, by which the former accepted from the latter £600,000 in lieu of all the debts rendered as a consequence of the war.

1. Stephen Conway, *The War of American Independence 1775–1783* (London: E. Arnold, 1995), 189,
2. Thomas Hansard, *Parliamentary Debates, Volume 21* (London: Longman, 1812), 802.

Unfortunately, this was a fraction of the money claimants had already made upon the Government. John Ingram Lockhart MP, who became something of a champion in Parliament for the Loyalists' compensation claims, wrote, "Had the commissioners pursued their labours to a successful termination, they would in all probability have needed at least two millions as the whole amount of that class of debts to which their investigation was directed."[3] This financial disparity caused increasing amounts of friction between Loyalists and successive governments, as the Treasury now had a finite amount of compensation it felt obliged to pay out.

In addition, some politicians believed Britain had no responsibility to the Loyalists at all. Most prominent amongst these was Whig leader Charles James Fox who blamed British and American Tories for misleading the public about conditions in America and perpetuating the war.[4] Fox, however, appears to have been in a minority. Far more typical were the comments of John Willmott MP, a like-minded Whig, who had abhorred the war and regularly voted against Lord North's Government. Upon his appointment by Lord Shelburne as one of the two commissioners to inquire into the sufferings of Loyalists, he declared 'I would share with them my last shilling and my last loaf." Despite his personal opposition to the war Wilmott worked tirelessly in parliament to arrange for Loyalists adequate compensation.[5]

As a class, Loyalists had included some of the colonies' most wealthy and influential citizens. It was no surprise, therefore, to find them organised in Britain as a vocal and resilient enclave in the immediate years after the peace. Most had lost something. A few had lost everything. All contended that they had a right to the full amount of their debts, guaranteed as they had been by the American government in the original peace treaty.

3. *The Parliamentary register: or, history of the proceedings and debates of the House of Commons, Volume 14* (London: John Stockdale, 1812), 481.

4. "We have lost thirteen provinces of America; we have lost several of our Islands, and the rest are in danger; we have lost the empire of the sea; we have lost our respect abroad and our unanimity at home; the nations have forsaken us, they see us distracted and obstinate, and they leave us to our fate. This *is* your situation, when you are under the conduct of Tory ministers and a Tory system, when you are disunited, disheartened, and have neither confidence in your ministers nor union among yourselves; when your cause is unjust and your conductors are either impotent or treacherous." Speech in the House of Commons (November 27, 1781), reprinted in J. Wright (ed.), *The Speeches of the Rt. Hon. C. J. Fox in the House of Commons*, J. Wright, ed. (London, 1815), 429.

5. *Cobbett's Parliamentary History of England: From the Norman Conquest to 1803, Volume 16* (London: Bagshaw, 1814), 564.

They coordinated themselves into an aggressive force of lobbyists producing sophisticated pamphlets and books to support their case.[6] Indeed they proved to be as vociferous and resolute in their claims against the British Government as they had been supporters of it during the war. Incredibly, Loyalists and their successors were still making claims in parliament well into the middle of the nineteenth century, with individual petitions being debated as late as May 1844 during Sir Robert Peel's Ministry.[7]

Each claim or memorial was considered by the commission and adjudicated upon. These memorials give an insight into how the most wealthy and influential Americans lived in the period up to the outbreak of war and provide a fascinating snapshot of the life of America's prosperous elite.

One of the most revealing and extensive memorials came from Mary Loring, then living in the semi-rural village of Highgate in North London. In 1783 she presented a claim "To the Commissioner appointed by Act of Parliament for enquiring into the Losses and Services of the American Loyalists." This memorial was on behalf of her late husband Joshua Loring whom she described only too accurately as "so obnoxious to the people that he was repeatedly mobbed and otherwise ill-treated in such manner as to oblige him to leave his house."[8]

Loring had been a commodore in the British navy and with the outbreak of the war proved to be an intractable foe to the Republican cause. Challenged about what he would do when faced by a choice between remaining loyal and supporting the revolt, Loring replied: "I have always eaten the King's bread, and always intend to."[9] He was de-

6. For the two most articulate publications produced on behalf of American Loyalists see *The case and claim of the American Loyalists impartially stated and considered* (London: "Published by their Agents," 1783), and Joseph Galloway, *The claim of the American Loyalists reviewed and maintained upon incontrovertible principles of law and justice* (London: G. T Wilkie, 1788).

7. "Mr Jervis rose to bring forward the Motion of which he had given notice, that this House will, on Tuesday next, resolve itself into a Committee to consider … the following claim made by John Hopton Russell Chichester, Esq., of Lincoln's Inn, as sole executor of Robert William Powell, an uncompensated American Loyalist, deceased, and that Her Majesty will be graciously pleased to advance to such claimant the amount of the balance due to the estate of the said Robert William Powell, for losses incurred in consequence of his adherence to his allegiance, as ascertained by the Commissioners appointed for that purpose, and to assure Her Majesty that the House will make good the same." House of Commons. May 30, 1844, api.parliament.uk/historic-hansard/commons/1844/may/30/american-loyalists-mr-powell.

8. Eva Phillips Boyd, "Jamaica Plain by Way of London," *Old-Time New England* XLIX (April-June 1959):

9. Chaim M. Rosenberg *The Loyalist Conscience: Principled Opposition to the American Revolution* (Jefferson, NC: McFarland, 2018), 127.

nounced by the Massachusetts Provincial Congress as "an implacable enemy to their country" on March 30, 1775. Despite this, the Lorings remained in Boston until 1776. When the army evacuated the city for Halifax, however, many Loyalists who had sought refuge within British lines went with them, the Lorings included. They travelled to Halifax and then on to England, where the commodore died suddenly in 1781 before the war's end.

From being the matriarch of one of the most wealthy and influential families in all of the American colonies Mary Loring was now in a state of financial penury, her husband's pension having been stopped in July 1781 even before his death. She wrote as a heartfelt introduction to her claim. "Your Memorialist has five Children, four Sons and a Daughter. . . . She was not able to procure any Allowance whatever as his Widow until 5th May 1782 when it commenced at one hundred pounds per annumn."[10]

Mary Loring's memorial then proceeded to itemise and value the fixtures, furnishings and working accoutrements of their estate at "Jamaica Plain in Roxbury within five miles of Boston." It was almost a forensic list with the largest claim in the schedule being for the house and land at £2500, down to £3 for "60 barrells of Cyder." Little was left uncatalogued from these two memorials presented by her and her son Joseph Royall Loring (then serving in His Majesty's navy) and which were considered in December 1783 and April 1784.

At the head of the schedule, Mary began her claim with "A large well-built House, out Houses, Coach House & Stable with Sixty Acres of Land under the best Improvement." It is easy to discern in this description of her home and farm a great familial pride. For "Well built . . . Under the best improvement" was no idle boast. The Lorings were very much at the forefront of Boston's landed gentry, and this social status needed to be reflected by their home. At many times in its life, the house (which still exists today) was described as a "manse."[11] Originally taken from an archaic Scottish word for the residence of a clergyman, by the revolutionary period the term had simply come to mean a large imposing residence. It was formally seized by the Provincial Congress on June 23, 1775, and converted into an infirmary for rebel troops during the siege of Boston. The entire estate was then confiscated in 1779 and sold at auction. The Lorings received nothing from the proceeds.[12]

10. For the full inventory of Loring's claim see Boyd, "Jamaica Plain by Way of London."
11. For the History and architecture of the Loring house see The Loring-Greenough House Boston Landmarks Commission Study Report, www.cityofboston.gov/images_documents/The%20Loring-Greenough%20House_tcm3-44535.pdf.
12. Boyd, "Jamaica Plain by Way of London."

Though the Loring House was an elite establishment, the property was very much an active farm and the manse stood at the heart of an expansive and flourishing agrarian estate. Farming remained the lifeblood of the everyday existence for even the most affluent in colonial America. It is not surprising then that most prolific items catalogued below the house refer to agriculture and include an extensive list of farm implements and livestock.

Significantly within these agricultural implements Loring consistently emphasises the word "iron," as in the £25 she claimed for an "Iron tooth harrow."[13] Today this metal is commonplace. But during the Revolution, ironworks were few and their finished produce costly.[14] Most of Loring's contemporaries would have farmed using implements made almost entirely of wood with only the very tip being covered in iron. That they had such metalwork in abundance illustrates not just wealth but also that the estate was at the forefront of the nascent agrarian revolution, with its owners prepared to invest in the most modern farming implements.

It is ironic then that the most expensive claim Loring makes is not for any of her many pedigree beast or sophisticated machines but £90 for "300 Loads of dung in the yard."![15] This may at first seem whimsical, but before modern chemicals, manure was used as a rich fertilizer, an efficient fuel and even a useful building material.

What is interesting about the claim is it that whilst it provides ample evidence of the wealth of the family it also illustrates how they spent that wealth. Loring's memorial is an extensive catalogue of opulence exhibiting many luxurious furnishings imported from all over the world.

Most modern depictions of Revolutionary period interiors fall into the trap of depicting them as staid and drab with muted colours. This was much more in keeping with later Regency or Federal America. In fact, during the 1770s the rich were keen to make their houses as colourful as possible. Loring specifically highlighted her many multicoloured "Chintz" furnishings. This calico fabric needed to be specially imported from India and was the rage in the decades immediately be-

13. Ibid.

14. "Iron refining was as much an art as a science in the colonial era." Though the colonies produced a sizable quantity of pig Iron, they were banned by Act of Parliament from turning it into finished goods in order to protect British foundries. Most of their good quality pig Iron was exported to Britain to be worked into finished goods. Herbert A. Applebaum, *Colonial Americans at Work* (Lanham, MD: University Press of America. 1996), 211.

15. Boyd, "Jamaica Plain by Way of London."

fore the war.[16] So expensive was it that the £8 she claimed for "Chintz Bed Curtains" and "Chintz Window Curtains" would have been the equivalent of around four months wages for a Massachusetts butcher or carpenter. Despite its cost, it remained so popular that in Britain its purchase was banned when it began to impact disastrously on home-produced textiles. These so-called "Calico Acts" however did not affect the British American colonies and they remained a prime export market for the East India Company.

Mirrors or "looking glasses" as they were then referred to are also noticeably abundant on the list. We take them for granted today, but until the middle of the nineteenth century, they were rare and expensive items of furniture and a luxury few could afford. No suitable plate glass was manufactured in the United States before the nineteenth century, so these continued to be shipped from Britain and France. The difficulty of shipping such a fragile cargo made them a precious commodity and only added to their expense.

Even small items of glass were phenomenally expensive. She troubles to note "a pyramid of Jelly glasses" at £5.[17] Glass for dining is now commonplace and passes without comment. However, in 1780 it was a notable extravagance. Though there were some glass producers in the colonies (mainly German immigrants) they were skilled artisans and their produce was scarce. Most fine or "clear" glass needed to be imported from Britain. Desert glasses for jelly and flavoured ices indicate not only that the Loring's could afford to buy such relative fripperies, but that they also dined in an aristocratic, formal style.

Pride of place in the inventory is given to an "8 Day Clock with mahogany" at £20.[18] These were cutting-edge technological marvels in an age when some people still told time by checking the position of the sun. The rich now had the ability to dissect time precisely into minutes. They were priced as mechanical wonders. Even the cheapest were expensive status symbols and Loring has deliberately emphasised the clock's wood and movement type. Mahogany was the most expensive case wood, and an eight-day movement the most technologically advanced. The more common oak thirty-hour clocks were driven by a single weight. Though these were much less expensive than Loring's mahogany eight-day example they would still cost the equivalent of two years of a farm labourer's wages.

16. The East India Company brought new goods and fashions to Europe, but North America became an increasingly valuable market. The light cotton chintz of India was particularly suited to the humid summers of the south-eastern states.
17. Boyd, "Jamaica Plain by Way of London."
18. Ibid.

As leaders in local society, the Loring's were expected to play an active part in the church. The claim lists both "a Pew in the Church in Jamaica Plain" and "a Pew in Trinity Church in Boston."[19] This illustrates the custom, now lost, of renting Church pews. It was common in Anglican churches to auction pews to families or individuals as a means of raising income, especially in colonial America where churches lacked government support through mandatory tithing. The practice was almost universal during Loring's time in Boston, but the Revolution had profound effects on not just politics, but religious practices too. Those lacking the money for luxuries such as pews were demeaned by their relegation to "free seats," a practice that began to die off in America during the nineteenth century.[20]

Perhaps the most startling item in Loring's list is the £50 she claimed for "A Negro Man named London."[21] Though he is not denoted as a slave, there can be little doubt that London was such. Boston is not associated in popular imagination with the practice of slavery, yet Massachusetts was the first colony in New England with slave ownership and was a center for the trade throughout the seventeenth and eighteenth centuries. Slave numbers in Roxbury increased with the progress of wealth in the town.[22] No legislation was passed in the state to abolish this practice until the Thirteenth Amendment in 1865. In reality, however, the institution had practically died out by the late eighteenth century through judicial actions litigated on behalf of individual slaves seeking manumission. These cases began just after Loring's departure in 1781 and in such numbers that no slaves were listed in Massachusetts by the 1790 census.[23] Unlike Virginia and the Carolinas, few slaves were employed in field work, the cultivation of crops being unsuitable to those labor-intensive methods common in the south. As such it is more likely that London was a domestic servant or footman.

Mary Loring's memorial presents itself as an intimate illustration of everyday life of the wealthy in revolutionary America. It also graphically illustrates how much some Americans lost as a consequence of their allegiance to the British crown. Mary did not live long enough to see her claims come to a full settlement, dying in Middlesex, England in

19. Ibid.

20. The practice was criticised as encouraging a class distinction at worship by creating a "rich man's aisle" and a "poor man's corner."

21. Boyd, "Jamaica Plain by Way of London."

22. Francis Drake, *"Roxbury in the Provincial Period,"* in *Memorial History of Boston*, Justin Winsor, ed. (Boston: James R. Osgood, 1881), 355.

23. Alden Bradford, *History of Massachusetts, from the year 1790 to 1820* (Boston: J. H. Eastburn, 1829), 30.

1795. Her family eventually received less than half of the £4815 they claimed. She was to never see her beloved Roxbury estate again. She did, however, rear sons who provided exemplary service to Great Britain, particularly within the Royal Navy. This service was recognised by the Admiralty during the Second World War when the destroyer escort HMS *Loring* was named in their honour.[24] Symbolically it was built in Boston under lend-lease arrangements and was, perhaps, the most fitting tribute that could be paid to this remarkable Anglo American family.

24. The ship was commissioned into service in the Royal Navy as HMS *Loring* (K565) under the command of Lt. Anthony d'Evelyn Sangster. She served on patrol and escort duty in the eastern North Atlantic Ocean for the remainder of World War II. The Royal Navy decommissioned *Loring* in 1945 after the conclusion of the war and returned her to the U.S. Navy.

The Revolutionary Memories of New York Loyalists Thomas Jones and William Smith

CHO-CHIEN FENG

The American Revolution produced different meanings for Patriots and Loyalists. After the end of the Revolutionary war, the pressing issue was no longer the problem of independence or the Imperial Crisis, but the problem of nationhood, and how this newly created nation should be run. Arthur Shaffer argued that the fact that "a diverse group of historians could produce . . . a nearly uniform picture of the American past can best be explained as a response to political and social conditions in the early republic." Partisanship and division in politics were two pressing political issues in the early republic. Under such political turbulence, the intellectual elites called for the unity of the new nation. Shaffer pointed out that as intellectuals in a new nation, the historians "were anxious to define those qualities that made the nation unique, to provide an identity that would set it apart from its former metropolis."[1] Attempting to solidify the accomplishments of the American Revolution and redefine the new nation, the intellectuals launched a series of endeavors, including writing new histories of America. Some chose to write a more general history of the American colonies, and some chose to write the history specifically about the American Revolution.[2]

Many scholars have focused on this patriotic phenomenon and explained how the history writings in this period consolidated a national

1. Arthur H. Shaffer, *The Politics of History: Writing the History of the American Revolution 1783-1815* (Chicago: Precedent Publishing, 1975), 1.
2. For the history of the American Revolution, two great examples are Mercy Otis Warren's *History of the Rise, Progress, and Termination of the American Revolution* (Boston, 1805) and David Ramsay's *The History of the American Revolution* (Philadelphia, 1789).

identity.[3] Loyalist historical writings, however, became the outsiders in this nationalist narrative.[4] Not only the Patriots recalled their revolutionary experiences and then created and solidified their memories, but the Loyalists also left writings to construct their own historical memories of the Revolution. The diverse experiences among these two groups inevitably generated differing explanations on the Revolution's causes and consequences. Most Americans today have been made familiar with the historical interpretations from the perspective of the winning side. In most cases, these interpretations came from the elites and attempted to establish an impression of a unified American nation. On the other hand, Loyalists attempted to justify their Loyalist cause by writing and publishing their descriptions of the Revolution.

Unlike the Patriots, the Loyalists did not have a new union to defend, but through writing histories and constructing historical memories, they attempted to justify their decisions and examine the origins of their miseries. They were the real losers of the American Revolution since they lost their properties, honor, and homes for the Loyalist cause. In their historical memories, they endeavored to defend their political decisions and demonstrated a view of the origins of the Revolution differing from the traditional Patriot view. The writings of two New York Loyalists, Thomas Jones and William Smith Jr., illustrate their historical perspectives.

Thomas Jones, a judge of the New York provincial Supreme Court, was the author of *History of New York during the Revolutionary War*.[5] He wrote it sometime between 1783 and 1788 while he was exiled in England. His manuscript was never published until 1879 in New York by the New York Historical Society. His work demonstrated the historical interpretations of Anglican Loyalists, of which he was one.

William Smith was a lawyer and pamphlet writer, but more than that, he was a historian of his own time. He published two volumes of

3. For examples, see Lester H. Cohen, *The Revolutionary Histories: Contemporary Narratives of the American Revolution* (Ithaca: Cornell University Press, 1980) and Shaffer, *The Politics of History*.

4. Most of the scholarly discussion has focused on the Patriots' history. However, some recent research starts to make the connection between Patriots' history and Loyalists' history. For example, Eileen Ka-May Cheng, "Plagiarism in Pursuit of Historical Truth: George Chalmers and the Patriotic Legacy of Loyalist History," in *Remembering the Revolution: Memory, History, and Nation Making from Independence to the Civil War*, edited by Michael A. McDonnell, Clare Corbould, Frances M. Clarke, and W. Fitzhugh Brundage (Amherst: University of Massachusetts Press, 2013), 144-61.

5. Thomas Jones, *History of New York during the Revolutionary War and of the Leading Events in the Other Colonies at That Period* (New York: New York Historical Society, 1879).

The History of the Province of New York,[6] and left plentiful historical memoirs during the Revolutionary years.[7] He was a fervent supporter of Whig principles during his political career and he was among the leaders of the resistance movement in pre-revolutionary New York. However, he ended up choosing to remain loyal to the British Empire. In 1780, he published a pamphlet, *The Candid Retrospect: Or the American War Examined, by Whig Principles*,[8] to examine the causes of the origins of the Revolution. Although both Thomas Jones and William Smith became Loyalists during the Revolution, their historical views were different.

THOMAS JONES'S *History of New York During the Revolutionary War*

The editor of Jones's *History of New York during the Revolutionary War* claimed in the beginning of the preface that this book was a Loyalist history, not "an English account." Being loyal to the British crown did not mean that Loyalists were less American. For Jones, remaining in the British Empire was the best option for the American colonies. He believed himself to be loyal to the American interest when he chose to remain loyal to the Crown.

As a member of the Church of England, Jones said that Episcopalians were "the friends of order, and good government, always making it a rule, never to interfere with, or molest the ruling powers, but ever to wait with patience till the time arrives which puts it in their power constitutionally to oppose their enemies."[9] However, he was not an inflexible advocate of the British government. In terms of the crisis stirred up by the Stamp Act, he said it "occasioned a universal tumult throughout the colony," and "all ranks of people appeared unanimous in opposing its execution." Therefore, "the peace of the province, as to any internal jarrings, or political tenets, among its inhabitants, was not in the least disturbed."[10] He did not welcome the British invasion of American rights, but he and other Loyalists preferred to protest within the boundary set up by British constitutional tradition. He was not a

6. William Smith, *The History of the Province of New York, from the first discovery to the year MDCCXXXII* (London, 1757). William Smith, *The History of the Late Province of New York, from Its Discovery to the Appointment of Governor Colden in 1762* (New York: New York Historical Society, 1829).

7. William H. W. Sabine ed., *Historical Memoirs of William Smith Vol. I: From 16 March 1763 to 9 July 1776* (New York, 1956). William H. W. Sabine ed., *Historical Memoirs of William Smith Vol. II: From 12 July 1776 to 25 July 1778* (New York, 1958).

8. William Smith, *The Candid Retrospect: Or the American War Examined, by Whig Principles* (Charlestown, 1780).

9. Jones, *History of New York during the Revolutionary War*, 17.

10. Ibid., 18.

fervent supporter of the latest parliamentary measures, but he was unquestionably an advocate of the British constitutionalism.

Convening the first Continental Congress was usually viewed by his contemporaries as an important event leading to American independence. Jones, however, recalled that it was not the original purpose of the Congress. He said that the New York Loyalists agreed to join the Congress to redress grievances and "to form a happy, perpetual, and lasting, alliance, between Great Britain and America." The New York delegates to the Congress included some Anglicans, so the New York Loyalists felt safe. He claimed that, "A redress of grievances, and a firm union between Great Britain and America upon constitutional principles was their only aim. This they hoped for, this they wished for, this they expected. To this purport they also verbally instructed their delegates." However, such hopes, Jones wrote, were "frustrated by the artful cabals of the republicans in Congress."[11] The New York Loyalists were disappointed to find their delegates were converted to "fixed republicans," and so they decided at a public meeting to oppose any future delegation.[12]

While the Continental Congresses were remembered to be the institutions that promoted American rights and played a crucial role at forming popular sovereignty, Jones remembered it in a very different way. He believed that the Congresses brought confusion and disorder, and even intruded on their rights. Jones wrote that the republicans "threatened destruction to any person who should oppose the election of delegates"[13] He wrote, "The whole city became one continued scene of riot, tumult, and confusion. Troops were enlisted for the service of rebellion, the Loyalists threatened with the gallows, and the property of the Crown plundered and seized upon wherever it could be found."[14] To appease the tumult, the Congress passed an Association to unify revolutionary efforts. The Patriots believed that it would maintain the peace and keep the power out of the hands of the mob. However, Jones thought it was the pretended reason, and the true reason was "to strengthen and cement the solemn league and covenant." Jones thought the Patriots wanted to claim power to control the government and society.[15]

As a Loyalist historian, Jones recorded some events not usually recorded in Patriot histories. For example, he wrote that in August

11. Ibid., 34-5.
12. Ibid., 37.
13. Ibid., 38.
14. Ibid., 40.
15. Ibid., 42.

1775, a group of "select party of republicans" "set off about midnight with a full design of seizing the Rev. Dr. Cooper," who was then President of Kings College. A student overheard their conversation and warned Cooper just in time to allow him enough time to run out of his house. About this Dr. Myles Cooper, Jones wrote, "I knew him well. He was honest, just, learned, and liberal; judicious, sensible, friendly, and convivial; he loved good company, and good company loved him; he was by no means dissipated. He loved God, honoured his King, esteemed his friends and hated rebellion."[16] By depicting the unfair treatment of Cooper by the Revolutionaries, he painted an image in which the Revolutionaries were the brutal villains.

Jones reflected on a pamphlet written in response to *Common Sense*, "in which the fallacy of every argument contained in *Common Sense* was fully refuted." He asserted that "great pains had been taken in its fabrication, and all the sophistry of Congress could never have made a proper reply to it." However, the revolutionary leaders did not allow the response to be published. "A meeting was summoned, the parties met, . . . attacked the house of the printer, broke open the doors, pulled him out of his bed, and forcibly seized upon and destroyed the whole impression with the original manuscript." Jones wrote, "This act was publicly boasted of . . . as an act of heroism, of patriotism, and of virtue." Sarcastically, he said, "These were the people contending for liberty." He chided the Revolutionaries that they "engrossed the whole to themselves and allowed not a little to their opponents, they published whatever they pleased, and threatened destruction to any printer who should dare to print an answer to any of their inflammatory, detestable publications."[17] He condemned such violations of freedom of publication. He pointed out that the day after this raid, every printer received a notice, saying, "Sir, if you print, or suffer to be printed in your press anything against the rights and liberties of America, or in favour of our inveterate foes, the King, Ministry, and Parliament of Great Britain, death and destruction, ruin and perdition, shall be your portion." He recalled that if any printer tried to publish anything in favor of Britain, "his life would not only have been in danger, but his property would have been destroyed, and his family ruined."[18]

Jones did not recall the Revolutionary history as a Briton, but as an American Loyalist. He complained about British measures during the Imperial Crisis and during the war. He believed that the British gov-

16. Ibid., 59-61.
17. Ibid., 63-65.
18. Ibid., 65.

ernment made many mistakes. For example, in 1776, in an attack on the revolutionary fort at Sullivan's Island, the British navy and army failed to coordinate the attack as planned but was seriously damaged. The army was unable to cross a stretch of water because the depth had been greatly underestimated. Jones criticized the incompetence of British military leaders. He blamed the British general for failing to discovered the depth of water before the attack. "This occasioned the failure of the attack, and of course all prospect of success in the Southern Colonies at that time."[19]

Jones also complained about the British treatment of Loyalists. He recorded what happened to Dr. Tredwell when General Howe occupied Long Island. Lieutenant Colonel Birch accidentally met Dr. Tredwell, who was "a gentleman of fortune, of character, and of one of the first families upon the island, and as warm and steady a Loyalist as ever had an existence." Birch saw Tredwell's horse and wanted it. Seeing Tredwell was alone, Birch ordered him to dismount and unsaddle his horse. Tredwell was angry and disclosed his identity. However, Birch still ordered him to dismount and had a servant to unsaddle the horse. Birch gave him the saddle and told him "to carry home the saddle upon his own back and be damned." Jones complained, "There was no civil law. . . . instead of being suffered to present a memorial to the General upon the occasion, upon his application at headquarters for that purpose, the aides-de-camp charged the Doctor with being a rebel and threatened him with the prevost."[20] Jones recognized that the British treated Loyalists as "others" rather than as fellow citizens. Lack of self-restraint and discipline not only hurt military honor, but also hurt the sentiment of the Loyalists.

In his *History*, Jones blamed partisan conflict as the cause of the rebellion. Throughout his *History*, he highlighted the Presbyterians headed by William Smith Jr. and his family. Whenever he mentioned the mob who plundered and pursued the Loyalists, he rarely forgot to remind his readers of the link between William Smith and the Presbyterians, even though he never alleged that William Smith had actually joined the mob.

Even though Smith later chose the British side, Jones did not trust Smith's motives for remaining loyal. He argued that if Smith were truly loyal to the Crown, he should have returned to New York when New York was taken back by the British. But, he did not. Jones asserted that

19. Ibid., 100.
20. Ibid., 114-5.

the intelligence brought in by the Loyalists indicated that Smith "was warmly attached to the American cause, though acting with as much cunning, art, hypocrisy, and dissimulation as possible." He accused Smith of drawing a constitution for the "rebel Government of New York," at the request of the provincial convention.[21] Jones implied that Smith's loyalty to the Crown was controversial and not sincere.

Jones recorded many anecdotes to build up a suspicious image of Smith's personality. Through these anecdotes, Jones depicted Smith as someone who was unreliable and cunning, and who worked only for his own interests. He pointed out that Smith's property was not confiscated by Patriots, which was really suspicious in Jones's eyes. He wrote, "the rebel power . . . looked upon Smith as their real, true, and steady friend."[22] Even though Smith stayed in New York throughout the whole Revolutionary war and was exiled to Canada afterwards, Jones believed that he was still the same person he was in 1753, "except only, that after an experience of 30 years he has greatly improved in all that art, cunning, chicanery, dissimulation, hypocrisy, and adulation . . . the true characteristic of a person professing the religion of a New England dissenter, and the politics of an English republican."[23]

Jones disagreed with parliamentary taxation of the American colonies; however, he preferred to fix this unfortunate situation in harmony with the British Constitution. The way that he remembered and described the history of New York on the eve of the American Revolution showed that he valued social order and harmony more than he valued rights. He valued rights, but because of his belief in social order, he did not believe that the American Whigs, or in his own term, the republicans, stirred up all the tumult based on their pursuit of liberties. Rather, he believed that their actions were based on their desire for power. He prioritized social order and British Constitution as his political values; therefore, when he recalled the revolutionary years, he intentionally emphasized the disorder and confusion caused by the revolutionaries, as well as the paradox of the American Revolution: in order to fight against the tyrannical rule of the British Parliament, the Revolutionaries established arbitrary institutes to carry out the revolution and produced more injustice to promote their own interests.

WILLIAM SMITH'S *The Candid Retrospect*

While Jones chose to write a history to demonstrate what he remembered, William Smith, Jones's life-time rival, even though he had dili-

21. Ibid., 142-3.
22. Ibid., 153.
23. Ibid., 168.

gently kept a diary, never wrote a history of New York during the Revolutionary era. In 1780, he published a pamphlet, *The Candid Retrospect*. In his title, he claimed to examine the Revolution by "Whig principles." Although he did not write this pamphlet in the form of history, the arguments therein regarding the origins of the Revolution reflected his historical memory, or, at least, what he wanted others to know and think about the Revolution.

In the beginning of this pamphlet, Smith summarized the Americans' political claims in twelve articles. In these, he included the principles that he believed to be fundamental to the bound between the Great Britain and the American colonies. He recognized that national sovereignty was absolute, and any endeavor to change the government that would lead to civil war was blameful. He emphasized that the grants, charters, and regulations that governed the colonies were "a great national covenant between the Mother Country and the Colonies" and were essential to the happiness of the whole empire. He argued that the national covenant "bound the parent country to protect and promote the Colonies, according to the good faith implied in the grants and charters." He further claimed that "neither of the contracting parties may dissolve this compact; as long as their joint aim in the union, to wit, their mutual prosperity, can be attained by it."[24]

Smith believed that both the Great Britain and America needed to be held responsible for this unnatural rebellion. Passing the Stamp Act, he asserted, was "a new and awful idea of the constitution" that "the Parent Country held up to her Colonies." This parliamentary act, he believed, sent out a message to the Americans: "You Americans are absolutely ours . . . The Privileges and securities of Englishmen cannot be yours unless you return to the old realm . . . All America is subject to our taxations; nor will we hear your complaints, until you first own our authority to deal with you as we please, and acknowledge that such benefits as you request, are to be expected not as of right, but of grace."[25] He blamed Britain for breaking the practiced rules that had guided the relationship between the American colonies and their mother country, and for attempting to redefine the imperial tie. Even though Smith recognized that Britain had the supreme authority to govern the whole empire, such an attempt to unilaterally and forcefully alter the imperial relationship was not acceptable to him.

Smith believed that the source of the animosity was "the pride and avarice of Great-Britain, in assuming an authority, inconsistent with

24. William Smith, *The Candid Retrospect: Or the American War Examined, by Whig Principles* (Charlestown, 1780), 3-4.
25. Ibid., 5.

the compact by which the empire had been long profoundly united." Although the Americans aroused great turmoil protesting the Stamp Act, they had returned to peace after Parliament repealed it. However, the Townshend duties revived the previous unwelcomed claims and also revitalized colonial resistance. Smith claimed that colonial resistance was justifiable since "representations and petitions having been tried without effect, what could be expected from the mere influence of dissuasions against the purchase of the duties article?" The British reaction to colonial resistance, such as the Coercive Acts, for him, was "utterly unjustifiable, and an infraction of the league." He believed that "it was the duty of the American Assemblies, and of the Congress acting for the whole continent . . . to tender a plan to the Mother Country, for restoring peace."[26]

Instead of declaring war against colonies, Smith thought Britain should rebuke the colonial denial of its authority in all cases respecting domestic polity and should be specific in where the American colonies should or would return to, "on condition of their contributing to the necessities of the Empire." He asserted that Britain and the American colonies would have a better chance to reach reconciliation, "had it explicitly asserted, that the right reserved to Parliament, of approving the quantum of the Colony contributions toward the common defence, was not claimed upon the supposition, that Parliament authoritatively command levies, but only on her right to judge of the exercise or defect of a due sympathy in any branch of the empire, to the general necessities of the whole body."[27] He believed that while the British Parliament had to claim the supreme sovereignty of the whole empire, it should specify the rights and obligations it would enforce. It should not, Smith insisted, claim the right to tax the American colonies directly, but should claim its right to approve the quantum of colonial contribution. It would maintain the status of the Parliament, fund the common defense, and at the same time ease the animosity. He blamed Britain for trying to redefine the imperial relationship, and did not try to find middle ground. Smith took a typical Whiggish stand. He cared about constitutional rights and tried to be flexible in terms of the application of those rights in order to maintain the integrity of the British Empire. In his historical memory, he blamed the British government for lack of flexibility, but assigned more blame for the Patriots.

Smith accused the Patriots of overstating their claims of rights. Patriots claimed an exclusive right of legislation not only in taxation, but

26. Ibid., 6-7.
27. Ibid., 8.

also in internal polity. Smith believed such claim "was a departure in terms from the original league; since it left no authority to the Parliament of Great-Britain over the Plantations." America would therefore become the ally of Britain, not a member of the Empire.[28] Even though he thought the Continental Congress was justifiable, he did not believe it was legal. Smith suspected Congress's action was directed by their desire for power. He blamed Congress for radicalizing the conflict while there were still chances for reconciliation. He insisted that Congress's "continuance of hostilities after the petition to the King . . . confirmed the charge of her commencing a war to maintain an illiberal dominion." He believed that Congress would have done better if, while it expressed its complaints to the King, it had also shown that it did not mean to "exclude Parliament from participating in the regulations respecting the internal polity of the Colonies." Not doing so, Congress confirmed the suspicion that it designed "to involve the Empire in blood." He blamed both Britain and America for "inattention to the obligations they were under to pursue the measures requisite to a reconciliation."[29]

In retrospect, Smith earnestly wished that these two parties could have reached an agreement to avoid eventual separation and war. He believed that Britain's best hope was founded on the dependence and union of America. He contended that Britain had also made efforts by repealing the Boston Port Act and two other coercive statutes in 1775, and thus "opened a door to pacification" and offered ways to communicate. Congress, however, did not respond and did not make the American public aware of the British attempt. Smith thought such concealment explained Congress's true intent, which "favour the perilous design of drawing the people into the precipitate renunciation of the dependency of the Colonies . . . and of plunging their countrymen into a tedious and desolating war." He criticized the Patriots for turning "the quarrel to their own emolument, at the expense of the blood and treasure of their country," and ruining those who "have taken no part in the controversy" and were eager for "a return to their ancient union, according to that compact which eminently advanced the common prosperity, antecedent to the year 1764."[30]

He argued that Congress needed to take the most responsibility for the unfortunate war, and that Congress should retract the declaration which renounced the whole Parliamentary authority in civil polity, "when but few of the Colonies had thought of even temporary estab-

28. Ibid., 7-8.
29. Ibid., 9-10.
30. Ibid., 11.

lishments for common order, nor any of them had authorized their Delegates to vote for a disunion." He further stated that Congress had no right "to give success to the unwarrantable project for dismembering the Empire, then concealed from the multitude, can bind the rest of their countrymen, . . . to support a weak and wicked faction, in an obstinate prosecution of the war." He asked his readers to consider: "Who then are the real enemies of America, if not they who have perverted the virtuous aims of the main body of the people for the defence of their rights and privileges, into a war for dominion?" He accused the Patriots of opposing all peaceful negotiations and forming a league with France to "gratify the corrupt aims of private ambition and interest." Congress, he argued, "by force and fraud" prevented people's return to "the blessings of peace, liberty and safety, under a most generous plan tendered by Great-Britain . . . for advancing and perpetuating the prosperity of the whole Empire."[31] Because Congress refused the negotiation due to their own pursuit of power and interests, Smith believed that Britain was justified in exerting its power to suppress the American rebels, and the American Revolution had "degenerated from a struggle for liberty, into an Unnatural Rebellion."[32] In sum, Smith appropriated his historical knowledge in his political argument, in which he blamed the Patriots for breaking away from their historical experiences and inventing a new political system. The rebellion was "unnatural" because it was not a fight for liberty, but a break from tradition and a product of political ambition.

CONCLUSION

Smith was more empathetic to the American claims. Actually, he was among the first people who made those claims. In his historical memory and his justification of the Loyalist cause, he did not alter this basic assumption: the British government made mistakes in altering their imperial policies and breaking the old norm that had sustained this imperial relationship. However, when he recalled the origins of the Revolution, he remonstrated the Patriots for overstating and over-expanding those arguments of rights. The assumption that guided his judgement was that the Parliament held supreme sovereignty over the whole empire; therefore, the colonists could hope to limit the exercise of parliamentary authority in colonies, but could not and should not completely exclude parliamentary authority. This given defined his perception of American rights and restricted the development of his argument of liberty. Bound by such embedded concepts, Smith could

31. Ibid., 12.
32. Ibid., 13.

not have joined the Revolution. When he recalled the origins of the Revolution, he argued that the British government, even though it made several mistakes, held the legitimate sovereignty over the American colonies, and the rebellious colonists overstated their appeal to rights.

On the other hand, Jones's historical memory was affected by his experiences of political struggles he had in 1750s and 1760s which contributed to his anger and suspicion towards William Smith and his colleagues. His witnessing of the struggle to establish an Anglican college solidified his suspicions of the motives of the revolutionaries, and reinforced his desire for peace and order. He agreed with the theoretical attacks on parliamentary taxation, but could not support the protestors. He suspected their motives, attacked their morality, and doubted their real intents. His accounts and judgements were filled with the language of honor. While the Patriots claimed that it was honorable to defend liberty, Jones implied that the Patriots had lost their honor as they gave up their moral standards for political and social interests. Jones built his attack on partisanship on the foundation of taken-for-granted moral principles that suffused his historical narratives. Historical memories are not just memories, but are another form of political argument. Therefore, Jones's and Smith's embedded cultural apperceptions that were the foundation of their political ideologies also shaped their historical memories.

The Day Nôtre Dame Cathedral Hosted Thomas Jefferson, John Adams, and King Louis XVI

JOHN L. SMITH, JR.

1785 was a rare year in Paris—it was safely nestled between revolutions. The American Revolution had come to an official end right there in Paris one and a half years before, while the French Revolution was still four years off. And for the past 440 years—since the 1345 opening of the Cathédrale Nôtre-Dame de Paris occurred on the Île de la Cité island in the Seine River—Nôtre Dame Cathedral had also witnessed its share of strife and turmoil.

But one particularly beautiful, but chilly day—April 1, 1785—had been set aside as a day of joyous celebration within the walls of Nôtre Dame. A son, the Duke of Normandy, had been born to King Louis XVI and Queen Marie Antoinette a few days before out at Versailles. To give thanks, the French King and Queen declared that a *Te Deum* (a traditional Latin Christian hymn) was to be sung at Nôtre Dame Cathedral with most of the French nobility present. It was to be a happy day of magnificent fashion, grandeur, and royal pageantry.

Of course, Marie-Joseph Paul Yves Roch Gilbert du Motier, Marquis de Lafayette had been invited to the event, along with his lovely wife—Marie Adrienne Françoise de Noailles, Marquise de LaFayette (who went by the rather conventional name of "Adrienne" to friends). It was decreed that each Royal invitee could also extend a *Te Deum* invitation to their own select guests, provided, of course, their choices were in good taste. (Besides, the Royal Couple also had a vested interest to make sure Nôtre Dame was packed to the rafters for the occasion). So the Marquise de La Fayette invited some of the American delegation living in Paris, which included Thomas Jefferson and the four members of the Adams family—John, Abigail, daughter "Nabby" and son John Quincy.[1]

THE ADAMSES AND JEFFERSONS ARRIVE IN PARIS

Ending lonely stretches abroad that John Adams endured during the Revolutionary War, and now with the conclusion of the peace treaty signing, by 1784 it was safe for John Adams to send for his family to be around him while he and Franklin were still completing American governmental business[2] from Paris.

Abigail and daughter—Abigail the second, (Abigail Amelia Adams, nicknamed "Nabby")—sailed to London in late June, 1784, arriving July 21; with seventeen-year-old John Quincy arriving on July 30. (The other Adams children, Charles and Thomas, stayed behind in Haverhill, Massachusetts with the family of Abigail's younger sister—Elizabeth and Rev. John Shaw). Arriving from his diplomatic business work in the Netherlands,[3] John met up with his wife and two children in London in early August, 1784. Together they all crossed the channel to Paris—settling in the western Parisian suburb of Anteuil.

Also in August 1784, Thomas Jefferson arrived in Paris accompanied by his daughter Martha ("Patsy") and William Short, his personal secretary. Jefferson had been appointed by Congress as minister plenipotentiary to help Franklin and Adams negotiate treaties of amity and commerce. During this time in Paris, Jefferson would grow close to both John and Abigail Adams.

In late January, 1785, Marquis de Lafayette also was converging upon his home town of Paris. He had just finished a four-month long visit[4] to the new United States of America, which he had played a small part in creating. Just before leaving his adopted country, he received honorary American citizenship from Congress. His American departure had been tearful as he hugged goodbye to generals Knox, Hamilton, and Greene, knowing that they probably would never see each

1. The other American delegation members invited and attended the April 1 *Te Deum* were Mrs. John Rucker, David Humphreys, Charles Williamos, and Benjamin West. I cannot find out exactly why Benjamin Franklin didn't attend the event. He most certainly would've been invited. And the very next day, April 2, Nabby recorded, "April 2d. Mrs. Hewston and Mr. Franklin came and drank tea with us." Franklin might not have attended the long event because at this time he was suffering from severe kidney stones and gout which would cause his departure back to America a few months later.
2. Mostly securing loans, and signing amity and commerce treaties with more than twenty European states.
3. John Adams was still officially minister to the Netherlands and treaty commissioner.
4. Lafayette would visit America once again in 1824 and 1825 where he would also lay the cornerstone for the Bunker Hill Memorial.

other again. The most poignant goodbye, though, had been between Lafayette and George Washington; the extent of the farewell had affected both men very deeply.

PARISIAN ROYAL "RUMOURS" ABOUND

The sound and spectacle of fireworks lit up the Parisian Sunday night sky on March 27, 1785. It heralded the announcement that Louis Charles de France, the Duke of Normandy had been born (he also would have been King Louis XVII if things had lasted that long). Using the dry sarcasm of his father, John Quincy recorded the event in his diary for that day,

> at about seven o'clock in the evening the Queen, was delivered of a Son, who is Monseigneur le Duc de Normandie: this is one of the most important events that can happen in this kingdom; and every Frenchman has been expecting it, as if the fate of his life depended upon it.[5]

John Adams and David Humphreys had previously been invited to the annual "Ambassadors' Day" at Versailles on Tuesday, March 29—which now fell two days after the Duke's Sunday birth. So, the visit to the French court was also punctuated by the two Americans "where they were presented for the first time, to the new born Prince, who received them in bed,"[6] "though only two days old."[7] It may have been the sarcastic, anti-monarchial side of John Adams who then wrote to a friend the next day, "last night on my return from Versailles and the Sight of the gallant young Duke of Normandy[8]

Daughter Nabby Adams noted the event in her journal and included a rather sharp indictment of her own for the lack of female equality in the system:

> 29th. Papa went to Versailles, it being Ambassador's Day; upon such an occasion there was much company. The young Duke of Normandy received all the ambassadors and ministers, though only two days old; he was lying on a bed, and attended by two or three ladies; if this had happened to have been a princess, she would have been scarce noticed.[9]

5. "27th.," Founders Online, National Archives, founders.archives.gov/documents/Adams/03-01-02-0007-0005-0023, accessed April 11, 2019.
6. "29th.," Founders Online, National Archives, founders.archives.gov/documents/Adams/03-01-02-0007-0005-0021 , accessed April 11, 2019.
7. *Journal and correspondence of Miss Adams, daughter of John Adams, second president of the United States. Written in France and England, in 1785* (New York: Wiley and Putnam, 1841-42), 64.
8. John Adams to C. W. F. Dumas, March 29, 1785, Founders Online, National Archives, founders.archives.gov/documents/Adams/06-16-02-0341, accessed May 17, 2019.
9. *Journal and correspondence of Miss Adams*, 64-65.

Son John Quincy's diary take on the situation focused on the political weaknesses in the same system: "Yet the Capital point is that the crown should pass down eternally from father to Son: insomuch that they would prefer being governed by a fool or a tyrant."[10]

On Monday, March 28, the day following the royal birth, John Quincy was dining at Lafayette's house[11] and some Royal Dirt gossip came to light once Lafayette arrived back from Versailles. It was prime filler material for J. Q.'s diary:

> He told me a curious Circumstance. The Queen was so large, that it was suspected she might have twins, and Mr. de Calonne, the controuler general had prepared two blue ribbands, in case two Princes should be born, for the kings children must be decorated with those badges, immediately after they come into the world.[12]

But the real bombshell that John Quincy was told was the eye-opening rumor that was being hushed up in the Versailles hallways. It was being whispered that the *Duc de Normandie*, whether one or two of possible twin babies, may in fact have been the offspring of Count Axel de Fersen, the Royal Swedish Regiment colonel commandant attached to the French army. Apparently, Queen Marie Antoinette and Count Axel may have been engaged in some amorous dangerous liaisons. Maybe. But it made for sensational "rumours" anyway.

ROYAL *Te Deum* INVITATIONS ARE SENT OUT REGARDLESS

Unfounded rumors aside, invitations for the *Te Deum* went out the week beginning March 28. The celebratory mass was going to be held Friday, April 1 at the Cathedral of Nôtre Dame and it was sure to be one of the grandest spectacles ever beheld, in the world center of all grand spectacles. Extended invitations filtered down to the guests of nobles by Thursday, March 31. John Quincy made this diary notation: "31st. Madame de la Fayette sent a Card to offer us places for the Te Deum, which is to be sung tomorrow at Nôtre Dame, when the king is to be present."[13]

10. "[March 27, 1785]," Founders Online, National Archives, founders.archives.gov/documents/Adams/03-01-02-0007-0005, accessed April 11, 2019.
11. The Lafayettes entertained a salon at their "Hôtel" home every Monday for visiting American representatives and merchants.
12. "28th.," Founders Online, National Archives, founders.archives.gov/documents/Adams/03-01-02-0007-0005-0020.
13. "31st.," Founders Online, National Archives, founders.archives.gov/documents/Adams/03-01-02-0007-0005-0023, accessed April 11, 2019.

THE DAY OF THE GRAND EVENT ARRIVES

Mme. Lafayette's logistics plan as hostess for Friday, April 1—the day of the late afternoon gala event—was set. Everyone was to meet at Lafayette's townhouse at 183 rue de Bourbon (called "Hôtel de La Fayette")[14] by 2:00 p.m. Confirmed attendees invited by Mme. Lafayette were the four Adams family members, Jefferson, Mrs. John Rucker, David Humphreys, Charles Williamos, and Benjamin West. Taking three to four carriages, Adrienne (Mme. Lafayette) would also ride in one of the carriages with her guests, since the Marquis de Lafayette "was with the King"[15] and would already be at Nôtre Dame.

Nabby recorded that to make it to the Lafayette's Parisian townhouse from the countryside area of Anteuil by "two o clock; we dined early and went. From Auteuil to the Barrier we met a number of people."[16] The "Barrier" Nabby wrote of was an iron gate which surrounded Paris. The city back then was a much smaller place and at each city entrance gate (or "Barrier") all entrants coming into the city selling goods were stopped and charged a toll. (The gate names live on today as the names of Metro stops: e.g. Porte de Passy, Porte Dauphine, Quai d'Issy).

Sitting next to Thomas Jefferson in their carriage, Nabby described the incredible crowds she saw alongside the streets for "at least three miles" toward Nôtre Dame, and what Jefferson leaned over and said to her about the crowds:

> every street was so crowded, that had it not been for the police, which upon every public occasion are as numerous as the people they are obliged to be very strict it would not have been possible for a carriage to have passed. I believe I may say with truth there were millions of people. Mr. Jefferson, who rode from the Marquis' with us, supposed there were as many people in the streets as there were in the State of Massachusetts, or any other of the States. Every house was full every window and door, from the bottom to the top.[17]

The next day in a letter, Thomas Jefferson himself kidded William Short, his private secretary, about missing the event (Short was twelve miles away in St. Germain learning the French language). Jefferson

14. Now on Rue Bourbon le Chateau—6th Arrondissement. While the word "Hôtel" in French can mean a hotel in the traditional sense, it can also mean any large building like a hospital, city hall, or as in the case of the Lafayette townhouse, a "mansion". Lafayette had purchased the townhouse in 1783 for 200,000 livres ($2 million).

15. *Journal and correspondence of Miss Adams*, 67.

16. Ibid., 66.

17. Ibid.

tongue-in-cheek guessed that the Nôtre Dame event had larger numbers of dignitaries than Washington had soldiers in some battles:

> You lost much by not attending the Te-deum at Notre dame yesterday. It bids defiance to description. I will only observe to you in general that there were more judges, ecclesiastics and Grands seigneurs present, than Genl. Washington had of simple souldiers in his army, when he took the Hessians at Trenton, beat the British at Princeton, and hemmed up the British army at Brunswick a whole winter.[18]

THE ARRIVAL AT NÔTRE DAME CATHEDRAL

Passing along the "Quai des Augustins" and the "Pont Neuf," the carriage finally arrived at Nôtre Dame Cathedral. Nabby continued,

> Before the Church there is a large square, which was lined with troops, drawn up in rows, and appeared very well. The Church of Notre Dame is of very ancient architecture; it is the most beautiful building I have seen. The churches have no pews, but are filled with chairs and benches. There are a variety of chapels in them, in which there always is a representation of the Virgin Mary and the child Jesus. On one side of the chapel there were seats, where all the judges were seated, dressed in crimson velvet robes, and large wigs. On the other side were lawyers in black habits; their dress is much the same as in our country, except that they wear their hair long behind, and without being tied, but waving, which is very graceful.[19]
>
> We were placed in a gallery that commanded the choir, and were in as good a place as any in the Church, which we owed to the Politeness of Mme. de la Fayette.[20]
>
> On one side of the altar were a number of ladies of rank; on the other side, were the ambassadors and public ministers; before the altar were placed seats, and under a canopy was a crimson velvet cushion, and seats all round with each a crimson velvet cushion; this was for his majesty to kneel upon. There were the bishops with the archbishop at their head, dressed in purple robes, with skirts which came as low as their knees, of the richest lace. There were a number of others of a different order, dressed with cloaks, wrought with gold.[21]

18. Thomas Jefferson to William Short, April 2, 1785, Founders Online, National Archives, founders.archives.gov/documents/Jefferson/01-08-02-0040, accessed April 11, 2019.
19. *Journal and correspondence of Miss Adams*, 66.
20. "Friday April 1st. 1785," Founders Online, National Archives, accessed April 11, 2019, founders.archives.gov/documents/Adams/03-01-02-0007-0006-0001, accessed April 11, 2019.
21. *Journal and correspondence of Miss Adams*, 67.

But apparently, one young man of the court in particular caught the eye of young, nineteen-year-old Nabby:

> Among these was the Abbe de Bourbon, an illegitimate son of Louis 15th. He appeared to be about 27 years old, a very handsome man. I observed all the gentlemen of the court paid particular attention to him.[22]

While Nabby was boy watching, John Quincy was observing the royal protocol unfolding from the seats of the gallery:

> The Archbishop of Paris had a mitre upon his head. When the king came, he went out to the Door of the Church to receive him: and as soon as his Majesty had got to his place and fallen upon his knees, they began to sing the Te Deum, which lasted about half an hour, and in which we heard some exceeding fine music. The voices were admirable. The Archbishop of Paris sung for about a Couple of Minutes, near the end, that it might be said, he had sung the Te Deum. His voice seems to be much broken. As soon as the singing was over the king and the Court immediately went away.
>
> I was however vastly pleased with the Ceremony; and should have been so, if it was only, that it gave me an opportunity to see so numerous an assembly of men, of the first rank in the kingdom. The king and all the court were dress'd in cloaths vastly rich but in no peculiar form.[23]

Although J.Q. was "vastly pleased with the Ceremony," Nabby wrote that hostess Mme. Lafayette didn't care for the Nôtre Dame gala: "Madame de la Fayette observed, she thought it was too magnificent, and there was too much noise and bustle for the Church; she said it was not peaceful enough."[24]

THE GREAT DAY ENDS WITH AN OMINOUS WARNING

Finally the *Te Deum* was over. Nobility, dignitaries and guests filed out of Nôtre Dame Cathedral *en masse* onto the large square in front of the church; and no doubt like an awards show of today—the celebrities were checking each other out while throngs of fans cheered nearby. And just like a post-awards show hassle, waiting for all of the transportation vehicles to pull up was a strict exercise in patience—or futility—even in 1785.

> After the Ceremony was finished, we had to wait a long time for our Carriages and could not at last get them all; so that we were obliged to

22. Ibid., 67.
23. "Friday April 1st. 1785," Founders Online.
24. *Journal and correspondence of Miss Adams*, 67.

go away, five in one Charriot. We returned to the Hôtel de la Fayette, and drank tea with Madam.[25]

But soon it was time to be getting back to Anteuil. John Quincy gives us one last account of a seemingly nondescript incident he noted from his carriage window near the riverbank park of *Cours la Reine*. It could be taken as just a historical example of impoverished peasants doing what they've always done. Or it could be taken as an omen of the simmering anger and discontent that was fuming between peasants and nobility, the underlying feelings of inequality that would erupt among the common people just a few years after this day and would explode into a full-scale revolution:

> We returned home at about nine, and were more than half an hour getting over the Pont Neuf, such was the crowd of Carriages: in the passage of the Cours la Reine, we saw a number of fellows, throwing up the sand, to see if there were no 12 sols pieces remaining for upon these occasions, when the Mob cry out vive le Roi, he throws out of his Coach handfuls of small pieces of money, and is thereby the cause of many a squabble, and some broken heads, though the Police is so attentive that few such misfortunes happen.[26]

Certainly below the surface, hidden social turmoil was festering. But for that brief, bright moment on that chilly spring day in April 1785, France was at peace and joyously celebrating a royal birth.

Nabby Adams closed her Nôtre Dame remembrances for that day, "In the eve the whole city of Paris was illuminated."[27]

25. "Friday April 1st. 1785," Founders Online.
26. Ibid.
27. *Journal and correspondence of Miss Adams*, 67.

The Constitution Counted Free Women and Children—And It Mattered

ANDREW M. SCHOCKET, KINZEY MCCLAREN-CZERR, COLIN J. SPICER

As adopted by the Constitutional Convention, Article I, Section 2, Clause 3 of the Constitution mandated that the population numbers forming the basis for calculating representation in the House of Representatives would "be determined by adding to the whole Number of free Persons, including those bound to Service for a Term of Years, and excluding Indians not taxed, three fifths of all other Persons." Contemporaries and historians have contested the meanings and consequences of the stipulation that three of every five enslaved people be counted. This formulation bolstered the House delegation size of states with considerable numbers of enslaved people and further demeaned those who suffered under slavery. We have paid much less attention to the Framers' innovation of including two other groups in addition to free white men. They also required the counting of non-Native American free women and free children when calculating representation. In doing so, the Framers tilted the House balance slightly back in favor of states with fewer enslaved people. Remarkably, no one at the time seems to have noticed the significant, lasting, practical ramifications of including white women and children, in addition to white men, when calculating each state's number of House members.

That representation at the national level would include the enumeration of white women and children was far from a foregone conclusion during the American Revolutionary period. The same summer that the Constitutional Convention deliberated in Philadelphia, in New York City the Articles of Confederation Congress passed the measure eventually known as the "Northwest Ordinance." This law established procedures for the area roughly bounded by the Ohio River, the Mississippi River, and the Great Lakes to progress from unincorporated land to statehood. At least in implicit conversation with the Constitution, the law's text demonstrates the Confederation Congress's muddied thinking on whom should be counted to calculate representation, and for what purpose.[1] On the one hand, it required that territorial governments be established when districts exceed "five thousand free male inhabitants of full age," and that there should be one elected representative "for every five hundred free male inhabitants." On the other hand, it mandated that districts could ascend to statehood upon reaching a total of "sixty thousand free inhabitants."[2] While there is evidence that in seventeenth-century New England the term "inhabitant" may have implied "landowner," that connotation seems to have faded, with the Confederation Congress intending the term to encompass men, women and children.[3] Thus the Confederation Congress both included and excluded free women and children when considering population for the purpose of representation.

State constitution writers were more clear: overwhelmingly, the state constitutions in force as of 1787 counted voting or taxable free men only for the purposes of future reapportionment. Rhode Island and Connecticut retained their colonial charters until well into the nineteenth century. Several states' constitutional framers pegged reapportionment to the number of taxpayers, usually white men. That included Vermont counting "taxable inhabitants" and Massachusetts "ratable polls."[4] Pennsylvania, where a small fraction of the population paid taxes, was most expressive in this regard, asserting that representation "in proportion to the number of taxable inhabitants is the only principle which can at all times secure liberty, and make the

1. Robert Alexander, *The Northwest Ordinance: Constitutional Politics and the Theft of Native Land* (Jefferson, North Carolina: McFarland & Company, Inc., Publishers, 2017), 10–12.
2. "An Ordinance for the Government of the Territory of the United States North West of the Ohio River" (1787), memory.loc.gov/cgi-bin/ampage?collId=lljc&fileName=032/lljc032.db&recNum=343.
3. John Frederick Martin, *Profits in the Wilderness: Entrepreneurship and the Founding of New England Towns in the Seventeenth Century* (Chapel Hill: Published for the Institute of Early American History and Culture, Williamsburg, Virginia, by the University of North Carolina Press, 1991), 217–28.
4. Francis Newton Thorpe, *The Federal and State Constitutions, Colonial Charters, and Other Organic Laws of the State, Territories, and Colonies Now or Heretofore Forming the United States of America* (Washington: G.P.O., 1909), 6: 3755; and 3: 1898, archive.org/details/cu31924019912074. Although the document says "ratable," it apparently means "rateable," that is, subject to taxation.

voice of a majority of the people the law of the land."[5] New York, Maryland, Virginia, and Georgia used "electors" or other terms tying representation to the number of eligible white male voters.[6] While New Jersey ratified the only constitution allowing women to vote, New Jersey's framers punted on reapportionment. They left to future legislators how to interpret their directive that changes in representation be decided "on the principles of more equal representation."[7] South Carolina's language most prefigured the federal arrangement, probably because, of all the states, it had perhaps the most similar problem to the federal one in being divided among jurisdictions with large enslaved populations and those with few. The great proportion of South Carolina's enslaved population resided in the low country parishes, while upcountry parishes were predominantly white. South Carolina's constitution called for future reapportionment "according to the particular and comparative strength and taxable property of the different parts of the same, regard being always had to the number of white inhabitants and such taxable property."[8] "Taxable property" in this case signified wealth in slaves. For all their experimentation, enumeration by counting the full population went beyond state constitution-makers' thinking.[9]

The Constitutional Framers blazed a path in prescribing reapportionment by a means other than by counting those of its residents theoretically eligible to bear arms and to vote (white men), or those who paid taxes (rateables and polls). The federal Constitution appears to be the first American document that explicitly tied future apportionment to an exact count of the total population, and certainly the first one that did so using such a complex formula. Perhaps this novelty contributed to lack of consideration of its mathematical complexities.

The Constitutional Framers generated their formula for the purposes of determining both states' respective federal privileges, in the form of House representation, and their federal obligations, in the form

5. Thorpe, *The Federal and State Constitutions*, 5: 3086; Gary B. Nash et al., "Notes and Documents," *The Pennsylvania Magazine of History and Biography* 99, no. 3 (1975): 362–75.

6. Thorpe, *Federal and State Constitutions*, 5: 2629–2630; 3: 1691–1692; 7: 3815–1816; 2: 779.

7. Ibid., 5: 2595.

8. Ibid., 6: 3252.

9. Rhode Island and Connecticut kept their colonial charters in force until well into the nineteenth century. For a longer discussion of the principles involved at the state level, see Marc W. Kruman, *Between Authority & Liberty: State Constitution Making in Revolutionary America* (Chapel Hill: University of North Carolina Press, 1997), 65–76.

of taxation. Consideration of the latter motivated the origin of what was proposed and adopted in the Constitution. According to James Madison's notes of the Constitutional Convention, the committee first tasked with considering the number of legislative representatives reported their recommendation on July 9, 1787. That committee came up with a plan for a total of fifty-six representatives, based upon a formula of one representative for every 40,000 people. When pressed on what data they used, committee member Gouverneur Morris implied that the committee considered both free and enslaved inhabitants, and admitted that, as far as exact numbers, "the Report is little more than a guess," although among William Paterson's notes for his own June 9 speech were the Confederation Congress's state-level population estimates as of 1785.[10] Because the Convention delegates from several states were displeased with the number of representatives their respective states were allotted, the committee was reconstituted. The next day, the new committee reported with a plan that was ultimately adopted, calling for sixty-five representatives.[11] No documents indicate what happened in that committee meeting, but the changes appear to have been designed to secure the support of states that gained representation, rather than based upon either different population estimates or a rationale for how representation was calculated.

Although that committee's numbers ended up being adopted for the makeup of the first federal Congress, James Wilson produced the exacting and ultimately successful plan concerning the future divvying of representation. According to James Madison's notes of the Convention, Wilson suggested that taxes and representation under the Constitution be calculated "in proportion to the whole number of white & other free Citizens & inhabitants of every age sex & condition . . . and three fifths of all other persons not comprehended in the foregoing description, except Indians not paying taxes." He noted that such had been "the rule in the Act of Congress . . . for apportioning quotas of revenue on the States."[12] Wilson was referring to the Article of

10. United States Department of State, *Documentary History of the Constitution of the United States of America, 1786-1870.*, vol. 3 (Washington: Department of State, 1900), 296, catalog.hathitrust.org/Record/100772439; William Paterson, "Papers of William Paterson on the Federal Convention, 1787," *American Historical Review* 9, no. 2 (January 1904): 332–324.

11. United States Department of State, *Documentary History*, 3: 299.

12. James Madison, *The Debates in the Federal Convention of 1787: Which Framed the Constitution of the United States of America*, ed. James Brown Scott and Gaillard Hunt, Journal of the Federal Convention (New York: Oxford University Press, 1920), 88, catalog.hathitrust.org/Record/010446630.

Confederation Congress's 1783 proposed amendment to the Articles of Confederation for the purposes of raising revenue more reliably and being able to calculate states' respective shares more easily than the prevailing method of relying on real estate evaluations. The Confederation Congress had decided that population could serve as a proxy for wealth. The three-fifths formulation resulted from a compromise among several possible ratios for the comparison of how much enslaved people contributed to wealth compared to free people, and had nothing to do with representation at that point.[13] Although there were several attempts in the Articles of Confederation Congress to move to representation by population, representation at the national level remained one vote for each state until the establishment of the federal government.[14]

Whether white women and children were counted in the Constitution may seem like a question that had no immediate practical consequences. One might guess that as long as the number of free men as a proportion of overall population did not vary much from state to state, whether or not white women and children were included would not affect the comparative size of different states' congressional delegations. That assumption is wrong.

Still, the delegates to the Constitutional Convention appear to have operated under this misguided notion. Hypothetical scenarios with simplified numbers illustrate the point. If free men comprised a third of the residents of State A, and a third of the residents of States B and C, then counting their whole populations would not change the comparative sizes of their Congressional delegations. Table 1 shows this stable ratio to be the case. The additional inclusion of free women and children in Table 1 means more representatives, but the proportional relationships among the states remains intact. In other words, in this scenario, adding white women and children does not make a material difference to the states' relative power in Congress.

Slavery's existence, though, and the southern Framers' desire to protect it, warped representation no less than it did all other facets of the early republic. The additional counting of three out of every five enslaved people rendered the inclusion of white women and children to be highly consequential. Let us look at another hypothetical scenario, this time with two fictitious states of equal population, State D half enslaved and half free, State E entirely free. In Table 2 we see that the

13. Robin L. Einhorn, *American Taxation, American Slavery* (Chicago: University of Chicago Press, 2006), 138–44.

14. Rosemarie Zagarri, *The Politics of Size: Representation in the United States, 1776-1850* (Ithaca: Cornell University Press, 1987), 63.

State	FreeMen	Representatives (on the basis of 1 per 100 represented)	Ratio to State A	White women and children	Total free population	Representatives (on the basis of 1 per 100 represented)	Ratio to State A
A	1,000	10	1	2,000	3,000	30	1
B	2,000	20	2	4,000	6,000	60	2
C	4,000	40	4	8,000	12,000	120	4

Table 1: Hypothetical Example of States Enumerating Only Free Population.

State	Free men	Enslaved people	Delegates (on the basis of 1 per 100 free represented, 3/5 of every unfree)	Ratio to State D	White women and children	Total free population	Total population	Delegates (on the basis of 1 per 100 free represented, 3/5 of every unfree)	Ratio to State D
D	500	1,500	14	1	1,000	1,500	3,000	24	1
E	1,000	0	10	0.71	2,000	3,000	3,000	30	1.25

Table 2: Hypothetical Example of States Enumerating Free and Enslaved People.

ratio of representation between states does indeed vary according to whether white women and children, in addition to free men and a portion of enslaved people, would be included. Without white women and children counted, State D's delegation exceeds that of State E; with white women and children counted, State E's delegation proves larger than State D's. In short, counting a larger proportion of the free population increases the relative power of those states composed of more free people, and could do so significantly. Just as this is the case in our imagined scenario, it was true of actual Congressional apportionment in the early republic.

The first practical application of the Constitution's apportionment formula indicated the effects of including white women and children. As noted above, the Constitutional Convention somewhat arbitrarily set the initial number of House members for each state. In 1792, Congress faced the conundrum of how best to apportion House seats based upon the results of the 1790 census. That sparked a political conflagration, with heated debates both within the Washington administration and Congress, and initial legislation that drew President George Washington to wield his veto for the first time. Article 1, Section 2, Clause 3 of the Constitution of the United States mandated that "the Number of Representatives shall not exceed one for every thirty thousand" counted according to the formula that Wilson had proposed, with every state having at least one House member. Beyond that, it was silent, leading to two major questions. First, how large should the House of Representatives be? Second, by what mathematical formula would that number of seats be divided?[15] The first of those questions appears more philosophical than practical, and the second technical. But, in combination, they could mean the difference between a smaller state being limited to one seat or granted two, or a bloc of states having a slight deficiency or edge.

Congress eventually passed, and Washington signed, a plan devised by Secretary of State Thomas Jefferson. Jefferson called for the enumerated population of each state to be divided by 33,000, with the fractional remainders ignored.[16] In other words, if a state had an enumerated population up to 33,000, it was granted one representative. An enumerated population of anywhere from 33,001 to 65,999 also resulted in one representative rather than two, as fractions would not be counted. This method produced a House composed of 105 members. Perhaps not coincidentally, Jefferson's Virginia gained a seat compared to the formula proposed by Jefferson archrival and New Yorker, Secretary of the Treasury Alexander Hamilton.[17]

With the inclusion of white women and children, the makeup of the Third Congress of the United States looked very different than if only free men and enslaved people had been counted. Without them, if we were to use Jefferson's formula, the total number of seats would only have been 33, rather than 105. Some states would have lost influence with the inclusion of white women and children, while others would have gained leverage (Table 3).

The inclusion of white women and children substantially affected the balance of power in the House of Representatives along a line that deeply concerned Revolutionary-era Americans. Not surprisingly, including a higher proportion of free people in the total count benefited what Americans called at the time "eastern" and what we now call the "northern" states as opposed to the Southern states, as Table 4 indicates.

The inclusion of free women and children, as Table 5 shows, also altered the House balance of power in terms of another deeply contentious issue, especially during the Constitutional Convention. The

15. M. L. Balinski and H. Peyton Young, *Fair Representation: Meeting the Ideal of One Man, One Vote*, Second edition (Washington, D.C: Brookings Institution Press, 2001), 8.
16. Thomas Jefferson, "Opinion on the Apportionment Bill, 4 April 1792" (n.d.), founders.archives.gov/documents/Jefferson/01-23-02-0324, accessed May 10, 2019.
17. M. L. Balinski and H. P. Young, "The Jefferson Method of Apportionment," *SIAM Review* 20, no. 2 (April 1978): 278–84, doi.org/10.1137/1020040.

State	Enumerated population excluding free women, children, and all other free persons*	Number of representatives excluding free women, children, and all other free persons	Percent of House	Enumerated population including free women, children, and all other free persons*	Number of representatives with free women, children, and all other free persons	Percent of House	Gain/loss with free women and children included
Vermont	22,445	1	3.0%	85,533	2	1.9%	-1.1%
New Hampshire	36,181	1	3.0%	141,822	4	3.8%	0.8%
Massachusetts	119,837	3	9.1%	475,327	14	13.3%	4.2%
Rhode Island	16,588	1	3.0%	68,446	2	1.9%	-1.1%
Connecticut	62,181	1	3.0%	236,840	7	6.7%	3.6%
New York	96,494	2	6.1%	331,590	10	9.5%	3.5%
New Jersey	52,105	1	3.0%	179,570	5	4.8%	1.7%
Pennsylvania	113,030	3	9.1%	432,878	13	12.4%	3.3%
Delaware	17,115	1	3.0%	55,541	1	1.0%	-2.1%
Maryland	117,737	3	9.1%	278,514	8	7.6%	-1.5%
Virginia	286,512	8	24.2%	630,559	19	18.1%	-6.1%
Kentucky	22,612	1	3.0%	68,705	2	1.9%	-1.1%
North Carolina	130,331	3	9.1%	353,522	10	9.5%	0.4%
South Carolina	99,832	3	9.1%	206,235	6	5.7%	-3.4%
Georgia	30,661	1	3.0%	70,842	2	1.9%	-1.1%
Total	1,223,662	33	100.0%	3,615,925	105	100.0%	100%

Table 3: 1792 House Delegations Excluding and Including Free Women and Children. *Enumerated population includes free white men and three-fifths of enslaved people. Note: All population numbers taken from the 1790 U.S. Census. Source: United States Department of State, *Return of the Whole Number of Persons within the Several Districts of the United States: According to "An Act Providing for the Enumeration of the Inhabitants of the United States," Passed March the First, One Thousand Seven Hundred and Ninety-One* (Philadelphia: Childs and Swaine, 1791), 4.

	Number of Representatives excluding free women and children	Percent of the House of Representatives controlled excluding free women, children and all other free persons	Number of Representatives including free women and children	Percent of the House of Representatives controlled including free women, children and all other free persons
Northern States	14	43.2%	58	55.2%
Southern States	19	57.6%	47	44.8%

Table 4: Comparative Strength of Northern and Southern House Delegations.

	Number of Representatives excluding free women and children	Percent of the House of Representatives controlled excluding free women and children	Number of Representatives including free women and children	Percent of the House of Representatives controlled including free women and children
Seven smaller states	8	24.2%	18	17.1%
Seven larger states	25	75.8%	87	82.9%

Table 5: Comparative Strength of Smaller State and Larger State Delegations.

percentage of members of the House held by the seven smaller states declined with the inclusion of free women and children compared to what it would have been without them.

Furthermore, because the inclusion of free women and children tilted the balance of power northwards in the House of Representatives, it also did so for the Electoral College. That made no difference for the 1792 presidential election, when every elector cast a ballot to return Washington to office. But 1796 was much closer. Massachusetts man John Adams garnered seventy-one electoral votes, while Virginian favorite son Jefferson tallied sixty-eight.[18] By increasing the relative number of northern votes, the enumeration of free women and children probably threw Adams over the top.

Despite its novelty and that it held important consequences for representation, the decision to enumerate free women and free children,

18. National Archives and Records Administration, "U. S. Electoral College Historical Election Results: Electoral Votes for President and Vice President 1789-1821," U.S. Electoral College, www.archives.gov/federal-register/electoral-college/votes/1789_1821.html#1796, accessed May 24, 2019.

as opposed to only free men, appears to have been met with silence. It occasioned no recorded comment during the Constitutional Convention. The three authors of this piece conducted a thorough search of the index and text searches of *The Documentary History of the Ratification of the Constitution*.[19] We found no evidence of debate concerning this issue in any of the state ratification proceedings. A survey of the scholarly literature came up empty. We also emailed John Kaminski, longtime editor of the *Documentary History of the Ratification of the Constitution* project; Jan Lewis, the foremost authority on the representation of white women in the Constitution; and Rosemarie Zagarri, author of prominent books both on the issue of representation and on women's rights during the American Revolutionary period. None could recall coming across late-eighteenth-century Americans discussing the political ramifications of enumerating white women and children in the Constitution.[20] If the members of the wordy—sometimes prolix—Revolutionary generation discussed the issue, they left little or no trace, suggesting that they simply did not think of it.

This is not to say that no one considered the broader philosophical question of whom the Constitution represented. In her seminal article on this topic, historian Jan Lewis argued that the Framers considered white women as essential to representation in the Constitution.[21] Lewis concluded that James Wilson, who first drafted the clause mentioning women, intentionally included them in the body politic because the purpose of government, in Wilson's eyes, was to facilitate happiness for all of its citizens. Lewis's claim was like a wildly post-modernist house situated on an otherwise staid city block. Her question of whether women were represented was a major departure in terms of what historians had asked. Lewis's reasoning, though, fit squarely in the greater historiographic framework concerning the debates over representation, placing the representation of women as a logical consequence of late eighteenth-century republican and liberal

19. Merrill Jensen, John P. Kaminski, and Gaspare J. Saladino, eds., *The Documentary History of the Ratification of the Constitution*, 34 vols. (Madison: Wisconsin Historical Society Press, 1976), digital.library.wisc.edu/1711.dl/History.Constitution.

20. John Kaminski to Andrew M. Schocket, "Re: Query about Representation & White Women and Children," November 28, 2018; Jan Lewis to Andrew M. Schocket, "RE: Question from SHEARite Concerning "'of Every Age, Sex, and Condition,'"" April 21, 2018; Rosemarie Zagarri to Andrew M. Schocket, "Women as Part of the Counted Inhabitants in Constitution," July 23, 2018.

21. Jan Lewis, "'Of Every Age Sex & Condition': The Representation of Women in the Constitution," *Journal of the Early Republic* 15, no. 3 (Autumn 1995): 359–87.

thought.[22] But Lewis's articles on the subject did not consider the immediate political consequences of counting free women, much less the issue of doing so for free children. The political ramifications of including free women and free children for the purpose of apportionment have remained a lacuna in the literature concerning representation and the Constitution.

The above tables beg the question of how such a politically powerful innovation could slip by unremarked. During the debates within the states over the ratification of the Constitution, Americans hotly contested nearly every other consequential clause. Making claims concerning why something did not happen—in this case, controversy over a significant element of representation—requires more speculation than interpreting why events happened how they did. We suggest a combination of two factors, one having to do with the particular historical context, the other a broader human failing.

First, the context. Had the expansion of the expansion of enumeration beyond free men to include white women and children occurred on its own, perhaps there might have been comment, even if Americans had estimated that the proportionality of the increases rendered moot its political consequences. However, as we have noted, that did not happen independently. Rather, it occurred in tandem with the counting of three out of every five enslaved people. For white Americans, once enslaved people were being counted–and in such a strange and controversial way–to exclude white women and children would have been unthinkable, regardless of how it would have affected apportionment in Congress. The glare generated by the fractional inclusion of enslaved people perhaps blinded late-eighteenth-century Americans to the mathematical ramifications of including white women and children.

We suggest that the other, deeper reason for the inattention stems from what may be a timeless human shortfall when encountering this kind of quantitative problem. In one of their pathbreaking articles establishing the concept of implicit bias, psychologists Amos Tversky and Daniel Kahneman identified an interesting phenomenon: when simultaneously presented with gauging the probability of two events, they rate the chance of both happening more highly than the rate the

22. J. R. Pole, *Political Representation in England and the Origins of the American Republic* (New York: Macmillan; St. Martin's Press, 1966); Rosemarie Zagarri, *The Politics of Size: Representation in the United States, 1776-1850* (Ithaca: Cornell University Press, 1987); Gordon S. Wood, *The Creation of the American Republic, 1776-1787* (Chapel Hill: Published for the Institute of Early American History and Culture at Williamsburg, Va., by the University of North Carolina Press, 1969).

possibility of one or the other happening independently. For example, Tversky and Kahneman gave a group of students a description of someone with certain liberal political proclivities. They asked the students how likely the person was to be a bank teller. The students were then given the opportunity to consider the probability that the person would be a feminist activist bank teller. The respondents actually rated the latter to be more likely than the former–notwithstanding what would seem the obvious conclusion that the chances of someone being a bank teller, regardless of their politics, should be higher than that of them being both a feminist activist and a bank teller. Tversky and Kahneman labeled this failing of human reasoning the "conjunctive fallacy in probability judgment."[23] They and subsequent researchers have reproduced this research in a variety of settings, and found that even people highly knowledgeable in statistics can fall victim to this misunderstanding of basic probability.[24]

That may have been exactly what happened with the Framers and the inclusion of white women and children along with three fifths of enslaved people. The Framers likely assumed that, had only white people been counted, the probability that the inclusion of women and children would have left the comparative size of the various state delegations unaffected was very high. That guess turns out to be mostly correct. As the 1790 census indicates, adult males comprised no less than 30.66 percent and no more than 35.60 percent of any state's free population.[25] So far, so good. However, when presented with the familiar formula of white population plus three-fifths of enslaved people, the Founders, like the students in Tversky and Kahneman's study, may have assumed the probability of including white women and children not affecting apportionment was even more likely than without the three-fifths clause.

The authors' own experience reinforces our conjecture. Schocket had assigned Lewis's article as reading for a class session in an undergraduate course on the American Revolution. Perhaps prompted by his own coursework in demographics, Spicer asked how the inclusion of women impacted apportionment, a question McLaren-

23. Amos Tversky and Daniel Kahneman, "Extensional Versus Intuitive Reasoning: The Conjunction Fallacy in Probability Judgment," *Psychological Review* 90, no. 4 (October 1983): 23.

24. For a review of this literature, see Rodrigo Moro, "On the Nature of the Conjunction Fallacy," *Synthese* 171, no. 1 (2009): 1–24.

25. United States Department of State, *Return of the Whole Number of Persons within the Several Districts of the United States*, 4.

Czerr followed up on.[26] Crucially, neither were operating under the assumption that including free women would necessarily leave apportionment unaffected regardless of the three-fifths clause. They were thus less susceptible to the deductive fallacy under which Revolutionary-era Americans and previous historians, Schocket included, operated. Putting the 1790 Census numbers on the board during that class session revealed that the inclusion of free women and children in combination with three-fifths of enslaved people did indeed result in a surprising concatenation of affects.

The expansion of enumeration to include all white people in addition to three-fifths of enslaved people at the national level set an important precedent. As Lewis noted in her more recent article following up on her original one, it resulted in a nation in which all the nation's residents, rather than only propertied white men, were nominally represented constituents of and subjects to the federal government.[27] More immediately, the inclusion of free women and children resulted in higher representation of free states than otherwise would have been the case both in the House of Representatives and in the Electoral College. The failure of early Americans to notice the momentousness of that inclusion reinforces an important truth: in this as in every other way we have found to examine the Founders, rather than demigods, they were no less fallible than the rest of us.

26. Colin G. Spicer and Kinzey M. McLaren-Czerr, "A Revolution for All?" (class discussion, American Revolutionary Era, 1763-1789; Bowling Green State University, Bowling Green, OH; April 19, 2018).

27. Jan Ellen Lewis, "What Happened to the Three-Fifths Clause: The Relationship between Women and Slaves in Constitutional Thought, 1787–1866," *Journal of the Early Republic* 37, no. 1 (2017): 1–46.

America's Revolution Against Toleration: The Rise of True Religious Liberty

BRIAN PATRICK O'MALLEY

In 1793, a widely circulated American editorial observed, "A few years ago, to say of any man that he was 'a friend to toleration,' was to place his temper in the fairest point of view." By the 1790s, people knew better. "Now every friend to the rights of man perceives that toleration was founded on usurpation and oppression." The writer described a "revolution" in "the minds of the enlightened."[1]

Toleration, in this context, meant permitting the exercise of religion other than the established national or state religion, but only while still paying tithes to the national or state church. Also certain honors, like holding public office, were reserved only for members of the established church.[2] Toleration, as Americans then understood it, was inherently unequal both in terms of tithes and in the limits that it imposed.

The revolution against toleration was pioneered by revolutionaries like James Madison and Benjamin Franklin. The leader who most promoted the revolution in American thinking was Welsh economist and clergyman Richard Price. America's founding generation adored him. During the Revolutionary War, Price delivered sermons and published pamphlets defending the American cause. Grateful for his efforts, the Continental Congress offered Price American citizenship in 1778, along with a post as a financial advisor. Price politely declined the

1. *Federal Gazette* (Philadelphia), February 19, 1793; *General Advertiser* (Philadelphia), February 21, 1793; *State Gazette of South-Carolina* (Charleston, SC), March 22, 1793.
2. Exclusion from public office was unevenly enforced in Britain. Some non-Anglicans in the eighteenth century served in municipal offices and Parliament; James E. Bradley, *Religion, Revolution and English Radicalism: Non-conformity in Eighteenth-Century Politics and Society* (New York: Cambridge University Press, 2002 [1990]), 79-80.

honor, but the offer illustrated American admiration for the Welsh man.[3]

Before the tumult of the Revolutionary War, American colonists associated toleration with tax support for an established church. England's Toleration Act (1689) stipulated that non-Anglican Protestants still owed their tithes to the Church of England. Baptists, Quakers and others "dissenting" from the official church still owed their tithes to the established denomination, whether Congregationalist in much of New England or Anglican in much of the South.[4]

In 1760, Congregationalist minister and future Yale president Ezra Stiles tried to prove that colonies with Congregationalist establishments were more lenient than Episcopalian establishments. In colonies with Anglican establishments, Stiles wrote, taxes supported only the Church of England "and dissenters are not exempted from contributing." Stiles overestimated the ease with which New England Baptists and Anglicans could redirect their tithes from the local Congregationalist cleric to a pastor of their own denomination. Stiles thought "other sects scarcely know that they are tolerated dissenters, so happy and mild is our dominion."[5]

Stiles recognized a distinction between "toleration" and "liberty." Liberty meant no establishment, that is, no tax-supported denomination. A person was free to give as much or as little as he wished to the church of his choice. Rhode Island, for instance, enjoyed "universal equal protestant liberty" because no denomination could "enforce their ministerial contracts at law." New Jersey and Pennsylvania had "universal liberty as in *Rhode-Island*."[6] Baptist doctrine shaped Rhode Island. Quakerism shaped Delaware, Pennsylvania and New Jersey, colonies with no religious establishment. Stiles acknowledged religious

3. *The Virginia Journal, and Alexandria Advertiser* (Alexandria), October 13, 1785; Carl B. Cone, *Torchbearer of Freedom: The Influence of Richard Price on Eighteenth Century Thought* (Lexington: University of Kentucky Press, 1952), 88-89, 104.

4. Check "Proviso for Tythes," in Primary Resource, "An Act for Exempting their Majestyes Protestant Subjects dissenting from the Church of England from the Penalties of certain Lawes" (1688), *Encyclopedia Virginia*, www.encyclopediavirginia.org/_An_Act_for_Exempting_their_Majestyes_Protestant_Subjects_dissenting_from_the_Church_of_England_from_the_Penalties_of_certaine_Lawes_1688.

5. Ezra Stiles, *A Discourse on the Christian Union…* (Boston: Edes and Gill, 1761), 125, 127, Early American Imprints, Series 1 (Charles Evans), No. 9018; 89; Derek H. Davis, *Religion and the Continental Congress, 1774-178: Contributions to Original Intent* (New York: Oxford University Press, 2000), 28-30.

6. Stiles, *Discourse*, 125, 126.

liberty in certain colonies, but only in passing. Stiles focused on proving that Congregationalist toleration was better than Anglican toleration.[7]

In the 1760s, Presbyterian and Congregationalist debates with Anglicans made toleration an ominous word. The prospect of an Anglican bishop in the colonies worried the Calvinist denominations. In 1768, Boston Congregationalist minister Charles Chauncy warned that pro-bishop Episcopalians wanted to extend "no other privilege to dissenters but that of a bare toleration." A 1769 essay, probably by William Livingston, denounced "*laws* that secure to English dissenters" nothing more "than a bare *toleration* under *intolerably* burdensome impositions."[8]

Some Americans tried to redefine "toleration" in a way that precluded tax support for an established church. In 1765, North Carolina Lt. Gov. William Tryon, the acting governor, remarked, "I never heard Toleration in any Country, made use of, as an argument to exempt Dissenters from bearing their Share of the Support of Established Religion." In 1770, a baffled defender of New England's Congregationalist establishments complained, "In *Virginia* and *Maryland* all denominations pay ministerial rates to support the episcopal clergy, and did any man ever complain that the paying this tax was inconsistent with the act of toleration, or liberty of conscience?"[9]

In the 1760s, Americans struggled with the limits of toleration. In 1776, Americans accelerated their rejection of toleration. In May 1776, the Continental Congress urged the colonies to found new governments. In what became the first state constitutions, Americans began dismantling toleration. On May 15 the Virginia Convention assigned a committee to draft a Declaration of Rights as a preamble for a Virginia Constitution. The committee entrusted the work to George Mason. In one article, Mason wrote that "all Men shou'd enjoy the fullest Toleration in the Exercise of Religion." The committee edited Mason's draft and presented it to the Virginia Convention. On May 29, the Convention ordered the printing of the Declaration as a leaflet

7. Ibid., 125; Davis, *Religion and the Continental Congress*, 25, 30-31.

8. Charles Chauncy, *The Appeal to the Public Answered, in Behalf of the non-Episcopal Churches in America . . .* (Boston: Kneeland and Adams, for Thomas Leverett, 1768), page 202, Early American Imprints, Series 1, No. 10853; Sir Issac Foot, "A Kick for the Whipper, No. 39," *New-York Gazette, or Weekly Post-Boy*, March 13, 1769.

9. Legislative Journals, May 3, 1765, *The Colonial Records of North Carolina*, Vol. 7, ed. William L. Saunders (Raleigh: Josephus Daniels, 1890), 43; *The Pennsylvania Chronicle, and Universal Advertiser* (Philadelphia), March 19, 1770.

for the perusal of the delegates. For many years, the draft version was more well-known than the actual Declaration of Rights.[10]

The committee retained the word "toleration" from Mason's draft. In later years, James Madison speculated that Mason "inadvertently" used the term toleration, based on its familiarity from English law. For Madison, toleration was not enough.[11] Madison, twenty-five, was a delegate from Orange County. He long remembered being "young and inexperienced," and was reticent around his distinguished colleagues. He drafted an amendment to the article on religion and asked Patrick Henry to present it. [12]

Madison's first proposal was too radical for the Convention. He proposed a second revision and enlisted another intermediary, Edmund Pendleton, his cousin and a staunch Anglican. Madison's idea prevailed. Virginia lawmakers ratified the Declaration of Rights with an assertion that "all men are equally entitled to the free exercise of religion," with no mention of toleration.[13] James Madison and Virginia's rejection of toleration was largely unknown outside Virginia. The *Virginia Gazette* published the committee's preliminary version on June 1, and newspapers around the country reprinted the preliminary draft.[14]

10. *Journals of the Continental Congress, 1774-1789*, Vol. 4, ed. Worthington Chauncey Ford (Washington, D.C.: Library of Congress, 1906), 342, 357, 358; James Madison, "Madison's Amendments to the Declaration of Rights," May 29-June 12, 1776, *Founders Online,* National Archives, founders.archives.gov/documents/Madison/01-01-02-0054-0003, accessed April 11, 2019; James Madison, *The Papers of James Madison*, Vol. 1, ed. William T. Hutchinson and William M. E. Rachal (Chicago: University of Chicago Press, 1962), 171-172, 178.
11. James Madison, "James Madison's Autobiography," ed. Douglass Adair, *William and Mary Quarterly*, 3d ser., 2 (1945): 199; James Madison to George Mason, December 29, 1827, in James Madison, *The Writings of James Madison*, Vol. 9, ed. Gaillard Hunt (New York: G. P. Putnam's Sons, 1910), 293.
12. Madison to Mason, December 29, 1827, Hunt, *Writings*, 9: 293; Madison, "James Madison's Autobiography," 199; Madison, "Madison's Amendments," especially note 5; Daniel L. Dreisbach, "George Mason's Pursuit of Religious Liberty in Revolutionary Virginia," *The Virginia Magazine of History and Biography* 108 (2000): 12-18, www.jstor.org/stable/4249815; Irving Brant, *James Madison*, Vol. 1, *Virginia Revolutionist* (Indianapolis: Bobbs-Merrill, 1941), 247; Richard Brookhiser, *James Madison* (New York: Basic Books, 2011), 24-25; Jeff Broadwater, *James Madison: A Son of Virginia and a Founder of the Nation* (Chapel Hill: The University of North Carolina Press, 2012), 8-9.
13. Madison, "Madison's Amendments," and note 9; Brookhiser, *James Madison*, 24; Virginia Declaration of Rights, June 12, 1776, Avalon Project, avalon.law.yale.edu/18th_century/virginia.asp.
14. Madison, "Madison's Amendments;" R. Carter Pittman, Review of *Sources of Our Liberties* by Richard L. Perry, ed., *Virginia Magazine of History and Biography* 68 (Jan. 1960): 110-111; Jeff Broadwater, *George Mason, Forgotten Founder* (Chapel Hill: University of North Carolina Press, 2006), 90.

The Declaration of Rights appeared in four Virginia editions of the state constitution from 1784 to 1805, but United States Congressional compilations of the state constitutions did not include Virginia's Declaration of Rights. Jonathan Foster's 1811 edition of *The Constitutions of the United States, According to the Latest Amendments* was the first edition to include the Virginia Declaration of Rights.[15]

On January 11, 1777, Presbyterian minister William Tennent III spoke before the South Carolina House of Assembly in support of a petition from Dissenters. The petitioners objected to exclusive tax support for the Church of England and called for equal civil rights for Protestants of every denomination. Claiming Protestant dissenters "stand upon the same footing with the Jews," Tennent explained, "No body molests them. But would it, Sir, content our brethren of the Church of England, to be *barely tolerated*? That is, *not punished* for presuming to think for themselves."[16] Despite Tennent's denunciation of toleration, state lawmakers ratified the 1778 South Carolina Constitution with the provision that all monotheists "shall be freely tolerated." The 1778 Constitution also designated the "Christian Protestant religion" as "the established religion of this State." Despite a declared establishment, the 1778 Constitution eliminated tax support for churches.[17]

Writing under a pseudonym in 1778, New Jersey Gov. William Livingston compared his state's "free constitution" to "British tyranny." The New Jersey Constitution of 1776 did not eliminate religious tests altogether. Consistent with the colonial regulations excluding Catholics, the 1776 Constitution opened public office to every denomination of Protestant. In comparison, toleration in England ostensibly excluded Protestant Dissenters from military offices and most public offices. The New Jersey Constitution prohibited tax support for church and clergy, while England forced Dissenters to support the established church.[18]

15. Pittman, Review, 110; *Pennsylvania Packet*, December 13, 1787.

16. William Tennent, *Mr. Tennent's Speech on the Dissenting Petition* ... (Charles-Town [Charleston]: Peter Timothy, 1777), pages 14, Early American Imprints, Series 1, no. 15612.

17. Constitution of South Carolina-March 19, 1778, art. 38, Avalon Project, avalon.law .yale.edu/18th_century/sc02.asp.

18. New Jersey Constitution, 1776, arts. 18 and 19, Avalon Project, avalon.law.yale.edu/ 18th_century/nj15.asp; Cato [William Livingston], "For the New-Jersey Gazette," *New-Jersey Gazette*, February 18, 1778 (Livingston's Cato); William Livingston, *The Papers of William Livingston*, Vol. 2, ed. Carl E. Prince (Trenton: New Jersey Historical Commission, 1988), 234-235.

Livingston wrote of toleration, "I call it *persecution*, because it is harassing mankind for their principles." Livingston asked, "For what are the civil disqualifications, and the deprivation of certain privileges . . . but so many punishments?" Livingston explained, "As contradistinguished indeed from actual prohibition, a permission may doubtless be call'd a toleration." An English dissenter enjoyed the exercise of religion, but with "penalties and forfeitures," he "certainly does not enjoy it freely."[19]

In December 1778, Thomas Paine wrote, "The toleration act in England, which *granted* liberty of conscience to every man, in religion, was looked upon as the perfection of religious liberty." Paine called toleration "a species of tyrannic arrogance." Paine declared, "In America we . . . do not *grant* liberty of conscience as a *favor* but *confirm* it as a *right*." By rejecting toleration, Paine believed Americans "have in point of justice exceeded every part of the known world."[20]

In the pamphlet *Information to Those Who Would Remove to America*, Benjamin Franklin assured immigrants that in America, "serious Religion, under its various Denominations, is not only tolerated, but respected and practised." Franklin published the essay sometime before March 1784.[21]

From 1776 to 1784, American disparagement of toleration was varied. Livingston mentioned "civil incapacities" (banning religious dissenters from office) but he also mentioned fines and forfeitures. Tennent focused specifically on religious taxes. In 1784, Welsh clergyman and economist Richard Price focused anti-toleration on religious tests.[22] In his 1784 opus, *Observations on the Importance of the American Revolution, and the Means of Making it a Benefit to the World*, he included a chapter on religious liberty. He wrote, "In liberty of conscience I include much more than toleration."[23] According to Price, "Toleration

19. Livingston's Cato.

20. "A Serious Address to the People of Pennsylvania on the Present Situation of their Affairs," *The Pennsylvania Packet, and Daily Advertiser* (Philadelphia), December 1, 1778; *The Independent Chronicle* (Boston), February 26, 1778; Thomas Paine, *The Complete Writings of Thomas Paine*, Vol. 2, Eric Foner, ed. (New York: Citadel Press, 1945), 285.

21. Benjamin Franklin, "Information to Those Who Would Remove to America" (before March 1784), *Founders Online*, National Archives, founders.archives.gov/documents/Franklin/01-41-02-0391; Bernard Peach, *Richard Price and the Ethical Foundations of the American Revolution* (Durham, NC: Duke University Press, 1979), 26.

22. Livingston's Cato; Tennent, *Mr. Tennent's Speech*, 14.

23. Richard Price, *Observations on the Importance of the American Revolution* (1784), in *Richard Price: Political Writings*, D. O. Thomas, ed. (New York: Cambridge University Press, 1991), 130.

can take place only where there is a civil establishment of a particular mode of religion; that is, where a predominant sect enjoys exclusive advantages . . . but at the same time thinks fit to suffer the exercise of other modes of faith and worship."[24] He expressed his disappointment at religious tests for office in several American states. Eligibility for office, Price believed, should extend to people of every religion. Price wrote, "Montesquieu was probably not a Christian. Newton and Locke were not Trinitarians and therefore not Christians according to the commonly received ideas of Christianity. Would the United States . . . deny such men, were they living, all places of trust and power among them?"[25]

Price sent a bundle of the pamphlet to Richard Henry Lee, President of the Continental Congress, for distribution to every member seated in that body, and sent copies to Benjamin Franklin, Thomas Jefferson, John Adams and George Washington, who may already have received it from Lee. Thousands of other Americans had opportunities to read Price's *Observations*. American publishers printed the book in Boston in 1784; in New Haven, Trenton and Philadelphia in 1785; and Charleston in 1786. Newspaper publishers through the United States published *Observations* in serial form.[26]

The widespread publication of Price's *Observations* prompted Americans to link toleration with religious tests. In a 1786 essay for *The New-York Packet*, "S." wrote, "Though the United States of Holland enjoy the honor of having *first* introduced into Europe, a spirit of religious tolerance, neither this power, nor Great Britain, can vie with the American States in this article; as those of their subjects who are not of the *established religion*, are deprived of the advantages of sustaining offices of government."[27]

American clergymen echoed Price's message. In a 1786 sermon, Congregationalist preacher Thomas Barnard of Salem, Massachusetts, described an inglorious past: "The road to civil distinction and honours was barred against all, who were not of the same religious profession with the majority: One Church reigned supreme, and suffered others

24. Ibid., 131.

25. Ibid., 136-37.

26. Cone, *Torchbearer of Freedom*, 104, 111; *American Mercury* (Hartford, CT), February 7, 1785; *Falmouth Gazette* (Falmouth, Mass. [Maine]), March 19, 1785; *Massachusetts Spy: Or, Worcester Gazette* (Worcester, Massachusetts), April 21, 1785; Richard Price, *The Correspondence of Richard Price*, D. O. Thomas, ed. (Durham: Duke University Press, 1983-), 2: 271n1.

27. *The New-York Packet*, April 3, 1786.

to exist only by *toleration.*" Perhaps Barnard read Price's *Observations* in January 1785 editions of the local paper.[28]

In a July 4, 1787 sermon before the militia of Elizabethtown, New Jersey, Episcopalian cleric Uzal Ogden observed, "Some powers it is true, as England, and Holland, boast of their religious toleration; but if a subject is not of the established religion in those countries, can he sustain any office of government? Their spiritual liberty therefore is defective." Ogden had an opportunity to read Price's remarks on toleration in the local paper.[29]

In 1784, Philadelphia physician and signer of the Declaration of Independence Benjamin Rush published a pamphlet urging the revision of a Pennsylvania law passed on October 1, 1779. The 1779 law was not an explicit religious test, as it did not require a voter or an officeholder to espouse or disavow a certain doctrine (England's Test Act (1673), for instance, required officeholders to disavow the Catholic doctrine of Transubstantiation). The 1779 test law was still a violation of conscience for many Pennsylvanians, as it implied a willingness to participate in a war of defense. This requirement disenfranchised Quakers and German pacifists like the Mennonites.[30] No Pennsylvanian could vote or operate a school without taking the pledge. In his pamphlet denouncing the law, Rush begged state lawmakers to "open the doors of freedom in Pennsylvania to all her children, by revising the test-law."[31]

Rush sent a copy of his pamphlet to Richard Price. In a letter acknowledging receipt of Rush's pamphlet, Price confessed the news of the 1779 test act made him regret his "utopian" optimism for the United States. Price feared he "made myself ridiculous by what I have said of the importance of this revolution." Despite his disappointment, Price hoped the United States "will become those seats of liberty, peace and virtue, which the enlightened and liberal parts of Europe are ardently wishing to see them."[32]

28. Thomas Barnard, *A Sermon, Preached at the Ordination of the Rev. Aaron Bancroft …* (Worcester: Isaiah Thomas, 1786), 20, Early American Imprints, Series 1, no. 19494; *Salem Gazette* (Salem, Massachusetts), January 18, 1785.
29. *The New-Jersey Journal, and Political Intelligencer* (Elizabethtown), July 18, 1787; *The Political Intelligencer and New Jersey Advertiser* (Elizabethtown), March 19, 1785.
30. Benjamin Rush, *Considerations Upon the Present Test-Law of Pennsylvania: Addressed to the Legislature and Freemen of the State*, Second Edition (Philadelphia: Hall and Sellers, 1785 [1784]), 3 (pages not numbered), Early American Imprints, Series 1, No. 19230, 3; Charles II, 1672: An Act for Preventing Dangers which may happen from Popish Recusants, British History Online, www.british-history.ac.uk/statutes-realm/vol5/pp782-785.
31. Rush, *Considerations*, 4-6, 8, 15, 18, 23.
32. *The Pennsylvania Packet*, September 22, 1785.

Rush sent Price's letter to *The Pennsylvania Packet* with a note explaining the letter's provenance. In his note, Rush wrote of Price, "His invaluable writings during the late war, in favour of the liberties and independence of America, rendered his name dear to every lover of liberty and republican forms of government." The Philadelphia paper published the letter on September 22, 1785 with Rush's note as an anonymous introduction.[33]

Pennsylvanians responded swiftly to the circulation of Rush's pamphlet and Price's letter. On March 4, 1786, the Pennsylvania General Assembly ratified a law that effectively nullified the 1779 test act. The 1786 law declared every adult white male, who was not an active Loyalist during the war, "a free citizen of this Commonwealth . . . intitled to all and every rights and privileges thereof, any law of the Commonwealth to the contrary notwithstanding." In deference to objections of religious pacifists, the new law implied no requirement to do violence.[34] Rush, a physician, used a graphic surgical reference to tell Price the part he played in overturning the law: "Your letter to me upon . . . that unjust law was the instrument that cut its last sinew."[35]

Newspapers throughout the United States published Price's letter, often with Rush's introduction or a similarly laudatory note. For instance, a writer for *The Virginia Journal and Alexandria Advertiser*, perhaps publisher George Richards, composed an introduction to Price's letter patterned after Rush's note, offering that if states adopted "the sentiments of the venerable Doctor in this letter," the decision "will reflect a glory on our republican governments, and render them respectable to every free country."[36]

Price's *Observations*, and his exchange with Benjamin Rush, prepared the Constitutional Convention to ban religious tests for federal office under the new Constitution. Charles Pinckney of South Carolina advocated the ban on religious tests in a speech to the Convention, though the precise day of its delivery is now known. Pinckney declared

33. Ibid.; *The Carlisle Gazette, and the Western Repository of Knowledge* (Carlisle, Pennsylvania), October 3, 1785.

34. Price, *Correspondence*, 3: 22n1; Benjamin Rush to Richard Price, Philadelphia, April 22, 1786, in Price, *Correspondence*, 3: 22.

35. Rush to Price, October 15, 1785 and April 22, 1786, *The Founders' Constitution*, Vol. 4, Article 6, Clause 3, Document 8, press-pubs.uchicago.edu/founders/documents/a6_3s8.html.

36. *Pennsylvania Packet*, September 22, 1785; *The Virginia Journal and Alexandria Advertiser* (Alexandria), October 13, 1785; *The Newport Mercury*, October 1, 1785; *The Connecticut Journal* (New Haven), October 5, 1785; *The Falmouth Gazette*, October 15, 1785; *Massachusetts Spy*, October 20, 1785; *The Vermont Gazette* (Burlington), November 21, 1785 (without elaborate introduction).

"the prevention of Religious Tests" was "a provision the world will expect from you, in the establishment of a System founded on Republican Principles, and in an age so liberal and enlightened as the present."[37] The speech incorporated the words of Rice and Rush. Price wrote of "the enlightened and liberal parts of Europe;" Pinckney spoke of the "liberal and enlightened" age. Rush mentioned "republican forms of government;" Pinckney referenced "Republican Principles."[38]

On August 20, 1787, Pinckney submitted a list of legislative proposals to the Constitutional Convention. Pinckney's legislative blueprint included the provision, "No religious test or qualification shall ever be annexed to any oath of office under the authority of the United States." Pinckney's proposals emerged from the Committee of Detail on August 30, minus Pinckney's ban on religious qualifications for office. Pinckney moved to add the article, "but no religious test shall ever be required as a qualification to any office or public trust under the authority of the U. States."[39] Roger Sherman of Connecticut thought religious tests had become so unpopular that banning them outright was unnecessary. Sherman thought "the prevailing liberality" was "sufficient security against such tests." (That prevailing liberality, of course, was shaped by Richard Price.) Despite Sherman's confidence, two delegates seconded Pinckney's motion, Gouverneur Morris of Pennsylvania and Pinckney's second cousin, Gen. Charles Cotesworth Pinckney of South Carolina.[40]

On September 12, 1787, the Constitutional Convention's Committee of Style presented a draft Constitution featuring the final version of Article VI, clause 3. The Convention approved the final draft of the Constitution on September 15 and delegates signed it on September 17. Article VI stipulated that "no religious Test shall ever be required as a Qualification to any Office or public Trust under the United States."[41]

37. Charles Pinckney, "Observations on the Plan of Government Submitted to the Federal Convention, In Philadelphia, on the 28th of May, 1787," *The Records of the Federal Convention of 1787*, Max Farrand, ed. (New Haven: Yale University Press, 1911), 1: 122 (*Farrand's Records*).

38. Ibid.; *Pennsylvania Packet*, September 22, 1785; *Virginia Journal*, October 13, 1785.

39. *The Debates in the Several State Conventions on the Adoption of the Federal Constitution . . .*, Jonathan Elliot, ed. (Washington, D.C.: Printed for the Author, 1836), 1: 250 (*Elliot's Debates*); *Farrand's Records*, 2: 488.

40. *Farrand's Records*, 2: 335; *Elliot's Debates*, 5: 498; on Charles Pinckney and Charles Cotesworth Pinckney being second cousins, see note 15 at, Enclosure: James McHenry to Philemon Dickinson, September 3, 1800, *Founders Online*, National Archives, founders.archives.gov/documents/Hamilton/01-25-02-0081-0003.

41. *Farrand's Records*, 2: 590n8, 603, 663; *Elliot's Debates*, 1: 311-312, 317-318.

Maryland delegate Luther Martin disapprovingly informed his state's legislature that the ban on religious tests "was adopted by a great majority of the convention, and without much debate." Martin claimed only some delegates were "*so unfashionable*" as to want "some distinction between the professors of Christianity and downright infidelity or paganism." To Martin's chagrin, religious tests had become passé.[42]

The rejection of toleration became a founding ideal of the republic. In 1790, George Washington assured the Hebrew Congregation of Newport, Rhode Island, "It is now no more that toleration is spoken of, as if it was by the indulgence of one class of people, that another enjoyed the exercise of their inherent natural rights."[43] Baptist preacher John Leland implicitly linked toleration with religious tests. In 1790, Leland wrote, "The very idea of toleration is despicable, it supposes that some have a pre eminence above the rest, to grant indulgence; whereas all should be equally free, Jews, Turks, Pagans and Christians. Test oaths, and established creeds, should be avoided as the worst of evils."[44] Explaining popular sentiment in Vermont, Congregationalist Rev. Samuel Williams wrote in 1794, "It is not barely *toleration*, but *equality*, which the people aim at." Calling attention to the ban on religious tests in the 1793 Vermont Constitution, Williams wrote, "No man is chosen to, or excluded from civil offices, on account of his particular religious sentiments . . . The people are under no obligation to support any teachers, but what they choose to lay themselves under."[45]

Americans even expected immigrants to flee toleration as well as persecution. In 1791, Pennsylvanian Tench Coxe wrote, "Nothing can be more rational, than that persons of *sincere piety* should seek a country in which the assertion of *mere toleration* is deemed as absurd, as the denial of *religious liberty* is thought to be criminal." Also in 1791, Alexander Hamilton predicted that manufacturers would "flock from Europe" to enjoy "what is far more precious than mere religious toleration—a

42. *Elliot's Debates*, 5: 498; Luther Martin, *Genuine Information* (1788), *Founders' Constitution*, Vol. 4, Article 6, Clause 3, Document 18, press-pubs.uchicago.edu/founders/documents/a6_3s18.html (italics in original).

43. George Washington to the Hebrew Congregation in Newport, Rhode Island, August 18, 1790, *Founders Online,* National Archives, founders.archives.gov/documents/Washington/05-06-02-0135.

44. John Leland, *The Virginia Chronicle* ... (Fredericksburg: T. Green, 1790), 40, Early American Imprints, Series 1, no. 22617.

45. Samuel Williams, *The Natural and Civil History of Vermont* ... (Walpole, NH: David Carlisle, 1794), 336, Early American Imprints, Series 1, No. 28094.

perfect equality of religious privileges."[46] In 1803, Bermuda-born Revolutionary War veteran and American jurist St. George Tucker observed that many countries no longer tortured heretics but still attached "civil incapacities" to any "dissent from the national religion." Tucker wrote that "ceasing to persecute by more violent means, has in such nations obtained the name of toleration." Tucker then offered an extensive quotation from "the elegant Dr. Price."[47]

In his later years, James Madison tried to establish his pioneering work in the rejection of toleration. Madison mentioned it in an autobiographical essay and in a letter to George Mason's grandson. Historians recognize Madison's contribution now. In his lifetime, alas, Madison's prescience as a trendsetter was underappreciated.[48]

Americans rejected toleration and the establishment of state religion. It was a revolutionary break from the practice of much of the world. With the 1791 ratification of the Bill of Rights, the First Amendment prevented a national church and any tax support it would expect. Even before the Bill of Rights, Article 6 of the Constitution opened federal office to people of any religious persuasion. Article 6 eliminated the insult of exclusion that was often a hallmark of toleration.[49]

46. *The Daily Advertiser* (New York), July 22, 1791, reprinted in Tench Coxe, *A View of the United States of America . . .* (Philadelphia: William Hall [and Wrigley & Berriman], 1794), 202; Alexander Hamilton, *Report on Manufactures*, December 5, 1791, *Founders' Constitution*, Vol. 5, Amendment 1 (Religion), Document 56, press-pubs.uchicago.edu/founders/documents/amendI_religions56.html.

47. St. George Tucker, *Blackstone's Commentaries*, 1APP. 296-97, 2App. 3-11, *Founders' Constitution*, Vol. 5, Amendment I (Religion), Document 59, press-pubs.uchicago.edu/founders/documents/amendI_religions59.html.

48. Madison, "James Madison's Autobiography," 199; Madison to Mason, December 29, 1827.

49. In *Torcaso* v. *Watkins* (1961), the Supreme Court ruled religious tests at any level of government violated the First Amendment; Davis, *Religion and the Continental Congress*, 35.

The Decision that Lost Britain the War: An Enigma Now Resolved

IAN SABERTON

In this article I address the absurdity of Cornwallis's decision to march from Wilmington to Virginia and the light thrown on it by *The Cornwallis Papers*.[1] The central enigma of the southern campaigns, it had until their publication never been able to be satisfactorily resolved.

Lt. Gen. Charles Earl Cornwallis, the British General Officer Commanding in the south, arrived in the vicinity of Wilmington, North Carolina, on April 7, 1781 after the disastrous winter campaign and his pyrrhic victory at Guilford. His troops were badly in need of refitment. In the meantime Major Gen. Nathanael Greene, the opposing commander, had begun his march for South Carolina, leaving Ramsey's Mill on Deep River on the 6th.

As early as April 5 and 6 Cornwallis advised Lt. Col. Nisbet Balfour, the Commandant of Charlestown, that he would not remain at Wilmington but run all hazards if Greene attempted any serious move towards South Carolina.[2] As interpreted by Balfour, the letters indicated Cornwallis's intention of coming after Greene in case of his movement that way.[3] Indeed, they are capable of no other interpretation. And as late as the 22nd Cornwallis reaffirmed to Balfour his intention to return, stating that he could not positively ascertain whether he would keep as low as Georgetown or pass by the head of the Waccamaw.[4] He went on to direct that supplies coming from Charlestown had better be detained, so that sufficient appear to have been available at Wilm-

1. Ian Saberton ed., *The Cornwallis Papers: The Campaigns of 1780 and 1781 in the Southern Theatre of the American Revolutionary War,* 6 vols (The Naval & Military Press Ltd, 2010) ("*CP*").
2. *CP*, vol IV, 42-4.
3. ibid., 171 and 177.
4. ibid., 122.

ington for his march, a fact borne out by the ample provisions he took with him to Virginia and by the assessment of Major James Henry Craig, who commanded the post at Wilmington, that on May 5 the following were in store there for 1,500 men: "flour 150 days, rum the same, salt meat 60 days."[5] So much, then, for Cornwallis's protestations elsewhere that he found it impracticable to return overland to South Carolina, for clearly by these letters he is damned with his own pen. Therefore we must look to other reasons for his failure to keep his word.

Cornwallis was, in fact, in two minds as to what he should do. Not revealed to Balfour during this period but disclosed on the 10th to Major Gen. William Phillips, who was commanding a British diversionary force in the Chesapeake, was Cornwallis's preference to forsake South Carolina and Georgia in favour of desultory operations in Virginia.[6] Matters came to a head on the 23rd, perhaps at a council of war, at which Cornwallis's views would have been decisive. On that day he wrote to Lord George Germain, the Secretary of State, and to Sir Henry Clinton, the Commander-in-Chief in North America, advising them of his decision to march northward. Why?

If we are to take Cornwallis's words at face value,[7] he did not expect any considerable corps left by him in South Carolina to be lost by Greene's movement, so high was his opinion of Col. Francis Lord Rawdon, commanding at Camden, and the precautions taken by Rawdon and Balfour. Yet, contradictorily, he went on to fear the worst and cite it as a reason for his not marching southward. Yes, he could have provided no immediate assistance, but fulfilling his expectations, Rawdon maintained his post at Camden, defeating Greene in the Battle of Hobkirk's Hill, and would have remained there if Cornwallis had marched promptly to relieve him, sending messengers ahead. As to Cornwallis's protestation that he would have had to return by sea, it is controverted by his letters to Balfour. All in all, Cornwallis's words are not those of an officer desiring in a perfectly feasible way to retrieve the situation in South Carolina, but rather those of one who was seeking any excuse to shore up his preference to swan around the highways and byways of Virginia, a preference which, as he readily admitted to Phillips, was very unlikely "to overturn the rebel government [*there*] and to establish a militia and some kind of mixed authority of our own."[8] At the end of the day it does not take an accomplished strategist

5. ibid., 168.
6. ibid., 114-5.
7. ibid., 107-8.
8. ibid., 115.

to see that desultory operations which did not involve the possession of Virginia would in no way compensate for the loss of South Carolina and incidentally Georgia. Nor, contrary to Cornwallis's protestations, is it unreasonable to assume that, in line with Clinton's instructions,[9] they could have continued to be held defensively, albeit tenuously. So, if Cornwallis's stated reasons for his decision do not make sense, were there others propelling him on? Almost certainly, yes.

A dynamic officer best suited to offensive action, Cornwallis was, as stated in *The Cornwallis Papers*,[10] temperamentally ill at ease with defensive warfare, a prospect now facing him in his immediate sphere of operations. A humane, cultivated man, he was moreover sickened by the murderous barbarity with which the war was waged by the revolutionary irregulars and state troops of the Carolinas and Georgia. Deterrence was essential, but in keeping with his character he had no stomach for the disagreeable measures involved, a point also made elsewhere in *The Cornwallis Papers*.[11] In short, as the Wickwires make clear, "Cornwallis had no place in a civil war."[12] Also contributing to his malaise was the mental and physical fatigue of commanding a whole year's hard and solid campaigning, fatigue which can be glimpsed during his stay at Wilmington. In his letter to Phillips of the 10th he remarked in a jocular but nevertheless sincere way, "I am quite tired of marching about the country in quest of adventures," to which there need to be subjoined a few revealing words in the draft of his letter of April 18 to Jeffrey Lord Amherst, the Commander-in-Chief of the British Army: "I can with great truth assure your Lordship that I have experienced as much care, anxiety and responsibility as ever fell to the share of any commanding officer."[13] Altogether, it is fairly clear that the weight of his command was bearing down heavily on him. Against this background it is not entirely surprising that Cornwallis should have cast around, perhaps subconsciously, for reasons to release him from the predicament of dealing with a situation which he had come to detest. Always keen to act offensively, he simply opted for the more congenial alternative of doing so in Virginia, well way from the distasteful nature of the war farther south, an alternative, incidentally, which pricked his pride less than the perceived ignominy of conducting a defensive war to the southward after another unsuccessful campaign.

9. *CP*, vol I, 56-62.
10. ibid., 5.
11. ibid., 156.
12. Franklin and Mary Wickwire, *Cornwallis: The American Adventure* (Houghton Mifflin Co, 1970), 172-3.
13. *CP*, vol IV, 117, note 20.

These, then, were more likely the real reasons why Cornwallis took the absurd and fateful decision that he did.

It ill became Cornwallis to advise Balfour of his determination in an exceedingly offhand way.[14] Not only Balfour but Rawdon, Lt. Col. John Harris Cruger, Lt. Col. Thomas Brown and countless other officers and men, many at the expense or risk of their lives, had been valiantly involved in maintaining the British position in South Carolina and Georgia at a vast outlay to the exchequer. All was now to come to nought. However much we may sympathise with Cornwallis's reasons for not wishing to return southward, more weighty considerations were involved. That he chose to discount them or rationalise them away, and incidentally contravene Clinton's instructions, was at best a serious flaw in his character and at worst a gross dereliction of duty.

Lt. Col. Banastre Tarleton is not free of blame for placing Cornwallis in the situation in which he found himself. If the light troops had not been lost at the Battle of Cowpens, then there might well have been a favorable outcome to the disastrous winter campaign.[15] In that event Cornwallis would not have felt impelled to march into Virginia and the catastrophe at Yorktown would have been averted.

Intuitively convinced that Clinton would not approve of his decision, Cornwallis quite simply presented him with a *fait accompli*. He marched northward on the 25th. All in all, it is no exaggeration to say that his decision was critical in a series of events that cost Britain the southern colonies and lost it the entire war.

14. ibid., 122-3.
15. ibid., ch 39.

AUTHOR BIOGRAPHIES

J. L. Bell

J. L. Bell is an associate editor of the *Journal of the American Revolution* and maintains Boston1775.net, a popular website dedicated to history, analysis, and unabashed gossip about the start of the American Revolution in New England. His is author of *The Road to Concord: How Four Stolen Cannon Ignited the Revolutionary War* (Westholme, 2016) and *Gen. George Washington's Home and Headquarters–Cambridge, Massachusetts*, a comprehensive study for the National Park Service. He has been elected a Fellow of the Massachusetts Historical Society, a Member of the American Antiquarian Society, and a Member of the Colonial Society of Massachusetts.

Todd W. Braisted

Todd Braisted is an author and researcher of Loyalist military studies. Since 1979, Braisted has amassed and transcribed over 40,000 pages of Loyalist and related material from archives and private collections around the world. He is author of *Grand Forage 1778: The Battleground Around New York City* (Westholme, 2016) and has been a guest historian on episodes of "Who Do You Think You Are?" (CBC) and "History Detectives" (PBS). He is the creator of royalprovincial.com, the largest website dedicated to Loyalist military studies. Braisted is a Fellow in the Company of Military Historians and a past-president of the Bergen County Historical Society.

Alexander Cain

Alexander Cain graduated from Merrimack College in 1993 with a degree in economics and New England School of Law with a juris doctorate. He frequently lectures on constitutional and historical issues, and developments in the United States. He has published several research articles relevant to New England militias and loyalists during the American Revolution. He is sthe author of *We Stood Our Ground: Lexington in the First Year of the American Revolution* (Heritage Books, 2008) and I See Nothing but the Horrors of a Civil War. (Self-Published, 2019).

Frederic C. Detwiller

Frederic C. Detwiller is principal of New England Landmarks. He does restoration, preservation, and historic research throughout New England. He began his career in Boston on the Faneuil Hall Markets Project at Architectural Heritage, Inc./F. A. Stahl Assoc., Architects, with James H. Ballou, AIA, of Salem. He later was historical architect with McGinley Hart & Associates. He received the Bulfinch Award for Restoration and Preservation in 1981. He is a board member of Govs. Shirley-Eustis House, Massachusetts, the Lafayette Society, and the local historical society.

Gina Dimuro

Gina Dimuro is a New York-based writer and translator. She graduated from New York University with a degree in Foreign Languages and currently works as a freelance history writer for several different sites. She also runs a personal blog featuring articles on New York City history and culture at https://normannusurbanus.com/

Cho-Chien Feng

Cho-Chien Feng is a doctoral candidate at Saint Louis University. His academic interests include cultural, political, and intellectual history of colonial and revolutionary America. He is writing a dissertation on the cultural roots of New York Loyalist political ideology. He has received a residential research fellowship at Robert H. Smith International Center for Jefferson Studies in 2015 and he was a Library Resident Research Fellow at the American Philosophical Society in July 2016.

Michael Gadue

Michael R. Gadue practiced law in Vermont for 43 years, and served as a U.S. Army Officer in active and reserve components for 31 years, with his last active-duty as Chief, US Military Liaison Team, former Yugoslavian Republic of Macedonia 1996-1997. He is a graduate of the U.S. Army War College, and holds B.A., M.A., M.S., J.D., and LL.M. degrees. Mike has published articles on German Auxiliaries in the American Revolution and Highlanders in the French & Indian War, and has written for the *Bulletin of the Fort Ticonderoga Museum*. Mike is currently professor of law at Northwestern California University School of Law, Sacramento, California.

Katie Turner Getty

Katie Turner Getty, an associate editor of the *Journal of the American Revolution*, is a Boston-based lawyer, writer, and independent researcher. She earned her J.D. from New England Law Boston, cum laude, holds a B.A. from Wellesley College with a focus on revolutionary America, and is a graduate of Bunker Hill Community College. For more information, visit her website, www.katieturnergetty.com

Don N. Hagist

Don N. Hagist is managing editor of *Journal of the American Revolution* and an independent researcher specializing in the British army in the American Revolution. His books include *The Revolution's Last Men: the Soldiers Behind the Photographs* (Westholme Publishing, 2015), *British Soldiers, American War* (Westholme Publishing, 2012), *Wives, Slaves, and Servant Girls* (Westholme Publishing, 2016), *A British Soldier's Story: Roger Lamb's Narrative of the American Revolution* (Ballindalloch Press, 2004), and *General Orders: Rhode Island* (Heritage Books, 2001).

Stuart Hatfield

Stuart Hatfield lives in Muskegon, Michigan. He earned his Masters in Military History from AMU (focused on the American Revolution) and is currently working in information technology. He has published three novels and currently curates an American Military History blog at historiamilitaris.org. He is currently researching the relationship between the Continental Congress and the Continental Army.

John Knight

John Knight received a joint honours degree in American History/Politics from Warwick University, England. He was a fine art valuer for a number of London-based auction houses, including Christie's and Bonhams, before taking up writing and lecturing full time. He writes on American culture, society, and history at his website, www.englishmanlovesamerica.com

Kinzey M. McLaren-Czerr

Kinzey M. McLaren-Czerr is pursuing her bachelor's degree in history at Bowling Green State University. She is a member of the Honors College, Student Advisory Board, Phi Alpha Theta, and the National Society of Leadership and Success. In addition to her primary focus of history, she also studies Women's, Gender and Sexuality Studies.

Jaume Sastre Moll

Jaume Sastre Moll is emeritus professor of history at the Universidad de Les Illes Balears and member of the Institut Menorqui d'Estudis section on archeology and history. He has authored many academic works on the medieval period and is recognized as a leading scholar on the medieval Balearic Isles. He has received numerous prizes for his work in that area, which comprises an extensive published bibliography in his field.

Matthew Moss

Matthew Moss is a British military historian with degrees from the Universities of Liverpool and Chester. In 2013, he established www.historicalfirearms.info, a website that looks at the history, development, and use of firearms, as well as wider military history. In 2017, he co-founded a new multimedia project, the Armourer's Bench (www.armourersbench.com). The project uses video, photos, and thoroughly researched articles to showcase the history of some of the world's most interesting and important firearms.

Steven Neill

Steven Neill is from Spokane Valley, Washington. He graduated from Whitworth University with a Bachelor's degree in Organizational Management and a minor in history and has served on the Spokane Valley Planning Committee for three and a half years. He is currently writing a book on the evolution of the U. S. Constitution.

Brian Patrick O'Malley

Brian P. O'Malley is a writer and real estate agent in Atlantic Beach, Florida. He earned a Master of Arts in history from the University of North Florida (Jacksonville). His writings include the occasional editorial in *Folio Weekly* (Jacksonville) and an Op-Ed piece in *The Washington Post*, "Lessons on Iraq From a Founding Father." He blogs on historical subjects at http://brianomalley1776.blogspot.com/.

Gene Procknow

Gene Procknow's research includes interpreting the lives and leadership of Revolutionary generals, widening our understanding of the Revolution from a global perspective, and assessing the contributions of Ethan Allen and the creation of Vermont. He maintains the website www.researchingtheamericanrevolution.com to assist in understanding Revolutionary War historiography and primary sources and is the author of the *Mad River Gazetteer* (2011), which traces prominent Vermont place names to Revolutionary War patriots.

Ian Saberton

Ian Saberton holds a PhD in history from the University of Warwick. He was an adviser on constitutional and political affairs, machinery of government, contingency planning, and devolution in the Northern Ireland Office (NIO) at the height of the Troubles. He is the author of *The American Revolutionary War in the South* (Grosvenor House, 2018), *George Hanger: The Life and Times of an Eccentric Nobleman* (Grosvenor House, 2018), and is editor of the Cornwallis Papers.

Andrew M. Schocket

Andrew M. Schocket is Professor of History and American Culture Studies at Bowling Green State University. He is author, most recently, of *Fighting over the Founders: How We Remember the American Revolution* (NYU Press, 2015) and an editor of the *Cambridge History of the American Revolution* (Cambridge University Press, in progress). His writing has appeared in the *Washington Post, San Francisco Chronicle, Newsday,* and *Slate,* and he is a co-creator of the Magazine of Early American Datasets.

Ken Shumate

The first two of Ken's careers were sequential: service in the Marine Corps, then software development in the aerospace industry. His third career in teaching overlapped the first two: public short courses on software engineering, and more formal courses at San Diego State and Chapman Universities. His fourth career overlapped the first three; the focus of his writing was the synthesis of techniques for developing large software systems, resulting in technical papers, a magazine column on software design techniques, and five popular books including *Software Specification and Design* (John Wiley, 1992).

John L. Smith, Jr.

John L. Smith, Jr. earned a B.S. degree from the University of South Florida and an M.B.A. from the University of Tampa. He is a Vietnam-era veteran and holds honorable discharges from the U.S. Air Force Reserve and the U.S. Army Reserve. His historical work has been featured by *Knowledge Quest*, *National Review*, CNN, and *Smithsonian Magazine*. Most recently, he was interviewed on Sirius XM about the American invasion of Canada, 1775-1776.

Colin J. Spicer

Colin J. Spicer is an undergraduate geography major at Bowling Green State University.

Eric Sterner

Eric Sterner is a national security and aerospace consultant. He held senior staff positions for the Committees on Armed Services and Science in the House of Representatives and served in the Department of Defense and as NASA's Associate Deputy Administrator for Policy and Planning. He earned a B.A. from American University and two M.A.s from George Washington University.

Sebastian Van Bastelaer

Sebastian van Bastelaer is the program manger at the Constitutional Sources

Project in Washington, DC. He earned a B.A. in History and Political Science the University of Wisconsin-Madison. An avid scholar of the Founding era, he has written pieces featured in the ARCHIVE journal at the UW-Madison and in the *Wisconsin Magazine of History*.

William M. Welsch

William M. Welsch, a United States Marine Corps veteran and retired university administrator, is the founding president of the American Revolution Round Table of Richmond and co-founder of the Congress of American Revolution Round Tables. He is a tour guide of Revolutionary War battlefields, frequent presenter, and author of multiple articles on the Revolution. His interest areas include the Revolution in New Jersey, Pennsylvania and the generals of the Continental Army.

Richard J. Werther

Richard J. Werther is a retired CPA and history enthusiast living in Novi, Michigan. He studied business management at Bucknell University in Lewisburg, Pennsylvania.

Jason Yonce

Jason Yonce is a 2018 graduate from Pittsburg State University where he completed his thesis work under the direction of Dr. Chris Childers. His interests include the later careers of the constitutional framers, constitutional history, and post-Reconstruction southern politicians. He lives in Alexandria, Virginia.

Andrew A. Zellers-Frederick

Andrew A. Zellers-Frederick earned a B.A. in History from Temple University, an M.A. in History from La Salle University, and a Historic Preservation Certificate from Bucks County Community College. He has served with the National Park Service at Independence and Colonial National Historical Parks; and as the executive director of Historic RittenhouseTown, the Masonic Library & Museum of Pennsylvania, the Woodlands Trust, and the Northampton County Historical & Genealogical Museum. Also, he was the Director of the Historic Jamestowne Fund for The Colonial Williamsburg Foundation.

INDEX